MORE ADVANCE PRAISE FOR *DIVINE FURY*

"As Darrin McMahon shows, the genius is the god among men—providing one of the last connections to the transcendent that our common secular culture retains, and setting up a struggle between our desire for exceptional beings and our leveling egalitarianism. In its absorbing and remarkable way, *Divine Fury* educates and entertains, vindicating the importance of grand history told over the long term." —SAMUEL MOYN, Columbia University, author of *The Last Utopia: Human Rights in History*

"It is rare to find an historian who writes in a style both so sure-footed and so light, and with such joy in the telling of a tale. In his engaging new book Darrin McMahon takes us on an intellectual adventure, tracing the transformation of the idea of genius as it shed its sacred garments to become the common property of our own democratic age. Ranging with ease across history—from the poets of Romanticism to the tyrants of the twentieth-century, from Einstein to the 'IQ Test,' and from Benjamin Franklin to the 'wiz-kid' inventors of Silicon Valley—McMahon invites us to consider a central paradox of our time: If anyone can be a genius, then perhaps no one is." —PETER E. GORDON, Amabel B. James Professor of History, Harvard University, and author of *Continental Divide: Heidegger, Cassirer, Davos*

DIVINE FURY

DIVINE FURY

A HISTORY *of* GENIUS

DARRIN M. MCMAHON

BASIC BOOKS
A Member of the Perseus Books Group
New York

Published by Basic Books,
A Member of the Perseus Books Group

Books published by Basic Books are available at special discounts for bulk purchases in the United States by corporations, institutions, and other organizations. For more information, please contact the Special Markets Department at the Perseus Books Group, 2300 Chestnut Street, Suite 200, Philadelphia, PA 19103, or call (800) 810-4145, ext. 5000, or e-mail special. markets@perseusbooks.com.

Designed by Cynthia Young

Library of Congress Cataloging-in-Publication Data
McMahon, Darrin M.
    Divine fury : a history of genius / Darrin M. McMahon.
        pages cm
    Includes bibliographical references and index.
    ISBN 978-0-465-00325-9 (hardback)—ISBN 978-0-465-06991-0 (e-book)
    1. Gifted persons—History.   2. Gifted persons—Biography.   3. Intellectual life—
History.   I. Title.
BF416.A1M35 2013
153.9'809—dc23
                                                                    2013016418

10 9 8 7 6 5 4 3 2 1

For Julien and Madeleine,
who have given me gifts, born *and* made.
May I offer them many in return.

THE GENIUS OF HUMANITY is the right point of view of history. The qualities abide; the men who exhibit them have now more, now less, and pass away. . . . Once you saw phoenixes: they are gone; the world is not therefore disenchanted. The vessels on which you read sacred emblems turn out to be common pottery; but the sense of the pictures is sacred, and you may still read them transferred to the walls of the world. . . . Once they were angels of knowledge and their figures touched the sky. Then we drew near, saw their means, culture and limits; and they yielded their place to other geniuses.

—EMERSON, *Uses of Great Men*, 1850

AMONG MODERN CIVILIZED beings a reverence for genius has become a substitute for the lost dogmatic religions of the past.

—WILHELM LANGE-EICHBAUM, *The Problem of Genius*, 1931

NOW THE WORD "genius," though in some sense extravagant, nonetheless has a noble, harmonious, and humanely healthy character and ring. . . . And yet it cannot be, nor has it ever been denied that the demonic and irrational have a disquieting share in that radiant sphere, that there is always a faint, sinister connection between it and the nether world, and for that very reason those reassuring epithets I sought to attribute to genius— "noble," "humanely healthy," and "harmonious"—do not quite fit, not even when . . . it is a matter of a pure and authentic genius, bestowed or perhaps inflicted by God. . . .

—THOMAS MANN, *Doctor Faustus*, 1947

CONTENTS

INTRODUCTION

The Problem of Genius

GENIUS. SAY THE WORD OUT LOUD. Even today, more than 2,000 years after its first recorded use by the Roman author Plautus, it continues to resonate with power and allure. The power to create. The power to divine the secrets of the universe. The power to destroy. With its hints of madness and eccentricity, sexual prowess and protean possibility, genius remains a mysterious force, bestowing on those who would assume it superhuman abilities and godlike powers. Genius, conferring privileged access to the hidden workings of the world. Genius, binding us still to the last vestiges of the divine.

Such lofty claims may seem excessive in an age when football coaches and rock stars are frequently described as "geniuses." The luster of the word—once reserved for a pantheon of eminence, the truly highest of the high—has no doubt faded over time, the result of inflated claims and general overuse. The title of a BBC television documentary on the life of the Nobel Prize–winning physicist Richard Feynman sums up the situation: "No Ordinary Genius." There was a time when such a title would have been redundant. That time is no more.[1]

Genius: we are obsessed with the word, with the idea, and with the people on whom it is bestowed. We might say that we are obsessed with ourselves, for seemingly all can be geniuses now, or at least learn to "think like a genius," as the cover of a recent *Scientific American Mind* proclaims, if only we "discover" our genius within. No shortage of titles promises to help us do just that, while a thriving industry of educational products tempts well-meaning parents with the prospect of raising Baby Mozarts™ and Baby Einsteins™, liberally dispensing advice on how to cultivate the gifted. Flipping through the pages of such ephemera, the reader may find it difficult to detect the aura of anything sacred. And yet that aura is still there, barely detectable, however faintly it glows.[2]

Consider the example of Einstein, the quintessential modern genius. As the author of a popular children's book rightly explains, "Einstein" is no longer just the last name of a gifted scientist. "It has become a common noun. 'Einstein' means genius." Dozens of biographies link the two words in their titles, and images of the man—at the blackboard, on a bicycle, with his wild hair and protruding tongue—spell out genius by themselves. Hebrew University of Jerusalem, which owns the copyright for the use of Einstein's image, generates millions of dollars a year in royalties paid by the manufacturers of an impressive array of T-shirts, postcards, and other schlock bearing the master's likeness.[3]

What exactly do we see in these images? What do we see in genius? On one level, the answer is straightforward. For Einstein's mass-produced image is like that of any other icon of modern celebrity or fame. Whereas a silkscreen of Marilyn signifies tragic beauty in a flash, and the silhouette of Che Guevara conveys romantic revolution, the image of Einstein bespeaks brilliance in the blink of an eye. It triggers other associations, too. If the core of Einstein's genius was creative intelligence, we also associate him with a certain playful eccentricity, the "carefree manner of a child," as a leading psychologist describes it, allegedly a common characteristic of truly gifted minds. There is Einstein's absentmindedness— forgetting to eat while working on a complex problem, or to put his socks on before his shoes—and his famous slovenliness of manner and dress. There are his diversions—playing Mozart on the violin, sailing in his little boats, or chasing after women who were not his wives. There are his emotional difficulties with loved ones and family, his introspection, his capacity for long and sustained toil, his stubbornness, his rebelliousness, his "mystical, intuitive" approach to problem solving. But finally, and most revealingly where genius is concerned, there is Einstein's role as a protector and "saint" (a label he resisted, but came to accept), the possessor of ultimate knowledge and seeker of transcendent truths, who warned the free world of the apocalyptic potential of nuclear fission and then helped to harness its destructive force. Or so the legend goes. A 1946 story in *Time* magazine captured this image well, featuring Einstein the "Cosmoclast" on the cover before a mushroom cloud bearing the equation $E = mc^2$. "Through the incomparable blast and flame" following the fatal release of the first atomic bomb, the article declares, was "dimly discernible, . . . the features of a shy, almost saintly, childlike little man with the soft brown eyes, . . . Professor Albert Einstein."[4]

The depiction of Einstein as a guardian protector and avenging angel—at once saintly creator and righteous destroyer—hints at a central theme of this book: the profound religiosity associated with genius and the genius figure. "I want to know how God created the world," Einstein once observed. "I want to know his thoughts." It was, to be sure, a manner of speaking, like the physicist's celebrated line about the universe and dice. Still, the aspiration is telling. For genius, from its earliest origins, was a religious notion, and as such was bound up not only with the superhuman and transcendent, but also with the capacity for violence, destruction, and evil that all religions must confront.[5]

This book tells the story of those surprising connections, tracing the history of genius and the genius figure from the ancient world to the present day. I pay close attention to the many fascinating individuals who brought ideas of genius to life, considering philosophers, poets, artists, composers, military strategists, captains of industry, inventors, scientists, theologians, rulers, and tyrants. But notwithstanding this attention, this book is above all a history of ideas of genius, or better still, a "history in ideas." A form of long-range intellectual history that examines concepts in multiple contexts across broad expanses of time (the intellectual *longue durée*), this is an approach to the past that until recently might have been glibly dismissed as old-fashioned or methodologically suspect. Lately, however, a revivified history in ideas has shown encouraging signs of new life. Perhaps historians have taken note of the dangers of diminishing returns from an overinvestment in subjects, contexts, and time frames too narrowly conceived. Perhaps their readers have, too. In any case, one of the potential benefits of the kind of approach adopted here is to correct for excessive specialization, showing connections and continuities, ruptures and breaks, across disciplines, time, and place. If this can be done in a style that is accessible to anyone with a bit of curiosity, so much the better. The benefits may be worth the risks.[6]

A long-range history in ideas is particularly well-suited to teasing out genius's intimate connection to the divine, a connection that few serious analysts of the subject have explored. On the one hand, natural and social scientists since the nineteenth century have attempted to unlock genius's secrets, to understand its nature and develop its nurture, probing the conditions that might bring it about. But in their relentless efforts to identify the many attributes of genius—and then to quantify and compare them—these researchers have tended to dismiss genius's religious reception and appeal as so much superstition. A very different group of scholars, on the other hand, working in the fields of literary theory, art history, and criticism, has been inclined to reject the notion of genius altogether, toppling it from the privileged place it once held as an arbiter of aesthetic distinction. Genius and geniuses, they have argued, are myths that should be deconstructed and then dismissed, like so many ideological relics from the past. The impetus behind this work was certainly instructive—for the notion of genius, like many religious notions, has undoubtedly served a mythic role. But to simply write it off as an outmoded aesthetic ideal or a vestige from the days when history was concocted as the story of great men is to miss much that is interesting in this potent force.[7]

Finally, a third group of scholars, far from dismissing the religious appeal of genius, has embraced it. Writing in the 1930s, the American popular historian Will Durant noted that "in an age that would level everything and reverence nothing," the worship of genius was the "final religion," demanding obeisance, not critique. "When genius stands in our presence," Durant declared, "we can only bow down before it as an act of God, a continuance of creation." More recently, if no less reverently, the well-known critic Harold Bloom has imagined geniuses as Kabbalistic representations of God. "We *need* genius, however envious or uncomfortable it makes many among us," Bloom affirmed. "Our desire for the transcendental and the extraordinary seems part of our common heritage, and abandons us slowly, and never completely." Bloom is right about the stubborn desire for transcendence; it will draw close attention in this book. But rather than reproduce the religion of genius, or treat it as a myth that merits only dismissal, the phenomenon must first be understood on its own terms and explained.[8]

The failure to do so is surprising, given that genius was so long construed in religious terms. The word itself is Latin, and for the ancient Romans who first used it and then bequeathed the term to us, a *genius* was a guardian spirit, a god of one's birth who accompanied individuals throughout life, connecting them to the divine. The Roman *genius*, without question, was very far from the modern "genius," conceived as an individual of exceptional creativity and insight. The latter understanding of the word only gained currency in the eighteenth century, for reasons that will be explained. Yet notwithstanding this long passage of time, and the many changes in meaning that intervened as ancient understandings of *genii* gave way to modern understandings of geniuses, the connection to religion endured, persisting well into the twentieth century. "Genius never loses its religious sub-flavour," the prominent German psychiatrist Wilhelm Lange-Eichbaum observed in 1931, the very year that Will Durant was declaring genius to be the "final religion." "Beyond all question," Lange-Eichbaum insisted, "the notion, or rather the emotionally-tinged conviction, that genius has a peculiar sanctity is widely diffused throughout the modern world."[9]

Unlike Durant, Lange-Eichbaum refused to prostrate himself before this mystical power. Proposing instead to look it in the eye, he argued, in his aptly entitled *Das Genie-Problem* (1931), that the "problem of genius"—human beings' age-old quest to search out the extraordinary in special human beings—was misconceived. Genius did not dwell as a sacred force in prodigies waiting to be discovered—its "sanctity," rather, was imputed and ascribed, the product of an inveterate human need to fabricate idols and of an "inborn delight in the exalted, the extreme, the absolute." The making of a genius was a process akin to the "origination of a god," a process of "deification" in which human beings invested others with mysterious powers and then bowed before them in awe. It followed that genius was invariably a "relationship" between the many and the one, a relationship that had come into being for specific historical reasons and that would, Lange-Eichbaum ventured, disappear in time. At the present moment, however, the relationship to genius was one of "semi-religious dogmatism." Therein lay the problem. Charged with supernatural authority and invested with mystery and power, the notion of genius was dangerous.[10]

Lange-Eichbaum's judgment was by no means beyond reproach in all matters concerning genius. But his insight regarding the potential danger of deification was prescient. Only two years later, in fact, Germany gave rise to a "genius" who more than fulfilled his fears, an evil genius with whom the good genius of Einstein would clash in apocalyptic struggle. That man was Adolf Hitler, who regarded Einstein as an adversary and threat, and who was strangely obsessed with the intelligence of Jews. He, too, featured on the cover of *Time* magazine, the man of the year for 1938, an "unholy organist" composing a hymn of hate. Like his rival, he changed the course of history. And, like him, he drew the label "genius" throughout the better part of his professional career.[11]

To speak of Hitler as a genius may seem unsettling, even shocking. Revelations that the singer Michael Jackson did so several years ago provoked an international outcry. But whatever the warped musings of the late pop star, to describe Hitler as a genius here is not to condone his actions or character in any way, or even to comment on his abilities, such as they were. It is simply to call attention to the fact that the label was crucial to his rise to power and public cult. *Time* employed it freely, albeit ironically, in an article entitled "Genius Hitler," reporting how the Führer was "being pictured as a military as well as political genius" in broadcasts throughout Germany that marked the celebration of his birthday in 1938. Such descriptions were commonplace. Hitler gave voice to them himself as early as 1920, commenting, in a speech delivered on

April 27 of that year, that Germany needed a "dictator who is a genius." He developed the thought at length in his autobiography *Mein Kampf*, judging that "true genius is always inborn and never cultivated, let alone learned," while daring to suggest that he was so begotten. A former artist, soldier, and lover of Wagner, it seemed, was the genius Germany needed to save and redeem its people. Germans prepared the way, proclaiming from the nineteenth century onward a cult of genius that critics and followers alike did not hesitate to describe as a "religion." A visionary creator and breaker of rules, the genius would summon in his person the spirit of the people and make of it a masterpiece, using force to shape the material. As Hitler's eventual minister of propaganda, Joseph Goebbels, observed in his novel *Michael* in 1931, "the people are for the statesman what stone is for the sculptor." "Geniuses use up people," he added chillingly. "That is just the way it is."[12]

If such claims seem outrageous to us today, that is not only because of their reprehensible content, but also because we are less familiar with the darker, irrational side of the history of genius than with the heroic image that triumphs with Einstein. That lack of familiarity is itself a product of Einstein's victory, for just as the *genius* of Augustus Caesar was said by Plutarch to have cowed the *genius* of his rival, Marc Antony, on the eve of their final battle, the good genius of Einstein has largely succeeded in imposing itself on the field. Historians, by and large, have abetted this triumph, showing themselves little inclined to think of genius in connection with a man like Hitler. Their reluctance is understandable. Yet if we wish to appreciate the role that genius has played in the modern world, we must recall the evil with the good, bearing in mind as we do so the uncomfortable thought that genius is ultimately the product of the hopes and longings of ordinary people. We are the ones who marvel and wonder, longing for the salvation genius might bring. We are the ones who pay homage and obeisance. In a very real sense, the creator of genius is us.

Which is not to deny that geniuses almost always possess something special, something real, however elusive that something may be. But it is to recognize the commonsense fact that genius is in part a social creation—what historians like to call a "construction"—and, as such, of service to those who build. That fact reminds us further that for all their originality (and originality is itself a defining feature of genius in its modern form), extraordinary human beings not only define their images but embody them, stepping into molds prepared by the social imaginary and the exemplars who came before. Even outliers as remarkable, as deviant, as Einstein and Hitler are no exceptions to this rule:

however inimitable—however unique—their genius was partly prepared for them, worked out over the course of generations.[13]

This book recounts the long history of that preparation, following the emergence of the genius as a figure of extraordinary privilege and power. It begins in classical Greece, when poets, philosophers, and statesmen first entertained the question of what makes the greatest men great, initiating a conversation that was continued by the Romans. What power did Socrates possess to make him the wisest of all men? What godlike force moved through Alexander or Julius Caesar as they leveled all before them? Why was the poet Homer able to sing like no other? What special something did these great-souled men possess? What special something possessed them? Christians took up these and related questions in a centuries-long rumination that continued into the early modern period, adapting the language of the ancients to suit their own image of the God-man Christ and the prophets and saints who struggled to imitate his perfection. Possessed by the Holy Spirit, or lifted up by the heavenly angels, the great-souled man might aspire to be perfect as God was perfect. But how could he be sure that an angel was not a demon; that the holy ghost was not a specter, sent by Satan, to tempt him, the way Satan tempted Faust, offering the key to all knowledge in return for one's soul? How could one be sure that those seized by higher powers were not mad, their souls stirred by dark humors and melancholy fits? Well into the Renaissance, when men like Michelangelo and Leonardo da Vinci sought to render God's beauty and reproduce the perfection of his creation, these remained vital questions.

It is worth listening closely to the answers. For although there is no single notion of genius that coheres magically over time, there are coherent ways of imagining how the highest beings might appear and what a beautiful mind might entail. Those early imaginings were present at the modern genius's birth, and they lend insight into what the genius in the nineteenth and twentieth centuries would become.

The modern genius was born in the eighteenth century—conceived, in keeping with long-standing prejudices, almost exclusively as a man. There were precedents for this birth, stretching all the way back to antiquity. But that the birth itself occurred in the bright place of deliverance we call "the Enlightenment" is clear. Scholars have long recognized the genius's emergence in this period as the highest human type, a new paragon of human excellence who was the focus of extensive contemporary comment and observation. What is far less clear is *why* the genius emerged. Why, at that time, in the long eighteenth century? And why there, in the West broadly conceived?[14]

Those who have bothered to ask these questions have focused on a number of factors, ranging from the advent of capitalism to new notions of aesthetics to new understandings of the author and the self. There is something to be said for each of these explanations. But this book adopts a different approach, seeking to understand the genius's emergence and subsequent flourishing in terms of two broad transformations. The first has to do with religious change, and, more specifically, with what has been described as the "withdrawal of God," along with the disavowal and dismissal of a range of spiritual companions—spirits and angels, prophets, apostles, and saints—who had long served human beings as guardians and mediators to the divine. That dismissal was by no means uniformly accepted. But the scale was nonetheless significant and the consequences profound. For not only did it leave men and women alone in the world with their Creator; it did so at the very moment that the Creator was appearing to many to be more distant, more remote, more withdrawn, and less likely to intervene in human affairs than he had been (or so it seemed) in earlier times. To reach the realm of the sacred, to get to God—if indeed he even existed, as an emboldened minority was inclined to wonder—was more difficult than ever before. A vast space opened up, and there were no longer helpers on hand to guide human beings across the way. It was in that space that the modern genius was conceived and born.[15]

In assuming his modern form, the genius assumed powers that once had been reserved exclusively for God and the gods and those exalted beings—the prodigies and prophets, the angels and *genii*, the saints and great-souled men—who had long been trusted to lead us to him. Occupying the space of their classical and Christian fore-bears, geniuses performed a number of their functions even as they took on new roles and even when, as was often the case, they denied any explicit connection to religion at all. Geniuses served as guardians and founding fathers, saviors and redeemers, legislators and oracles of the people. Geniuses mediated between human beings and the divine. Chosen to reveal wonders, geniuses were conceived as wonders themselves, illustrating perfectly the proposition that the gradual dis-enchantment of the world was accompanied from the outset by its continual re-enchantment. Geniuses pulled back the curtain of existence to reveal a universe that was richer, deeper, more extraordinary and terrible than previously imagined. The baffling beauty of space-time was no different in this respect from the sublime majesty of Byron's poetry, Beethoven's symphonies, or Poincaré's theorems, as radiant as an Edison light bulb or the explosion of the atomic bomb. Genius was a flash of light, but its brilliance served to illuminate the dark mystery that surrounded and set it apart.[16]

Geniuses, then, were believed to possess rare and special powers: the power to create, redeem, and destroy; the power to penetrate the fabric of the universe; the power to see into the future, or to see into our souls. Detectable already in the eighteenth century at the time of the modern genius's birth, these powers were significantly expanded in the nineteenth and early twentieth centuries as geniuses assumed an ever greater cultural authority. Enhanced by the pervasive influence of European Romanticism, which further stylized and mystified the genius, this authority was also fortified by an extensive science of genius, which appeared to give sanction—through the measurement of skulls, the analysis of brains, and the identification of pathogens and hereditary traits—to the genius's exceptional nature. The effort to quantify genius that culminated in the elaboration of the intelligence quotient (IQ) at the beginning of the twentieth century seemed to confirm the presence of a power—an exceedingly rare power—that scientists had assumed for over a century, and that a chorus of "genius enthusiasts" was then preaching self-consciously as a basis for worship. It was power that could be put to political ends—for the better, as some hoped, or for the worse, as others feared. The two great political religions of the early twentieth century, communism and fascism, attempted to do just that, sanctioning the legitimacy of Joseph Stalin and Adolf Hitler by means of the religion of genius.

If broad religious transformations, and the responses to them, provide one essential context for understanding the emergence of modern conceptions of genius, the other is sociopolitical and involves the no less sweeping advent of the belief in human equality. Widely proclaimed on both sides of the Atlantic from the end of the seventeenth century, the view, as Thomas Jefferson put it famously in the Declaration of Independence, that "all men are created equal" could pass by the end of the eighteenth century as a self-evident truth. By the middle of the century that followed, it was being hailed by astute observers such as Alexis de Tocqueville as a "providential fact," an unstoppable force that leveled all before it. And yet the assertion of equality was qualified and challenged from the start, with whole categories of human beings singled out as exceptions to the general rule. Historians have devoted close attention to these exceptions, showing how women, people of color, Jews, and others were systematically deprived of their rights in strategies of exclusion that aimed at denying some the inherent equality granted to others. But what have received less attention are the justifications used to elevate the few above the many, granting privileges and rights beyond the norm. Jefferson himself spoke of a "natural aristocracy," composed of individuals of talent, creativity, and intelligence, that might replace the old aristocracy of birth and blood, and many in nineteenth-century Europe would conceive of artists in a similar fashion, as beings endowed by nature with special abilities and so entitled to special privileges. Such assertions were often linked to corresponding claims of the natural inferiority of others, and together these notions formed part of a "shadow language of inequality" that accompanied the bright proclamation of the equality of all. Modern discussions of genius were most often conducted in this idiom, serving to justify new forms of hierarchy while registering a profound protest against doctrines of universal equality. Conceived as an extreme case of inherent superiority and natural difference, the genius was imagined as an exception of the most exalted or terrible kind, able to transcend or subvert the law, and to liberate or enslave accordingly.[17] The evil genius, too, is a modern figure with roots deep in the past, and he is inextricably bound to his more righteous brother and twin. Both reveal traces of the sacred in their modern incarnations. And both have haunted those who have dreamed of human equality since the centuries that first proclaimed it.

The particular circumstances of the genius's birth and subsequent development thus help to account for the predominately European focus of this book. For it was in Europe that men and women first experienced the drama of disenchantment in a significant way, a development without precedent in the whole of human history. And it was in Europe and the Americas that the doctrine of equality first gained significant traction.

But what about method and scope? Why, that is, undertake a history of genius, as this book does, as a history in ideas spanning the course of several thousand years? An alternative approach would be to dispense with gestation altogether and begin directly with the birth, commencing at the moment when modern genius first saw the light and was quickly put to use. The approach has much to recommend it—for some time it has been the industry standard among historians studying ideas in context—and in the present case it would undoubtedly have simplified the task. And yet, despite the claims of some in the eighteenth century, few ideas— even ideas of genius—emerge from nothing, ex nihilo, without any precedents at all. To begin at the "beginning" would be to do no such thing and would also run the risk of overlooking continuities, connections, and departures that a broader sweep stands a chance of taking in.

Another approach would be to follow the history of the word "genius," which, after all, stretches back to the Romans. Or, better yet, to go in search of analogues to modern geniuses in the past. If the creature in question is ultimately the brilliant, creative individual widely recognized for unmatched talents and skills, doesn't it make sense to seek out the modern genius's historical counterparts—the poets and scientists, the statesmen and artists, in a word, the "geniuses"—who came before? That thought, too, has much to recommend it, as does tracing the history and genealogy of the word, and both approaches will be given due attention here. But just as critics rightly caution that words and concepts are not things, there are also strong reasons for resisting the temptation to write the history of genius as a moving tableau of eminence, a historical pantheon of geniuses *avant la lettre*. In the first place, such history has been written before—many times. Indeed, virtually all history composed until the twentieth century represents one variation or another on the dominant theme of outstanding individuals—great men, far less often great women, of deed and thought—who were said to have shaped the world and everything in it. The shortcomings of such an approach have been chronicled ad nauseam (without, it seems, hurting the sales of biographies)—so much so that it is refreshing to see scholars take up the history of the "great" in new ways. I attempt to do some of that in this book, paying close attention to the many stellar individuals who embodied ideas of human greatness before the modern genius was born.[18]

Yet there is one other, even stronger, reason to be wary of the effort to write the history of genius exclusively as the history of eminent achievement. Not only would such an approach risk repeating much that has been said before, it would risk anachronism, envisioning the past through the perspective of a type—the modern genius—who only comes into being in the eighteenth century. Before that time, there were no geniuses in our modern sense. And though it is undoubtedly true that the eminent artists, thinkers, poets, and sages who preceded the genius played a role in shaping the genius's later image and reception, so did a group of less likely forebears. These were the apostles, prophets, saints, and sorcerers whom the modern genius superseded and replaced, as well as the sundry spiritual beings—the demons, angels, and *genii*—who were once held in their power. In this respect, the *genii* of the ancient world and their various Christian successors have more to do with modern genius than has been acknowledged. To focus solely on the outstanding individuals of the past who resemble the geniuses who came after them would be to miss that vital connection.

It would also be to miss what is right before our eyes. For genius is seemingly everywhere today, hailed in our newspapers and glossy magazines, extolled in our television profiles and Internet chatter. Replete with publicists, hashtags, and "buzz," genius is now consumed by a celebrity culture that draws few distinctions between a genius for fashion, a genius for business, and a genius for anything else. If the "problem of genius" of yesteryear was how to know and how to find it, "our genius problem" today is that it is impossible to avoid. Genius remains a relationship, but our relationship to it has changed. All might have their fifteen minutes of genius. All might be geniuses now.[19]

In the conclusion to this book I analyze our changing relationship to genius in the aftermath of World War II in terms of its long and complex relationship to democracy and equality, pointing out that a world in which all might aspire to genius is a world in which the genius as a sacred exception can no longer exist. Einstein, the "genius of geniuses," was the last of the titans. The age of the genius is gone. Should citizens of democracies mourn this passing or rejoice? Probably a bit of both. The genius is dead: long live the genius of humanity.

CHAPTER I

THE GENIUS OF
THE ANCIENTS

Every age, and every culture, has its heroes of the mind. The ancient Egyptians told tales of wise men, such as Djedi and Setna, who had so mastered the ancient books that they knew everything there was to know. In China, aspiring scholars performed incredible feats of learning for thousands of years, memorizing the archaic texts of the classical tradition in heroic cultural acts. In India, Japan, and Tibet, Hindu Brahmins and Buddhist monks astonish to this day with their mental gymnastics, reciting sutras and vedas with perfect recall for days on end. Jewish tradition celebrates the mental dexterity of rabbis who can put a pin through a page of Torah and say, without looking, what letter it pricks, just as Muslims take pride in the *mufti* or *ulama* who can recite every verse of the Koran. And many of these traditions possess analogues to the great African bards—the *griots*, *doma*, and "masters of knowledge," living libraries who aspire to gather all that is known in their heads, preserving in oral tradition what would otherwise be forgotten.[1]

For those of us who find it hard to remember our anniversaries or where we left our keys, such examples serve as painful reminders of our own inadequacies. But they also illustrate nicely the simple fact that intelligence knows no bounds. Whatever the vagaries of the statistical laws that distribute human aptitude across time and space, they pay little heed to nation, culture, or race. Many in the West long denied these basic continuities, boasting, as some do still, of an inherent superiority of mind. But this book defends no such claims, even (and especially) when it tries to understand them. In short, if we take genius to mean exceptional intelligence or high IQ, great learning, performance, or presence of mind, then "the genius" is both a creature of all seasons and a citizen of the world.[2]

It is now perfectly common to speak of genius in this general way. But that hasn't always been the case. Only relatively recently, in fact, and above all since World War II, have genius and intelligence been so closely coupled, as if the one were a simple synonym for the other. At the time of its emergence in Europe, by contrast—and for centuries thereafter— the ideal of genius was most often predicated on the belief that this rare capacity entailed something other than mere learning and intelligence, acquired mastery and knowledge. Genius—and the genius—embodied something else.

What was this something, the distinguishing power or possession that set the genius apart? This entire book will treat of efforts to answer that elusive question, and this chapter begins by examining some of its earliest formulations, a series of Greek and Roman reflections on just what it was that made the greatest men great. For though the *genius* of the ancients was not at all the "genius" of the moderns, early attempts to wrestle with the problem of what set the classical paragons apart influenced later discussions. What was it exactly that made Socrates the wisest of all men? Why was Homer, the blind bard, gifted with such piercing poetic sight? Why were Alexander and Caesar masterminds of statecraft and war? Were they possessed by a higher power? Or did they themselves possess a different nature, a special kind of soul? Were they gods, or were they men? Or beings in between? Focusing such questions on the lives of eminent individuals, ancient commentators worked out a range of responses that would resonate down through the ages, informing subsequent considerations of what divided the many from the few.

But before considering further these early reflections and the out- standing men who prompted them, we must appreciate what these ancient exemplars—what *all* ancient exemplars, whether Greek or Roman, Persian or African, Indian or Chinese—were not. For only in this way can we fully grasp the novelty of the subsequent departure and see clearly what separates modern Western paragons of genius from the heroes of the mind who came before. The wise men and sages who open this chapter provide a perfect foil for the modern creative genius, for in every instance the embodied ideal is one of recollection and retrieval, a preservation and calling to mind of what was first revealed long before. Mental prowess, in this understanding, is essentially an act of recovery, a rearticulation of words earlier spoken, of thoughts previously known. The same is true in art, where imitation and mimesis long structured the human gaze. To reproduce the eternal forms, to render in its ready perfection the world revealed to us, was the great goal of the artisans whom we now describe as "artists," those skilled craftsmen who for centuries confined themselves to tracing the patterns and following the lines inscribed in the world by the ancestors and the ancients, by nature, the gods, or God. To create originally, without precedent, pattern, or model, was never the ideal of the ancient artist or sage, and indeed the ancients frequently denied the very prospect. As early as the third millennium BCE, the Egyptian scribe Kakheperresenb could comment on the impossibility of writing phrases that "are not already known," "in language that has not been used," with "words which men of old have not spoken." And in the eleventh-century Sanskrit epic song-cycle the *Katha sarit ságara*, or *Ocean of the Streams of Story*, the god Shiva's lover Parvati begs him to tell her a tale that has never been heard before and that will never be heard again. Shiva was a god of great talents (among his remarkable feats, he maintained an erection for eons). But the best he is able to muster is a pastiche of well-worn tales that are in turn quickly recycled. In this case, true originality is impossible even for a god.[3]

The moral of the story is that "there is nothing new under the sun," a sentiment that will be familiar to readers of Jewish and Christian scripture, but is in fact common to virtually every ancient account in which God or the gods are held to have created the universe and all that it contains, or in which the universe is understood to have always existed. In either instance, genuine originality is, strictly speaking, impossible, for mere mortals must confine themselves to recovering and reproducing what already exists. And insofar as the defining characteristic of modern genius is original creation, it follows that the ancient sage cannot a modern genius be. Rather than look to the horizon of the original and new, the ancient's gaze is focused instead on the eternal recurrence of perennial forms, or on a "time of origins" in a mythic past that demands constant vigilance. For there in the "absolute past" lies the key to all understanding in the present and future, which will but be an eternal return, as it was in the beginning in a world without end. In the past lie the answers to all questions. In the past lie the solutions to all riddles. In the past lies the map of our fortune and fate.[4]

Students of ancient mythology and religion have taken pains to show that this general temporal orientation was common to the wisdom traditions and great world religions that took shape in the so-called Axial age that spanned the first millennium BCE. Its sway was extensive, and it proved lasting, enduring well into the early modern period in the West and elsewhere besides, a fact that has important implications for the emergence of genius as a cultural ideal. For only when the primacy of the past was challenged and the gods' monopoly on creation contested could human beings truly conceive of themselves as creators of the new. Only then could the ideal of modern genius assume form.

Much of this book will be devoted to explaining the emergence of that ideal and to developing its implications, but the basic point may be grasped quickly enough simply by considering the etymology of the words "discovery," "invention," and "creation." Into the eighteenth century, the first two of these terms retained in the various Indo-European tongues their root meanings of "uncovering" or "finding." To "dis-cover" was to pull away the covering cloth, disclosing what may have been hidden, overlooked, or lost, but that was in any case already there. To "invent," similarly, was to access that *inventory* of knowledge long ago assembled and put into place: an invention was just a dis-covery, a re-covery of an object forgotten, now an *objet trouvé*. The word "creation" provides an even more striking illustration of the point. "To create" was long deemed impossible for mortal human beings; creation—the supreme act—was reserved for the gods. *Solus deus creat*, the medieval theologian Saint Thomas Aquinas affirms in a typical refrain. "God alone creates," for God as the *creator omnium* was the creator of all. As late as the eighteenth century, French jurists drew on that principle to justify the king's authority over copyright on all books and ideas. Seeing that God was the author of everything in the universe, it was only just that his representative on earth should oversee how *royalties* were collected and dispersed on behalf of their true creator. Human ideas were but imperfect imitations of the divine original.[5]

It followed from these same assumptions that those who took it upon themselves to approximate the divine act of parturition—bringing into existence something new—flirted with danger, for they risked usurping a sacred prerogative. The classical myth of Prometheus imparts this message well. The wisest of the Titans, gifted with "forethought" (the literal meaning of his name), Prometheus hailed from a race of monstrous gods who had been defeated by Zeus and the pantheon of Mount Olympus, but who then took vengeance by stealing their fire. He bestowed on humanity that elemental power, which served in turn as the source of many more inventions—language and agriculture, metallurgy and carpentry, medicine, astronomy, and prophecy. But Prometheus was severely punished for his audacity, chained to a rock for all eternity as an eagle pecked out his liver again and again.[6]

The consequences of usurping creation were no less severe in Judeo-Christian myth. The apocryphal book of Enoch, for example, found among the Dead Sea Scrolls, tells a tale not unlike that of Prometheus, elaborating on the biblical account in Genesis 6 of a race of fallen angels, "the sons of man," who were moved by lust to couple with women of the earth. The fruit of their unnatural union are giants, part human, part divine, who bring evil and oppression to the world while disclosing knowledge stolen from God—metallurgy, agriculture, writing, and "other eternal secrets made in heaven." God's anger is uncompromising. Just as Zeus punishes Prometheus for his theft and disclosure, Yahweh lays waste to the giants and their misshapen world in the great flood that spares only Noah. Christian legend elaborates on a similar theme, telling how Lucifer, the "bringer of light" and wisest of the angels, became Satan, "the enemy," by daring to usurp the function of creation, which is prohibited even to the angels. In John Milton's *Paradise Lost*, in fact, Satan is depicted famously as a kind of Prometheus himself, a dangerous source of innovation and imagination, justly punished, to be sure, but not without a tragic heroism in his doomed attempt to aspire to godhood. Indeed, the message in these mythic examples is often mixed—for though aspiring to creative prowess is dangerous, hubristic, redolent of sin, it is also heroic. Those who challenge the gods may be monsters and giants, but they tower above ordinary men. And yet those who are raised to great heights have a tremendous way to fall.

The seduction and allure of the ascent is bound up with the attraction of genius, which helps to explain why so many of the powers first attributed to it—creativity, imagination, originality, and "invention," in the modern sense of making something new—were long regarded as taboo: they were a challenge to the gods. It is largely for that reason that the ideal of creativity only began to emerge as a modern value in the eighteenth century, and that in earlier times imagination was viewed with deep suspicion as a faculty to be controlled and even feared. That is not to say that there was no imagination prior to this point, any more than it is to suggest that people throughout the world somehow lacked creativity of their own. One need think only of gunpowder, the pyramids, or printed paper to dispel such thoughts. Yet to draw attention to the eighteenth century's novel claims to creativity and genius is to suggest that it was only in this period—and, above all, in the advanced dominions of Europe—that the pervasive belief that there *was* something new under the sun was first put forth in a sustained and systematic way. If, as has been claimed, "the existence of the Creator deprives human beings of their own creativity," then it could only be where the Creator's existence was called into question that human creativity could fully emerge. In this respect, genius as a cultural ideal, an embodiment of imagination, innovation, and creative capacity, was a product of a specific time and place, born in the West and given birth in the long eighteenth century, amid the very first period in the whole of human history to launch a sustained attack on the gods. Undoubtedly, there are analogues and approximations to this ideal in other traditions. But it was above all in Europe and its dependencies that it first assumed widespread prominence, with revolutionary consequences for better and for ill.[7]

How then to chart the long gestation leading up to the birth of this new being, the slow and sometimes painful delivery? There are, no doubt, different ways. But surely any satisfying account must make sense of that special "something" that set the special apart. Scholars and sophists will make their appearance, along with men of intelligence and learning, poets and bards. But the individuals who must focus our attention are those who were believed to be more than men, those who in their audacity or divine election approached the summit of Mount Olympus and reached up to the heavens. At once dangerous and seductive, monstrous and beautiful, ominous in their power, these special beings were creatures apart. They possessed—or were possessed by—what no other human being could claim. And though there are many examples of such lofty beings among the ancients—from Pythagoras to Archimedes and beyond—one man fascinated and perplexed his peers and posterity like no other. With a philosopher from Athens—the wisest of mortals, who claimed to know nothing—does this history of genius begin.

W̲E HEAR OF HIS STRANGE companion only obliquely, in snippets and asides. "Just as I was about to cross the river," Socrates explains in one of Plato's many dialogues, the primary source, however imperfect, of the master's own beliefs, "the familiar divine sign came to me which, whenever it occurs, always holds me back from something I am about to do." Elsewhere, Socrates refers to this "sign" (*sêmeion*) as a "voice" that has spoken to him since childhood. But the word that he invariably uses to describe it is *daimonion*, the diminutive of *daimon*, ancestor of our own "demon." The term had not yet taken on the exclusive connotation of evil that it would develop with the advent of Christianity. Yet that there was already something potentially menacing—something dangerous and revolutionary even—about the *daimonion* in question is given dramatic illustration by the setting in which Socrates was forced to account most fully for its existence. As Socrates's pupil, the Athenian soldier and historian Xenophon, explained, "It had become notorious that Socrates claimed to be guided by 'the *daimonion*': it was out of this claim, I think, that the charge of bringing in strange deities arose." Accused by prominent citizens of Athens of having introduced "new demonic beings" (*daimonia kaina*) into the city, Socrates was put on trial as a heretic and corrupter of youth, whose appeal to an unfamiliar power threatened the very stability of the state. He himself denied any such explicit political intent, though he candidly acknowledged that the *daimonion* was the source of his urge to "interfere" in the affairs of others. "I experience a certain divine or daimonic something," he confessed, "which in fact [has been] caricatured in the indictment. It began in childhood and has been with me ever since, a kind of voice, which whenever I hear it always turns me back from something I was going to do, but never urges me to act. This is what has prevented me from taking part in politics." Ironically, the very power that kept him from power proved his political undoing. And so the man who "of all men living" was the "most wise," as the Pythian priestess at Delphi famously declared, was found guilty of introducing strange demons into the city and sentenced to death in 399 BCE. Socrates apparently drank his hemlock in peace, for, as he told his friends in the hours before his death, his *daimonion* approved his actions, never once holding him back. "That which has happened to me is undoubtedly a good thing," he concluded, making himself a martyr, if not, strictly speaking, to genius, then at least to his own *daimonic* power.[8]

But what exactly was this power, this *divinum quiddam*, as Cicero would later call it, struggling like Socrates to find the words to capture this divine and mysterious thing? Generations of scholars once passed over the question in embarrassed silence, or sought to explain it away, as if a man as rational as Socrates could never have believed anything so strange. The simple truth, however, is that this same man, who sought by the power of his intellect to clarify what was obscure, recognized the existence of mysterious forces, and obeyed them. Socrates, we can be certain, believed in his inner *daimonion* and heeded its call.[9]

In that respect, at least, this extraordinary man was not all that different from the great majority of his contemporaries, who also believed in spirits hidden and unseen. Invoking *daimones* as a way to explain the silent forces that moved through their lives, they conceived of these powers as akin to fortune or fate, affecting their actions despite their explicit intentions, for better or for worse. That human beings were attended by guardian *daimones* of sorts, whether evil or good, was in fact a widely shared belief among ordinary people, who held that although a mischievous *daimon* might lead them astray, a "good *daimon*" (an *eu daimon*), could make them "happy" (*eudaimon*). The two words were one and the same.[10]

Socrates's own understanding of his *daimonion* likely drew on these broader beliefs, which were also sustained by widely received legends, myths, and poems. In the verses of Homer, for example, Greeks would have encountered scattered, if conflicting, references to the *daimones*, which the bard equates on occasion with the gods of Mount Olympus themselves. Homer's rough contemporary, the poet Hesiod, was more specific, claiming that the *daimones* were originally heroes of the Golden Age, transformed by Zeus when their race died out into guardians and "watchers of mortal men." And the followers of the sixth-century philosopher and mathematician Pythagoras maintained that they could see and hear *daimones* as a consequence of their superior enlightenment. When we bear in mind that a similar ability was attributed to soothsayers, priestesses, and priests, the mysterious *daimonion* of Socrates begins to seem rather less a mystery. As Xenophon insists, in defending the apparent normalcy of his master's sign, "he was no more bringing in anything strange than other believers in divination, who rely on augury, oracles, coincidences and sacrifices."[11]

Xenophon's claim to normalcy, however, is an exception, and even he cannot sustain it. Whereas other men skilled in prophecy read in natural occurrences like the flight of birds the signs of the gods' will, Socrates, Xenophon conceded, observed the sign in himself, and the sign was invariably right. Was this not a tacit admission that the wisest of all men had been specially touched, that his spiritual something was something special? Socrates himself seemed to acknowledge as much, observing, in a passing reference in Plato's *Republic*, that few, if any, had ever possessed such a sign. In this respect, Socrates's accusers had a point: his *daimonion* was strange, unlike any the world had known.[12]

It was that understanding that came to dominate Socrates's legend, which was perpetuated both by his detractors and his proponents. On the one hand, his detractors insisted on the essential monstrosity of this man possessed and apart. The point was given graphic illustration by Socrates's notorious physical appearance. He was, by all accounts, "strikingly ugly," short and squat with a broad, flat face, bulging eyes, swollen lips, and a deep-set nose. A bald head and an unkempt beard completed the picture, rendering Socrates the very antithesis of conventional Athenian beauty, like a university professor gone to seed. And given that it was common to relate physical appearance to character, Socrates's ugliness was used by his detractors to highlight the base and demonic nature of his soul. Socrates as satyr, Socrates as monster, Socrates as sorcerer who trafficked with demons to seduce the young and threaten the stability of the state—these were the images that haunted the memory of a man who, by his own admission, was an annoying gadfly, disturbing the peace with unsettling questions and impertinent remarks. It is revealing that the earliest known representation of Socrates—a bust executed within ten to twenty years of his death—depicts Socrates as Silenus, the drunken and unattractive tutor of the wine-god Dionysius, whose ecstatic trances were legendary.[13]

The depiction of Socrates as Silenus, however, cuts another way. For the companion of the god was also renowned for his piercing insight and prophetic power. And though Silenus's "frightening wisdom," as Friedrich Nietzsche would later describe it in *The Birth of Tragedy*, may have heralded dismemberment, nothingness, and death, it was privileged wisdom all the same. In the hands of Socrates's admirers, the prophetic and oracular forces allegedly mediated by the demon could be extolled. Thus Plutarch, a Greek writing under the Roman Empire in the first century, has one of his characters observe, in a celebrated dialogue devoted to Socrates's sign, that his *daimonion* was heaven sent, a divine source of revelation and prophecy, illuminating him in "matters dark and inscrutable to human wisdom." Despite Socrates's insistence that his sign acted only negatively, characterizations of this kind, building on Xenophon's early intimation of divination and prophecy, assumed considerable importance. Cicero reports on a collection in his possession by the Greek Stoic Antipater that gathered together "a mass" of stories regarding Socrates's *daimonion* and its "remarkable" premonitions. And later classical commentators, such as Apuleius, Proclus, and Maximus of Tyre, devoted entire treatises to the subject, which were often frank in their embrace of an explicit demonology linking Socrates to higher powers. As Maximus explains, typically, in this vein, in the second century CE: "God himself, settled and immobile, administers the heavens and maintains their ordered hierarchy. But he has a race of secondary immortal beings, the so-called *daimones*, which have their station in the space between earth and heaven." These *daimones* are the "middle term" of the universe. Some heal diseases, some "descend from their station above the earth to inhabit cities," and still others "are assigned homes in different human bodies; one Socrates, another Plato, another Pythagoras, another Zeno, another Diogenes." The greatest minds of the ancient world, in short, were singularly chosen and possessed. The indwelling presence of the *daimon* was what explained their superior powers.[14]

Maximus's understanding of Socrates's demon was both literal and crude, and in this respect it was not unlike a great many Platonic and later Neo-Platonic accounts that speculated with lavish imagination about the sundry spiritual beings who filled the universe, interacting with the gods and human beings alike. They found the basis for such speculation in Plato himself, who dwelled at considerable length in a number of his dialogues on the function and role of the *daimones*, describing them as angelic "messengers" who "shuttle back and forth" between the gods and men, or spiritual beings who were themselves "a kind of god," existing "midway" between the human and the divine. Read literally, these descriptions offered a banquet of materials on which later admirers could feast in speculation about the *daimonic* forces that filled the cosmos. But more refined delicacies were also hidden in their midst, providing the basis for a different kind of reflection, an explanation of the *daimonic* man that dwelled less on the nature of the demon than on the nature of its host. For if outstanding individuals like Socrates excited wonder about the nature of the forces that might possess them, they also excited speculation about the nature of the forces they possessed. On whom did the gods lavish their powers, and why, anointing some while spurning others? These are questions even older than the *daimonion* of Socrates, and in the ancient world, it was poets as much as philosophers who begged them.[15]

"SING, O GODDESS, OF THE ANGER of Achilles." "Sing, muse, of the man of twists and turns." So begin the two most celebrated poems of the ancient world, Homer's *Iliad* and Homer's *Odyssey*, the epic tales of the exploits of Achilles and Odysseus during and after the Trojan War. Both men are heroes, favored by the gods. But the poet who conjures them is also divinely attended. A different translation hints at how: "Sing *in* me, Muse, and through me tell the story. . . . " A séance, petition, and prayer, the words are a summons to the goddess to take possession of the poet and command his voice, to settle and dwell in his person. The founding texts of the Western literary canon open with an incantation.[16]

The conception of the poet as a medium who reveals divinely inspired words is by far the oldest understanding of this exalted being in the Greek tradition, and many others besides. Homer himself writes of the blind bard Demodocus, who moves Odysseus to tears and others to laughter when "the spirit stirs him on to sing." "God has given the man the gift of song," Homer declares, "to him beyond all others." Generations of Greeks said much the same of Homer himself, who was also frequently represented as blind, though uniquely gifted with special sight. Hesiod, Homer's only equal for early poetic fame, spoke similarly of the source of his power, recounting how the Muses appeared before him atop Mount Helicon and "breathed into me a divine voice so that I might celebrate the events of the future and the past. They bade me sing of the race of the blessed, eternal gods, but always to sing of themselves first and last." Poetry of this kind, invoking the gods even as it is dictated by their emissaries, provides a perfect illustration of what later writers will call *inspiration*, from the Latin verb *inspirare*, meaning "to breath into." Hesiod uses a different word, a variant of the Greek verb *pneo*, to breathe, but his stress is on the same pneumatic source of poetic revelations, which are blown directly into the mind by the Muse. When we consider that poetry itself comes from the verb *poeien*, to create, it follows clearly enough that poems are the creation of the gods, realized through their human artisans and agents.[17]

It is partly for this reason that poetry was so often likened to prophecy and prophets to poets. The famous priestesses at Delphi, who declared Socrates the wisest man, delivered their oracular pronouncements in bits of verse, filled with the breath of the gods and the sulfurous vapors that wafted up from the vents below their temple, inducing prophetic states of trance. And just as Hesiod "might celebrate the events of the future" when he was properly inspired, prophets frequently spoke in poetic language, serving, like the much older Hebrew *nabi* (one who communicates the thoughts of God), as divine ventriloquists, blending beauty and revelation. In the beginning was the word, and the word, in many traditions, was with the gods and from God, imparted to poets and prophets alike.[18]

But though the Greek poet-prophet was by no means unique, he was accorded unique status within ancient Greek society, singled out as a special being. Painters, for example, or architects or sculptors, enjoyed no such favor, despite the ancient world's admiration of their handiwork. Deemed craftsmen—artisans who labored with their hands—they were judged inferior to those who labored with their minds, a prejudice that would endure until at least the time of the Renaissance. In ancient Greece, poets were privileged. It was they who kept alive the memories of the past. It was they who told the stories of the gods and heroes. And it was they who served as the principal educators of the youth, imparting morals and models of conduct in what was still a predominantly oral culture. In the greatest masters—Hesiod and Homer above all—the culture conceived its spokesmen, and as the many surviving busts of these two men indicate, they were held in particularly high esteem.

But why should Homer and Hesiod have been singled out by the gods? Any simple answer to the question is complicated by the fact that the works of "Homer" and "Hesiod" were not composed by single "authors." The thousands of lines we attribute to them, in other words, were a blend of different voices, worked and reworked by many as they were handed down orally over the centuries. Still, contemporaries believed that the poems were the product of that special in-breathing conferred on those who exhaled them. Which only begged the question of why the Muse should choose to settle here and not there. Were the greatest poets like lightning rods, drawing energy from the sky? Perhaps there was special metal in their souls, a "conducting" agent that summoned this power? Or were they merely empty vessels, filled from on high?

The earliest Greeks seem to have had no notion of innate poetic ability, a perspective that would have harmonized well with the common observation, by no means confined to Greece, that the gods—or God—worked in mysterious ways, frequently conferring power on the unsuspecting. The greatest of the ancient prophets, Moses, for example, was "slow of speech and tongue" until God filled him with words. "Who gave human beings their mouths?" replies Yahweh in answer to Moses's fumbling protests that he was not worthy to speak for the Lord. God himself decides whom to fill with his breath, and he needn't give an account of his choices, however unlikely they might seem. In the same way, the gods and Muses inspired where they would.[19]

This ancient notion of the utter passivity of the poet was given its most explicit formulation well after the fact by Socrates's pupil Plato, who develops in his early and middle dialogues, the *Ion* and the *Phaedrus*, a theory of inspiration that would exert a tremendous influence on later understandings of genius. There Plato puts forth the view that poets and rhapsodists who recite their works are inhabited and taken over by the Muse in moments of production and performance. "God takes away the mind of these men," he says, "and uses them as his ministers, just as he does soothsayers and godly seers." Like ecstatic prophets, poets are filled by the divine breath—they are inspired, possessed. God is the source of their power.[20]

Nor is that all. For to be possessed, Plato insists, is to lose one's mind, to cede one's self entirely to the god. "Unable ever to compose until he has been inspired and put out of his senses, and his mind is no longer in him," the poet experiences radical alienation in the enthusiasm of composition. He is caught up in the grips of *mania*, a form of madness or inspiration that Latin commentators, on Plato's example, would later describe as the *furor poeticus*, the poetic "fury" or "frenzy" that claims a poet in the midst of impassioned composition or recital. In such an enthusiastic trance, the poet's mind is literally not his own. Temporarily insane, he is in ecstasy (from the Greek *ek-stasis*, literally a standing outside of oneself), a condition that Plato explicitly relates in the *Phaedrus* to other forms of divine alienation. Playing on the close similarity in Greek between the words for madness (*manike* or *mania*) and prophecy (*mantike*), Plato describes there how the Sybil and other priestesses in the ancient world delivered their ecstatic pronouncements while possessed, predicting the future, and granting oracles, inspired by the god Apollo. This "prophetic madness," like "poetic madness," bore a direct affinity to what Plato describes as a kind of "mystical madness," induced by the god Dionysius during cultic rites, which filled religious devotees with ecstasy and enthusiasm, taking them temporarily out of themselves.[21]

Plato insisted that these forms of "divine madness" owed not to sickness or disease, but to a divinely inspired presence. As such, they were gifts of the gods. And yet it should also be clear that his account was not without its ambiguities, particularly where poets were concerned. For by taking the position that poets were nothing but empty vessels—and totally out of their minds!—Plato denied them any merit or knowledge of their own. And while there was ample precedent for that claim, by the time Plato formulated it in the fourth century BCE, the Greeks had also elaborated a notion of poetry as an art—a *technê*, or craft—whose rules could be learned and intricacies perfected by practice and the accumulation of skill. The poet needed inspiration, to be sure, but that divine gift could be refined through cultivation.

Plato, however, explicitly denies that poetry is an art of this kind, taking pains in the *Ion* to demonstrate that all good poets compose and utter their work "not from art, but as inspired and possessed." And if the poet, like the prophet and the religious ecstatic, practices an art that is no art, he can have no real knowledge of what he does, no wisdom at all. His madness may be divine, but it is madness all the same, irrational and potentially dangerous. Poets, Plato seems to suggest, are a little bit crazy and so must be watched, and indeed in the *Republic* he makes that suggestion explicit, calling, in an oft-cited discussion, for the poets to be censored in his ideal community, and even banished, until they can give a proper account of their benefit to the state. Ironically, the theory of poetic inspiration that would later prove so influential among poets was used by Plato to challenge their claim to authority.[22]

Plato's subtle critique of the poets, however, should not be read as animus toward poetry per se—his entire oeuvre resounds with a love of poetic language and skill—but rather as a frank acknowledgment of poetry's seductive power. The divine gifts of language and imagination, he recognized, may easily be abused, above all in a political setting, where they can quickly inflame the passions and sway the soul. If the poet, in Plato's celebrated description, was a "light, winged, holy thing," this same angelic being could prove a demon.

Which raises an interesting question. What was the difference between a poet driven mad by the Muse and a philosopher like Socrates, whose *daimonion* whispered in his ear? Weren't they likewise possessed, and so equally dangerous? The question takes on added drama when we bear in mind that one of Socrates's principal accusers, the Athenian citizen Miletus, was a poet himself. Was Plato simply avenging his master in banishing the bards from the Republic? Or worse, was he committing the very same crime that the rulers of Athens had committed against his beloved teacher, condemning the appeal to a god he could not control?

The distinction between the two cases becomes clearer when the divine madness of poetry, prophecy, and religious ecstasy are contrasted with what Plato describes in the *Phaedrus* as a fourth type of mania, the divine madness of love, which offers a glimpse of yet another way of conceiving that special something said to distinguish the most exalted human beings. Love, too, is a potentially dangerous force, which may possess us utterly and completely, as a shuddering orgasm or a jealous rage make only too clear. But though the gods who impart it—Eros and Aphrodite—can be the bearers of a fury and frenzy of their own, Plato maintained that they could be channeled and controlled, given direction and course. By choosing an exalted object of desire, we might not just be led along, but lead ourselves, learning to love in a process that Sigmund Freud would later describe as sublimation, the redirection of erotic energy to "higher" things. This is a theme of much of Plato's work, but immediately following his discussion of divine madness in the *Phaedrus*, he gives it a particularly arresting articulation by focusing on the vehicle of ascent. That vehicle is the soul, he says, "immortal," "self-moving," and endowed metaphorically with wings, "which have the power to lift up heavy things and raise them aloft where the gods all dwell." The soul, he claims further, is composed of three parts—reason, will, and desire—which he likens in a famous image to a charioteer hitched to two winged horses, one white and noble, the other black and unruly. The driver, who occupies the place of reason, attempts to goad the two horses—his will and desire—ever upward in an effort to return the soul to the place whence it came: the realm of the immortal gods. But those souls that get weighed down by earthly things—their dark horse led astray—will never soar to the heights of truth. Only those led successfully by reason can do so, and in Plato's view, it is the philosopher (*philosophos*), the passionate lover of truth, who achieves the greatest heights. Striving to discipline his will and curb his unruly desires, the philosopher orients himself toward lofty things, standing "outside human concerns" in order to "draw close to the divine." Ordinary people will "think he is disturbed and rebuke

him for this, unaware that he is possessed by god." They will "charge
that he is mad." But his madness is in truth the highest form of wisdom.
"Perfect as perfect can be," he knows the *furor divinus*, the divine fury,
and is privy to extraordinary vision and power. Like Socrates, this philosopher lives in the "grip of something divine."[23]

Here then was a form of divine inspiration that, while unruly and
potentially dangerous, like all forms of possession, could nonetheless be
cultivated and at least partially controlled by the appropriate forms of
training. Philosophy, unlike poetry or prophecy, was a craft that could be
learned, and throughout his works, Plato places a good deal of emphasis
on the kind of education necessary to acquire it. Which is not to imply
that Plato believed that philosophy could simply be imparted to any and
all: the vision of truth that it afforded could only be glimpsed by the
special few. On several occasions, Plato suggests that Socrates alone had
succeeded in training his eye to see in this way. To "live in the grip of
something divine"—and to see accordingly—was a privilege of very special souls.

Did that mean that Socrates's own philosophical soul was constitutionally different from that of other men? That his nature—and that of
other great-souled individuals like him—was somehow distinctive and
unique? To put the question another way, can it be said that Socrates was
not only possessed by, but in possession of, a special power? Any speculation to that effect in the context of Plato's thought must bear in mind
that he likely shared with other early Greeks, such as Pindar and Protag-
oras, a belief in metempsychosis, or the transmigration of the soul. If all
souls are shaped by their past experiences, and are born into the world
bearing the imprint of prior knowledge, then it follows that they would
indeed be "unequal" at birth, endowed with varying capacities. It is also
true that in a famous passage in the *Republic*, Plato acknowledges the
expediency of conceiving of human beings as constitutionally unequal in
this way. It would be useful, he maintains, to perpetuate the belief that
social hierarchies are natural, that the body politic reflected the composition of souls. The rulers of his ideal republic are taught to believe that
they have souls of "gold," while their auxiliaries possess souls of "silver,"
and the lowly workers and craftsman, souls of "iron" or bronze. Plato
describes this fiction as a "magnificent myth" or "noble lie"—politically
useful, if not true.[24]

Men's souls, clearly, are not composed of gold. But that their "metal"
might be measured in another way is suggested in a fascinating aside in
Plato's dialogue *Timaeus*, where he repeats an assertion made elsewhere
that every man has a *daimon*, an attendant guardian, linking him to the

divine. Rather than describe this *daimon* as a separate being, as he does on other occasions, however, Plato equates it directly with the rational part of one's soul, whose seat, he says, is in the head. It is that part of us—human reason (*logos* or *nous*)—that is most heavenly and divine, the part that can be "fed" and nourished by learning and contemplation. Critically, Plato adds that insofar as one is "forever tending his divine part and duly magnifying that *daimon* who dwells along with him, he must be supremely blessed," he must have a great *daimon*. The suggestion would seem to be that a man like Socrates, who cultivated the rational part of his soul more assiduously than anyone before him, should be singled out not just for his state of possession but also for what he possessed. His special sign, his *daimonion*, on this interpretation, was not an extrinsic spirit or god, but his own elevated soul, his own beautiful mind.[25]

Plato never made that suggestion perfectly clear. But others did. The pre-Socratic philosopher Heraclitus, for example, observed cryptically in a surviving fragment that "man's character is his *daimon*" (*ethos anthropoi daimon*), implying that soul and spirit were one. And later the Roman Platonist Apuleius argued in his celebrated treatise on Socrates's *daimonion*, *De Deo Socratis*, that "in a certain sense even the human mind itself, even while still located in the body, can be called a *daimon*." But if there was thus some basis in Platonic terms for thinking of the mind as the possessor of its own exalted power, posterity would tend to seize on the more arresting image in Plato of the mind possessed—of the prophet, poet, mystic, or philosopher seized in divine fury by an alien power, whether a *daimon*, an angel, or the Holy Ghost. For the contrasting model of the mind as the generative source of its own imaginings, posterity turned to a different tradition—one that also originated with the poets, but that culminated not in the tradition of Plato, but in that of his leading student, Aristotle.[26]

THE TRADITION CAN BE TRACED to the poet Pindar, who lived about a hundred years before Plato in the second half of the fifth century BCE, and who seems to have been the first to formulate a view of innate talent in Greece. Suggesting that the gods endowed "different men with different skills," and that each should strive to live "according to his nature" (*phusis*), Pindar contrasted inborn capacities with learning, art, or craft and came down decidedly on the side of the former. Nature trumped nurture: "Everything that is natural is best." Extraordinary poetic ability, on this view—and by extension supreme talents of every kind—must be present from birth. The great-souled or great-natured individual—the *megalophues*—could lay claim to an inherent capacity that could never be acquired simply by practice or rivaled by learning and craft.[27]

This opposition between the skill acquired by learning and the gifts conferred by nature was invoked by many critics in the ancient world, and eventually served as the basis for a particularly modern prejudice— that true genius is always born, never learned—with Pindar himself held up in the eighteenth century as a case in point, a paragon of the original genius. In the ancient world, however, and for centuries thereafter, nurture and nature (*ars et ingenium*) were most often seen as complementary, and the same is true of the belief in natural endowment and the theory of poetic inspiration. For though the two views of the creative process could be contrasted as competing ideal types, more frequently they were paired. Nowhere does Pindar himself, for example, present nature and inspiration in opposition. Natural gifts, after all, were themselves divinely conferred, bestowed on the individual at birth by the gods. In this sense, there was nothing "natural" about the man of natural endowment. Just like the man possessed, the possessor of great nature was divinely touched, singled out and chosen by the gods. There was no good reason why a man so favored should not receive further offerings from the Muse, blown directly into his soul. Those who have shall receive.[28]

It was only later, in fact, in Aristotle's *Poetics*, written in the middle of the fourth century BCE, that one finds an explicit, if still tentative, distinction between natural endowment and inspiration. There Aristotle briefly contrasts poetry written as a "happy gift of nature" with that conceived through a "strain of madness" of the sort that lifts one "out of his proper self." And though he does not elaborate on the difference, it is safe to say that Aristotle was more comfortable with possessors of natural talent than with men possessed. His matter-of-fact mind tended to eschew the sort of soaring flights of ecstasy that characterized the divine fury, and he was also forthright in his assumption that human natures were differently formed. The souls of women were manifestly inferior to those of men, he believed, and nature had shaped many individuals to be "natural" slaves. What Plato presented as a useful fiction—that some minds were constitutionally different from others—Aristotle held to be a simple truth. At the very least, an outstanding man must be that—a man—born free and with a soul amenable to the kind of training that could make for true greatness and virtue.[29]

Yet notwithstanding these basic differences of temperament and outlook, Aristotle left behind a theory that could accommodate elements of his master's teachings: the possessor of natural talent might still be conceived as a man possessed. True, Aristotle himself did not write the critical text in question, the *Problemata*, or *Problems*, though it was assumed until recently that he had. The work is representative nonetheless of an "Aristotelian" tradition of great influence regarding matters of the mind.[30]

The *Problems* is a collection of ruminations on perplexing questions of "science," such as why some women are bald or some men hairy. And Book 30 opens by inquiring, "Why is it that all those who have become eminent in philosophy or politics or poetry or the arts are clearly of an atrabilious [melancholy] temperament, and some of them to such an extent as to be affected by diseases caused by black bile? . . ." The assumption and point of departure—that men of eminence across various fields share what we would describe as a common physiological makeup—reflects not only a belief in a natural or inherent disposition to excellence, but also the influence of a broader tradition of medical speculation that was evolving at the same time that Aristotle and his students were active. Best expressed in the writings of the ancient physician Hippocrates (c. 460–377 BCE) and later systematized by Galen (c. 130–200 CE), this tradition set forth the powerful humoral theory of the body, which explained the operation of the human constitution according to the interactions of four vital fluids, or humors: blood, phlegm, yellow bile, and black bile, the latter rendered in Greek *melan* (black) + *chole* (bile), or, in Latin, *atra bilis*. In healthy individuals, these humors were thought to flow in harmony and balance. But a disequilibrium could strongly affect mood, creating (in names we retain to the present day) phlegmatic, sanguine, choleric, and melancholy types. The latter were thought to be particularly prone to anxiety, sadness, and morbid delusions, and so those born with a superabundance of black bile were at risk for a variety of afflictions. But as the author of the *Problems* maintains, such individuals were also comparatively rare, and when black bile was present in just the right proportions and at just the right temperature, it could have extraordinary effects, inducing states of "frenzy and possession" like that which gripped "the Sibyls and soothsayers and all inspired persons." Conducive to prophetic powers, a melancholy temperament could likewise spur imagination, poetic invention, and mental prowess of various kinds. Ajax and Heracles were men of this type, along with "many others of the heroes," "most of the poets," and philosophical giants on the order of Plato and, not least, Socrates.[31]

And so the *Problems* provided a quasi-scientific account of the nature of eminent men, explaining how certain individuals were inherently predisposed to greatness. But it did so while at the same time affirming key aspects of Plato's theory of possession. Those of a particular constitution were susceptible to states that closely resembled the *furor divinus*, privy to ecstatic visions and prophetic flights. Reaffirming a connection to mental instability and even madness, the *Problems* offered grounds for thinking of the possessor as possessed, of the man of natural talents as specially inspired, just as Plato's own theory provided grounds for thinking of the possessed as a possessor, with the anointed figure of Socrates attended by the strange demon that was his exalted mind. The two main perspectives on human mental prowess to emerge from Greek antiquity were thus mutually reinforcing to a considerable extent, together consolidating a view of the godlike individual who was at once divinely anointed and potentially dangerous and unstable in his special election: a man who was more than man, but who could also be less. As Roman interpreters incorporated these accounts into their own understandings of human nature and special possession, the collective picture of that special something that attended men of eminence emerged in even more vivid terms.

L ISTEN ONCE AGAIN to the poets, this time of Rome, who sing also of man and what sets him apart. Tibullus, in the first century BCE, writes of paying homage to his *genius*—the god of his birth—with unmixed wine, cakes soaked in honey, incense, dancing, and games. For Ovid, the usual kinds of honors include propitious prayers and fine words, together with cakes and

> *a white robe hanging from my shoulders,*
> *a smoking altar garlanded with chaplets,*
> *grains of incense snapping in the holy fire. . . .*

Horace celebrates the *genius* of a friend by throwing a great party on his "natal day." A "full bottle of old wine from the Alban Hills" is set aside for the occasion, and garlands are prepared:

> *The household is getting ready; the silver is polished,*
> *The cups and flagons gleam; the household altar,*
> *Adorned with leaves, is ready, awaiting the offerings,*
> *Everyone hurries.*

All those who have attended a birthday celebration or the feast of a patron saint will know something of this elemental excitement, the festive commemoration that attends birth and being in the world. They also will have participated, however unwittingly, in the last remnants of a once flourishing pagan rite. For what Ovid describes as the *festum geniale*, the annual ritual and sacrifice to one's *genius*, is the distant ancestor of the birthday party. The cake that now features so centrally there was once a primary offering, along with flowers and wine. Even the wish that we make as we close our eyes to blow out the candles recalls the prayer once offered before the flicker of the altar. An act of homage and sacrifice to *genius*.[32]

The word is Latin, spelled precisely as it is in the subtitle of this book, though its modern meanings only faintly recall the ancient ones. And yet the Roman rumination on what this power was, who it attended, and how it might express itself closely tracked the Greek discussion of the *daimonic* forces that moved through human beings. To inquire after a person's *genius* was to ask what kind of man he was, what nature he might possess, or what force might possess him, connecting him to the gods.

Genius, from the Latin verb *gigno*, *gignere*, meant to generate, father, beget. Its cognates are abundant, multiplying in words like *gens* (people or clan), *genus* (birth, descent, race), and our own "gene" and "genital," from whence all else derives. *Genius*, a begetter, one who begets. *Genius*, the father of us all. The origins are obscure. The oldest surviving literary references to *genius* are from the Roman playwright Plautus, who describes, in the third century BCE, an aging miser who, upon the theft of his gold, regrets pleasures never spent. "I have cheated myself, my soul (*animus*) and my *genius*," the character pines, like many before him and many since. Elsewhere, Plautus's comic personae speak of making war on *genius* by starving it of food and sex. But "to indulge one's genius" (*indulgere genio*) would also become, if it was not already, a common Latin idiom, meaning "to yield to passion," to indulge in the good things of life. "Indulge the genius, let us seize the sweet things of life" ("Indulge genio, carpamus dulcia"), advises the first-century Roman satirist Persius. The idiom would remain in use until at least the sixteenth century, when Erasmus saw fit to include it in his *Adagia*, a vast annotated compendium of Latin and Greek proverbs.[33]

But if to feed one's *genius* was to give it sustenance and sex—and to deny it, to deny natural desires—what was this *genius* itself? Plautus's invocation of the word gestures to meanings now covered over by time. Yet this much is clear: *genius* from its earliest origins was power—an elemental "life force," in one classicist's description, a "ubiquitous divine power penetrating the world of appearances," in the words of another. *Genius* was energy, a sacred presence akin to what the Romans called *numen*, the aura of a god, or the *mana* of animistic cultures, strange spirits and forces of nature. In the Roman case, however, the power of *genius* seems always to have been linked to generation. And so there are indications, stretching all the way back to the time of the Etruscans in the eighth century BCE, of a connection between this propagating life force and the phallus, the Etruscans' lord and giver of life. The Romans associated it in art with the horn of plenty and the snake, both symbols of reproductive capacity. The horn, with its undulating shaft, was a ubiquitous sexual metaphor in its own right, and of course still is (Are you feeling horny?). And even more plainly, the serpent, close to the ground and all things that rise from it, was seductive by virtue of its shape alone: it is an archetypal symbol of fecundity and procreation in many ancient cultures.[34]

In early Italian religion, probably preceding even the founding of the Roman Republic at the end of the sixth century BCE, the snake appears to have served as a totem of *genius*, a sacred creature that watched over the family and clan, embodying its reproductive power and guarding its lands. It is revealing that two of Rome's greatest chroniclers, Plutarch and Livy, took pains centuries later to comment on the persistence of the legend of the begetting of Alexander the Great by an immense serpent-*genius*. A snake, Livy reports, was often seen in the bed chambers of Olympia, Alexander's mother, and evidently possessed her. Livy's successor, Suetonius, recounts a similar tale, telling of the magical serpentine origins of the emperor Augustus. Following his reptilian conception, a serpent-shaped mark appears on the body of Augustus's mother, Attia, and in the requisite time—ten months in Suetonius's reckoning by the lunar calendar—the future emperor is born as young Octavian, his genius engendered by *genius*.[35]

An enduring symbol of reproductive power, the snake was also closely associated, as these examples suggest, with the space in which that power was transmitted. Romans would eventually come to see the *genius loci*, or "genius of the place" as inhabiting a great variety of spaces, from mountain springs to military barracks to entire cities. But if all such places could have their presiding spirits, the original haunt of the snake was the bounded property of the clan's paterfamilias: the earliest dwelling of *genius* was the home. It seems to have been considered early on as one of a number of minor household deities and protectors, including Vesta, the goddess of the hearth; the Penates, the spirits of the storeroom; and the Lares, the gods of the homestead. Even more specifically, the power of the *genius* gathered about the *lectus genialis*, the marital bed, which served as a magical site of generation. It was here, at the point of procreation, where the clan and the family were conceived—where its "genes" were passed from one "generation" to the next—that the sacred power of *genius* revealed itself and was fully disclosed.[36]

Just how and when, precisely, the free-flowing life-force of the early Italian *genius* became a personal spirit and individual protector of the sort invoked by Ovid and Horace is not altogether clear, though it is easy enough to imagine the general progression: a power initially associated with procreation, and believed to course through the body of the paterfamilias, was gradually envisioned not just as the divine energy of the one who maintained the family, but as divinity itself, accompanying, watching over, and protecting all men from the moment of their birth. What we do know is that by the late second century BCE, and probably well before, the personal life-force invoked by Plautus with the coming of the word had been transformed into a personal protector, a guardian and tutelary spirit. It is altogether revealing of the early sexual connection that this *genius* was considered by Romans as exclusively a guardian of men. Even when the concept was extended from the patriarch and his dominions to other corporations and places, the *genius* retained a strongly gendered sense, conceived as the originating principle of the institution, the founding father and enduring source of its "life" that preserved continuity over time. Such instances only reaffirmed the active male character of *genius*, an association that would long outlive the Roman cult.[37]

A guardian and protector, the *genius* was simultaneously conceived as an intercessor to the divine and a spiritual embodiment of what was unique to the character of each man. Horace reflects this dual sense in a well-known passage from the *Epistles*, when he asks what determines the difference in temperament between two brothers, the one lazy and fancy-free, the other serious and hardworking. Only our *genius* knows, Horace responds,

> *that companion who controls our birth-star,*
> *the god of human nature, mortal throughout each man's life,*
> *variable in features, bright and gloomy.*

The *genius*, an individual's intimate "companion" (*comes*) and spiritual double, is aware of, and responsible for, the differences that shape human personalities and determine their fates. And fate is written in the stars. That, at any rate, was the assertion of ancient astrologers, whose influence on popular Roman religious beliefs was extensive. Horace's invocation of the birth-star (*astrum natale*) reflects that influence, which precisely in this period was giving to the concept of *genius* a pronounced astrological inflection. The connection is understandable: a *genius* was the god of our conception, honored on our birthday, the day on which the stars aligned in such a way as to assign our fate and form our character, giving us a "personality" and particular traits. And so it was natural to conclude that this god was a powerful force in the zodiac, guiding the alignment of the planets that influenced our temperament and predicted our destiny.[38]

It was also natural to conclude that this god—who might soar through the heavens to intercede with the divine forces of the universe— was also resident within us. Roman commentators disagreed about the precise dwelling place of the *genius*—whether it hovered continually about us, or was resident within, whether it took its seat in the head, or the knees (*genua*), or suffused the entire body like a breath or soul. But given that the *genius* helped to form a unique temperament and character in us from birth—and was invariably represented in statuary and painting as an individual's exact likeness—the relationship between this divine companion and one's inborn nature was close. Already in Roman times, *genius* was intimately related to a cognate word with which it would much later be conflated entirely, the classical Latin *ingenium*, meaning our inborn nature, disposition, or talent. Formed from the prefix "in" and the accusative form of the noun *genius*, the word literally meant the *genius* within—the nature of the god that shapes us. And as every man has a different *genius*, a different guardian and companion, so, too, does each man have a different personality, a different nature and fate. The two notions, *genius* and *ingenium*, tended to merge.

And so a line of inquiry that had preoccupied the Greeks—what makes the nature of men, and, more specifically, what makes the nature of great men—also exercised the Romans, who drew freely on the answers of the predecessors they so admired. As they did so, they conflated their own reflections on *genius* and *ingenium* with Greek speculation about the *daimon* and natural talent (*phusis*). Thus can a Roman author like Seneca observe, in a much-repeated gloss on the Pseudo-Aristotelian *Problems*, that "there can be no great *ingenium* without a touch of madness." Others embraced Plato, giving his divine enthusiasm the Latin name by which it would resound through the ages, the *furor poeticus*, that divine *afflatus* or breath that served as a species of the more general *furor divinus*. Still other influential commentators refused to take sides. Cicero, for example, sings the praises of *ingenium*—that natural talent that cannot be learned—while also endorsing the enthusiastic transports of divine inspiration. Horace, in his *Ars Poetica*, invokes the madness of outstanding poets, conflating the Pseudo-Aristotelian and Platonic accounts. And the author known as Longinus, in a treatise on the sublime that would have a major impact on later thinking about genius, describes how writers of great natural talents were in possession of a force that could carry them out of themselves "above all mortal range," lifting them "near the mind of God."[39]

In all of these ways, Roman subjects carried on and kept alive the Greek discussion about what outstanding individuals had in their possession—or what it was that possessed them—to make them more than ordinary men. But the best example of such syncretism is the Romans' reflection on what they came to call the *genius* of Socrates. Already in the first century, Plutarch's treatise *On the Sign of Socrates* was being called, in Latin, *De Genio Socratis* (On Socrates's *genius*), a convention that the English poet John Dryden adopted when he translated Plutarch's writings into English in the seventeenth century. Not long after Plutarch, Apuleius asserted in his own reflection on the "god" of Socrates the direct correspondence of the Greek *daimon* and the Roman *genius*. The coupling allowed Romans to see their own *genii* in Greek demons, and vice versa. Thus can the learned Varro speak of the *genius* in terms that borrowed from Plato's conception of the *daimon* as the rational part of the soul. "*Genius,*" he writes, in a now lost manuscript cited by Saint Augustine, "is the rational soul (*anima rationalis*) of each man." Apuleius maintained that position while further incorporating the received Greek notion that human beings were guided not only by a good god, a friendly *daimon-genius*, but an evil one as well. Whereas the good *genius* was simultaneously the god and soul of each man—dwelling "in the inmost sanctum of the human mind in the function of consciousness itself"— the evil *genius* represented our potential for wickedness and depravity. Plutarch, similarly, recounts in a famous passage how Brutus, the slayer of Caesar, sat alone in his camp one night during the Second War of the Triumvirate with "a dim light burning by him," as the other soldiers slept: "Reasoning about something with himself and very thoughtful, he fancied some one came in, and, looking towards the door, he saw a terrible and strange appearance of an unnatural and frightful body standing by him without speaking. Brutus boldly asked it, 'What are you, of men or gods, and upon what business come to me?' The figure answered, 'I am your evil genius, Brutus; you shall see me at Philippi.'" Philippi is the place where Brutus dies. His evil *genius* is his angel of death. The Roman soul in this reckoning becomes the site of a great war of *genii*, a battlefield of conflicting forces of the divine. By the fourth century, the Roman grammarian Servius was perfectly explicit on the matter, writing that "when we are born, we are allotted two *genii*: one exists which urges us toward good things, the other which corrupts us towards evil things." To the stronger would go the spoils.[40]

Not everyone, to be sure, affirmed the existence of twin *genii*. A single *genius* could just as easily be made to do the work of two, leading men wisely, or leading them astray. But whether conceived as a single or double agent, a procreative urge or the highest faculty of the soul, a guardian spirit, an emissary of evil, or a fragment of the great World Soul, the governing spirit that some said permeated the universe, the classical *genius*, was, in all its forms, a piece of the divine in man—with him, in him, about him, animating his existence, enchanting his world. Serving to connect the individual to a form of being that was different from and beyond human existence, it assured him that he did not walk alone in the universe, but shared his journey with his private god, his *comes*, his companion double and friend. With his *genius*, the individual was in the presence of a force other than himself that was greater than himself, a divine expression of his nature that linked him to the gods.[41]

All men had a *genius*. But no man's *genius* was the same as any other's. And just as the *genius* of Socrates was conceived as a special being—a reflection of his own uncommon nature and self—the *genii* of the greatest Romans were imagined as extraordinary and unique. One, in particular, that of Brutus's adversary at Philippi, came to dominate all others, seeking to subsume the *genius populi*, the *genius* of the Roman people. Whereas Socrates's *daimonion* forbade him to enter politics, the *genius* of Octavian, the future Augustus Caesar, urged him to extend his sway over all.

THERE WERE OTHERS BEFORE him who had been moved in this way, other god-men and heroes who sought to impose their will on the world. The model of the kind was Alexander. Both Octavian and Julius Caesar were captivated by the man, who had paraded in triumph across empires in the mid-fourth century BCE, seizing the imagination, while shedding the blood, of the ancient world. Alexander, who unraveled the Gordian Knot, slashing with his sword, where others lost themselves in loops. Alexander, the brilliant commander, who conquered much of the world before he was thirty, and kept a copy of Homer close to his person at all times. It was a gift from his teacher, Aristotle, and an ever-present reminder of what men who were more than men could be. Alexander, who longed not only to do extraordinary things, but to have them remembered, to be a man of whom the Muses would sing. Alexander, who died, half mad, claiming to be a god.

It has been said that Alexander was the first famous person. His fame was very much willed, the product less of position, dynasty, or tradition than of who he was and who he aimed to be. In this respect Alexander differed from earlier divine rulers, the Chinese emperors or Egyptian pharaohs, who also claimed to rule as gods on earth, but who did so on the basis of what had come before or what had always been. Vast pyramids and terracotta armies, still standing, recall their names. But Alexander's renown was different; he made it largely for himself. His example inspired all who yearned for fame in the ancient world, and fame was highly coveted, above all among Alexander's Roman successors. "The nobler a man is, the more susceptible he is to the sweets of glory," Cicero maintained. Cicero was more susceptible than most, wondering aloud how he would be remembered 1,000 years in the future, and marveling at the example of Alexander, who had the foresight to bring along historians to record the details of his campaigns. Cicero did him one better: he did his own recording. But those who coveted the very highest glory were drawn directly to the source, traveling to Alexander's tomb in the city he had founded in Egypt, Alexandria, as if one might glean his secrets simply by being in the place. Pompey went there, and Julius Caesar, and, most famously of all, Caesar's grand-nephew and adopted son, Octavian, the future emperor Augustus, who made the journey after defeating his rival, Marc Antony, at the Battle of Actium in 31 BCE and deposing Antony's consort, the queen Cleopatra. Unsealing the tomb, Octavian placed a crown on Alexander's corpse and covered it with flowers, inadvertently breaking off the nose. Octavian was only thirty-three. Standing before this prodigy, he must have wondered: How does one account for this marvel of a man? How can one explain Alexander's greatness?[42]

Contemporaries could only have done so in the way they explained all extraordinary achievement, by reference to the divine. Today we would call it "genius," "charisma," or both. The terms are ours, though the roots are ancient, in the latter case from the Greek *kharis*, meaning divine favor or grace, a gift of the gods. Charisma is, by definition, a thing apart—as its first and still most famous analyst, the German sociologist Max Weber, took pains to observe, a certain ineffable something, a quality of the personality or soul, that created the illusion that one was touched by supernatural, superhuman, or exceptional powers. Alexander had this thing—this *numen*, this aura—and to such a degree that it was easy to conflate the giver with the gift.[43]

Octavian was no Alexander when it came to moving men on the battlefield, and no Julius Caesar either. But as a strategist of power, he was at least their equal, and like them seems to have recognized in a penetrating way a paradox of eminence in the ancient world. Greatness, and the fame it conferred, must be willed. But greatness must depend, and must seem to depend, on what was not—on what was ineluctable, fated, foreordained. Men of eminence took their breath from the gods; they were in their nature unnatural; they possessed extraordinary *ingenium*, strange demons, uncommon *genius*. The man sired by a snake understood this, and believed it, too, as a man of the ancients must. And in that combination of calculation and conviction, he wrought something without precedent. If the worship of the *genius* of Augustus is a turning point in the history of fame, it is no less a landmark in the history of genius itself.[44]

Already, there were intimations in his youth. The historian Suetonius recounts how, as a young man, Octavian visited an astrologer with Agrippa, his close friend and ally, the future general of renown. When the astrologer predicted the commander's brilliance, Octavian remained silent, withholding the details of his own birth for fear that he might be shown to possess a less exalted fate than his friend. But when he finally agreed to share them, the astrologer jumped up and venerated him, overcome by the brilliance of his destiny. "Soon," Suetonius writes, "Augustus had acquired such faith in fate that he made public his horoscope and had a silver coin struck with the image of the star sign Capricorn, under which he was born." Later, famously, when a comet appeared at games sponsored by Octavian in honor of the slain Julius Caesar, the young man interpreted the celestial disturbance as a sign that Caesar's birthstar, his *genius*, had returned to signal his favor, urging the adopted son to fulfill his father's fate. Henceforth, he would claim the *sidus Iulium*, the "Julian star," as his own.[45]

Octavian's faith in his own destiny was only reaffirmed by the stunning victory at Actium against Mark Antony, whose *genius*, Plutarch recounts—and Shakespeare would later repeat—continually cowered before Octavian's own. The battle brought to an end a prolonged period of civil strife and left Octavian sole ruler of Rome, allowing him to complete the task initiated by Julius Caesar—that of emasculating the institutions of the fractious Republic, in effect bringing it to an end. Gradually, he consolidated his rule by investing it with divine authority, stressing his proximity—even likeness—to the gods. His official title, "Augustus," reflected this ambition. Conferred by the Senate in the year 27 BCE, the title had strong religious connotations. Ovid claims it was synonymous with *sanctus* or *divinus*—holy or divine—and though that was probably a flattering exaggeration, the term does seem to have been used to describe holy places and consecrated ground. In the popular

mind, in any case, the word was linked to *augurium* (augury), a connection that led, in turn, to another. For as everyone knew, the power
of Rome's mythical founder Romulus had been confirmed by a divine
augury—the appearance of twelve vultures in the sky—a sign of the
gods' will that Romulus should be father of Rome. And as Octavian's
promoters were well aware, educated Romans would have known the
line from the poet Ennius indicating that by "august augury," glorious
Rome was founded ("Augusto augurio postquam incluta condita Roma
est"). Octavian, too, would be a founder, a new father of his people and
a prophetic man, whose very spirit would gather in its midst the spirit of
all Rome.[46]

It was the public cult of his private *genius*, the *genius Augusti*, that consolidated that role. If, as Max Weber says further of charismatic authority, the "genuine prophet, like the genuine military leader and every true
leader in this sense, preaches, creates, or demands new obligations . . .
by virtue of oracle, inspiration, or of his own will," then the revelation
of Augustus's *genius* was a fundamental disclosure. Like all Roman men,
Octavian possessed a tutelary spirit, a personal god of birth. But it was
his crucial innovation to transform his private god into an object of public worship, conflating it in practice with the *Genius populi Romani*, the
Genius of the Roman people that had been worshipped from at least the
third century BCE. Livy recounts how, with Hannibal across the Alps and
threatening the very survival of the Republic, the Romans sacrificed "five
adult victims" (*maiores hostiae quinque*) to "Genius." It is the earliest reference to a collective or public *genius*—what later sources describe variously as the *Genius urbis Romae*, the *Genius publicus*, or the *Genius populi
Romani*. And while scholars have suggested that these gods of the city
were likely an adaptation from Hellenistic models—the cult of the *demos*
of Athens, for example, or the Tyche of the city of Antioch—the collective
genius was also a perfectly natural extension of the *genius* cult of the family, *gens*, and place. Were not Romans, too, a family of sorts, an extended
people or clan? And did not that family also have a birth, a beginning, a
generation? If a genial power could watch over the body of a person, then
a *genius* could maintain vigilance over the body politic.[47]

Something like this logic seems to have been at play in the emergence of the cult of the *genius populi* and a great many other corporate
bodies and places. But Augustus made it explicit, identifying his own
genius with the *genius populi*, rendering it the father of all. As early as
30 BCE, his compliant Senate decreed that a libation of wine should
be poured out at every meal in the fatherland in honor of the emper-
or's *genius*—a sacrifice to be conducted alike in the humblest private

dwelling and at the most lavish public banquet. Not long after, coins were struck bearing the image of Augustus's *genius*, and over the course of his long reign, various other measures and practices were put into place. In 12 BCE—the year in which Augustus assumed the title of *pontifex maximus*, the highest priestly office in the realm—a law was passed requiring that all official oaths be sworn in the name of Augustus's *genius*. Whereas members of private households had previously sworn by the *genius* of their master, and ordinary Romans frequently had sworn by the *genius* of Jove or some other god, they were now asked, indeed required, to invoke their emperor's *genius* in matters of solemnity, as Christians would later swear by the angels and the saints. At roughly the same time, Augustus introduced the cult of the crossroads (*compita*), reviving and significantly altering an ancient practice that had been abandoned during the Republic. At the crossroads of every district in Rome, the emperor ordered the construction of sanctuaries containing a sacrificial altar and images—usually statues—of his *genius* and familial Lares. A regular cult was maintained there by magistrates of the administrative districts of Rome, and a yearly festival, the Compitalia, was held involving sacrifice, feasting, and games. The carefully crafted message was clear: as crossroads marked the boundaries of territories, and the Lares and *genius* were the keepers of family and space, the cult of the *compita* united the whole of Rome with the household of Augustus. His private *genius* was the *genius* of all.[48]

The man sired by a snake thus laid claim to a god far more expansive, and far more powerful, than that of any other man. Fittingly, it was nourished, like the *Genius populi Romani*, by a victim of flesh—in this case, a great bull—sacrificed on special occasions and on Augustus's *dies natalis*, which was celebrated as a public holiday, with games and hymns in honor of the emperor's *genius*. Whether an official state cult to the *Genius Augusti* was maintained in Rome itself is debatable. But in the provinces, and the more indulgent East, special temples were undoubtedly erected in Augustus's honor, overseen by their own priesthoods. And the image of Augustus's *genius*, indistinguishable from Augustus himself—was ubiquitous on paintings, coins, public monuments, and statues. Ovid claims that in the crossroads chapels in the city of Rome alone, there were more than 1,000 figures of his *genius*, perfect likenesses of Augustus.[49]

By conflating the private god of his birth with the *genius* of the public writ large, Augustus effected an important and powerful union. *Genius* remained what it had always been—a means of connecting individuals and families to the divine. But in Augustus's hands, the *genii* of the countless inhabitants of the empire were channeled through his person, or rather, through the divine embodiment of his person, his private companion and double, which represented his innate qualities and gifts. Just as members of the Roman household had originally joined in honoring the *genius* of the paterfamilias, swearing oaths by the father's guardian spirit, so now did the Roman people honor the *genius* of their collective father, their *pater patriae*, swearing by him. The *genius* of Augustus was the spiritual force that brought together the private spirits of each member of the empire with the spirit of Rome, creating a god that towered above all others of its kind.

Augustus's flirtation with apotheosis was an innovation of major consequence. For although there were Greek precedents, as well as the short-lived examples of Alexander and Julius Caesar, both of whom were widely acknowledged as gods after their death, proud Roman republicans had never been inclined to worship their living leaders as gods. Whether they actually did so in the case of Augustus remains a matter of debate. Officially, he joined the immortal ones only at his death. But clearly the cult of his *genius* was conceived to affirm the transcendent character of his rule. The fate of Augustus was indistinguishable from that of the Roman people; his rule was inscribed in the stars, divinely consecrated and conferred.

Augustus's innovation—his revolution—put in place a regime and cult of personality of potentially dangerous consequences that would be abused by successors like Nero and Caligula, who had no compunctions about openly declaring themselves gods. To rule divinely, however, requires the genius to pull it off, and the evil *genii* of Nero and Caligula were manifestly perverse, calling attention to the poverty of their directing spirits. Few, in the end, could live up to the standard of Augustus, yet the Roman Empire lived on regardless, and with it the cult of the emperor's *genius*, which would receive libations and oaths for centuries to come. In this respect, Augustus was more successful than either Alexander or Julius Caesar before him. If charismatic authority, like the authority derived from one's genius, is always unstable—a "specifically revolutionary force" in its repudiation of the past, as dangerous as the demon in us all—Augustus provided simultaneously for its containment. He was a master of bureaucratic and administrative organization, which served to "routinize" and contain his *auctoritas* and so to survive the waning of his *genius*. Even in his innovation, he looked continually to what had been, inventing laws, discovering traditions, re-creating precedents that had long been forgotten or overlooked. By resurrecting republican morals at the very moment that he destroyed the Republic, he could thus credibly present his rule as a return to established forms.

So did the past constrain the present, and imitation of what had been hold in check what was yet to be.[50]

Yet Augustus had generated a precedent, and it was one that brought together centuries of classical reflection on the *divinum quiddam* that makes a great man truly great. The mysterious, generative force that coursed through the souls of special men might serve as the basis of a superhuman authority. The *genius* of a great man might rule as the *genius* of the people, uniting the all to the one. That this force was volatile, even dangerous, virtually all agreed—it could lead the unsuspecting to madness, take possession of the mind, divert the course of the soul. Men of eminence, Pseudo-Aristotle warned—whether poets or politicians, philosophers or practitioners of the arts—were in possession of a common power that rendered them unstable, prone to dark tempers of the soul. Plato insisted that those seized by the *daimonic* force of divine inspiration were similarly at risk, susceptible to the madness and alienation of possession. Largely for that reason, Plato would ban the poets from the public sphere as dangerous conjurers of words. And though he held out hope that in a perfect world a philosopher who knew the *furor divinus* might rule as a philosopher-king, his model of the kind refused the temptation. Socrates's *genius* kept him from politics, and the people of Athens agreed. Not all would prove so prudent. But as the twists and turns of the *daimon* led those who would be more than men to the throne of the Christian God, a new thought was born along with a new model of the highest human type. The *genius* of the individual might be worshipped in glory as an angelic force ascending to the heavens, or be consumed as an idol in the fires of hell.

CHAPTER II

THE GENIUS OF CHRISTIANITY

BUT WHEN THE GOVERNOR pressed him and said: "Take the oath and I will let you go, revile Christ," Polycarp said: "For eighty-six years I have been Christ's servant, and he has done me no wrong. How can I blaspheme the King who saved me?" But when the Governor persisted, and said, "Swear by the genius of Caesar," Polycarp replied: "if you vainly suppose that I will swear by the genius of Caesar, as you say, and pretend that you are ignorant of who I am, listen plainly: I am a Christian."

—EUSEBIUS

So POLYCARP, THE BISHOP of Smyrna and a direct disciple of the apostle John, sealed his fate before the Roman proconsul in the year 155 CE. Promptly burned at the stake and run through with a sword, Polycarp triumphed as a martyr, earning the celestial glory of a saint by refusing to acknowledge the *genius* of the pagans.[1]

Polycarp's encounter is a wonderfully concise illustration of the place of *genius* in the confrontation between pagans and Christians. It was hardly an isolated occurrence. Roman administrators used the oath as a test of allegiance during their periodic persecutions, and Christians gloried in their refusal to take it—with predictable results. "We certainly do not swear by the genius of the emperor," the prominent theologian Origen declared in the early third century. "The so-called genius of the emperor is a demon . . . and we ought rather to die than to swear by a wicked and faithless demon that commits sin with the man to whom it has been assigned." Christians ought to render unto Caesar his due, but, as Origen's contemporary, Tertullian, insisted, Caesar's evil *genius* did not figure in the allowance. Still, in denying the *genius*'s authority, both men affirmed its existence and acknowledged its power, even as they called it by another name.[2]

That ambivalence—belying at once affirmation and denial—would characterize Christian attitudes toward the pagan inheritance for centuries to come, sustaining a tension that continued well into the Renaissance. And so, even as they put forth powerful new models of the God-man Jesus Christ and those extraordinary individuals, the martyrs and the saints, who aspired to his perfection, they continued to countenance the *divinum quiddam* of the ancients. Reinventing divine possession and divinely planted power as gifts of the one true God, Christians searched for signs that set the Lord's anointed apart. Prophets were possessed by the Holy Spirit. Saints and apostles kept the company of angels. And a beautiful mind that flowered in the light of God's grace was seeded in a beautiful soul.

Christians thus conceived of their paragons in familiar terms. But they worried, too, about the dangers of a mind possessed. For to seek to be perfect as God was perfect was to expose oneself to the temptations of Satan; to court the divine fury that could lift one ecstatically to God risked calling forth the furies of the demons. The contrast was clear between a sorcerer and a saint, an angel fallen and an angel ascendant. But the line of separation was thin. The holy men of late antiquity who did battle with the demons understood that truth, as did the mystics and doctors of the medieval church, and the early modern magi, who strove, like Faust, to know God's secrets and to speak with his angels in their cryptic tongue. The divine poets and artists of the Renaissance, finally, who moved in spaces that the saints had sanctified, recalled the *genius* and *ingenium* of the ancients. And in the persons of men like Michelangelo, they joined them together, bearing the pains of inspiration and the humors of their souls as they struggled to raise themselves to God by imitating his creation. Heirs to the *daimonic* powers of the ancient world and ancestors of the modern genius: they became men who would be more than men, for better and for worse.

In the fourth-century basilica of a Roman citizen and saint, we may still catch a glimpse of this nascent Christian model of transcendence that would develop into the Renaissance, a model of inspiration and grace, of the souls of human beings spectacularly endowed, possessing or possessed.

Iᴛ ᴄᴀᴍᴇ ᴛᴏ ʜɪᴍ ɪɴ ᴀ ᴠɪsɪᴏɴ, he told his sister in a letter: the place where the bones of the martyrs Gervasius and Protasius lay. Their remains had been lost since the second century at the time of their glorious deaths. They must be found now and moved to a fitting place of rest. And so the bishop of Milan, Ambrose, sent his servants to find the spot and clear away the ground, revealing, as in the dream, "two men of marvelous stature, such as those of ancient days." The heads of the martyrs were separated from the bodies, but all the bones were perfect, and there was much blood. The witnesses assembled could feel the sacred presence, and as they stared in wonder, the "power of the holy martyrs" came upon them: one man was "seized and thrown prostrate"; others shuddered, shook, and cried out in reverence before this awesome sight.[3]

There was a great new basilica being built in the city, and a tomb beneath the altar lay empty, intended for the bishop himself. The martyrs must have his place, the bishop announced. And so, born aloft in solemn procession, the relics were carried to their new home in what Catholics describe as a "translation." Demons fled screaming from their hosts. A blind man, the butcher Servius, recovered his sight. The scripture was sound: "Whereas I was blind, now I see." Others, too, would have their eyes opened by the power of these holy martyrs, these men who were more than men, saints touched and suffused by the Holy Ghost.

Unearthed on June 17, 386, the relics of Saints Gervasius and Protasius were deposited in the newly built Basilica Ambrosiana two days later. They lie there still. Ambrose's friend Saint Augustine was on hand to observe the proceedings, and he attested to the healing of the blind man, adding that "several persons who were tormented by evil spirits were cured, for even the demons acknowledged the holy relics."[4]

Although little is known of the mortal lives of Gervasius and Protasius, their subsequent fortunes are well documented. For what is most extraordinary about their discovery and deposition is how they were later put to use. Twin overseers of the basilica, the men were embraced as its guardians—"protectors" and "defenders," as Ambrose describes them—heroic "champions," "soldiers of Christ." They also served as intermediaries, conduits to the divine, who opened the eyes of those who beheld them to "the numberless hosts of angels" and the majesty of God. Their "patronage is powerful," Ambrose affirmed. As he later declared in a sermon delivered on the third anniversary of their discovery, they were like two "good serpents" (*boni serpentes*) guarding the boundaries of their space.[5]

The description of the martyrs as serpents is striking given the fact that the image generally recalls for Christians the snake in the Garden of Eden, who slides in the grass of human sin. But Ambrose's reference in this case is literary, not scriptural. It is taken directly from a line in Virgil and evokes a classical connotation: that of the *genius loci*, whose venerable Roman symbol was the snake. The two good serpents, Gervasius and Protasius, Ambrose asserts, are good *genii*, guardians of the Basilica Ambrosiana, fathers attendant at its birth.

Ambrose was the first figure in Latin Christianity to use the term "patron" (*patronus*) in connection with Christian martyrs. Romans had employed the word to describe their own guardian protectors, whether men of power and influence, looking after their retainers, or *genii*, presiding over corporations and towns. Following Ambrose's example, Christians extended the word's sway to the martyrs, whose glorious deaths had singled them out as among God's chosen. As they did so, they joined the description to another, employing a term that Saint Paul had used in the New Testament in reference to the righteous: *agios* in Greek, *sanctus* in Latin, words that literally meant "holy." But as the word *sanctus* was applied in sermons and hagiographies extolling the lives and deaths of the Christian heroes, it began to take on the associations that it now has of "saint." The martyrs were the first such *sancti*, "holy ones" endowed with special powers that set them apart from ordinary human beings. They could ward off demons, in death as in life, because their relics retained their sacred force. And they could intercede before God, petitioning on our behalf, because they stood close to his throne. Over time, other men and women remarkable for their holiness were added to the lists of the special dead. They, too, were remembered and invoked as saints, and the sites of their remains were venerated as loci of sacred power. Patrons and protectors, intercessors to the divine, the saints followed Gervasius and Protasius in assuming the role of the Roman *genius* of old.

That process of co-optation is well attested. With their conversion to Christianity, Roman emperors in the wake of Constantine proscribed the cult of *genius*, rendering the act of sacrificing wine to the god of birth an offense punishable by death. The old ways lingered, of course; Christian missionaries in Europe complained for centuries of their stubborn persistence, singling out such practices as throwing bread and wine into springs, placing shrines at crossroads, or otherwise honoring the *genius loci* of some local place. But gradually, in late antiquity, men and women transferred much of the language and longing previously reserved for the *genius*, *daimon*, and other invisible companions to the saint. The saint was the *genius*'s heir, watching over people and places alike and protecting their human charges from birth until death. Saints bore messages and prayers, interceding for the people before God. And like the classical *comes*, saints were friends, consoling the afflicted and comforting the sick. Gradually, if steadily, the saints assumed prominence over their classical predecessors, and the signs of their triumph were abundant: in art and iconography, where the patron saint replaced the votive renderings of the *genius*; in the ubiquitous "lives of the saints," which lovingly recounted the miraculous deeds of patron protectors; in the practice of assigning saints' names to children at birth and ensuring that all, at baptism, acquired an individual patron; and finally, in the celebration of saints' days—literally the anniversary of the saint's death, but called, revealingly, their *dies natalis*, the day of their "birth" into heaven. The feast of one's patron saint replaced the birthday, the *festum geniale*, as the principal day of celebration in individual and corporate lives. It was on this day that Christians sought to propitiate those who watched over them and who interceded before God on their behalf. By the Middle Ages, every soul in Christendom had a patron, and nearly every corporation, too—guilds, clubs, confraternities, cities, countries, platoons—each with its own little shrine or sanctuary, a private altar, image, or fragment of bone. Whereas Servius had once said of the Roman Empire, "nullus loci sine genio," there is no place without a *genius*, now it could be said of Christendom, "nullus loci sine sancto," there is no place without a saint.[6]

But the patron saint was much more than simply a classical *comes* in disguise. Most obviously, the saint was a *human* mediator—indeed, very often a woman—of flesh and blood. All saints were dead, it is true, and so, strictly speaking, they were spirits of sorts, souls in the heavenly spheres until they would be reunited with their bodies at the time of the resurrection. But unlike the *genii* or *daimones*, the saints left their mortal remains behind, and those relics—venerated with tremendous passion throughout the Middle Ages—were a continual reminder that the saint had lived in flesh and bone, providing in death an image of the higher self that few could emulate but all might ponder or strive to attain. In this respect, the Christian saints resembled less the invisible companions of the ancients than a range of human exemplars common to different peoples at different times. Like legendary heroes, they underwent trials, tribulations, and tests, suffering bravely in self-sacrifice in the face of adversity. Like Hebrew prophets and bearers of the law, they were filled by the voice of God and aspired to follow his ways, striving like Abraham to lead lives of righteousness, or to keep God's commands on the model of Moses, "the greatest and most perfect man that ever lived." And like holy men of many kinds—whether Hindu *sadhus* or Buddhist *bodhisattvas*—the saints embodied the ideals of their contemporaries while going beyond and even contradicting them in the service of a higher calling. Very often they conducted their quests in isolation, for the saints, like virtually all human paragons, were deemed to be persons apart.[7]

In these and other ways, the Christian saint stood on a continuum of related types that encompassed the hero and the prophet and that one day would include the modern genius. And yet the saint was charged with another, and quite specific, demand. "Be perfect as your heavenly father is perfect," Jesus tells his disciples in the Gospel of Matthew (5:48). The example of his life drove home the point. God had become man, appearing in flesh and blood as the embodiment of divine perfection and human striving, the conquering hero par excellence. He was a living reminder of what an individual charged with divine power could be. And so to take up his cross in imitation of his life was to strive to be god-like. There were precedents for that aspiration, to be sure. All Jews knew that God had formed man after his own image and in his own likeness, suggesting a certain approximation. And the ideal of the "divine man" was well known in the ancient world, where the gods were regularly portrayed in human form and where the highest human beings, such as Alexander or Caesar, claimed to be gods incarnate. Yet the Christian injunction was more explicit, more sweeping, and more direct. Strive to be perfect as God is perfect, to participate in God's mystical body, to become a divine man like Christ. To aim for perfection in the *imitatio Christi* was to attempt to become God himself.[8]

That, it may seem, was an impossible quest, and indeed, Saint Ambrose and his great contemporary and disciple, Saint Augustine, endeavored to show that it was. Augustine devoted his enormous theological energies to proving that human nature had been fatally damaged by original sin and so could never attain perfection unaided—or in this life. Our primal transgression, he reminded his contemporaries, was precisely Adam and Eve's indulgence in the face of the serpent's promise, "You will be like God" (Gen. 3:5). Such aspirations were perilous, redolent of hubris and pride. Human beings could never attain transcendence on their own, but only be raised higher by the mystery of God's freely given grace.

Augustine's forceful articulation of this point largely succeeded in silencing for a time those who read Jesus's command to be perfect as if it were possible to fulfill. But it could not dispel the longing or the quest—nor was it, in the end, intended to do so. All who would follow Christ must seek to be Christlike, even if the goal was impossible to fulfill. The divine example of Jesus was at once a limiting condition and an ideal. And yet, the very effort to take up one's cross raised a series of nagging questions: If human beings were incapable on their own of overcoming their fallen natures, how might they advance on the road to perfection? Did those destined to be saints possess in their persons an inherent power, implanted or infused by God? To what extent could one cultivate God's gifts? And how might our own labors and works, the painstaking efforts to be Christlike, contribute to our salvation?

To take up these questions in earnest would be to recount much of the history of Christianity. Theologians have debated the answers for centuries, seeking a definitive solution to the mystery of salvation and grace that not only sundered the Catholic Church at the time of the European Reformation but has generated a range of competing positions ever since. But from the perspective of the history of genius, the salient point is that Christian debates on how human beings might attain transcendence tracked closely with the classical discussion of what it was that made a mere mortal more than a man. What was that special something, this *divinum quiddam* of grace, that made a saint a saint, and how could it be had? Was it present, like superior *ingenium*, from birth? Was it infused by a ministering spirit? Imparted directly by God to those who had earned it through sacrifice and the sweat of their brow? Affirmative answers to all these questions were possible, and they were put forth over the centuries with an explicit awareness of the classical precedents. But regardless of one's position, it was meant to be clear what the *divinum quiddam* was not. For in the context of the early church there was no escaping a direct confrontation with those mysterious beings who were said by the ancients to have raised human beings to heights that were out of reach for ordinary individuals, and who, in the special case of Socrates's *daimonion*, were able to endow a man with unsurpassed wisdom and clarity of sight. For Christians, a divine something could not a demon be.

THE WORD *DAIMONION* APPEARS often in the Greek New Testament— fifty-five times, to be exact. And though the preference for the diminutive likely reflects Christian condescension—for all pagan *daimones* were "little" before the towering majesty of Christ—the word could not help but bring the *daimonion* of Socrates to mind, making plain, for those who considered such matters, that Socrates's vaunted sign was a devil in disguise. The first Latin theologian, Tertullian, points out, for example, that "the philosophers acknowledge there are demons. Socrates himself waited on a demon's will. And why not?, since it is said that an evil spirit attached itself specially to him even from his childhood—turning his mind no doubt from what was good." Tertullian's contemporary Lactantius, a Christian author and adviser to the emperor Constantine, reminds his readers similarly in the early third century that "Socrates said that there was a demon continually about him, who had become attached to him when a boy, and by whose will and direction his life was guided." And Saint Augustine, though kindly disposed to Socrates and Plato in many ways, nevertheless sought to emphasize, in an extended discussion of the subject in his *City of God*, that Apuleius's work was misnamed: *De Deo Socratis* should rightly have been called the *Demon of Socrates*, for that is what possessed him.[9]

Tertullian, Lactantius, and Augustine all wrote in Latin, not Greek, and so employed the Latinized *daemon* to describe Socrates's guiding spirit. None chose a diminutive form to distinguish Socrates's *daimonion* from other, more general spirits, and that choice was repeated by Saint Jerome when he translated the Bible into Latin. Readers of the Vulgate, as the church's canonical text is now known, will find *daemon* used for both the Greek *daimon* and *daimonion* throughout. The choice is perfectly defensible in light of the fact that early Christians themselves were sweeping in their understanding and dismissal of the spirits that haunted the mind. The pagan gods, the tutelary *daimones* or *genii*, devils and malignant spirits—all could (and did) fall under the general Christian category of *daemones*, "demons." What for the ancients had been a neutral term was split off and transformed: in the Christian understanding, all "demons" were evil.[10]

That redefinition—or what we might call today "rebranding"—had a curious consequence, preserving at the heart of a nominally monotheistic religion the remnants of a polytheistic conception of the world. Alongside God the Father hovered untold legions of little "gods"—never, to be sure, described by Christians as such—but present nonetheless. No wonder that early Christians saw demons everywhere! The whole of the pagan pantheon—from the Olympians to the most insignificant local *genius* or sprite—was reconceived as the product of mass illusion wrought by the work of conniving spirits. Demons had corrupted souls for centuries before the coming of Christ, and they continued to do so still in a great war for hearts and minds. They lurked about the body and haunted all manner of places, laying traps of temptation, snares of iniquity and sin. Even Jesus is approached by the demons' dark lord, the master tempter, Satan himself, who after forty days and forty nights dangles before him the "kingdoms of the world" (Matt. 4:8). Jesus resists, but not all are so strong. With legions at his command, the "prince of the demons" can lay siege to the most formidable soul.

FIGURE 1.1. Peter-Paul Rubens, *Prometheus Bound*, early seventeenth century. The Prometheus myth is an archetype of the dangers, as well as the temptations, of usurping divine creativity and knowledge. *Philadelphia Museum of Art / Art Resource, New York.*

FIGURE 1.2. William Blake, *Satan Calling Up His Legions*, c. 1805. Inspired by John Milton's *Paradise Lost*, the painting presents Lucifer, the wisest of the angels, in quasi-heroic terms as a being who dared to rival God. *National Trust Photo Library / Art Resource, New York.*

FIGURE 1.3. A fresco from first-century Roman Pompeii depicting a guardian *genius* (top center) with trademark cornucopia and offering plate, surrounded by household gods (Lares). Below are two serpents, common representations of the *genius* and *genius loci*. *Museo Archeologico Nazionale, Naples, Italy. Copyright © Vanni Archive / Art Resource, New York.*

FIGURE 2.1. Michelangelo Buonarroti, *The Torment of Saint Anthony,* c. 1487–1488. The earliest known work of "Michael of the Angels," completed when he was still an adolescent, the painting depicts a great Christian saint in combat with the demons. *Kimbell Art Museum, Fort Worth, Texas / Art Resource, New York.*

FIGURE 2.2. Albrecht Dürer, *Saint Jerome in His Study*, 1514. The translator of the Bible as a scholar-saint engrossed in contemplation, privy to special revelations. *Bpk, Berlin / Kupferstichkabinett, Staatliche Museen, Berlin / Joerg P. Anders / Art Resource, New York.*

FIGURE 2.5. Rembrandt Van Rijn, *Faust in His Study*, c. 1652–1653. The legendary Germanic myth of Faust, who sells his soul to the devil in return for occult knowledge, may have been based on an actual German magus of the fifteenth century. The legend was recycled continually thereafter, most notably by Christopher Marlowe and Goethe. *The Victoria and Albert Museum, London / Art Archive at Art Resource, New York.*

FIGURE 2.6. From Andreas Vesalius's celebrated anatomical atlas *De humani corporis fabrica* (On the structure of the human body), first published in Basel in 1543. The Latin caption reads "Genius (*ingenium*) lives on, all else is mortal." *Wellcome Library, London.*

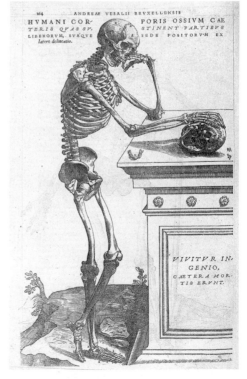

FIGURE 3.1. Louise Elizabeth Vigée-LeBrun, *The Genius of Fame*, 1789. In art, particularly iconography and painting, *genii* were prevalent in the eighteenth century, even as they were banished from life. Commonly used to depict the governing spirit of a place or an abstract entity, they were most often represented as winged cherubs or angels, a convention that dates to the Renaissance. *Bpk, Berlin / Gemäldegalerie, Staatliche Kunstsammlungen, Berlin / Joerg P. Anders / Art Resource, New York.*

FIGURE 3.2. The genius (Voltaire) with his *genius*, source of inspiration and light. The frequent coupling of *genii* and men of genius in the eighteenth century perpetuated the conflation of their powers. The Latin epigraph translates loosely as "One day he will be as dear to all, as he now is to his friends." Engraving by J. Balcchou after a portrait of Jean Michel Liotard, 1756. *Collection of the author.*

FIGURE 3.3. The prodigy of genius. A nineteenth-century re-creation of Mozart and his sister performing for the Empress Maria Theresa. *Album / Art Resource, New York.*

FIGURE 3.4. The frontispiece to Voltaire's *Elémens de la philosophie de Newton* (1738). Newton transmits the divine light of the heavens to Voltaire by way of Madame de Châtelet, the French translator of Newton's *Principia Mathematica* and Voltaire's mistress. *Florida State University Libraries, Special Collections and Archives.*

It was for that reason that men and women needed powerful protectors like Gervasius and Protasius, Christian militants who could rout the demons and put them to flight. Ambrose describes them unambiguously as soldiers, but the saints also engaged in combat as exorcists, on the model of their master, Christ. Repeatedly, in the synoptic gospels, Christ commands demons, rebukes them, and drives them out of people and places by the power of the Holy Spirit and the force of the "finger of God" (Luke 11:20). So closely are his miraculous powers linked to the expulsion of demons that he is accused by the Pharisees of being possessed himself. "It is by the prince of demons that he drives out demons," they charge before the people (Matt. 9:34). The people, nevertheless, are in awe, as are Jesus's own disciples when they learn that their master's power is being transferred to them. The "authority to drive out demons" (Mark 3:14–16) is part of Christ's legacy and gift, bequeathed to the apostles, and then to holy men such as Gervasius and Protasius, men of power who continued the work of Christ. Well into the Middle Ages, the tombs of the martyrs would serve as important sites of exorcism, noisy howling places where, as Augustine gloated, the demons "are tormented, and acknowledge themselves for what they are, and are expelled from the bodies of the men they have possessed."[11]

But if the saints thus exorcised and purged demons—serving as soldiers on the front lines of a great cosmic battle with evil—their triumph was not simply one of brawn. For the same power that allowed them to detect and defeat the many *daimones* of the world provided them with a piercing clarity of vision, the capacity to see through ephemera in order to penetrate to the eternal truths of existence. The soul of the saint was a highly developed instrument that put its possessor in direct contact with the divine. Saints were privy to a higher order of knowledge and understanding: they could relay messages and dispatch wisdom, utter prophesies, petition miracles, and disclose truths with epiphanic power. Privileged to see and hear where others were blind and deaf, saints had access to the deepest verities of existence and so could lay claim to insight and inspiration that no ordinary mortal could attain.

It was in part to honor this aspect of the holy ideal that the church singled out a class of saints renowned for their immense learning and vision, the so-called "doctors" of the church (from the Latin verb *docere*, to teach). Employed somewhat loosely by patristic writers, the title was eventually formalized around the four founding "great doctors," the church fathers Ambrose, Augustine, Jerome, and Gregory, who were widely recognized as such by the early eighth century. In time, the church added others as well, including celebrated Scholastic philosophers such as Aquinas, Albertus Magnus, and Bonaventure as well as visionary mystics and seers like Theresa of Avila and Catherine of Siena. Albrecht Dürer's famous sixteenth-century engraving of Saint Jerome at work in his study—glowing with beatific wisdom and inspiration—attests to the power of the image of the saint as inspired scholar and seer. Jerome's own fourth-century *De viris illustribus* (*On Illustrious Men*) did the same. The work was a self-conscious attempt to do for Christians what classical authors had done for the "illustrious men of letters among the gentiles," a direct response to Suetonius and the many other pagan authors who had written panegyrics of philosophers and *viris illustribus*, extolling their wisdom and virtue. Let "they who think the Church has had no philosophers or orators or men of learning," Jerome challenged, "learn how many and what sort of men founded, built and adorned it, and cease to accuse our faith of such rustic simplicity, and recognize rather their own ignorance." The good doctor and patron of librarians had a point, and in pressing it home, he and his fellow Christians could appeal with confidence to another source of illumination. For in displacing the guardians and god-men of the ancients, the saints could call on the assistance of their own special protectors to supplement Christ's *numen* and help carry them to God: every saint had a *genius* of his own.[12]

M ALACHI IN HEBREW, *angeloi* in Greek, "angels" were the benevolent counterparts to the demons in the stark division of the Christian universe, and in the end even more powerful. Of course, Christians were hardly the first to detect the presence of such beings. The notion had deep roots in many traditions, including the Greek, which, in addition to the concept of *daimones*, possessed its own understanding of the *angeloi* as divine messengers or emissaries. But it was above all the long and rich heritage of Jewish reflection that helped open Christian eyes. Angels fill the pages of the Hebrew Bible, where from the Book of Genesis forward the "angel of the Lord" and the "angels of the Lord" make frequent appearances, calling out or revealing themselves to the favored. In his famous dream in Genesis 28:12, Jacob sees a ladder to heaven "with the angels of God ascending and descending on it," and later wrestles with a strange being in the night, said in the Book of Hosea to have been an angel. The God of Israel sends an angel to "prepare the way" for the flight of his children from Egypt, and he frequently employs angels as agents of destruction—such as the "band of destroying angels" he unleashes "in hot anger" against Pharaoh in Psalm 78. There are cherubim with flaming swords, winged seraphs, and countless evil angels, too, minions of Satan. And in the Septuagint, the Greek translation of Hebrew scripture produced in the third century BCE, we hear of angels who attend the throne of the Lord.[13]

Such precedents gave Christians ample material on which to draw, and their own scriptures, not surprisingly, abound in angelic references. The most famous example is Gabriel, who appears before Mary with the good news of Jesus's impending birth. And though he is one of only three named angels in the Bible, along with the archangels Michael and Raphael, the angels are evidently great in number. Jesus explains to the apostles that, were he so moved, he could call upon his father to send "more than twelve legions of angels" to vanquish his enemies (Matt. 26:53). Stalin would later scoff at the paltry number of the pope's divisions, but the Lord of hosts himself has ample resources at his disposal, angels "numbering thousands upon thousands, and ten thousand times ten thousand," according to Revelations 5:11. Well into the Renaissance, Christians and Jews alike constructed elaborate hierarchies that ranked the various angels and archangels, cherubim and seraphim in order of importance while speculating freely on their origin and function. Ministering to the faithful and punishing the wicked, conveying messages and otherwise carrying out God's commands, angels played a variety of different roles. But they were most present to Christians as guardians of souls and protectors of the Lord's anointed. "Are not all angels ministering spirits sent to serve those who will inherit salvation?" Paul asks in his Letter to the Hebrews (Heb. 1:14). Similarly, in the Acts of the Apostles, when Peter escapes from prison and knocks on the door of a friend, the household is incredulous, believing him dead. "It must be his angel," they exclaim (Acts 12:15). Peter's angel, we are meant to infer, is his perfect likeness, his spiritual double, his guardian *genius*.[14]

Early Christians, it is true, seldom used that word in this connection, given its pagan connotations, though over time *genius* would reemerge as a direct synonym for "angel." But the broader point is that early Christian commentators frequently remarked on the presence of guardian companions in ways that belied a debt not only to the Jewish, but also to the classical inheritance, and particularly to the extensive cult of *genius* in the Roman world. The second-century *Shepherd of Hermas*, for example, a popular and influential work read out in churches and regarded as divinely inspired by many of the early fathers, describes "How to Recognize the Two Spirits Attendant on Each Man, and How to Distinguish the Suggestions of the One from those of the Other." "There are two angels with a man," the text affirms, "one of righteousness, and the other of iniquity." In the first half of the third century, the Alexandrian theologian and early church commentator Origen observes typically that "two angels attend each human being. One is an angel of justice, the other an angel of iniquity. If good thoughts are present in our hearts and justice springs up in our souls, the angel of the Lord is undoubtedly speaking to us. But, if evil thoughts turn over in our hearts, the devil's angel is speaking to us." Descriptions of this kind highlight the point that angelology was early psychology, a way of understanding competing urges and making sense of the conflicting forces of the mind. But they also draw attention to the transmutation of the belief in a good *genius* paired with an evil twin. Right through the Middle Ages, in fact, commentators would warn of the presence of a personal evil demon, an angel of iniquity, present from birth, who could infiltrate our innermost thoughts and lead us into sin. This was all the more reason to seek the protection of divine guardians. The saints served that function, of course, but the guardian angels did, too, and were ever ready to come to our aid. "The dignity of a soul is so great," Saint Jerome assured the early Christians, "that each has a guardian angel from birth." Elsewhere, Jerome describes the guardian angel as a *comes*, employing Horace's familiar description of the *genius*. It is a revealing conflation, and was repeated in other ways. Instead of swearing an oath by one's *genius*, for example, or the *genius* of another, early Christians took to bearing witness by angels, substituting the form *per angelum tuum* for the old Roman *per genium tuum*. Similarly, they addressed their sisters and brothers formally as "Your angel." Funeral inscriptions reveal that early Christian tombstones often used the form "The Angel of [the departed]" in a way that directly copied the pagan practice of marking graves by reference to the *genius* of the departed.[15]

The earliest Christian depictions of angels even looked like *genii*. For, despite the fact that biblical passages describe angels in flight, their trademark wings were only introduced later in visual representations, beginning in the fourth century. The very first Christian images of angels show them as young men, generally clean-shaven (though sometimes with a beard), and clad in white tunics, in striking resemblance to the Roman *genii*. Finally, just as the Roman *genii* served as guardians not only of people, but also of places, the dominion of the angels was interpreted on scriptural authority to extend to cities, nations, and "all things that pertain to us"—even, some said, animals, plants, and the winds.[16]

Although a number of the more overtly pagan aspects of the angel cult drew suspicion on grounds of idolatry, and were gradually abandoned, the cult of individual guardian angels flourished well into the early modern period, with Pope Paul V establishing an official feast day in their honor as late as 1608. Together with the patron saint, the guardian angel functioned as a higher self, serving, like the *genii* and *daimones*, to mediate between heaven and earth. All human beings had a guardian angel—conferred in utero at conception, Tertullian believed—just as all were granted a patron saint at baptism, our spiritual birth. But it was the saints themselves who enjoyed the most powerful protectors and the most intimate relations with these higher beings. It was chiefly the saints who could see them, or who opened the eyes of others to their presence. The relics of Gervasius and Protasius were said to have revealed "the numberless hosts of angels" to Ambrose and his flock, for example. As the fourth-century historian Ammianus Marcellinus pointed out, although "the theologians maintain that [guardian angels] are associated with all men at their birth, as directors of their conduct," these angels "have been seen by very few, whom their manifold merits have raised to eminence." Marcellinus was a pagan, but his broader point—that the spiritually eminent maintained particularly close relations with their angelic companions—was widely shared. As Gregory Thaumaturgus, one of Origen's pupils, could write, almost boastfully, "for a long time, the angelic presence has nourished me, and led me by the hand." Intimacy was not only a sign of divine presence, but of special favor, and before Origen, Gregory sensed a particularly exalted presence, "the angel of the great counsel," an angel of Christ himself. Just as pagans such as Socrates or Augustus were thought to be served by a superior *genius*, men of great faith possessed angels of a higher order.[17]

Not only were such eminent individuals in fellowship with their angelic companions, but they resembled them, serving as spectacular reminders of Christ's promise in Matthew, Mark, and Luke that at the time of the resurrection, the saved shall be "like the angels in heaven" and know no death. Man, Saint Paul affirms, "is a little lower than the angels." But his guardian could raise him. To become "angelic" was the glorious end of the righteous, and for the saints, that end was assured. With reason do the saints and angels stand together in church portals and on the facades of cathedrals. With reason do the faithful pray to "all the angels and the saints."[18]

Over time it became commonplace to call a saint "angelic," and some were singled out for special designation. The learned saint Thomas Aquinas—said to have possessed a mind so quick that he could dictate to several scribes at once—earned the title the "Angelic Doctor" in the Middle Ages. Saint Bonaventure became the "Seraphic Doctor," and in Bonaventure's considered opinion, Saint Francis of Assisi was not just angelic, but an angel himself, the sixth angel of the apocalypse, to be exact, who had apparently descended to earth to tend to the faithful in bodily form. As the medieval church's leading authority on angelic phenomena, Bonaventure was in a position to know. But this particular piece of information was revealed to him directly by a heavenly voice, dispatched, he explained, by an angel.[19]

Indeed, to an even greater degree than the pagan tutelary spirit, the Christian angel was understood to be a bearer of privileged truths, an emissary of epiphany and revelation. Clement of Alexandria maintained in the second century that angels had been active on earth at God's command long before the coming of Christ, dispatching "the secret and occult philosophy of the Egyptians," the "astrology of the Chaldeans," Hindu knowledge "pertaining to the science of the most High God," and philosophy to the Greeks.[20] Now, with the coming of Christ, they were more active than ever before, imparting God's infinite wisdom directly to the chosen. To feel the breath of an angel in one's ear was to be filled with heavenly insight—"inspired," as we still say, catching a breath from afar. Just as God had blown life into Adam, he could fill our souls with knowledge in a whisper. In revelation, inspiration, and epiphany, the angels had the power to disclose the deepest secrets of the universe.

Here was the basis for a uniquely Christian *furor divinus*. And yet how could one be sure that it was an angel of the good who whispered in the ear and not an angel of iniquity—that one was possessed by God and not simply possessed? The demons delighted, did they not, in disguising themselves in angelic garb, all the better to deceive? This was the learned opinion of Tertullian, who judged that wings were the "common property" of angels and demons alike, allowing the demonic imposters to be "everywhere in a single moment," and so to seduce with the appearance of foreknowledge and omniscience. Had not Satan himself been an angel once—the greatest of God's troupe—and all the demons, too? Even after their fall, Satan and his servants retained their vast knowledge of the universe, along with craftiness and cunning, all the better to tempt and to lead astray. It is revealing in this connection that early Christian apologists followed Plato in tracing the etymology of the word "demon" (*daimon*) to the Greek *daêmôn*, "knowing," a derivation that Augustine saw fit to repeat in the *City of God*. Isidore of Seville pointed out the connection in his sixth-century encyclopedia the *Etymologiae*, which was widely read into the Middle Ages. And though not all Christians were concerned with the derivation of words, the association between the demons and knowledge was reinforced by popular accounts of *magi* (magicians) and *malefici* (sorcerors) who allegedly put the demons' knowledge to work. The pagan world had teemed with such figures—wizards, astrologers, soothsayers, and diviners who were famed for their great knowledge and spellbinding powers. Hermes Trismegistus, the most famous of the lot, was popularly identified with Thot, the Egyptian god of learning. He could bring stone statues to life and raise the souls of the dead. Others, such as Asclepius, were highly regarded even by their detractors for their intellectual prowess (in Asclepius's case, in medicine and healing), and their feats of magic, though regularly condemned by Christians, were credited as real. The Acts of the Apostles tells of another such figure, Simon Magus, who tries to purchase the power of the Holy Spirit from Peter. He is, of course, rebuked, but his powers were considerable nonetheless. "All the people of Samaria, both high and low," the Acts insist, "gave him their attention. . . . They followed him because he had amazed them for a long time with his magic" (Acts 8:9–13).[21]

Such legends helped to perpetuate an image of the dark magus as a kind of anti-saint, a sorcerer who trafficked with the demons, whereas the true saint lived in fellowship with the angels, drawing on their knowledge and power. The line between the two was theologically clear, and in hindsight easy to determine: saints were canonized as saints precisely because they resisted the demons and drew angelic favor. But in the chaos of spiritual combat, the line was far less distinct, blurred by the simple fact that even the best-intentioned might fall prey to a demon's deceptions. To consciously summon an angel, then, was always to risk idolatry and incantation, mistaking an angel of iniquity—a demon—for an angel of the good.

It was largely for this reason that the cult of angels generated such consternation in the early church. Already in the first century, Saint Paul saw the need to warn the inhabitants of the city of Colossae in Asia Minor of the dangers of "false humility and the worship of angels" (Col. 2:18), and authorities reiterated his warning in the centuries to come. The regional Council of Laodicea in 380 judged that "it is not right for Christians . . . to invoke angels," pronouncing "anathema" on such "secret idolatry." And a late fifth-century council forbade the practice of "calling on angels for protection against illnesses or evil spirits," concluding that the "angels are themselves demons." Whatever they were, they were not easily exorcised, and in the end the church was forced to settle on an uneasy compromise. Belief in angels was dogma, but their worship could be dangerous. Let the angels appear to the chosen and come to the aid of the saints. But to summon them directly risked imperiling one's soul by conjuring a demon instead.[22]

Such strictures were given force by well-publicized condemnations like that of the French priest Adalbert in the mid-eighth century, who boasted of receiving holy relics, a letter from Jesus, and revelations from the angels, with whom he claimed to be in regular contact. But condemnations of the sort could no more stifle the yearning to ascend to angelic heights than the doctrine of original sin could eradicate the desire to be like Christ. The angels existed, did they not? They were higher than man, closer to God, and could come to the aid of the exalted, imparting wisdom and divulging truths. Why one should refrain from seeking their assistance in the purest of faith was never entirely clear. And so, alongside the more orthodox channels of transcendence, at the margins and in the shadows, Christians sought furtively to draw on the power of angels to raise themselves to God. Those who did so by consciously cultivating "demonic magic"—magic involving the medium of an angel or a demon—were always a tiny minority. But a great many more pursued the esoteric secrets of "natural magic." The distinction, always subtle, turned on the means of transmission: whereas demonic magic involved soliciting an immaterial force to perform actions in the material world, natural magic was held to be the result of matter acting on matter in a hidden or occult way. It was widely believed, for example, that the planets could exert an influence on human beings and animals, just as certain minerals or medicinal herbs could be manipulated to induce bodily cures. By this reasoning, all therapeutic medicine was a type of natural magic. And so, though it was clear that the church condemned magic of the demonic kind, it took a more indulgent view toward the natural variety. The Gospel of Matthew, after all, spoke of the glorious wise men from the East, good magi guided by a star, whose knowledge of the heavens helped lead them to Christ (Matt. 2). The tale provided a scriptural basis in support of a tradition of good magic, and that tradition was defended further by Scholastic philosophers in the Middle Ages, who drew elaborate distinctions between magic evil and good, helping to carve out a place in which various forms of hermetic wisdom might flourish: the study of medicine, alchemy, astrology, and the practice of the occult.[23]

Such practices generated considerable interest in the Middle Ages, but it was in the Renaissance that they came into their own. Countless works of ancient magic and the occult were recovered alongside the many Greek and Roman classics that were "reborn" in the age. Works of alchemy and astrology competed for space on early-modern shelves alongside dense ruminations on Kabbalah, Arab treatises on divination, and the scattered writings attributed to the mythical Egyptian magus Hermes Trismegistus. The latter, in particular, with his talk of shape-shifting and the ability to animate statues, made orthodox minds uneasy, but in truth, the line between natural and demonic magic was always thin. And though few of the Renaissance's magi ever engaged in outright demonolatry, they did show a worrying tendency to talk of spirits, crowding their cosmos with legions of beings who might heed their call.

That tendency long predated the Renaissance. Christians sought from late antiquity forward to complete the Great Chain of Being that connected the lowliest creatures to God. The effort to integrate Platonist and Neo-Platonist cosmological accounts, in particular, with their elaborate descriptions of the angels and *daimones* that animated the universe, encouraged speculation, and in the wake of the Neo-Platonist revival of the twelfth century commentators grew increasingly bold in imagining *genii* at every level of the cosmos. Some spoke, in a turn of phrase that would have shocked the earliest Christians, of "good demons" (*bonos daemones*) who staffed the celestial hierarchy along with the choirs of the angels and the saints. Others invoked *genii* of various classes and kinds, and still others wrote of the tutelary *genius* in a way that was more than a synonym for the guardian angel. Finally, poetic and literary accounts described the figure of Genius as an artist (*artifex*) and priest who presided over reproduction and gave form and shape to all beings—the scribe of the universe, sketching their outlines on a magical parchment. The account of the Genius in the latter case was allegorical. But the speculation about the place of *genii* in the universe was not.[24]

Thus the Renaissance magi of the fifteenth and early sixteenth centuries confronted a cosmos teeming with spiritual beings. And with all those beings bumping about, it was hardly surprising that some should have slipped inside the pathways of their purportedly natural magic. The German Benedictine Johannes Trithemius is a notorious case. Although he repeatedly denied any involvement with demonic magic, his treatises read today like manuals for conjuring. Trithemius classified the various ranks of spirits of the holy hierarchy and detailed the means to call upon angels through the recitation of chants composed in a secret, angelic tongue. He astonished with his claims to have uncovered techniques enabling magi to perform incredible feats of learning, such as mastering the entire Latin language in two hours. And when a private letter of 1499 boasting similar skills was intercepted and made public in Germany and France, Trithemius was forced to deny publicly that he was able to forecast the future and raise the dead. Even more astounding were the pretensions of Trithemius's acolyte Heinrich Cornelius Agrippa, who asserted in his *magnum opus, De occulta philosophia libri tres* (*The Three Books of Occult Philosophy*), the existence of not just one good *genius*, but three, the so-called *triplex homini daemon bonus* watching over men. Composed of a *daemon* like Socrates's, sent by God to shepherd the rational soul, this "three-fold keeper" also included a "genius of nativity" controlled by the "circuits of the stars" and a "daemon of profession" dictating our natural aptitudes and strengths. It was the complex interaction of the three that formed individual character and produced the highest qualities in the highest men, a point that Agrippa sought to illustrate by reference to the varied gifts of the holy prophets and the saints, noting that Abraham excelled in justice, Jacob in strength, Solomon in knowledge, Peter in faith, John in charity, and Thomas in prudence. The magus who could learn to control his demons, speaking their language and interpreting their signs, might similarly rise to great heights. Throughout his work Agrippa gave detailed instructions as to how this might be accomplished.[25]

Neither Trithemius nor Agrippa was ever formally censured, and in their own estimation they acted in the fullness of faith. Yet the collective impact of the rumors of the inquiries of these men and of other magi across Europe was to stir up fears of a threat to orthodoxy, and arguably with good reason. For the speculations of the magi challenged the central Christian belief that there were limits to what could be known of the divine world without divine favor. Rarely do the magi speak of grace. Their presumption, rather, is that one can plumb the secrets of the universe and even rise to supernatural power (performing miracles) through a mastery of knowledge applied in such a way as to command the angels and manipulate the divine. But this presumption carried the attendant threat of ecclesiastical displeasure, and for this reason, virtually all of the leading magi of Europe came, in the end, to repudiate magic, bowing like Agrippa to the authority of their superiors. In an age when charges of witchcraft or traffic with the demons could lead to imprisonment or death, as the celebrated persecutions of the hermetic scholars Giordano Bruno and John Dee later in the sixteenth century made clear, magic was dangerous.[26]

Yet the impact of the magi was by no means short-lived. In the long run, they left behind powerful images and myths focusing on the hazards of the quest for superhuman knowledge and wonder-making power. Providing the basis for such literary archetypes as Shakespeare's Prospero, Mary Shelley's Frankenstein, and the figure of Faust, the magi called attention to the tenuous space that lay between the demons and the angels, reaffirming what the saints in their struggles and Christ in the wilderness knew: that the line separating those who would be more than men from those who would be less was perilously thin. The dark magus and the luminous saint were brothers of sorts, a lesson in chiaroscuro that harkened back to a founding temptation. *Eritis sicut dii*, the serpent says in Jerome's translation (Gen. 3:5): Eat from the tree of knowledge, and "you will be like God [or the gods]." The attempt to go beyond ourselves was fraught with peril, and yet there could be no higher calling than to seek to imitate God. This was a primordial and perennial conflict that would replay itself in modern times. For if the saints and the sorcerers were descendants of those in the grips of the *daimones*, they are ancestors, too, of the modern genius and his evil double and twin.

The influence of the magi was no less profound in the nearer term. For although overt efforts to draw the powers of the *genii* and *daimones* may have waned in the suspicious climate induced by the Reformation and its Catholic response, those beings nonetheless turned up in the writings of humanists throughout the sixteenth and seventeenth centuries. Some, like the physician and man of letters Girolamo Cardano, dwelled at length on the ministration of his own personal *genius*, noting that "guardian spirits have clearly been operative" throughout history, and citing the cases of Socrates, Plotinus, Caesar, and Brutus as proof. The temptation to master the guiding force of our nature endured, but there were other ways besides sorcery to divine it, as the magi themselves well knew. "The ancient philosophers teach us to know the nature of the Genius of every man," Agrippa remarked. Yet their instructions for making inquiries, through the use of astrology and other means, were generally so vague, so conflicted, and so difficult to understand that Agrippa reasoned we could "far more easily inquire into the nature of our Genius from ourselves," examining those habits and instincts that heaven and nature instilled in each of us from birth. Agrippa's injunction to "Know thy Good Genius" became, in effect, the Socratic command to "Know thyself." Others agreed, stressing that by seeking self-knowledge and turning within we might dispense with the services of the angels and the demons altogether and be raised aloft by the motive power of the mind. In their recovery of the ancient past, the Renaissance magi stirred up not only the classical *genius*, but the classical tradition of the great-souled man, whose divine fury and superior *ingenium* would come to constitute the genius within.[27]

M ARSILIO FICINO WAS a prime mover in this process. He, too, was a magus, and also a priest, and in the fullest sense of that overused phrase, a Renaissance man. A fifteenth-century Florentine humanist and theoretician of music, a physician, philosopher, and student of the soul, Ficino worked at the behest of his patron, Cosimo de Medici, to translate the whole of Plato's recovered writings into Latin, along with a host of Neo-Platonic authors and many other ancient texts, including the scattered writings attributed to Hermes Trismegistus. A man of deep faith, Ficino also harbored a lifelong interest in the occult.

Ficino's interests generated suspicion at the time (and controversy to this day) as to whether the magic he practiced was truly natural. But his more important legacy where matters of genius are concerned has less to do with the angels and demons that flutter through his work than with what he did to render their services obsolete. His initial guide in this respect was Plato. For, almost single-handedly, Ficino restored Plato's doctrine of the *furor divinus* to European awareness, translating and writing formal commentaries on the *Symposium* and the *Phaedrus* and producing a massive synthesis of Platonic and Christian thought, the *Platonic Theology* (1474). In so doing, he drew out a line of inquiry implicit in Plato himself. Substituting the beautiful soul for the angels as the agent of ascent to God, Ficino ventured that our true *genius* was the glorious mind, caught up in the rapture of divine embrace.

Ficino followed Plato in elaborating four distinct varieties of divine madness. He subscribed to a more favorable view of poetry than his predecessor, but he concurred with him in ranking the divine fury of love—prepared by philosophy, the love of wisdom—as the highest type. "The most powerful and most excellent of all [forms of madness] is amatory," Ficino stressed in his commentary on the *Symposium*, fittingly entitled *De Amore*—"most powerful, I say, on account of the fact that all the others necessarily need it. For we achieve neither poetry nor mysteries, nor prophecy[,] without vast zeal, burning piety, and sedulous worship of divinity. But what else do we call zeal, piety, and worship except love?" For Ficino, the divine madness of love permeated all the furors—it lay behind true oracular, prophetic, and mystical power just as it animated the ecstatic visions of the genuine poet, who was blessed by God with the ability to see and re-create the beauty of the world. All those special abilities were divine gifts, which raised us to something higher than ourselves. That was the transformative power of the *furor divinus*, without which, Ficino judged, "no man has ever been great."[28]

But how was this power conferred? Plato, recall, had been somewhat ambiguous on the point, entertaining the notion that the heavenly seeker was possessed by a higher being while also suggesting that this *daimon* might simply be the rational part of our soul. He himself never fully developed the thought, but it had been kept alive by Platonic and Neo-Platonic interpreters with whom Ficino was intimately familiar. In a chapter devoted to "Our Tutelary Spirit" in the *Enneads*, for example, a work that Ficino translated in full, Plotinus explains how, for the fully developed philosopher (the "achieved Sage"), it does not suffice to have only the *daimon* allotted to all men as a "co-operator in life." "The acting force in the Sage," rather, is the "diviner part of the human Soul," which is "itself his presiding spirit (*daimon*) or is guided by a presiding spirit of its own, no other than the very Divinity." The genius of the highest man, in other words, was his own rational soul, guided directly by God.[29]

Ficino developed this same thought with greater precision than anyone before him. His language is technical, and the details are involved, but the final consequence is perfectly clear: in Ficino's account, the soul becomes the sole intercessor between the individual and God, occupying the place of the angels. Despite Ficino's flirtation elsewhere with the prospect of engaging the angels through magic, and despite his own unquestioned belief in their existence, he largely dispenses with their services in his articulation of the *furor divinus* and the soul's divine ascent. The soul becomes its own messenger and mediator, what Ficino explicitly calls the "middle term of all things in the universe," a *genius* or angel unto itself.[30]

Although there were certainly precedents for this understanding—in mystical practice as much as in Platonic and Neo-Platonic thought—Ficino's account was no less influential for that. Clearing the space between heaven and earth, it presented the human soul as the true miracle of the universe. Man could be anything he wanted, it seemed, if he loved the right things, a thought that was given famous expression by Ficino's student Giovanni Pico della Mirandola in his celebrated *Oration on the Dignity of Man* (1486). God had planted in man "every sort of seed and sprouts of every kind of life," and man could cultivate them as he best saw fit, living vegetatively like a plant, sensuously like an animal, or intellectually, like "an angel and a son of God." The miracle of man was precisely that he had no established place on the Great Chain of Being, no fixed and determinate nature. A shape-shifter, he was a "molder and maker" of himself who might soar beyond the highest of the angelic orders and every created being, to the very throne of the Creator.[31]

But did all souls, all minds, really possess such angelic seeds? In the aftermath of Martin Luther's initial confrontation with the church in 1517, the Protestant Reformers would trample on such optimistic accounts, recalling, with Augustine, the limitations on human freedom and the necessity of God's redeeming grace. When the Reformers spoke of seeds, it was more often to recall Christ's parable of the sower: God's word could be scattered freely, but in most cases it fell on barren ground (Luke 8:1–15). Only those who received his grace could begin to imitate God.

Yet even before this point, those grappling with the implications of Ficino's account—including Ficino himself—were generating pointed questions about the nature of the *furor divinus*, asking why it was that some, and not others, should receive it. Aided in their inquiries by a renewed engagement with the writings of Aristotle, whose own vast oeuvre underwent a major recovery in this period, they focused, in particular, on his doctrine of the soul, conceived as the "act" or expression of the body. Aristotle seemed to offer a less ethereal, more corporal account than Plato, his Athenian master, a point that was particularly apparent in the pages of the *Problems*, a work universally, if falsely, attributed to Aristotle himself. Could it really be true, as the opening line of Problem 30.1 declares, that "all those who have become eminent in philosophy or politics or poetry or the arts are clearly of an atrabilious [melancholy] temperament"? In weighing this question in the extensive debates of the fifteenth and sixteenth centuries, Renaissance observers cut to the heart of an issue bound up with genius as we now conceive it, asking where extraordinary intellectual and creative capacity came from.[32]

Ficino had already provided one answer to that question: great artists, philosophers, poets, and prophets were inspired directly by God, who kindled their souls and enlightened their minds, which they could use to raise themselves to Him. Ficino never abandoned this position, but in wrestling with the *Problems*, he came to modify his views, and in so doing he introduced the seeds of another. Reading the text through the prism of his Platonic assumptions, Ficino came to believe that it provided a physiological account of the convulsion of the soul, described by Plato as the mania of divine possession. The Pseudo-Aristotelian melancholy and the Platonic *furor*, in short, were the same phenomenon, only differently described.[33]

This was a seminal insight. For although medieval commentators had been familiar with the theory of the humors and some of the writings of Hippocrates and Galen, they tended to regard the superabundance of black bile as an affliction—a condition to be avoided or cured—styling melancholy as the "devil's bath." It was only with the rediscovery of the Pseudo-Aristotelian *Problems* and the wide dissemination of Galen's humoral theory during the fifteenth and sixteenth centuries that critics began to consider in earnest the potential benefits of the disease. Here, again, Ficino's contribution was crucial. His great final work, the *Three Books on Life* (1489), was devoted to helping scholars use knowledge of the humors to help maximize their intellectual strengths. A melancholic himself, born under the sign of Saturn, the planet thought to exert the greatest influence on the fluctuations of black bile, Ficino was acutely sensitive to the suffering this condition could bring. And yet, as he also made clear, melancholy was the natural counterpart to the supernatural impetus of divine illumination: "Divine madness," he affirmed, "is never incited in anyone else but melancholics." And so it was incumbent on those who would aspire to the heavenly heights to manage this humor effectively. As a "doctor of the soul," Ficino dispensed counsel ranging from advice about diet (for "the mind that is choked up with fat and blood cannot perceive anything heavenly") to warnings against the "monster" of intercourse, which "drains the spirits" and "weakens the brain." He urged scholars to initiate study at the most propitious hours ("right at sunrise" or an hour or two before) and advised on a whole range of pills, syrups, electuaries, and elixirs to manage the effects of melancholy and the other afflictions to which scholars were prone. Finally, and critically, he gave detailed instructions in the idiom of natural magic about mediating the influence of the planets: Venus, Mercury, and the Sun, which favored reflection and eloquence, and, above all, Saturn, at once dangerous and alluring to the melancholy mind.[34]

Conceived at a time when Renaissance humanists were making concerted attempts to reconcile the two greatest thinkers of antiquity, Ficino's effort to harmonize the Platonic, Aristotelian, and Pseudo-Aristotelian accounts was hugely influential in moving others to think of melancholy as potentially beneficial; it even gave rise to a "vogue" for that condition among humanists and literary elites, ensuring that for centuries thereafter, melancholy and madness would figure centrally in discussions of genius. Yet it also prompted a critical response, led on the one hand by Christians, who continued to worry about the dangers of the devil's bath, and who argued that the melancholy humor was more conducive to a *furor daemonicus* than a furor divine, and on the other by Aristotelian purists who questioned the need to resort to any supernatural explanations at all in accounting for melancholy's extraordinary effects. Had not Ficino himself declared, in the *Three Books on Life*, that "black bile makes people intelligent"? If that were the case, surely an account like that of the *Problems*, which explained intellectual operations in terms of the bodily humors alone, was more compelling than that of Plato or Ficino, with their recourse to a divinely inspired (or demonically bestowed) fury acting on the soul. As one of the more robust polemicists of this position, the medically trained Paduan philosopher Pietro Pomponazzi, insisted superabundance of black bile and its natural effects could alone account for the various "gifts"—prophetic, poetic, philosophical, and creative—that such a condition conferred. "It is a custom of the vulgar," he stressed, "to assign to demons or angels that of which the causes are unknown."[35]

Thus, even though the revived Aristotelian theories of melancholy might be employed to contest Ficino's Platonically inspired understanding of the *furor divinus*, they only strengthened his general tendency to banish the angels from accounts of extraordinary mental achievement. Together, they drove the *genius* within, and because both theories focused on the soul as the source and site of human prowess, they had the further effect of emphasizing the fortunes of birth. This was particularly the case with the Aristotelian theories. For although it was certainly possible to manipulate the humors, through medicine or other means, all individuals possessed a particular humoral constitution that impinged on their souls, shaping their intelligence and natural endowments—what the ancients had called *ingenium*. Drawing on their example, Renaissance authors employed the word widely to describe an inborn capacity for mental activity, natural talent, innate intelligence, and inherent ability. They also used the word more broadly to describe a person's natural bent, something akin to individual character or personality, the kind of human being each of us was born to be. As Pomponazzi put it, *ingenium* is "nothing else but the product of the birth of a man, so that those who have good birth have good *ingenium*, and those who have bad birth have bad *ingenium*."[36]

A great many humanists developed the implications of that thought over the course of the sixteenth century, but the most famous was the Spanish physician Juan Huarte, whose treatise on *ingenium*, the *Examen de Ingenios* (1575), was quickly translated into every major European language, going through more than sixty-five editions in Spanish alone. Huarte was an Aristotelian naturalist who read the *Problems* with special care. He cites the work over fifty times, using it to deny that the furors described by Plato are born of divine inspiration and to help justify a rigorously physiological view of human intelligence. As any schoolmaster will confirm, he claims, some pupils are quick and bright and others useless and slow, a difference that no amount of instruction can overcome. Such differences are rooted in nature, determined by the humors and what Huarte calls the "temper" of the brain, the particular balance between its heat, dryness, and humidity. "From these three qualities alone, proceed all the differences of *ingenium* observed among men," he concludes. And though Huarte acknowledged that such factors as environment, upbringing, and climate may affect the brain's temper, his overwhelming emphasis was on the fate of one's birth.[37]

Huarte took a great interest in educational reform, and so part of his aim was to be able to identify and direct students toward the vocations that best suited their natural aptitudes. In this respect, he was a pioneering psychologist, engaged in one of the first formal efforts to evaluate personality types. Not unlike many later practitioners, he was supremely confident in his ability to identify a person's unique endowments, even attempting in the book's final pages to apply his theories to the brain of Christ: of "subtle *ingenio*," its temper was undoubtedly humid as a young man, Huarte assures us, but dried as he grew older. Less daringly, he drew on the prevailing Galenic and Aristotelian assumption that women were but imperfectly formed men to stress that "they should not be blamed for their simple nature" (*rudeza*), as this was due to the coldness and humidity of their constitutions, which were "at odds with all talent and *ingenio*." He advised parents who desired intelligent children "to seek to have boys"—and in the work's final chapters he gives detailed instructions about choosing mates and the sexual techniques most conducive to spawning children of superior birth.[38]

The work, in this respect, is an early manual of eugenics, and it is significant in that connection that Huarte took pains to ruminate in a revised edition on the etymology of *ingenium*, a word, he believed, that in Latin, as in Spanish (*ingenio*) and Italian (*ingegno*), likely derived from one of three Latin verbs: *gigno* (to beget), *ingigno* (to engender), or *ingenero* (to seed or implant). All three possible roots related to a procreative capacity, and for Huarte that was hardly a coincidence. For *ingenium* also referred to a "generative power" (*potencia generativa*), and man possessed two such powers by virtue of his special place on the Great Chain of Being. The first—the power of physical reproduction—he shared with the animals and plants below him. But the second he held in common with "spiritual substances, God and the angels," and it enabled him to produce "children" of another sort: ideas, notions, and concepts with which he became "pregnant" and to which he then gave birth. Those who first employed the word *ingenium*, Huarte speculated, were surely conscious of this fertile connection between innate human mental capacities and the spiritual power of angels and of God.[39]

In describing *ingenium* in this way—as a seminal, creative force linking man to the divine—Huarte echoed the pronouncements of his countrymen and contemporaries, who were writing of the possession of *ingenium* in ecstatic terms as a God-given tool of invention, left over to man after the Fall, to make use of for better or for worse. "The inventor of all arts and sciences is *ingenium*," observed the humanist Juan Luis Vives, a friend of Erasmus, whose works were almost certainly known to

Huarte. "All the inventions and discoveries of man have their origin here; the useful and the harmful, the good and the bad." Speaking variously of *ingenium* as the life force of the soul (*vigor animi*) and the "whole general strength of our mind," Vives also stressed *ingenium*'s capacity to observe, compare, and seek out the "truth in every thing." But it was above all his emphasis on creativity and invention that influenced Huarte, and indeed it was this aspect of his work that bore witness to something new, testifying to the emergence of a wider understanding of *ingenium* as the source of what we now think of as "ingenuity," the ingenious capacity to invent, create, and conceive.[40]

Neither Huarte nor Vives nor any other of the many theorists of *ingenium* of the fifteenth and sixteenth centuries were Romantics *avant la lettre*. The medieval dictum that God alone can create still resonated in the minds of theorists and practitioners alike, who regarded all art and thought as in large measure an act of recovery and imitation, a re-creation of what God in his perfection had already conceived. Huarte put it well when, employing a loose translation of Aristotle, he defined the man of perfect *ingenium* "as one who knows everything and understands all things." Adam before the Fall was such a man, born "perfectly instructed with all scientific knowledge infused"—from which it followed that "there is not a phrase or a sentence, in any domain of learning[,] that has not been uttered before."[41]

Notwithstanding these qualifications, *ingenium* was put to innovative uses, and in Huarte's likening of the mind to the procreative power of God one finds the seed of a genuine innovation. For those who possessed the very finest *ingenium* could "give voice, without art or study, to things that had never been seen, heard, or written—such subtle, truthful, and prodigious things that no one had thought of them previously." And while it was understandable that Plato and his followers might think such seminal thoughts to be poured into us from above, the seed, in fact, came ready planted at birth, and required no divine fertilization. To believe that the thoughts of men of great *ingenium* were "divine revelations," and not products of their particular nature, was a "clear and manifest error." In Huarte, we see a glimmer of what others in the sixteenth century were beginning to discover for themselves: men—special men—could create on their own, bringing into being the genuinely new.[42]

Which is not to say that Huarte, or any of the other apologists for *ingenium*, would have denied that our in-built natures were, at the moment of their inception, divinely conferred. Ficino spoke for the majority when he remarked in a letter to a friend on the subject of our natal endowments, "I shall in agreement with Aristotle say that this nature itself is a unique and divine gift." *Ingenium*, the seed that was planted in us at birth, was an offering from God, and most considered the question of why some should receive a more bountiful offering than others as mysterious as why some, and not others, should be saved. Indeed, the notion of *ingenium*, no less than the *furor divinus*, tracked in interesting ways with the Reformation's debates about grace. Just as the *furor divinus* could be given either a Protestant or Catholic inflection—conceived as an active grace poured into a passive vessel, or as the heavenly reward of the soul that raises itself to God—so *ingenium* could be thought of in Protestant or Catholic ways. For some it was a perfect analogue to the Protestants' *gratia*—a divine seed sown in us, without which we could achieve nothing of worth. But it also lent itself to a more Catholic interpretation, with an emphasis on the "works" required to cultivate our natural gifts. As the celebrated architect and man of letters Leon Battista Alberti affirmed, "the gifts of Nature should be cultivated and increased by industry, study, and practice." Whatever one's religious persuasion, that was a message with which most before the eighteenth century would have agreed. As the Roman poet Horace famously emphasized in a widely repeated rule, *ingenium* must be coupled with *industria* and *ars*, the hard work and acquired mastery necessary for perfection. Given their immense respect for the models of the ancients, early modern men and women invariably agreed.[43]

Theories of divine inspiration and *ingenium* could thus be appropriated by Protestants and Catholics alike. People of both persuasions adapted these theories to suit their needs, emphasizing nature or nurture, inspiration or works, as they best saw fit. The two theories might still be combined (as Ficino had done)—if, say, inspiration is conceived as descending only on those of great nature, and those of great nature are seen as summoning gifts from on high. Or, they could be maintained separately and in isolation. Well into the seventeenth century and beyond, unrepentant Platonists vigorously denied that the configuration of the bodily humors could ever be the cause of divine fury, great poetry, or art. Aristotelians countered with equal vehemence that fanciful notions of men possessed did little to explain the true possession of excellence, man's divine *ingenium*.[44]

Yet where all three variations converged is on the soul of the unique individual, the mind of the great man, which was slowly assuming powers that for centuries had been entrusted to the angels and the demons and to those men and women—the sorcerers and the saints—whose bidding they performed. That process of assumption was clearest in Ficino's concept of a heavenly soul that could wing itself upward in the madness of possession, soaring like an angel or *daimon* to God. But it was also apparent in the special *ingenium* of the great-souled man, the man who, on the strength of his natural powers, could perform the very same feats—prophetic, philosophical, poetic—as the man taken up in fury. *Ingenium*, too, was a *genius* of sorts, an angelic power imbedded in our persons, a higher source of self.

In the Protestant countries, at least, this process of co-optation and displacement was accompanied by a far more extensive clearing of the space between heaven and earth. Men and women, Protestants believed, were saved by faith alone: nothing else should stand between their savior and their souls. And so they abolished reliquaries and the cult of the saints as divine companions and intercessors before God. They scoffed at what they saw as the ludicrous speculations of medieval angelology, frowning particularly at the cult of the guardian angel, which smacked dangerously, in their view, of idolatry. Those "who limit the care which God takes of each of us to a single angel," Calvin observed, "do great injury to themselves and to all the members of the Church." The Reformers did not dispense with the angels altogether—there were far too many references in Scripture for that. And the Baroque piety of the Catholic Counter-Reformation strongly reaffirmed a belief in personal guardians and angelic beings. Yet it remains the case that the collective impact of the Reformation helped to clear the space between heaven and earth, downplaying, where not discounting altogether, the role of mediators, messengers, and angelic friends. This was an important precondition for the appearance of the genius, in our more modern sense—a being who would succeed in displacing the souls, saints, and spirits who had come before.[45]

The appearance of the modern genius was still some way off. But an annunciation of sorts could be heard in the declaration of the word, which gradually over the course of the sixteenth century relinquished its exclusive association with the angels and *daimones* of old. *Genius* was used in the 1500s as a direct synonym for the *furor poeticus*, as in the title of a Latin text that reflected this change perfectly: *Genius, sive de furore poetico* (Genius, or the Divine Fury). And in a further sign of such coupling and combination, authors writing in Italian and Latin began to equate *ingenium* and "genius" (*genio* or *genius*) as well. Slowly, over the course of the century, they conflated the two words, employing genius, or *genio*, to signify not a *daimon*, poetic fury, or angelic friend, but our in-built nature and intelligence, our *ingenium*, the genius of man.[46]

This was a usage that gained currency first in Latin and Italian from the middle of the sixteenth century, and then spread slowly across Europe in the centuries to come. In English, *ingenium* was initially translated as "wit," and in French as *esprit*, but in the seventeenth century "genius" and *génie* were used with increasing frequency. Jean Nicot's *Thresor de la langue françoyse* (Treasure of the French language) of 1606, for example, defines *génie* as the "natural inclination of each of us," and Elisha Coles's *English Dictionary* of 1676 describes genius as "nature, fancy, or inclination." The older senses of the word did not simply disappear, of course, but lingered about like disembodied souls. "A good angell, or a familiar evill spirit, the soule," is the lone entry for "genius" in Henry Cockeram's *English Dictionarie* of 1623. For the rest of the century those meanings coexisted with the newer sense of the term, a testament to the conflation of *ingenium*, inspiration, and genius carried out over the course of the Renaissance. When the English poet John Dryden paused to reflect in 1695 on the contemporary meaning of the word, he unwittingly (or rather, with wit) summarized over two centuries of debate: "A happy genius is the gift of nature: it depends on the influence of the stars say the astrologers, on the organs of the body, say the naturalists; 'tis the particular gift of heaven, say the divines, both Christians and heathens. How to improve it, many books can teach us; how to obtain it, none: that nothing can be done without it all agree." Genius, for Dryden, was still a power, not a person, something one had. But though all might have a genius for something—a natural inclination that led them along—those who were led to the very highest heights were held aloft as special men, beings of another order, angelic and divine. Michelangelo provided a vivid illustration of a being so uplifted, an individual blessed with such wondrous *ingenium*, that his contemporaries could only proclaim him at the hour of his death a being apart. Michael of the Angels, a man who was more than man. A creature whose *genius* was himself.[47]

T HE BODY ARRIVED in the early spring of 1564, borne from Rome across the Apennines to the Tuscan town on the Arno—the same town where Donatello had died and Ficino had lived and Michael of the Angels had first entered the world under a "fateful and fortunate star." He was coming home to a place of rest after a life of sacrifice and devotion, a life of beautifying God's world. The people of Florence were grateful. They lined the streets as the coffin passed, and filled to overflowing the great church of Santa Croce, which was prepared to receive the "saintly old man." When the casket was opened on March 11 in the sacristy, it "seemed a great thing to everyone that he was not at all disfigured nor his body in the least decomposed," wrote Don Giovanni di Simone, a direct witness. Another observed that "touching his head and his cheeks, which everyone did, they found them to be soft and life-like, as if he had died only a few hours before, and this filled all with amazement," for in truth, he "had been in the coffin for 22 days or more, and from the day of his death 25 days had passed." The priest who presided over the preparations for burial declared this a "divine sign," and Michelangelo's close friend, the painter-author Giorgio Vasari, echoed that sentiment in the revised edition of his celebrated *Lives of the Artists*. "We were tempted to believe," he noted there, "that [Michelangelo] was only resting in a sweet and tranquil sleep."[48]

Whatever the actual condition of the body, claims of its incorruptibility and the vague suggestion of thaumaturgic power implicit in the laying on of hands called to mind the long-standing belief that the flesh of saints was impervious to decay. And that, in turn, further confirmed what Michelangelo's contemporaries believed to be the immaculate state of the soul that it housed. Michelangelo claimed to have been born under the sign of Saturn. But could melancholy alone account for the extraordinary nature of his powers? Could mere nature explain the wonder of his work? For here, truly, was a man who could animate statues, endow stones with souls, and impart, as one observer marveled, "living form even to marble." Everywhere Michelangelo's magic evoked expressions of incredulity and awe—*stupendo, stupore, meriviglia, mirabilia*—words that testify eloquently to the inability of observers to fully believe their eyes. Surely, the *ingenium* that produced such marvels could not be wholly of this world. A miracle of perfection, this *ingenium* was, in a word, "divine."[49]

That sacred epithet had once been reserved exclusively for the saints, but in the fifteenth century it was applied more broadly to characterize the *ingenium* of great men. Poets such as Dante, and humanists such as Petrarch, were described as "divine" well before the word was granted to those working in the plastic arts; Filippo Brunelleschi appears to have been the first of the latter, his "*divino ingegno*" invoked to explain the architectural brilliance that spanned the massive dome of Florence's cathedral. Other "super-artists" were then duly sanctified as "divine"— Dürer, Leonardo, Titian, Raphael—drawing the epithet that Michelangelo drew like no other. Vasari described Michelangelo as *divino* no fewer than twenty times in the first edition of the *Lives of the Artist*, published in 1550 while Michelangelo was still alive (nearly forty times in the second edition of 1568). He was, the poet Ariosto famously punned, "Michael, better than a mortal, an archangel divine," and at the moment of his death, his saintly and angelic gifts appeared more radiant than ever. In keeping with custom, mourners affixed messages and fragments of verse to his coffin, spontaneously giving voice to their reverence for this angelic bearer of divine *ingenium*. "Unequalled through all ages past," Michelangelo was a "true angel" (*vero Angelo*), a "divine angel" (*Angelo divino*), whose "lofty *ingegno*" was ready with its glance and wings for so high a flight. Later, at the official memorial services held at the Basilica of San Lorenzo—an honor hitherto reserved for princes—the humanist Benedetto Varchi pronounced a eulogy that soared to even greater heights. Michelangelo, endowed with the "very strongest" and "most capacious" *ingegno*, was not just a human being of the highest excellence, but a "celestial and divine man," "more divine than human," "singular and unique," a producer of "marvels" and "miracles." "Should I call him an angel," Varchi wondered, "or an archangel even more divine?" "Not only can we believe," he insisted, "but we must believe" that Michelangelo was "chosen in heaven, and sent to earth by God."⁵⁰

It is important to be sensitive to the rhetorical license of such pronouncements, bearing in mind a point that art historians have emphasized of late when they remind us that in 1550, for instance, the very year that Vasari published his apotheosis of Michelangelo, the "divine one" was still performing routine jobs, receiving six *scudi* to gild eight bedknobs on Pope Julius III's bed. The point is that declarations of divinity need to be brought down to earth, understood in a social context in which artists were still shaking off the stigma of being artisans, manual workers, and hired help. To declare divinity in this setting was to affirm the power and prestige of artists with respect to patrons and social betters. It was an act of self-promotion and self-fashioning, a way of "inventing" oneself and one's friends.⁵¹

Not that Michelangelo himself was inclined toward self-love. Generally contemptuous of such praise, he was painfully aware of his own limitations. "Michelangelo had such a perfect and distinctive imagination," Vasari explains, "and the works he envisioned were of such a nature that he found it impossible to express such grandiose and awesome conceptions with his hands." He suffered as a result, his mind ranging beyond itself, haunted by the perfection that he conceived, but could not perfectly render. Leonardo da Vinci experienced this curse to an even greater extent: forever unsatisfied with his work, he slashed canvases, took hammers to marble, and struggled in isolation, locking himself in his studio for days. Michelangelo, too, withdrew from the company of men. Working constantly, he neglected food and drink and slept in his clothes, bathing so infrequently that when he removed his boots, the skin came off. Independent and defiant, he refused the entreaties even of the pope.[52]

It was qualities like these—a proud and incessant striving coupled with a sense of tragic failure and anomie—that would later endear the artists of the Renaissance to the Romantics. "Oh sublime genius!" Delacroix declares in looking at a Michelangelo sketch. It was a common response, and seems natural to us today, for in fact the Romantics largely succeeded in imposing their own categories on the past. In the godlike artist of the Renaissance, they saw an image of themselves, an image of the genius who strives for originality, who creates in defiance of convention and the rules—an eccentric, a rebel, who suffers for his art, even unto madness and despair. Scholars influenced by the Romantics long reinforced the picture. It was in the Renaissance, they believed, that the Romantic genius was born, and they found evidence of that seminal creation in men of great *ingenium*, a word they translated invariably—as many do still—as "genius."[53]

But neither Renaissance *ingenium* nor Renaissance *genii* can be equated with genius in its modern form. *Ingegno* was still too tightly bound by *ars* and *industria*; the power to create by the compulsion to imitate; the imagination by the example of the past. For all their talk of approaching God, Renaissance artists still inhabited a universe of limits. One might travel upward along the Great Chain of Being, but the links remained, separating and binding together the whole. And though a winged soul like Michael might appear to his fellows as an angel or a saint, and even assume a portion of their powers, it was rare to confuse such creatures with their Creator. Only when the *genii* were put to flight and God himself had receded and withdrawn would human beings occupy their sacred space. In the sixteenth century, a man could be said to possess genius, but even Michelangelo was not yet a genius himself.

Still, in their rumination on the angels and the demons, *ingenium* and the soul, melancholy and mind, Renaissance commentators did clear a space in which the modern genius could begin to assume form. Summoning the *genii* from the classical past, they shifted their shapes and transferred their powers to the souls of outstanding men, men who were moved by inspiration or endowed at birth with special gifts. And notwithstanding the rhetorical license, to describe a man of genius as "divine" was to say more than that he belonged in the company of the esteemed. As Vasari observed of Leonardo, another man whom posterity would call a genius before the time: "The greatest gifts often rain down upon human bodies through celestial influences as a natural process, and sometimes in a supernatural fashion a single body is lavishly supplied with such beauty, grace, and ability that wherever the individual turns, each of his actions is so divine that he leaves behind all other men, and clearly makes himself known as a thing endowed by God (which he is) rather than created by human artifice."[54]

Here was a creature set apart, elected and chosen, different in kind. Whereas once the feats of such men were chronicled exclusively in lives of the saints, they now featured in lives of the artists or other compendia of *viris illustribus*, of which Vasari's was but a single, if prominent, example. Scholars, poets, and architects occupied a central place in works such as Paolo Giovio's 1564 collection of the lives of illustrious individuals, the *Elogia doctorum virorum* (Sketches in praise of learned men), whereas Polydore Vergil's vast 1499 treatise on discovery, the *De inventoribus rerum* (*On Discovery*), celebrated great inventors and their inventions throughout history, attributing to them the "glory" of being first. Their presence in the company of cardinals, commanders, and kings was evidence of innovation in itself. But the terms in which they were described were truly without precedent since the coming of Christ. The humanist critic Julius Caesar Scaliger could hail the poet as an *alter Deus*, like another God, whereas the great sixteenth-century poet Torquato Tasso maintained that "there are two creators, God and the poet." Vasari, similarly, begins his *Lives* by drawing an explicit comparison between the artist and God, a comparison he extends throughout the work by using the term *artefice* for his subjects, in place of the more common Italian *artista* or *artigiano* (artisan). The word recalled the Latin *artifex*, long employed in theological writings to describe God the Creator. Just as God, by "shaping man, discovered in the pleasing invention of things the first form of sculpture and painting," so did artists partake of godlike powers in performing acts of creation. In the case of Michelangelo, the analogy was abundantly clear. To a greater degree than any other artist, ancient or modern, he dispensed with precedent and imitation, doing away with the "measures, orders, and rules men usually employ" to guide their work. Michelangelo "broke the bonds and chains" that held other men down, freed himself to create ex nihilo. He was, in this sense, a "mortal god."[55]

Staring upward at the Sistine Chapel—that "great picture," as Vasari says, "sent by God to men on earth so that they could see how Fate operates when supreme intellects descend to earth and are infused with grace and divinity of knowledge"—viewers might well have countenanced the comparison. And as they did so, they might have recalled the words of Ficino: "Since this person sees the order of the heavens, whence they are moved, whither they proceed, with what measures, and to what they give rise, who will deny that he has almost the same genius [*ingenio*], so to speak, as the author of the heavens, and that he is capable in a way of making the heavens, should he ever obtain the instruments and the celestial material." Ficino worked in words, Michelangelo in plaster, paint, and stone. But together they and their contemporaries seeded a thought, at once exhilarating and terrifying. One day a genius might come who dared, like God, to fashion not only art, but the world itself in his own image.[56]

CHAPTER III

THE GENIUS OF
THE MODERNS

TOWARD THE END OF THE OPENING section of René Descartes's *Meditations on First Philosophy*, genius makes a spectacular, if fleeting, appearance. "I shall then suppose," Descartes writes in this foundational work of modern thought, that "some evil genius not less powerful than deceitful, has employed his whole energies in deceiving me; I shall consider that the heavens, the earth, colours, figures, sound, and all other external things are nought but the illusions and dreams of which this genius has availed himself in order to lay traps for my credulity." The "deceiver," Descartes then supposes, is "very powerful and very cunning," employing all its energy in deceiving him. Yet, despite its greatest efforts—or rather, despite Descartes's worst imaginings—the malicious specter cannot shake him of the conviction that he is a *res cogitans*, "a thing that thinks." "Ego sum, ego existo," Descartes writes in a variation of his earlier (and more famous) statement in the *Discourse on Method*, "Cogito ergo sum" (I think therefore I am). "I am, I exist." No demon deceiver can make him believe otherwise.[1]

First published in Latin in 1641, the *Meditations'* specific reference to a *genius malignus* (*un mauvais génie*, in the French translation of 1647) is often treated today as a curious thought experiment designed to test the limits of radical skepticism. It was, in part, just that. Yet it is not at all surprising that Descartes should have resorted to the hypothesis of the demon deceiver, for the belief in demons was still very much alive. Descartes himself had experienced a series of dreams involving *genii* as a young man. And in the century or so since the Renaissance magi had attempted to conjure the classical *genius* and summon guardian angels from on high, Europeans had witnessed the great panic of the early-modern witch craze, with its feverish rumination on demons

67

and the occult. Gradually, Descartes convinced himself that demons were but phantoms of a fevered imagination, chimera that would disappear when one distinguished clearly between reality and illusion. And the *Meditations on First Philosophy*, like the earlier *Discourse on Method*, aimed to fulfill that end, seeking to eliminate all threats to the certainty of knowledge. The fictive evil genius, Descartes declares, might deceive us in everything save that we are thinking. And on the bedrock of that "clear and distinct" idea, he proceeds to rebuild the structures of thought that his doubts had torn down, positing the existence of a new mechanical world of cause and effect in which there would be no room for *genii* at all. The Cartesian universe retains a place for God as its architect and creator. But it admits of no *Mittelsmächte*, no mediating forces or occult powers of any other kind.[2]

It would be silly to assume, as later hagiographers were sometimes wont to do, that Descartes succeeded in banishing the demons single-handedly, putting the angels to flight. Europeans did not go to sleep dreaming of *genii* only to wake up thinking like Voltaire. And yet, to those horrified by the seventeenth-century witch hunts that had turned up devils on every door, the rational doubt cultivated by both men was appealing. It was indicative of a new and emboldened skepticism toward the spirits that for centuries had mediated the universe's powers. *Genii* might still embellish rococo canvases, or grace neoclassical marbles, books, and prints. It is a *génie*, after all (for the Arabic *jinn*), who emerges from the bottle when rubbed in the first (and widely reproduced) European translation of *One Thousand and One Nights*. But banishment to such exotic locales was itself an indication that the *genii* were being driven to the margins as creatures of fantasy, amusement, allegory, or myth. When educated Europeans surveyed their own mental universe, they were far less likely to grant them a place. Voltaire spoke for many in the new age when he declared, under the entry *"genii"* in his *Philosophical Dictionary*, that "all that can be said is reduced to this: I have never seen a genius, and no one of my acquaintance has ever seen one; . . . therefore I do not believe a thing of which there is not the least truth." The same logic was dutifully applied to demons, angels, fairies, and satyrs, who Voltaire confessed might exist in principle, "with little turned-up tails and goats' feet." "But I would have to see several to believe in them," he stressed, "for if I saw but one, I should still doubt their existence." If seeing was believing in the eighteenth century, then Voltaire and many like him simply did not believe.[3]

That (lack of) belief significantly transformed their understanding of special individuals and eminent men. Voltaire scoffed at the notion that Socrates had a "good angel" or "genius." If anything, he joked, his angel must have been bad, since it prompted him to make the rounds of Athens, interrogating his fellow citizens to show that they were imbeciles. Voltaire's irony, however, concealed a serious question, one that confounded an age otherwise inclined to make the ancient philosopher a hero. If Socrates possessed no *daimonion* or special sign, just what was it that possessed him? Had he lied about his little demon in order to deceive his followers? Perhaps they had invented the story after the fact to accentuate his greatness? Or was he simply deluded? And what of the other great men who had long been regarded as divinely touched or inspired? "So much has been written about this by so many sophists," the German critic J. G. A. Hamann complained in 1759, himself adding to the cascade of words, that "no cultivated reader of our day lacks talented friends" who could hold forth on the subject at length.[4]

Hold forth they did, and in doing so they contributed to a process of consecration that had been under way since the Renaissance, conflating the spirits of men like Socrates with the men themselves. The same period that drove off the angels in droves, dispelling the *genii* and the saints, gave birth to a genius of its own, the genius conceived in flesh. His name was familiar, as were a number of his functions. And yet this new creature was no mere replacement of the guardians of old. The genius was an altogether new creation, a new type of being, a modern man. In a century that dared to proclaim the equality of all, he would be like no other—the great exception.

Why this exceptional figure should emerge in the eighteenth century as a new type of cultural hero—and just what that emergence might mean—are the questions that animate this chapter, which examines the causes and consequences of the genius's birth and consecration. Considering the lives of some of the outstanding individuals of the age, the chapter also treats a host of lesser known figures who were present at the delivery or who played a key role in the genius's rise to prominence. Scientists like Newton, musicians like Mozart, and philosophers like Immanuel Kant make their appearance alongside others who garnered attention as geniuses or who reflected on the phenomenon: men of letters, men of commerce, men of state. For although the genius was the century's singular being, he assumed many forms.

THERE WAS NO SHRIEKING ENTRY into the world on this occasion. No wise men from the East to follow his star or pay homage at his feet. No frankincense and myrrh. Yet a new being was born to humanity all the same, in circumstances similarly humble. In time, notice would be taken by wise men of the East and West alike—women, too—of a word made flesh and come to dwell among us. A true light to enlighten the world.

And so we find him, nestled amid the third entry of the word, in Antoine Furetière's *Dictionnnaire universel* of 1690. "Cet homme est un vaste génie, qui est capable de tout." "This man is a vast genius, capable of all." Intended as an illustration of current French usage, the annunciation is offered without further comment or remark. And yet, in light of what precedes it on the page—and for the better part of human history—the definition is remarkable. "Genius," the first entry reads familiarly enough, is "a good or bad demon whom the ancients believed accompanied illustrious men." "Genius," a second definition follows, is "used in Christianity to refer to the good angels who accompany men, or who are assigned to states and churches to protect them." And "genius," a third continues, is "used as well to refer to natural talent, and to the disposition that one has toward one thing, and not another." Such descriptions are by now familiar enough to readers of this book, charting as they do the history and genealogy of the term. "Genius" in all of these instances is an object, something one has (a spirit, an angel, a talent), rather than something one is. The entry that follows, however, is a striking departure. "This [particular] man is a genius," it reads. An example of how the word might be used in speech, the statement is ontological, a proclamation of what special men could become.[5]

Tucked away in the manger of its words, Furetière's description might well have passed into obscurity had its central gospel not been taken up elsewhere. But commentators embraced the new meaning alongside the older variations, speaking—like the eulogist at the Académie Française, who referred to Cardinal Richelieu, in passing, as *ce puissant Genie*, "this powerful genius"—of outstanding individuals as if they were geniuses themselves. Although the academy's own dictionary failed to acknowledge the new usage in its first edition of 1694, it recorded it in the second edition of 1718: "One says that a man is a fine, a great genius, a superior genius, in order to say that he has a fine, a great genius." A man is a great genius when his genius is great. In French usage, a new type of being, *l'homme de génie* (the man of genius), was born.[6]

France was far from alone in its fecundity: one may trace similar evolutions throughout Europe, from England (where the astute spectator Joseph Addison was observing, as early as 1711, that "there is no Character more frequently given to a Writer, than that of being a Genius") to Germany (where by the second half of the century, leading participants in the aptly named "Age of Genius," the *Geniezeit*, were complaining of the overuse of the term). Even in the New World, Benjamin Franklin was hailed in the 1770s as the "distinguish'd genius of America."[7]

In all these places, observers detected geniuses where previously they had seen only wise men or gifted souls. And they lavished attention on these special beings in a public cult without precedent, recording the intimate details of their lives and their works; reproducing their images in paint, print, and stone; and seeking them out in their homes like the celebrities they gradually became. Enlightened men and women even discovered geniuses who were long dead and gone. It was in the eighteenth century that Shakespeare was christened a genius, "one of the greatest geniuses the world ever saw," in the estimation of John Dennis's *Essay on the Genius and Writings of Shakespeare* of 1712. Homer was another, along with the wild and audacious Pindar, greatest of the lyric poets of classical Greece, and a host of other individuals, ancient and more modern, who were discovered as "geniuses" for the first time. They included philosophers and men of letters, natural scientists and musicians, orators, statesmen, and bards, though it bears emphasizing that in all of these cases—virtually everywhere that genius assumed form and flesh—the genius was assumed to be male. Women might have a genius for skills in keeping with their sex, but to be a genius in the eighteenth century was largely a male prerogative, even if there were notable exceptions and spirited dissent. The English poet Mary Scott, for example, boldly spoke of "female geniuses," while the authors of the 1766 *Biographium Faemineum*, a compendium of the lives of illustrious women, noted that "souls are of no sex, any more than wit, genius, or any other of the intellectual faculties." It was an early articulation of a view later attributed to the *femme de lettres* Madame de Staël—that "genius has no sex." An inspiring thought, but in the context of the eighteenth century, it was ahead of its time. More of the moment was the German thinker Hamann, who confessed in a letter to a friend, "My coarse imagination has never been able to imagine a creative spirit without [male] genitalia."[8]

Yet before considering the body of geniuses—and with the body, its gender—the more pressing task is to make sense of the embodiment. What accounts for this striking incarnation? Why did the Age of Enlightenment give birth to genius in the flesh? The matter is more than just a simple case of what literary scholars would call metonymy or synecdoche—the substitution of a part for the whole. For while the use of the term "genius" to refer to those who possessed genius was in some sense a natural linguistic evolution—an outgrowth of the Renaissance's fusion of *genius* and *ingenium* in the mind—this evolution doesn't explain why the figures who had it—men of genius—were so widely hailed in the eighteenth century, celebrated as new models of the highest human type. The birth of the genius as a figure of extraordinary privilege and exception, in short, is a process that needs to be explained.[9]

Given the importance of the question, scholars have not failed to address it. Some have focused on matters of aesthetics, linking the rise of the original genius to the gradual emergence of Romanticism and the corresponding decline of neoclassicism and the mimetic imperative in poetry and art. Only when artists were freed of the constraints of mimesis—the need to imitate nature, to faithfully reflect God's creation, and to hold true to the pristine models and conventions of the past—could the cult of the original creator, the man of genius, come into its own. Others have attempted to explain the emergence of the man of genius and the valorization of his principal qualities—originality and individual creative freedom—as a reflection of underlying material causes, the result of social and economic change. In its crudest, Marxian form, this explanation presents the genius as a hero of the rising bourgeoisie, who assailed established norms in science, literature, and art in the same way that the middle class was said to have attacked the last vestiges of feudal restrictions with the advent of capitalism and economic laissez-faire. Finally, scholars have retained an interest in underlying social and economic transformations while shifting the focus to the plight of the individual author or artist. Deprived of powerful patrons and increasingly dependent for survival on the proceeds of their work, writers and artists strove to define unique personalities and styles in order to highlight claims to the ownership of their creations. Originality and copyright developed in tandem, and the new creator of "genius" dramatized the emergence of the modern artist and self.[10]

There is something to be said for each one of these explanations: a development as complex and wide-ranging as the rise of the genius necessarily had multiple causes and effects. Certainly, there can be little doubt that the genius figure—individual, autonomous, self-legislating— would come to reflect a new, idealized conception of the self. The decline of mimesis and the rise of notions of original genius, moreover, were undoubtedly linked both to evolving aesthetic notions and to the plight of creators eager to free themselves from patrons and to protect the ownership of their work. Nor, in the final analysis, should the crudeness of an older Marxian rhetoric prevent one from appreciating the role that nascent commercial society played in precipitating the rise of the genius as a being celebrated for his capacity for discovery, invention, and creativity. It is no coincidence that the verb "create" was applied to commercial activity in the eighteenth century; that commercial activity itself was taken as a model for innovation; and that genius was thought of as a force applicable to enterprise and trade. As the French *Journal de commerce* maintained in 1759, the successful man of business must have "the same kind of genius" as a Locke or Newton to successfully pursue his craft—inventiveness and original insight. Tellingly, it was in this same general period that the French and others took to calling engineering "genius" (*génie, ingeniero, ingegneria*). An *ingénieur* was simply one with "ingenuity," with genius dwelling within, an individual who could conceive and create, fabricate and build ingeniously. It is no less telling that "the inventor" emerged in this same period as a new cultural hero, one frequently associated with genius. Such examples highlight the undeniable fact that the new world of nascent capitalism celebrated original creativity and individual invention. The genius figure, in this respect, if not in all others, served nicely as an embodiment and ideal type of values central to an emergent capitalist world.[11]

And yet, to leave the matter at that would be to omit a crucial aspect of the story. For what these explanations have all overlooked is the way in which the rise to prominence of the genius figure was the product not only of evolving aesthetic norms and a changing social and economic space, but of an altered religious and political environment—the consequence, on the one hand, of the unprecedented clearing of the heavens of mediating powers and the attendant withdrawal of God, and the related advent, on the other, of the ideal of universal equality. Whereas the one development opened up a space in which the genius could emerge and spread his wings, the other provided a crucial context of dialectic and counterpoint. For the genius was by definition an anomaly—singular, unique, constitutionally different from ordinary men. In a world that heralded human equality he would be the great exception.

A number of the causes of the first set of developments have already been discussed: the innovations introduced by Renaissance philosophers, who imagined genius not as an angelic being, but an indwelling power; the Protestant critique of the cult of the saints and its discounting (though seldom total disavowal) of the angels and their guardian role; and the concerns about magic raised by the Reformation and its Catholic response. Each of these factors played its part in fostering skepticism toward divine companions, mediators, and those who invoked them. The reaction to the excesses of the European witch craze had a similar effect, as did the process of critical inquiry initiated by men like Descartes and the ensuing movements of the Enlightenment that swept across Europe and the New World in the seventeenth and eighteenth centuries, casting doubt on demons, angels, and spirits of all kinds. But the very same period that put the angels to flight also experienced the presentiment and perception that God was growing more distant, more remote, and less concerned with the affairs of human beings in the world here below. In this account—and it is one shared by observers who are by no means unsympathetic to religion—this "withdrawal" of God was felt even (and especially) among believers, who likewise struggled to detect the Creator's presence and despaired of the absence of their "hidden God." But wherever it was felt, God's withdrawal had powerful, and contradictory, effects. Positively, it allowed for the emergence of a new type of human agency in a more autonomous and malleable universe. It left "the human community completely to itself," a development that a number of leading historians have linked to the emergence in the eighteenth century of concepts like "society," "nation," and "public opinion," conceived as autonomous realms largely free from divine manipulation, and subject overwhelmingly to human control. In God's absence, human beings were free to assume elements of his power, taking upon themselves capacities that they had long attributed to him. Yet this same withdrawal also had a more negative effect, inducing a haunting sense of loneliness and abandonment that was all the stronger for the flight of the angels and the retreat of the guardian companions. To those whom God had partially forsaken, to those without a *comes* or friend, the universe could seem a lonely and disorienting place.[12]

Bear in mind that this was a predicament without precedent in the history of the world. At no time had human beings lived alone in this way, without mediators and intercessors to the divine. And it was at just this moment (and for closely related reasons) that they began to turn their gaze in earnest from the "always already there" to the "yet to be realized," focusing intently on the future as the privileged place of human making, the site of the disclosure of the new and the unknown. Rather than dwell solely on the patterns and revelations of old, they began to look forward on time's horizon, seeking the unexpected, the original, the unknown. It should hardly surprise us that in the midst of this temporal reorientation and in the vast space opened up by God's withdrawal and the guardians' flight, a new figure was seized upon to provide a portion of God's power and an element of the guardian's comfort. Geniuses offered assurance that special beings still animated the universe, that someone stood between the ordinary and the unknown, the sacred and the profane, that a privileged few could see where the many were blind. Revealing, disclosing, guiding, creating, the genius enchanted a world threatened by disenchantment.[13]

The emergence of the cult of the genius was thus in part a response to the tectonic shifts of an evolving religious landscape. But the cult also emerged in a changing political environment, one that witnessed a development as unprecedented and monumental in human history as the withdrawal of God. The proclamation of universal equality was, of course, long just that—a proclamation—that only garnered grudging (and imperfect) acceptance after centuries of struggle. Nor were its first, explicit formulations without precedent. As a host of novel theorists in the seventeenth and eighteenth centuries—from Thomas Hobbes and John Locke to Baruch Spinoza and Jean-Jacques Rousseau—would themselves point out, some form of equality was arguably our oldest human endowment, an original condition that had reigned in the state of nature long ago, only to have been surrendered or usurped. Christians, too, could claim, with the Apostle Paul, that all were one in Christ and equal before God—Jew and Gentile, male and female, slave and free (Gal. 3:28). Indeed, it was radical Christians, first in the Reformation and then in the upheavals of the English Civil War of the mid-seventeenth century, who initially pushed the claim, turning the world upside down in their effort to realize God's equality on earth. Yet notwithstanding these important precedents, the broad assertion of human equality—of opportunity, of rights, of general endowments—was largely a novel one in the seventeenth and eighteenth centuries. And as polemicists pressed it with increasing insistence—in theory in the Enlightenment, and in practice in the American, French, Haitian, and Latin American revolutions of the late eighteenth and early nineteenth centuries—they challenged centuries-old privileges of aristocrats based on birth and blood while begging the question of the equality of women, religious minorities, indigenous peoples, and African slaves. The ideal was far from reality. But the thought had been broached: all human beings were equal, or should be treated as if they were so.[14]

Scholars are quick to point out—and rightly so—how these sweeping assertions of natural equality elicited equally sweeping claims of natural difference, with anthropology and a host of nascent disciplines pressed into service to justify new forms of racism, sexism, and anti-Semitism in the nineteenth and twentieth centuries. But what these observers have missed is how the new cult of the genius—with its central claim of natural human superiority and difference—also constituted a response to the doctrine of human equality, a protest and reassertion of innate and inherent distinctions, albeit on wholly modern terms. The genius was no aristocrat reborn (though some would claim aristocratic privileges and exceptions), and the relationship to equality was not without its ambiguities and concessions. But, on the whole, the cult of the genius was reactive, bound up dialectically with the assertion of equality from the late seventeenth century onward, just as it was bound up with the complex process of disenchantment. The two developments, in fact, were reaffirming. For the genius's exception to equality was a product of his exceptional nature, his rare endowment as a being who walked where the angels and god-men once trod. The creator of genius was no mere mortal, but a "second Maker, a just Prometheus, under Jove." The line is that of Anthony Ashley Cooper, the third Earl of Shaftesbury, from his essay "Advice to Authors," written at the very beginning of the eighteenth century. It is often repeated, and with reason, for it captures nicely an emergent sense of the exalted and exceptional status of the creator. What is less often remarked, however, is Shaftesbury's explanation of this process, which tracks closely with the account of the rise of the genius offered here.[15]

Indeed, in the very same essay in which he hails the power of the poet as a higher being, a "second maker" under God, Shaftesbury calls attention to an ancient opinion that "were it literally true, might be highly serviceable." The opinion in question was the doctrine "that we have each of us a daemon, genius, angel, or guardian spirit, to whom we were strictly joined and committed from our earliest dawn of reason, or moment of our birth." As a newly Enlightened man, Shaftesbury refused to countenance the veracity of that opinion, but he keenly felt its loss. For the idea of the spiritual double was the ancients' way of setting up one part of the mind as a "counselor" and "governor" over the other. By entering into discourse with this better self in the pursuit of "morals and true wisdom," the ancients sought self-knowledge and that proper "subordinacy, which alone could make us agree with ourselves, and be of a-piece within." And they regarded this quest for wholeness and self-understanding as a sacred task, "a more religious work than any prayers, or other duty in the temple."[16]

Moderns, of course, no longer believed in spirits of this kind, and so neglected the ancient rituals and rites, just as many, too, were setting aside the Christian cult of the guardian angel and the patron saint. But rather than celebrate that fact—cheering the onset of Cartesian clarity and doubt—Shaftesbury drew attention to the costs of disenchantment. For those who denied the existence of the doubles and *daimones* who had guarded humanity from its birth now found it hard to know their own minds, to divine that "obscure implicit language" that all of us harbor within. Alienated and alone, moderns were lost to themselves and the world, and "for this reason," he mused, "the right method is to give [our thoughts] voice and accent." This, "in our default, is what the moralists or philosophers endeavor to do . . . when they hold us out a kind of vocal looking glass, draw sound out of our breast, and instruct us to personate ourselves in the plainest manner." In other words, great writers and thinkers translate our innermost thoughts by holding up a mirror—a vocal mirror of words that not only speaks the sounds of truth to us, but allows us to comprehend the secret language of our souls, to see ourselves and the world about us more clearly than we otherwise would. Geniuses, in effect, became our *genii*, serving as our guides and better selves, our guardian protectors and moral spectators, who help us negotiate the mysteries of the self and of the world.[17]

Shaftesbury was far from the only observer in the eighteenth century to make this connection explicit. "Genius is *genius*," the Swiss founder of physiognomy, Johann Caspar Lavater, declared amid a soaring enco-mium to that special individual who could feel, think, speak, act, com-pose, create, and build "as if he were dictated to by a *genius*, an invisible being of a higher kind, as if he himself were this being of a higher kind." The German philosopher and theologian Johann Gottfried von Herder likewise conflated the ancient *genius* with the modern genius in his writ-ings, speaking interchangeably at times of *der Genius* and *das Genie*. There were others, as well, though to draw attention to the fact is not to insist on any crude or direct correspondence between the ancient *genius* and the modern incarnation. Lavater himself was promiscuous in his comparisons, describing the modern genius as the "counterpart of the divine," a "king of the world," and a "human god." Others pressed the comparison with saints, prophets, and apostles. In truth, the modern genius was none of these things, but rather a being sui generis, an origi-nal who dared imitate only himself. [18]

That said, it is the case that the genius preserved in his person— and was perceived to do so—something of this former sacred aura and calling, and thus continued to mediate between ordinary human beings and whatever might dwell above or beyond them. Geniuses translated, decoded, and deciphered the mysteries of the universe, even as they ren-dered the universe deeper, more complex, and more profound, reveal-ing it to be at once marvelous and terrible in its sublimity. Wonders themselves, they made the world wondrous with their revelations and creations, enchanting at the very moment that they enlightened, clar-ified, and explained. Geniuses reassured that the universe was still a magical place, and they provided in the absence of the guardians of old a compensation for the loss and dislocation identified by Shaftesbury. Higher beings, men exalted, geniuses were in possession of a rare and special power.

B
UT WHAT WAS THIS POWER, this special capacity that bid contemporaries to make of those who possessed it a new type of being, a creature apart? What was it, precisely, that modern geniuses had? The difficulties that contemporaries displayed in responding to that question are themselves revealing of the answer. For despite a discussion that spread across Europe, and spanned the whole of the eighteenth century, the power of genius remained as much a mystery at its end as it had been at the beginning. Nor was this simply the result of the imprecision of language, the fact, as one observer pointed out in 1799, that "genius is a term, like many others, too complex to admit of a regular or precise definition." Mystery, rather, was central to the thing itself, bound up with its power in the most fundamental way. The poet and critic Edward Young put it best, observing in his influential *Conjectures on Original Composition* of 1759 that "a genius differs from a good Understanding, as a Magician from a good Architect; that raises his structure by means invisible; this by the skillful use of common tools." Even in the Age of Enlightenment, the genius possessed a hint of magic.[19]

Talk of this kind—invocations of mystery and magic, divine inspiration and special revelation—had, of course, attended eminent men from the outset. Thus does Young stress in the very next sentence, "Hence Genius has ever been supposed to partake of something divine." He hastens to illustrate the point with two suitably ancient quotations. "Nemo unquam vir magnus fuit, sine aliquo afflatus divino," he quotes from Cicero's *On the Nature of the Gods*: "No man has ever been great, but by the aid of divine breath." And he offers a line attributed to Seneca, "Sacer nobis inest Deus," which he glosses as "Genius is that god within," the divinely implanted *ingenium*, seeded in our souls. The two understandings of human greatness—genius as divine inspiration and genius as divine gift—lived on in the eighteenth century, illustrating the surprising extent to which modern discussions of genius were themselves a product of the rediscovery and reinterpretation of themes first elaborated in the ancient world. The long reach of Renaissance humanism helped to ensure that the Enlightenment, too, was heir to the venerable classical tradition of the possessor and the possessed.[20]

Yet there is something more interesting going on in the eighteenth-century discussion than simply continuity and persistence. For the widespread invocation of genius was not merely an atavism, but an innovation, a novel response to the effort to understand extraordinary human achievement rationally, in purely human terms. The cult of genius as it emerged from the eighteenth century, in other words, constituted a *reaction* to efforts to demystify human experience, and as such provides a perfect illustration of the proposition that the progressive disenchantment of the world was accompanied from the start by its progressive re-enchantment. But what was it that the possessor possessed? And, in a post-Enlightened world—a world without spirits, demons, or divine breath—what could it be that actually possessed him?[21]

Consider first the efforts to strip genius of its magic, to comprehend it in terms of reason and science alone. For there *was* such an effort in the Age of Enlightenment, and it was not without considerable influence. Seventeenth-century critics may have been content to treat genius as a "vague, undefined power"—frequently associating it with that indefinable something, the "Je ne sais quoi" of great art. But their eighteenth-century counterparts sought repeatedly to pin that power down, dispelling the mists that obscured it. Already in the 1650s, the English philosopher Thomas Hobbes was casting scorn on the notion that artistic prowess was infused by inspiration—whether by God, the Muses, or the mystical possession of the *furor poeticus*. Why should a man want to believe he is being played like a "bagpipe," he scoffed, blown up by someone else's breath, when he is "enabled to speak wisely from the principles of nature and his own meditation"? Hobbes's dismissal of such windy theories reflected a distrust of "enthusiasm," a word that was increasingly on the lips of his contemporaries, almost invariably as a pejorative. Coined in the seventeenth century, the term meant literally, as its Greek etymology suggested, "to be possessed by a god" (*en* + *theos*), but it was most often used in post-Reformation Europe as a blanket term for religious "fanaticism." "Enthusiasts" were those who lay claim to direct revelation or the power of the Holy Spirit, those moved to quake and shake, prophesy and preach, speaking in tongues or declaiming in public. Hobbes held them accountable for the religiously inspired upheavals that had wracked Great Britain and the European continent for decades, and his critique of enthusiasm was consistent with his broader suspicion of indwelling "spirits" of any kind—Aristotelian essences, Platonic forms, innate ideas, or even, many suspected, the Christian Logos itself. That suspicion was in turn linked to an evolving empiricism, the view that the mind and its contents were shaped primarily by experiences in the world, as opposed to whatever might be gleaned from inspiration or acquired, innately, at birth. Hobbes's contemporary, John Locke, gave this empirical view its most forceful articulation in his celebrated *Essay Concerning Human*

Understanding (1689), in which he compared the newborn mind to a *tabula rasa*, a "blank slate," like a piece of white paper. Everything we know in life, Locke argued, comes to us via the senses. Only later do we reflect on these initial impressions, recombining them and building them up into more complex ideas. There was more to the theory than that, but the essential point is that our direct encounters with the world form the primary basis of all we know.[22]

Elaborated by a host of leading thinkers in the eighteenth century, Locke's empiricism became one of the most influential epistemological theories of the Enlightenment. And although the reception of Hobbes's views was restrained by suspicion of his atheism, his radical critique of enthusiasm nonetheless provided an opening salvo of what proved a sustained barrage. Locke himself condemned enthusiasm as a disease of the "warmed or over-weaning brain," and many others joined him, transforming enthusiasm in the course of the eighteenth century into a "powerful term of opprobrium."[23]

By casting doubt on both the theory of divine inspiration and the special *ingenium* of the mind, Locke's empiricism and the critique of enthusiasm opened the way for a sustained attack on the mystery surrounding genius. That attack was waged throughout Europe, and by a host of different combatants. But it was given its most vigorous statement at mid-century by the Anglican clergyman William Sharpe, in his *Dissertation upon Genius* (1755), and by the celebrated French *philosophe* Claude Adrien Helvétius, who pursued a similar line of inquiry in several major sections of his *De l'esprit*, or *On the Mind* (1758). Both authors were deeply indebted to Locke's epistemology and empirical psychology and drew from it a conclusion that Locke himself had suggested in his popular treatise on pedagogy, the *Letter Concerning Education* (1692). "Of all the men we meet with," Locke noted there, "nine parts of ten are what they are, good or evil, useful or not, by their education. 'Tis that which makes the great difference in mankind." Sharpe took this proposition even further, drawing the logical conclusion that if the mind was a blank slate at birth, then all it could become was a product of what it might acquire. The implications for genius were clear: "Genius is not the result of simple nature, not the effect of any cause exclusive of human assistance, and the vicissitudes of life; but the effect of acquisition in general." Genius, in short, was made, not born, a conclusion that Helvétius came to as well in answering the question posed in the title of the opening chapter of the third part of *De l'esprit*: "Whether genius ought to be considered as a natural gift, or as an effect of education." Coming down firmly on the side of education, Helvétius argued that natural differences in intelligence were negligible and that every man was endowed with a memory "sufficient to raise him to the highest degree of mental abilities." Inequality of the mind, it followed, was a consequence not of birth, but of what came afterward: education, exposure, and application as well as a degree of chance, which "has a greater share than we imagine in the success of great men." Helvétius illustrated the latter point with the example of seventeenth-century French drama, which "successively acquired many degrees of perfection," and specifically, with the example of Pierre Corneille, a leading tragedian of the age. Though many individuals had contributed to the development of the art, "Corneille was born at a time, when the perfection he added . . . rendered it complete; Corneille is therefore a man of genius," wrote Helvétius. The genius was one who brought an evolving process of discovery to a head, and the same "law of continuity" operated in other domains, including statecraft and science. Just as Napoleon Bonaparte, Charles Darwin, or Albert Einstein would later crystallize a host of developments in their respective fields, men of genius like Corneille benefited from being in the right place at the right time. Where matters of genius were concerned, timing and fortune were crucial.[24]

Although Helvétius spelled out other criteria of genius, the essential point is that he, like Sharpe, sought to remove genius's mystery, presenting it as something we could rationally comprehend and explain. Geniuses were not constitutionally different from ordinary men; nor were they the recipients of special favor, furor, or gifts. They simply had different experiences and better training, worked harder, and benefited from the serendipities of time and place. This was a view both novel and prescient. An important branch of the psychological profession to this day posits that geniuses, or statistical "outliers," are largely what they are through "deliberate practice," intense training and exposure, begun at an early age. Nor should these continued efforts surprise us. For the Lockean position developed by Sharpe and Helvétius—or others, such as the French *philosophes* Condillac, Turgot, d'Alembert, and Condorcet—put forth a view of human possibility that fit nicely with a developing belief in human equality and progress. If, as Hobbes and others suspected, men were equal in "faculties of the mind," if genius was made, not born, then "education" and "institutions," as Sharpe argued, were the critical factors in shaping it. All men (if only men) were equal at birth, and so all might be made better by cultivation. To improve social conditions, widen access to education, and enhance human possibilities was to extend the frontiers of the republic of genius, enhancing the potential of all.[25]

The position espoused by men like Helvétius and Sharpe, then, was "modern"—progressive and potentially democratic in its recognition of basic human equality and widely inclusive in its view that nurture, as opposed to nature, was the deciding factor in shaping the human mind. The position enjoyed robust defenders throughout the eighteenth century and continues to do so today. And yet the irony that a consideration of the long history of genius imposes is that neither modernity nor democracy has ever been wholly at ease with it, continually reverting instead to the antithetical claim that genius is born, not made. Emphasizing the inherent and fundamental difference of extraordinary beings whose original genius set them apart at birth, this discourse received its most forceful statements in the second half of the eighteenth century, in direct response to the positions put forth by Helvétius and Sharpe. Its principal themes, however, were being rehearsed well before. An important article, published in the London *Spectator* in 1711 by the journal's editor, the well-known man of letters Joseph Addison, provides an early glimpse.[26]

Addison set out to inquire "what is properly a great genius," and responded that there are two types. On the one hand are what he calls "natural" or "original" geniuses, "who by the mere strength of natural parts, and without any assistance of arts or learning, have produced Works that were the delight of their own time and the wonder of Posterity." Never "disciplined," and "broken by rules," these natural geniuses include the likes of Homer, Pindar, and Shakespeare, and can be contrasted, on the other hand, with what Addison describes as "imitative" geniuses, geniuses of learning, such as Aristotle, Virgil, Francis Bacon, or Milton, who "have formed themselves by Rules, and submitted the Greatness of their natural talents to the Corrections and Restraints of Art." Addison affects a strict neutrality between the two, claiming that "the Genius in both these Classes of Authors may be equally great." Yet his sympathies incline toward the natural type, an impression that is reinforced by his mildly chauvinistic tendency—repeated by others throughout the century, especially in Britain and Germany—to associate imitative genius with France. "There is something nobly wild and extravagant in these great natural Genius's," he notes, "that is infinitely more beautiful than all the turn and polishing of what the French call a Bel Esprit, by which they would express a genius refined by conversation, reflection, and the reading of the most polite authors." The "great danger" of imitative geniuses, Addison continues, is that they can "cramp their own abilities too much by imitation, and form themselves altogether upon models, without giving the full play to their own natural parts." In short, "an imitation of the best authors is not to compare with a good original."[27]

Addison's distinction between natural and imitative genius had precedents in the seventeenth century and reflected in part an effort to mediate the concerns of the two warring parties in the ongoing battle of the ancients and the moderns (or, as it was commonly known in England, the Battle of the Books). The dispute pitted defenders of the supremacy of ancient poetry and learning against those who pressed the rival claims of more recent luminaries. And though the two sides in the conflict do not easily correspond to positions on the question of genius—indeed, if anything, the ancients, with their praise of the noble wildness of men like Homer, and their defense of the firstborn, were often more amenable to the claims of originality than their counterparts—what matters most is the way in which Addison's distinctions were seized upon by later polemicists to justify an invidious comparison. The preference for originality over imitation, for noble wildness over polish, and for the strength of natural parts over learning, acquisition, and established rules anticipated the positions taken up, albeit more sharply, by those arguing against Helvétius and Sharpe in the second half of the eighteenth century. Dispensing with the category of imitative genius altogether, those who championed this view insisted that the defining characteristic of original genius was precisely that it was original, that it couldn't be learned. It was for this reason that men such as Shakespeare, Homer, Pindar, or the mythical Celtic bard Ossian assumed such an importance in their writings, for they seemed to present unambiguous cases of individuals whose creative prowess owed nothing to formal schooling, the imitation of examples, or the mastery of rules.[28]

It was for this reason, too, that the partisans of original genius tended to be drawn to epistemological models that conceived of the mind as something more exalted than a blank slate or sheet of paper. The mind of the genius, in their reckoning, was no mere scribe, faithfully recording impressions of the world and recombining them in novel ways. Genius was of another order. As Young maintained, in laying out a qualitative distinction, "learning we thank, genius we revere; That gives us pleasure, This gives us rapture; That informs, This inspires; and is itself inspired; for genius is from heaven, learning from man." The stark contrasts are revealing in their emphasis on the special, even superhuman, aspects of this powerful force. Genius defied the limits of human understanding, and so could never be explained by recourse to context or circumstance, learning or acquisition alone. Gradually, these distinctions hardened into the fixed and invidious opposition between "talent" and "genius" to distinguish mere skill from the more exalted power conferred on nature's chosen. "Talent is an inferior faculty," the German critic Friedrich

Gabriel Resewitz declared, in what was a common eighteenth-century refrain. Or, as the philosopher Arthur Schopenhauer would later remark, in developing this same distinction, "talent is like the marksman who hits a target, which others cannot reach; genius is like the marksman who hits a target, which others cannot see." Genius was the power to perceive what lay beyond the mortal horizon.[29]

The new theoreticians of genius, then, articulated their views in pronounced opposition to the effort to demystify genius by attributing it to learning, acquisition, or cultivated skill. Achieving prominence first in Great Britain beginning in the late 1750s, when Young and others emerged as forceful "heralds" of the new view, they established themselves slightly later in the German states, where British theorists of genius were widely admired and read. In France, by contrast, the respect for imitation, tradition, and the rules of art continued to exert a more pronounced influence, as Voltaire's notorious judgment of Shakespeare makes clear. The Bard may have possessed "a genius full of force and fecundity," Voltaire conceded, but he lacked the "slightest spark of good taste [*bon goût*] and the least knowledge of the rules."[30]

Yet in France, too, there were strong opponents of the positions espoused by Helvétius (or less dogmatically by Condillac and Turgot), and by the second half of the eighteenth century they could count among their number two of the most forceful and inventive minds of the age: Jean-Jacques Rousseau, who, wild and unkempt, defiant and irrepressibly creative, seemed to embody the belief in original genius; and Denis Diderot, who proved to be one of its most penetrating and eloquent analysts. History, moreover, was on their side. For although they and their contemporaries could do little more than intuit these long-term transformations, the century as a whole was engaged in a gradual, if steady, shift away from *ars*, in Horace's sense of acquired mastery and knowledge of the rules, toward greater *ingenium*, in the modern sense of individual genius and creative subjectivity. European art had always, it is true, operated to some extent along a spectrum defined by poles of imitation and originality, reason and imagination, reflection and intuition, tradition and innovative boldness. It continued to do so in the eighteenth century, and would continue to do so long after that. Even the most original genius, after all, must apply himself and learn in order to become what he is. Yet it remains the case nonetheless that, as the years went by, the eighteenth century inclined toward the second of each of these oppositions, downplaying mimetic imperatives and neoclassical restraint in favor of greater creative freedom and license. Though still held in check by judgment and taste, good sense and the need to pay heed to established rules, the artist was gradually becoming a rule unto himself, less responsible for following the laws than for laying them down. In this climate, original genius—not genius that was acquired and learned—was of the avant-garde, despite the many battles still left to fight on the front lines.[31]

Thus, however much it might draw on ancient precedent, the articulation and embrace of the notion of original genius constituted a modern doctrine in its own right, a bold assertion of genius's qualitative difference and power. Genius was an extraordinary departure from the norm, its advocates agreed—something different, something else—even if they could seldom concur on how precisely to explain it. "A great and admirable genius will be allow'd to result from some curious structure of the brain . . . [and] from the different dispositions of the humors," an English commentator observed, with characteristic vagueness, in 1725, drawing still, as many did, on the long-standing humoral vocabulary. An influential French commentator, the abbé Dubos, could scarcely do much better, observing that genius was the consequence of a "happy arrangement of the organs of the brain," contingent upon good blood and a favorable climate. Later in the century, Diderot was still wondering whether genius was a "certain conformation of the head and the viscera," or "a certain constitution of the humors." Gradually, the language of humors was replaced in medical circles by talk of "sensibility" and theories of the nerves. Others invoked vital energy or a creative life force. But such talk did little to clarify the matter. Was genius a particular faculty of the mind, or the combination of several, as Kant maintained? Was it coextensive with the vital force of human nature itself, as Kant's former student Herder argued, or a specific aptitude of the soul? The point is that although there was general consensus in the eighteenth century regarding genius's importance, there was comparatively little agreement on what it actually was. The inability to say with certainty would make ample work for scientists in the years to come. In the meantime, it reinforced the profound sense of wonder and mystery that genius evoked.[32]

That mystery revealed itself in many places, even, ironically, when genius was employed to clarify the world, to further enlighten and explain. But it assumed its most powerful impact in the presence of "the sublime." A classical concept, first articulated in a Greek manuscript attributed to the ancient author known as Longinus, the sublime attained widespread prominence as a category of criticism only much later, in the seventeenth century, when the poet Nicolas Boileau translated *Peri hypsous* (*On the Sublime*) into French, with an extensive commentary, in 1674. Earlier translations of Longinus's work had fallen more or less stillborn; Boileau's made a splash, and it was followed by a number of vernacular editions in the succeeding decades. By the mid-eighteenth century, the sublime was being treated as an essential category of aesthetics.[33]

Boileau was a partisan of the ancients, but he read Longinus's manuscript in a manner in which the ancient author himself probably did not intend. A treatise on the rules of composition and rhetoric to be followed by writers eager to imitate the lofty achievements of the past, the work was effectively a user's manual, a primer that fit nicely in the tradition of Aristotle's *Poetics* and Horace's *Ars Poetica*, with their stress on imitation and mimesis, classical balance, and laws. The sublime, in this reading, was the mood induced by the proper deployment of stylistic conventions and rhetorical "figures." And yet Boileau insisted on something else, emphasizing the sublime's awesome power, its upsetting and revolutionary effects, its capacity to "ravish" and "transport." An ecstatic and supernatural force, the sublime was wild and unpredictable. It could not be summoned simply by following the rules. Acting on and through the passions, the sublime was marvelous, defying logic and understanding, inducing wonder and disbelief, while imparting meanings that transcended the letter of the words that disclosed them. Finally, the sublime emanated not just from the poet's language, but from his person. On Boileau's understanding, the sublime would more often be born than made or learned.[34]

As classical Greek possesses no precise equivalent of the term "genius," it is hardly surprising that Boileau's translation made only occasional use of the word. But in the various English translations that followed, genius's presence is striking. The poet Leonard Welsted's 1712 edition of *On the Sublime*, based largely on Boileau's own, speaks of that "natural superiority of Genius," which "be rather the Gift of Heaven, than a Quality to be Acquire'd." "Genius," in Welsted's words, is a reflection of inner loftiness, the "Mirrour, which represents a great soul." William Smith's 1739 translation of *On the Sublime* employs the term even more freely. In a key passage in the first chapter of Longinus's work likening the effect of the sublime to a bolt of lightning, Smith adds that this shows at one stroke the "Compacted Might of genius." And even in passages that treat of the effects of imitation, Smith places the emphasis on the power of the original: "So from the sublime Spirits of the Ancients there arise some fine Effluvia, like Vapours from the sacred Vents, which work themselves insensibly into the Breast of Imitators, and fill those, who naturally are not of a towering Genius, with the lofty Ideas and Fire of others." The allusion is to the oracle at Delphi, said to have contained a rift in the earth that emitted divine vapors and prophecy-inducing fumes, a source of the priestess's power. In the same way does the sublime force of genius induce oracular pronouncements and ecstatic states, while setting even those who do not possess it afire.[35]

Smith's translation went through five editions by 1757 and was reprinted down through the century. It so succeeded in effecting a link between genius and the sublime that later translators continued to adopt it as a matter of course. As one modern edition of Longinus observes, typically, the sublime "effect of genius is not to persuade the audience but rather to transport them out of themselves. Invariably what inspires wonder, with its power of amazing us, always prevails over what is merely convincing and pleasing." "Writers of genius are above all mortal range," it adds later, and whereas "other qualities prove their possessors men, sublimity lifts them near the mind of God." Whether or not such sentiments are consistent with the intentions of the original text, they do reflect nicely the reading of it introduced by Boileau and subsequently embraced by defenders of original genius. In their hands, the sublime served as a vivid illustration of genius's wondrous and wonder-making power, of its unique ability to transcend mortal limits and to carry others along toward something greater than themselves. Heavily enlisted, as a result, it was used as a weapon to assert the marvelous exception of genius against those who would reduce it to the rules or seek to explain it in purely rational terms.[36]

A similar rhetorical use was made of the genius's enthusiasm, "a very common, if not an inseparable attendant of genius," in the opinion of the Scottish theorist Alexander Gerard. Gerard is a complicated figure. He occupies something of a middle ground between the positions staked out by Sharpe and Helvétius and the more robust proponents of original genius. But his embrace of enthusiasm seems all the more striking in light of the fact that enthusiasm was, in many respects, the "anti-self" of the Enlightenment, invoked in virtually every other connection to cast aspersion on the delusions of "fanatics," who insisted on presenting themselves as directly inspired by God. When employed by eighteenth-century proponents of genius, however, "enthusiasm" became a term of the highest praise, a sign and confirmation of the special power that burned within the chosen. "The man of genius feels the presence of a flame of enthusiasm that animates all his soul," the Swiss philosopher and mathematician Johann Georg Sulzer observed typically, echoing the earlier observation of the German critic Carl Friedrich Flögel, who declared that "genius is a fire that burns without limits; not a tranquil source, but a furious torrent, because an overflowing enthusiasm animates it." The

British critic John Gilbert Cooper described genius similarly as that "glorious Enthusiasm of Soul, that fine Frenzy, as Shakespeare calls it, rolling from Heaven to Earth, from Earth to Heaven." What proponents of the Enlightenment were inclined to treat contemptuously in other instances as fanaticism, they granted to the man of genius as a special privilege, banishing the "in-breathing of God" from the front door, while admitting enthusiasm through the back. To be in the grip of the enthusiasm of genius was to be seized by a marvelous power.[37]

Descriptions of these kinds—linking enthusiasm to frenzy, furor, and fire—recall, of course, venerable discussions of the divine inspiration of the possessed, just as talk of the sublime recalls long-standing traditions of the possessors of special *ingenium*. Eighteenth-century authors were no less inclined to conflate these descriptions than their ancient predecessors were, noting, with Diderot, that it "is impossible to create anything sublime in poetry, painting, eloquence, or music without enthusiasm," a "violent movement of the soul." But the crucial point is that in either mode, commentators on genius retained and reasserted, often despite themselves, a language replete with allusions to possession, transcendence, rapture, and special revelation, even as they denied the existence of possessing demons or the possessive power of divinely conferred gifts. So does Diderot, an atheist and materialist, describe the genius's mind in a poetic fit: the spirit "becomes engrossed, agitated, tormented. The imagination heats up; passion rises and grows disturbed. . . . The poet feels the moment of enthusiasm. . . . It announces itself in him with a shudder that sets out from his chest, and passes quickly and deliciously through his entire body." On one level, Diderot attempts to give a physiological description of the *furor poeticus*, describing it clinically and empirically. But on another he reproduces that discourse's oldest tropes, freely blending a pseudomedical vocabulary with images of heat and convulsion and transport that are as old as Plato's *Ion*. The physical description serves to explain a process that is ultimately not physical, but mystical: the genius's capacity to go beyond the ordinary limits of human nature, to do what no other can do.[38]

Through the rapture of enthusiasm and the sublime, genius revealed aspects of the world otherwise hidden to the naked eye, dazzling with the capacity to summon the marvelous, to move and enchant and inspire. Yet there was more to the power of genius than just the ability to reveal and disclose: genius also possessed the capacity to conceive and bring into being what did not already exist. To some extent, genius's creative fecundity was an old association, tracing back to the Roman root *gignere*, to generate, father, beget. That original sexual connotation, linking the *genius*, as the god of one's birth, to procreation, was tied to the creative faculty in the late Middle Ages. Well-known chronicles—such as the *Romance of the Rose*, or Alain de Lille's *The Plaint of Nature*—depicted the figure of Genius as an allegorical artist (*artifex*), a priest who exercised mastery over the organs of reproduction, wielding his great spermatic stylus to summon the whole of creation into existence. A similar association—described as the "great analogy" between the artist and God—was implicit in the discourse around the divine Michelangelo at the height of the Renaissance. But although this analogy had deep roots, it was ultimately only with the waning of mimetic aesthetics—and the demise of the theological assertion that God alone could create—that creative and imaginative capacities came to be celebrated as the highest of human powers. Freed not only from the thrall of the ancients, but also from the sacred injunction to faithfully "re-present" God's world, creative genius dreamed of conceiving the unprecedented, conjuring worlds undreamed of. Imagination, which had long been viewed as a potentially dangerous force in need of vigilance and restraint, was enlisted as an indispensable partner in the creative act. Eighteenth-century critics continued to caution creators of the need to keep imagination within the bounds of reason, judgment, and taste. But whereas a man of the old school, such as Samuel Johnson, might decry imagination as a "licentious and vagrant faculty, unsusceptible of limitations, and impatient of restraint," an unabashed proponent of original genius, such as the Scottish writer and Presbyterian minister William Duff, was at least willing to entertain, if not fully accept, the proposition that "genius and imagination are one and the same thing." Increasingly, imagination was celebrated as the very source of genial power.[39]

It was precisely as bearers of imaginative and creative force, moreover, that men of original genius showed themselves to be just that—original, unprecedented, and new. Novelty—originality—was central to the genius's self-presentation and reception. For though genius was ever conceived as a mediating force that pushed those who came into contact with it across the "boundaries of the surrounding world," to catch glimpses of the universal, it was also, like the Roman god of old, particular to the person in whom it was embodied. The new embrace of genius placed a premium on individuality and uniqueness, heightening the growing eighteenth-century appreciation of the self. As Diderot observed, "the man of genius has a way of seeing, of feeling, of thinking that is unique to him alone." It was a belief that imparted courage to challenge tradition. "Let not great examples, or authorities, browbeat thy reason into too great a diffidence of thyself," Edward Young implored in the *Conjectures on Original Composition*. "Thyself so reverence, as to prefer the native growth of thy own mind to the richest import from abroad." Young did much to cultivate the metaphor of organic growth in connection with genius, emphasizing that what was new or original pushed up its shoots from the seed of the soul. "An Original may be said to be of a vegetable nature; it rises spontaneously from the vital root of genius. It grows, it is not made," he wrote. Or, as the philosopher Sulzer observed, the expression of genius was like a flowering plant, which "ripens gradually within us," and then "emerges suddenly into the light." Each flower, each petal, was one of a kind.[40]

Hence the widespread use of the term "original" to imply both point of origin and individual particularity, the ability to do what no one else had done or thought or seen. Duff spoke for many when he explained that, "by the word original, when applied to Genius, we mean that native and radical power which the mind possesses, of discovering something new and uncommon." Voltaire, though by no means an unqualified proponent of original genius, could nonetheless agree that, "however perfect [an artist] may be[,] . . . if he be not original, he is not considered a genius." Young put the stress the other way around, saying that "originals can arise from genius only." And Kant, who crystallized advanced reflection on the subject toward the end of the century, observed, in a celebrated discussion in his *Critique of Judgment*, that "everyone agrees that genius must be considered the very opposite of a spirit of imitation." From which it followed, naturally enough, that "originality must be its foremost property."[41]

Here was a profound departure from the mimetic impulse that had guided Western reflection for centuries, and the principal source of what would become a Romantic fixation on creative autonomy and the indispensable need to be new. "Genius is the introduction of a new element into the intellectual universe," William Wordsworth would famously declare in his 1815 edition of the *Lyrical Ballads*. With our reverence for novelty and innovation in the twenty-first century, we have so assimilated the assumptions behind the thought that it is easy to overlook how radical a departure it really was. Rather than simply register the truth and beauty of God's world, imitate the classics, or "re-present" nature, the man of genius was called upon to create, to bring something new and unprecedented into being. It is hardly a coincidence that it was precisely at this moment that questions of copyright, plagiarism, and intellectual property came to the fore. For the decline of the mimetic ideal opened the way to seeing an imitation as a cheap "knock-off" or worthless "copy." "Copying" came to be regarded as a transgression and even a crime. Only with the demise of mimesis did authors begin to demand acknowledgment in footnotes and a stake in the financial rewards of their labor. To bring something new into being, after all, to harvest fruit that one had cultivated within, implied ownership and a stake in the pickings.[42]

But there was another implication just as dramatic as the genesis of intellectual property, and in the long run perhaps even more profound. For the power of creation was a power hitherto reserved exclusively for God. In the Renaissance, the humanist scholar Julius Caesar Scaliger and a handful of other intrepid souls had dared to suggest that the poet could be an *alter Deus*, a comparison that the third Earl of Shaftesbury echoed in the eighteenth century with his reflection that the true poet was a "second Maker, a just Prometheus under Jove." But Shaftesbury's claim was bolder than that of the Renaissance humanists, for if Prometheus was "just," he had committed no crime; in stealing from the gods, he had taken what was rightfully his. The creative flame belonged to man; seizing it was a heroic act. Men of genius, like God the Father, now created for themselves.[43]

Claims of this kind could still provoke outrage and charges of blasphemy in the eighteenth century. But in an age that was more conscious than earlier ones of the possibilities and predicament of human autonomy, in an age of a withdrawing God, committed Christians could reconcile themselves to the new notion easily enough. In many cases, they actively embraced it. It is revealing that Edward Young, Alexander Gerard, and William Duff were not only enthusiastic commentators on genius, but also Protestant clergymen. Jews, too, would show themselves amenable to the faith, proudly embracing such heroes of the mind as the "Jewish Socrates" Moses Mendelssohn, as well as the "*Gaon* [Genius] of Vilna," the Rabbi Elijah Ben Solomon, as contrasting images of Jewish genius in a cult that took on increasing importance in the nineteenth century. If nothing else, the genius filled a need, occupying a space that had long been kept exclusively by God and his ministering powers, those higher beings, the prophets, angels, apostles, and saints, who shared in his glory and partook of his power. Hovering between this world and whatever might lie beyond it, the genius was a testament to the miracle of creation, and so could be deemed a miracle himself, an exception to the ordinary laws of nature. Geniuses, as the critic Joseph Addison put it, were the "prodigies of mankind." In the person of Wolfgang Amadeus Mozart, the world was offered the possibility of observing a genius in his infancy, with all his newly assembled powers.[44]

"HERE THE BOY'S GENIUS first came to light," recounts Mozart's earliest biographer, Franz Niemetschek. The prodigy was but three years old, and "he would often sit at the clavier of his own accord and amuse himself for hours harmonizing in thirds, and when he found them he would play them and was greatly delighted. So his father began to teach him easy pieces; and he saw with delight and astonishment that his pupil exceeded all human expectations." By age six, the boy was composing his own music, which was published the following year, and soon he was astonishing the courts and concert halls of Europe. In Paris in December 1763, he dazzled with his improvisational skills, which gave "free rein," as Friedrich Melchior von Grimm declared in his *Correspondance littéraire*, to "the inspiration of his genius." Helvétius, who was little inclined to marvel at the wonders of nature, nonetheless felt moved to describe the boy to a correspondent in London as "one of the most singular beings in existence." And when the singular being himself traveled to London the following spring at the advanced age of eight, he amazed the king and queen with his virtuosity and invention. A concert announcement published shortly thereafter proclaimed that "the celebrated and astonishing" child was "justly esteemed the most extraordinary Prodigy, and most amazing Genius, that has appeared in any Age."[45]

Mozart continues to serve as a consummate "symbol of genius." We are so accustomed to thinking of him in these terms that it is difficult to conceive of him in any other way. Surely, it must be the case that Mozart's "genius" was self-evident from the start? In certain respects, it surely was, as all these exclamations attest. Yet, Mozart's contemporaries demanded confirmation. After seeing the prodigy perform in 1767, Father Beda Hübner, a librarian at St. Peter's Abbey in Salzburg, observed in his diary, "Nobody can believe it, and it is indeed inconceivable, except to those who have themselves heard him play, who can and must believe it." The real presence of Mozart's genius compelled assent. In Mantua, before "civic authorities" and "distinguished professors," the *Wunderkind* gave such "proofs" of his gifts as to "astonish everyone," a newspaper reported. And in Rome, in a much recounted feat, Mozart was said to have memorized Gregorio Allegri's entire *Miserere*—a piece of exquisite beauty and complexity, for two full choirs of nine voices each—after one hearing in the Sistine Chapel. The popes had long guarded the secrecy of the score, preventing it from being published outside the Vatican's walls. But the fourteen-year-old recorded it in his mind, and later committed it to paper. Or so the story goes. The feat seems to have been slightly less prodigious in point of fact, with Mozart remembering only parts of the score, not the whole. But the point is that the miracle was believed and recounted again and again. After scores of direct sightings, firsthand reports, and eyewitness accounts, Europeans were ready to accept such tales of genius on faith.[46]

It wasn't always so. Indeed, what is curious about many of these early reports is how much they sound like the testimonies of scientific demonstrations. Published in great volume, and circulated widely in the republic of letters, scientific accounts of this kind were likewise reported firsthand, providing evidence of experimental veracity and truth. Mozart's recitals, seen in this light, were not just musical performances; they were public spectacles, scientific demonstrations of a wonder of nature. When an announcement "To All Lovers of Sciences," published in London's *Public Advertiser* in 1765, invited spectators to confirm the "miracle" of Mozart firsthand—to see "the greatest Prodigy that Europe, or that even Human nature, has to boast of"—it was asking witnesses to verify with their own eyes what they might not otherwise believe.[47]

The Honourable Daines Barrington, a member of the British Royal Society and an amateur natural philosopher, took this process of investigation even further, performing a series of experiments on the eight-year-old prodigy while Mozart was still in London. In a report sent to the Royal Society several years later chronicling his "amazing and incredible" findings, Barrington described in detail how he had put the boy's genius to the test. Bidding Mozart to play a series of complex compositions, which he never could have seen before, Barrington marveled at his sight-reading abilities and improvisational skills, which "prove his genius and invention to have been most astonishing." In the end, Barrington assured the members of the Royal Society, there could be no doubt. He had verified the existence of a "very extraordinary genius" indeed.[48]

In this respect, Mozart's genius *was* self-evident. It proclaimed itself from the stage, offering to Europeans a perfect illustration of a theory developed over the preceding decades. As the German critic Christian Friedrich Daniel Schubart put it, looking back in 1784, a true musical genius like Mozart "announces himself already in his youth." "The heavenly flash of genius is of such divine nature that it cannot be concealed. It presses, forces, pushes, and burns so long until it bursts forth as a flame and glorifies itself in its Olympian splendor. . . . The musical genius awakes and rises heavenwards. Yet he has room enough also to carry up the listener on his cherubic wings." Such magnificent power of lift and ascent was present from birth; it could never be learned. It overwhelmed and imposed itself on its contemporaries.[49]

True, more recent observers have insisted on questioning this account, arguing that far from illustrating a theory of original genius,

Mozart, on the contrary, lends credence to the argument for nurture. The extraordinary number of hours he clocked as a young man playing the concert halls of Europe, these critics maintain, is an illustration of the "10,000-hour rule," showing that great achievements come only from great practice. Even in the face of what he acknowledged was a "singular being," Helvétius might still have had the last laugh.[50]

There is another, even clearer, way in which Helvétius might be vindicated by Mozart's example. Timing, the French philosopher had claimed, was all important when it came to genius, and Mozart's timing was good. Appearing before Europeans as a child, he seemed to substantiate what they already were coming to believe: "Genius nascitur non fit" (Genius is born, not made). Earlier in the century, the great George Frideric Handel had been hailed as the prodigy that he was, and biographers and eulogists had not missed the chance to use his case as confirmation of the presence of original genius. The boosters of Johann Sebastian Bach, too, had seized the moment, particularly at his death in 1750, emphasizing his originality and his genius while building a case for canonization, with which most would soon agree. But Mozart's timing was even better. Whereas Joseph Haydn, as Albert Einstein once observed, "became 'original' long before 'original genius' appeared in the poetry of the time," Mozart's timing was perfect. He embodied a belief.[51]

Yet for all that the spectacle of Mozart confirmed established opinions, it also raised questions—and in the end provoked incomprehension and disbelief. The quasi-scientific character of the demonstrations notwithstanding, there was something miraculous about them as well. Contemporaries said as much, describing the genius as a "miracle of nature," a point that the use of the word "prodigy" only underscored. For a prodigy was a wonder, an exception to the ordinary laws of nature, traditionally regarded as an omen and a sign. Prodigious individuals and events announced some impending work of God. But what, to Enlightened minds, could a prodigy like Mozart portend? Men and women of the Enlightenment, after all, were little inclined to wonder in this way. And they took a dim view of miracles, a sentiment that Mozart's father recognized explicitly, believing it his duty to "announce to the world a miracle"—his son—at a time "when people are ridiculing whatever is called a miracle and denying all miracles." As the French *Encyclopédie* of Diderot and d'Alembert declared, in a typical expression of the age, "whatever one may say, the marvelous is not made for us."[52]

Given these tendencies, it is all the more astonishing to behold the astonishment with which the Enlightened confronted genius, attributing to the prodigy Mozart the very qualities they disparaged in others:

imagination, enthusiasm, inspiration, the miraculous. The genius as *Wunderkind* was not only a wonder to behold, he generated wonder, raising questions that could not easily be answered by the science of the day. "What is it that lets anyone be born a Poet, a Musician, or a Painter?" one spectator of Mozart was moved to ask. "Metaphysics alone can tell us." It was the same question—and a similar response—that had motivated the ancients in their encounters with the special something of special men. In many ways, the moderns were no better equipped to provide an answer than those who had come before. As Denis Diderot was moved to remark, "in men of genius—poets, philosophers, painters, orators, musicians—there is some particular, secret, indefinable quality of the soul without which they can execute nothing great or beautiful." But what it was, exactly, he could not say. What did the apparition of genius mean? And how, precisely, could it be recognized when it revealed itself on earth?[53]

Like solicitous parents eager for signs that their children are gifted, or like Tibetan monks scouring the countryside for the next incarnation of the Dalai Lama, Europeans in the eighteenth century sought answers to these questions by probing the phenomenon of genius itself. The miracle of Mozart was apparently well attested, although, as he aged, many grew less certain that the child was the father of the man. Famously, at the full flowering of Mozart's genius—when he was no longer performing as a child but creating as an adult in new and original ways—many greeted his work with incomprehension. His decision to leave the comfortable position of court musician at Salzburg and to strike out on his own in Vienna proved perilous. Though he made a go of it for a time, the final movement of his life was tragic. Mozart died penniless in a pauper's grave, as is well known, coveting fame and the attention of the public he courted, yet sick in his heart at the inability of his contemporaries to recognize in his mature creations the fulfillment of his childhood promise.

At the time of his death, Mozart believed himself a failure. That tragic fate would feed its own mythology, leading, in the nineteenth century, to the idea of the suffering genius misunderstood, rejected by his contemporaries, and honored, if at all, only in death. In Mozart's day, it dramatized the fickleness of fame and the continuing power of aristocratic patrons to make and break fortunes. But it also highlighted the difficulty of detecting a genius in one's midst. If even an apparently confirmed case like Mozart's turned out to disappoint and deceive—or at least so it seemed—how could one ever be sure of the real presence of genius? For Jean-Jacques Rousseau, who himself could lay reasonable claim to the power, there was no use trying to spot genius from afar; it could only be known from within. "Don't ask, young artist, what genius is," he cautioned in his *Dictionary of Music*. "Either you have it—then you feel it yourself, or you don't—then you will never know it." The physiognomist Lavater was even more despairing of the possibility of detecting genius from afar, notwithstanding his own claims to be able to read signs of genius in the face. Those who have it, know it not, he affirmed. And those who do not have it will never know what genius is. Besides, genius was exceedingly rare. "The proportion of genius to the vulgar is like one to a million," Lavater maintained elsewhere, introducing a ratio that Francis Galton would later discover with the power of modern statistics in his own studies of genius in the nineteenth century.[54]

Immanuel Kant, for his part, avoided numbers, but when he set out to define genius at the end of the eighteenth century, he wholeheartedly agreed that it was a "rare phenomenon." For the genius was an anomaly, "nature's favorite," whose mind was a place of disclosure of nature's power, which worked through him to reveal original forms and to legislate new rules for art. Impressed directly by the "hand of nature," Kant writes, this power could never be learned or taught, but rather was a mystery, even to those who possessed it. "Genius itself cannot describe or indicate scientifically how it brings about its products," Kant stressed, adding that "this is why, if an author owes a product to his genius, he himself does not know how he came by the ideas for it; nor is it in his power to devise such products at his pleasure, or by following a plan." It was for that reason, Kant observed, that the "word genius is derived from the [Latin] *genius*, the guardian and guiding spirit that each person is given at his own birth, and to whose inspiration those original ideas are due." Whereas genius was once thought to be imparted by a mysterious being, it now revealed itself through nature, a similarly mysterious force.[55]

Kant gave eloquent expression to the eighteenth century's wonder before the prodigies of nature and mankind. But he departed from the norm in confining his perplexity exclusively to the makers of art. In Kant's idiosyncratic view, those who were able to give a reasoned account of the steps they took to achieve their discoveries could not be qualified as "geniuses." This precluded scientists, among others, and Kant singled out the century's greatest example—Isaac Newton—to illustrate the point. Newton's enormous achievement could be studied and learned—imitated—by a diligent person, and Newton himself "could show every one of the steps he had to take in order to get . . . to his great and profound discoveries," Kant said. But a great poet like Homer could never "show how his ideas, rich in fancy and yet also in thought, arise and meet in his mind." In Kant's view, the mystery of the creative process that gave rise to original production was genius's distinguishing trait. And so, despite his enormous respect for natural science in general, and Newton in particular, he confined the illustrious title of "genius" to the arts.[56]

It may well be argued that Kant's reflections belied an imperfect understanding of the process of scientific discovery. But the more important point is that his effort to confine the category of genius went very much against the tenor of the times. Although it is certainly true that self-conscious reflection on genius since the Renaissance had tended to focus on the letters and arts—whether poetry or prose, painting or music, oratory or rhetoric—the category as it developed in the eighteenth century was broadly conceived and widely applied. As Goethe observed of the use of the term in Germany in the 1770s, "in the common parlance of the day, genius was ascribed to the poet alone. But now another world seemed all at once to emerge; genius was looked for in the physician, in the general, in the statesman, and before long, in all men, who thought to make themselves eminent either in theory or in practice." Even though genius was exceedingly hard to find, contemporaries looked for it in many different places. Such profligacy, in Goethe's view, was an abuse, and Kant's effort to define the term with greater precision was likely a reaction to that development. But the majority of theorists were more eclectic. "The empire of Genius is unbounded," William Duff declared. "All the Sciences and Arts present a sphere for its exercise." Helvétius likewise understood genius and geniuses to occupy many different spheres, from philosophy to statecraft to science. The critic Alexander Gerard agreed. "Genius is properly the faculty of invention," he remarked, using "invention" in the modern sense of creative and original discovery. It was clear to him that human beings made use of this faculty in a great many domains, especially in science, where, as in art, invention was "the proper province of Genius, and its only certain measure." Indeed, to exclude scientific genius would have been unthinkable to all of these men (and many others besides), even if they generally admitted of distinctions when describing its powers. The genius of science, no less than the genius of art, as Duff confirmed, allowed humankind "to penetrate the dwelling of the gods and to scale the heights of Heaven."[57]

The man who illustrated this power more than any other in the eighteenth century, and the inspiration behind the lines just cited, was none

other than Isaac Newton, who was described by the astronomer Edmond
Halley (he of comet fame) in his eulogy of the great man as

> *Newton, that reach'd the insuperable line*
> *The nice barrier 'twixt human and divine.*

Notwithstanding Kant's estimation of the matter, Newton was
widely regarded as the genius of the century. In the words of the philosopher and historian David Hume, he was the "greatest and rarest genius
that ever rose for the ornament and instruction of the species." Newton's
very name, as an English biographical dictionary pointed out in 1807,
had become "synonymous with genius." A little more than a century
later, people would begin to say the same about Einstein, completing a
process that Newton himself initiated: the shift toward representing the
scientist as the quintessential embodiment of genius.[58]

Newton, though, was not a "scientist," properly speaking—at least
not in the way we are now inclined to think of the type. The word "scientist" itself was only coined in 1833, and it was not widely used until
much later in the century. And the perceived conflict with religion that it
came to imply—a conflict that our own age too often crudely imposes on
the past—was only scarcely conceivable in Newton's day. Newton's contemporaries referred to him as a "natural philosopher." The pioneering
chemist Robert Boyle, a friend of Newton's, described him as a "priest of
nature," someone whose very purpose was to learn more about God and
his ways by studying the natural world. Newton thought of himself in
this manner as well. Yet the role of genius that Newton came to embody
was in tension with the faith he professed, precisely because it pretended
to sacred power. When an ardent admirer observed, not long after Newton's death, that his "virtues proved him a Saint & his discoveries might
well pass for miracles," he no doubt exaggerated. But his comments capture nicely the semi-sacred awe that Newton's genius inspired.[59]

"Does he eat, drink and sleep like other men?" a French mathematician reportedly asked of Newton. "I cannot believe otherwise than that
he is a genius, or a celestial intelligence entirely disengaged from matter."
In conflating the two senses of genius, old and new, the observer gave
perfect voice to the way in which the one encroached on the other. And
although the oft-recounted anecdote may well be apocryphal—the sort
of mythic tale once told of the lives of the saints—it is no less significant
for that. Stories of this kind both contributed to and captured Newton's
"canonization." How fitting, then, that his body should be received at
his death in 1727 at Westminster Abbey, resting place of the saints of

old. And how fitting that his statue in the antechapel at Trinity College, Cambridge, should bear the inscription, "Qui genus humanum
ingenio superavit"—that is, by his genius—his *ingenium*—he surpassed
the human race. How fitting, finally, that the pedestal of his statue in
the Temple of British Worthies at Stowe should read, "Sir Isaac Newton whom the God of nature made to comprehend his work." Newton,
divinely touched, was a genius put among us to capture and reveal the
truth. Newton was a secular saint.[60]

The very presence of a statue of a man like Newton in the garden of
an aristocratic country house like Stowe is itself revealing of the process
by which the canonization of the modern genius was achieved. It also
helps to answer the eighteenth century's question of how genius could
best be detected. For, as historians of literary and scientific reputation
emphasize, extraordinary eminence seldom just appears, but is invariably
"constructed," "created," and "made," invented through a process of celebration and publicity that helps to bring it into being. Newton in fact
was shrewd in the art of "self-fashioning"—far shrewder than Mozart—
cultivating powerful patrons. He sat for more than twenty portraits and
busts, works that helped to spread his image, carefully controlled, to the
world. Even more importantly, a group of committed "disciples" worked
hard after his death to propagate his fame, celebrating his genius in biographies, images, anecdotes, and verse that emphasized his upward ascent.
Newton was a "pure intelligence," a cosmic traveler who

> . . . *wings his way*
> *Through wondrous scenes . . .*
> *of saints and angels.*

He was an "eagle," soaring aloft, high above other men. And he was
presented repeatedly alongside his comet, the Great Comet of 1680,
which played a crucial role in his theoretical calculations. Like the shoot-
ing star of Caesar, the comet symbolized the genius of a higher man.
Finally, in scores of mass-reproduced engravings and etchings, in min-
iatures and plaster busts, Newton's image was presented to the nation
and to the world. In an age when seeing was believing, it helped to have
genius pointed out.[61]

To suggest that Newton was a genius because others said so—
insistently, repeatedly, and with ever greater conviction—is not to detract
from his astounding achievements or evident brilliance. Genius is rarely
a function of self-fashioning or public relations alone. One might proclaim oneself a genius, as the author George Colman tried to do in the

pages of the *St. James's Chronicle* in 1761, when he announced, "I myself am an acknowledged GENIUS." Others have followed suit, including Oscar Wilde, who, when passing through customs in the United States, is said to have quipped, "I have nothing to declare except my genius." But when acknowledgment is not forthcoming, the proclamation is difficult to sustain. An unacknowledged genius is most often a contradiction in terms.[62]

Acknowledgment, moreover, is confirmed in death, and with far fewer restraints. To have explained in Newton's presence that he was a higher order of human being—another species or a saint—might have piqued his self-love. But it would undoubtedly have invited scorn. To do so after his passing ran no such risk, and it spared the genius the burden of having to pull it off. Miracles could now appear uncontested, places of pilgrimage could make themselves known, and all those who told tales of the master's inspiration and superhuman feats could benefit from the association. Newton assumed his sainthood only slowly, because geniuses, too, are canonized only when they are gone.

Others—from Homer and Shakespeare to Plato and Aristotle to Mozart in his pauper's grave—were beatified posthumously in this way. But although the eighteenth century continued to look largely to the past to furnish its models of greatness, the annunciation of the genius was also a call to something new. Genius was a summons to see what no one else had seen, to do what no one else had done, to create what had never before existed. The aesthetics of originality demanded innovation. So to search for genius in the past—finding the unprecedented in precedent, new creation in men who were dead and gone—was implicitly ironic, even if that irony was scarcely detected at the time. Occupying a space long inhabited by beings who were eternal, the eighteenth-century genius was conceived comfortably in the eternity of death. And yet, as historians and philosophers have long recognized, the temporal orientation of the eighteenth century was shifting gradually from the past to the future, with a new emphasis on becoming, on progress, on development and growth. The change of focus in art—from an aesthetics of mimesis to an aesthetics of originality downplaying the models of the past—was a symptom of that shift. To an age in transition, the child was the image of the man. And in the infant Mozart, one begins to catch a glimpse of what the future might hold: a genius imagined not in death, but in life, a living being of flesh and bone.[63]

It is at this point that the history of the genius merges with that of another being born in the eighteenth century—"the celebrity"—a figure of fascination whom the curious must see. The young Mozart was just such a type—and in the machinery of publicity that was used to reveal the genius of Newton, one witnesses an early deployment of what would later prove to be powerful tools. The same craning of the neck with which the curious sought out the prodigious child moved others to peer in café windows or through the curtains of private homes, titillated by the prospect of seeing genius in the flesh. Such curiosity sent Rousseau into hiding at the end of his life, and Voltaire's letters are filled with complaints about the fawning attentions of unwanted callers who interrupted his work. If *célébrité*, a word that first came into widespread use in the second half of the eighteenth century, was, as the French writer Nicolas Chamfort described it, "the privilege of being known by people who don't know you," it had its downside in the form of prying eyes. Such were—and are—the fortunes of fame.[64]

FAME HAD OTHER FORTUNES, too, as Chamfort well knew. As early as the 1760s, he was observing that the genius of a few great "masters of humanity" shaped the spirit of the age, "imposing its sovereignty on the mass of men." The statement was as much fantasy as fact, and yet it captured nicely how the celebrity of the genius might be employed. Insightful souls at the century's outset had perceived with Shaftesbury the conditions of the genius's consecration—they had seen and comprehended, even as they welcomed, how a new being was supplanting the guardians of old. But there were others, by century's end, who glimpsed in this same process of transference and consecration—of disenchantment and enchantment, and the attendant celebrity that the genius accrued—a tantalizing possibility: genius might rule the world. Some, like Chamfort, welcomed the thought; others were less sure. For although, as the philosopher Herder observed, geniuses were often adept at recognizing the good, they could also turn against it. And when they did so, abandoning reason and justice as means to channel their power, they were at risk of falling into "sublime madness" or "abomination," becoming a "nightmare." That was an ancient fear, the fear of the possession and alienation to which great minds were prone, and not even Descartes could dispel it in dispelling the *genius malignus*. It lingered on in the eighteenth century, especially among the devout, who continued to warn in familiar terms of the temptations and corruptions that preyed on the errant soul. The fear was also evident in the neoclassical insistence that the potential wildness and enthusiasm of genius needed to be bound by tradition, judgment, and taste. But it was a man of a more modern cast who spoke with the greatest clarity of the genius's propensity for aberration and evil. Denis Diderot's masterful dialogue *The Nephew of Rameau*—begun in the 1760s, though not published until after the author's death in an 1805 German translation by Goethe—opens with a rumination on precisely this subject.[65]

The work is a conversation between two men, the nephew of the celebrated composer Jean-Philippe Rameau and a *philosophe*, loosely modeled on Diderot himself. "If I knew history," the nephew declares, "I would show you that evil always arrives on earth by means of some man of genius." "Men of genius" are detestable, he adds; they are "bad citizens, bad fathers, mothers, brothers, parents, friends." Although he acknowledges that it is men of genius who "change the face of the globe," Rameau would still be inclined to rid the world of their presence. If a child bore from birth the sign of this dangerous "gift of nature," he reflects, "it would be advisable to smother him in bed, or to throw him to the dogs." Rameau's position is complicated by the fact that, although talented, he is a ne'er do well, a dissolute and resentful drifter who would like to be a genius himself. "I admit, I am jealous," he confesses. The *philosophe* points out by way of response that a "fool is more often an evil person than a man of intelligence," and he notes that ages which have produced no geniuses are held in low esteem. But what is striking is that the *philosophe*, in the end, essentially agrees with Rameau, observing that the genius is like a tall tree that shoots up into the sky, while causing other trees planted near him to wither and die, choking off their sunlight and nutrients. In his radical departure from the norm, the genius is an anomaly, a deviant in the eyes of his fellows. Geniuses, Diderot elsewhere insists, are "kinds of monsters."[66]

Why this should be the case is a question that Diderot sought to resolve without reference to demons or original sin. Instead he pointed out the inherent conflict between the radical originality of the solitary genius and the conformism of the many, who were, in his view, but pale copies and imitations of each other, inherently suspicious of those original innovators and "sublime men" who lived according to a law of their own. The genius, as a consequence, was always potentially at odds with society, and society both admired and feared him. It was for this reason that geniuses were frequently persecuted. Diderot presented Socrates as a case in point. He was a martyr to a higher truth who so contradicted the status quo and challenged the democracy of Athens that his contemporaries felt constrained to banish or destroy him. Like all geniuses, Socrates was a revolutionary, a prophet of the new. But for these same reasons, he was a threat to the old. All creators, in effect, are destroyers, too.

Diderot himself saw nothing inherently evil in the example of Socrates, a man he greatly admired. Yet his theory explained why so many of the Athenian's contemporaries regarded him as a monster, and it suggested that the many need not always be wrong. There was no guarantee of righteousness, that is, in the genius's confrontation with the powers that be, no assurance of goodness in his person or of justice in his private morality and law. Indeed, Diderot gave disturbing hints that just the opposite might be the case. For genius was an unstable force—like sexual energy or a violent storm—and as such could lead to fits of madness and enthusiasm or genuine evil and crime. As Rameau points out in the context of a discussion of great men, "if it is important to be sublime in anything, it is above all the case with evil. One spits on a petty thief, but it is impossible to refuse a certain consideration to the great criminal."[67]

In the power of the modern genius there continued to lurk, like the *genius malignus* of old, the prospect of temptation and transgression. Calling attention to that prospect, while broaching the connection to revolutionary change, Diderot proved himself a clairvoyant of sorts, a prophet of the new. For the theme he entertained in the private pages of an unpublished dialogue would soon occupy much of Europe and beyond. With the French Revolution, the question of genius and its evil twin became far more than a matter of conjecture.

The Dawn of the Idols

B ENJAMIN FRANKLIN ACQUIRED his claim to genius by literally wresting lightning from the sky. In 1779, he wrote to his daughter from France to complain that his image was everywhere—stamped on clay medallions, fashioned in all sizes, "set in lids of snuff boxes," and "worn in rings." The "numbers sold are incredible," and these, together "with the pictures, busts, and prints, (of which copies upon copies are spread everywhere) have made your father's face as well known as that of the moon." Franklin boasted as much as he complained. But his sense of humor prevented the celebrity of genius from going to his head. "It is said by learned etymologists that the name doll, for the images children play with, is derived from the word Idol." From the number of dolls now made of him, he punned, it could be truly said that he was "i-doll-ized." In an age that was building monuments to men of genius, and that reproduced their likenesses on dishes and plates, such lighthearted comments contained an unwitting warning that could still resonate with those who knew their scripture. "Little children keep yourself from idols"; parents, put an end to childish ways. The worshippers of idols "can be never the better for such worship," Franklin insisted elsewhere. Adults should know better than to play with dolls.[1]

If Franklin felt a touch of uneasiness in confronting the idol of his genius, the sentiment proved well founded, above all in Europe. To be sure, the American original was not without his admirers on native soil. But the process of "i-doll-ization"—of Franklin in particular and geniuses in general—went much further across the Atlantic, where the cult of genius flourished in singular ways. It was there, not at home, that Franklin was most likely to find a graven image of himself. It was there, not at home, that he was suspected of possessing supernatural powers, like a "new Prometheus," who drew "fire" from the sky. And it was there, not at home, that Franklin was most effective at parlaying the celebrity

of genius into political and diplomatic influence (to say nothing of success in the bedroom). In France, especially, Franklin was treated with the
reverence that was becoming the genius's due, fêted in life as America's
ambassador from 1778 to 1785, and regaled in death at his passing in
1790, amid the early euphoria of the French Revolution that had begun
the previous year. When the newly convened National Assembly received
word that Franklin had died, the revolutionary leader Mirabeau rose to
proclaim three days of official mourning. "The genius that freed America
and poured a flood of light over Europe" was no more, he lamented,
this "hero of humanity" who "restrained thunderbolts and tyrants" was
gone! Lauded at the rostrum and celebrated on the stage, this "avenger
of humanity," this "apostle of liberty," this "rival of the gods" had earned
the eternal gratitude of the French people by paving the way for the Revolution of 1789.[2]

Or so it was claimed. Franklin's actual role in precipitating the
French Revolution was minimal, at best, and the same might even be
said of his role in the American Revolution. "He has done very little,"
John Adams observed dryly in a diary entry of 1779, lamenting the fact
that "it is universally believed in France, England, and all Europe that
[Franklin's] electric wand has accomplished all this [American] revolution" on his own. Franklin was a "great genius," Adams conceded, a fine
philosopher, a man of science, a man of affairs. But of the Europeans'
belief, "nothing" could be more "groundless."[3]

Colored by envy and exaggerated by pique, Adams's remarks nonetheless capture nicely an evolving myth that was of a piece with the
evolving cult of genius: that the single individual could make history on
his own. Once, not long before, the gods and Fate had been held to rule
the world. And in the future, complex social forces and iron laws would
be invoked to replace God's providence. But in Europe, at the time of
the French Revolution and for many decades thereafter, history was well
imagined as the work of great men. Even in a country whose people
stormed the Bastille en masse and marched to Versailles to remove the
king and queen, the many revered the one.

Such reverence gave new impetus to the cult of genius that had
developed in Europe for close to a century, allowing it to burst forth in
spectacular new ways. The scale of the revolutionary celebrations was
impressive, their claims about genius bold. And in their repeated insistence that exceptional individuals were the true motors of history, who
had ushered in the glorious dawn of 1789, the revolutionaries worked
to drown out the doubts of skeptics like Adams. Consolidating a myth
of the genius's political power that even their opponents would come

to share, the revolutionaries elaborated a belief that would long outlive them. The genius could be a maker of revolutions, a leader of the people, a revolutionary man.

The timing of Franklin's death, in this respect, was propitious, coinciding not only with an amenable theory of history, but also with the emergence in France of a revolutionary cult of *grands hommes* (great men), men who were singled out for their service to humanity in preparing the glorious dawn of 1789. "Genius" and *grand homme* were not, strictly speaking, synonymous terms, but genius's presence amid the pantheon of greats was conspicuous all the same. Both French and foreign, the luminaries included Voltaire, Franklin's friend, that "immortal Genius, who prepared the Revolution in advance," as the French journal the *Mercure de France* proudly declared in 1790. There was Mirabeau, another of Franklin's acquaintances, the orator, writer, and statesman of genius, who led the Revolution in its early days. And there was the "divine" Jean-Jacques Rousseau, Franklin's admirer, though the two never met, who was hailed as both an architect of the Revolution and an archetype of genius. In temperament and belief, the three men could not have been more different, but they were frequently represented together with their American counterpart in the French Revolution's early years, reconciled in print and harmonized in death. Voltaire, Mirabeau, and Rousseau shared a common fate: each was interred by the revolutionaries in the Panthéon in Paris, the hallowed resting place of the Revolution's great men.[4]

Formerly the Church of Saint Geneviève, built by Louis XV to house the relics of his patron saint, the sprawling neoclassical edifice was transformed by the revolutionaries in 1791 to honor a different kind of protector. Its namesake was the Pantheon of Rome, completed during the reign of Augustus as an offering to the immortal gods. But those who were interred in the temple of the French Revolution would be men, great men, to displace the saints and guardians of old. Mirabeau went first in the spring of 1791, and he was followed shortly thereafter by Voltaire. The *philosophe's* heart and brain had been removed at his death in 1778 and were lovingly preserved apart. But Voltaire's other relics lay at his estate near Geneva. They were disinterred and carried back to Paris in a procession that self-consciously imitated the translation of a saint. No miracles were reported, and no demons fled screaming from their hosts, though the genius was accompanied by his *genius* along the way. There could be no better symbol of the Revolution's transfer of sacrality and of its consecration of a new type of man. Part hero, part *grand homme*, part guardian, part saint, the genius was a composite of the old and a creation of the new who would bear the weight of the nation on his remains. A patron of the fatherland, he was also a father of humanity who reflected the aspirations of men and women far beyond France, reconciling the universal and the particular. As the mathematician-cum-politician Condorcet observed, in seeking to secure a place for another genius—Descartes—in the Panthéon's hallowed ground, the man who had dispelled the *genii* had not only "brought philosophy back to reason," liberating the human mind, but also prepared "the eternal destruction of political oppression." He was, as Condorcet's friend d'Alembert declared, among the "small number of great geniuses whose works have helped spread enlightenment among men."[5]

In attributing such power to the thought and action of extraordinary individuals, Condorcet and his contemporaries necessarily built upon articles of faith put forth by commentators in the preceding decades. But whereas Chamfort had maintained wishfully in the 1760s that geniuses were "masters of humanity" who imposed their sovereignty on the people, revolutionaries found evidence for that assertion all around them. Were not the true fathers of the Revolution men like Franklin, Descartes, Rousseau, and Voltaire? The revolutionary upheaval was itself an illustration of a point made by the writer Antoine-Léonard Thomas before the Académie Française in 1767. "The man of genius," he declared, "has become the arbiter of the thoughts, of the opinions, and of the prejudices of the public."[6]

Yet if the Revolution's cult of genius was in this respect a natural continuation of the cult that had flourished in the Old Regime, it was also a new departure, in large part because the open attack on the church and the monarchy that accompanied it removed barriers to its full and free expression. Without priests to frown at excessive claims and warn of the dangers of blasphemy, without kings to trumpet their sovereignty and to posture as God's representatives on earth, geniuses could be hailed like never before. The contrasts are revealing. In the Old Regime, Voltaire had been denied a Christian burial; in the Revolution, he was made a saint in a church transformed. In the Old Regime, time was punctuated by the rhythms of the Christian calendar and the commemoration of its martyrs, saints, and kings. In the Revolution, men made haste to conceive time as marked solely by the interventions of human beings. An early revolutionary almanac reflected this change well, proposing to replace the saints of the liturgical year with "universal" figures, such as Leonardo, Descartes, Racine, Molière, and Voltaire. In 1793, when the revolutionaries abolished the Christian calendar altogether, they vowed to devote a day at the end of the revolutionary year to a "festival of the genius" (*fête du génie*). The *fête du génie*—one of five supplementary holidays established to conclude the revolutionary calendar—would recognize those who had benefited the nation. As the former actor Fabre d'Églantine explained in submitting the proposal to the revolutionary legislature, the National Convention, the "festival of the genius" would honor the "most precious and lofty attribute of humanity—intelligence—which sets us apart from the rest of creation." The "greatest conceptions, and those most useful to the nation," would be celebrated on this day, along with "all that relates to invention or the creative operations of the human mind," whether in "the arts, sciences, trades, or in legislative, philosophic, or moral matters." The proposal passed, though the *fête du génie* seems not to have been celebrated amid the turmoil of war and bloody factional strife.[7]

The genius did not lack for honors or indemnities, however. While defending legislation designed to secure the intellectual property of authors, the revolutionary deputy Joseph Lakanal proclaimed "the declaration of the rights of genius." And in a substitution that is wonderfully symbolic of the genius's newly exalted status, "Genius" took the place of kings on revolutionary playing cards, and "Genius" and the "genius of France" graced revolutionary coins, just as the *genius* of the emperors had once sealed the specie of Rome. Symbolically, the genius was usurping the place of sovereigns and claiming the right of kings.[8]

That belief, that myth—whether celebrated in the Panthéon or bemoaned in counterrevolutionary phrases, such as "the Revolution is the fault of Voltaire"—highlights a related way in which the revolutionary experience gave a new inflection to the cult of genius. By linking geniuses emphatically to politics and political change, the revolutionaries highlighted the capacity of extraordinary individuals not just to understand the world, but to change it. Only with the Revolution could a myth of revolutionary genius emerge, and with the propagation of that myth was born a possibility, still fledgling, but soon to be fulfilled: that genius might be used as the *basis* of political power, celebrated not only in death but in life, employed to justify an extraordinary privilege and license. The very possibility raised a question: What was the place of the genius in a free nation? To a regime that had declared liberty, equality, and fraternity as its founding ideals, it was not an idle concern.

In the early, heady days of the Revolution, the answer to the question seemed straightforward enough. "Nature has formed an intimate union between liberty and genius," the playwright, poet, and politician Marie-Joseph Chénier observed in his report recommending the transfer of Descartes's remains to the Panthéon. In Chénier's view, Descartes's exile and death in Sweden was a measure of the despotism of the Old Regime, a failure of recognition that he would later describe as a "crime against genius" requiring expiation and atonement. It was only natural to Chénier that a man whose "very existence marked out an extraordinary epoch in the history of the genius of men" should be honored as a friend of revolutions. Genius and liberty were one. The connection had long been implicit in the understanding of genius as a force that refused to bow to convention, to slavishly acquiesce to established rules, and already in the early eighteenth century, English commentators were making the connection explicit. Enlisting Longinus as an apologist for the Glorious Revolution that overthrew the despotism of the Stuarts in 1688, they cited with relish a line that the ancient himself had implied was already well established—the view that "democracy is the nurse-maid of genius," and that freedom alone "has the power to foster noble minds." Later in the century, the French *Encyclopédie* agreed, observing in its article on "genius" (*génie*) that "rules and laws of taste will only be obstacles to genius," which "breaks them to steal from the sublime." Before the sublime spectacle of the French Revolution, it was easy enough to conflate aesthetics and politics, envisioning genius as a revolutionary force for freedom that was capable of throwing off the shackles of tired formula and overturning arbitrary laws.[9]

But genius was not only a liberator and breaker of rules, genius was also a legislator. As Kant famously claimed in the *Critique of Judgment*, it "gives the rule to art." To conflate aesthetics and politics once again, was it not evident that genius might lay down the law? Just like the sublime force that moved it, genius could induce the spirit of liberty or impose the awe of authority, eliciting reverence, terror, and the fear of death. And, as Diderot had speculated, giving new articulation to a venerable concern, duplicity, domination, evil, and crime might be the genius's lot. Seen in this light, the "intimate union" between liberty and genius was not so clear. When it was revealed, after his remains had been safely laid to rest in the Panthéon, that Mirabeau was in truth a traitor who had entered into secret negotiations with the king, such thoughts were no longer mere conjecture. Mirabeau's spirit was exorcised and his relics were removed, translated to a cemetery for criminals. The example of the fallen saint prompted suspicion and fear: Was not genius always a temptation? And what prevented those who possessed it from abusing its power? As none other than Maximilien Robespierre pointed out in the National Convention in answer to Fabre d'Églantine's proposal to institute a festival of the genius as the *first* of the Revolution's supplementary holidays, "Caesar was a man of genius," but "Caesar was nothing but a tyrant." Cato, by contrast, possessed virtue, and Cato was of "greater worth than Caesar." Genius was no guarantee of justice or right conduct, Robespierre made clear, and for that reason, a "day of virtue should take precedence over the festival of the genius."[10]

Robespierre's motion passed, and though it proved in the end to be moot, it did succeed in registering a concern about the place of genius in a republic, raising the specter of what one legislator described in the ensuing debates as an "aristocracy of the genius" (*l'aristocratie du génie*). Some might claim wishfully that "true genius" was always of the people. But those who sided with Robespierre feared otherwise, seeing in the consecration of a hierarchy of the intellect the prospect of a dangerous new form of inequality. At a moment when France had abolished the aristocracy of blood, would republicans and democrats really genuflect before a natural force that set men so dramatically apart? The question was pointed, and it forced other republicans to confront it, too. Condorcet, for one, took the question seriously. And though he could not dispense altogether with a belief that nature distributed her talents in unequal parcels, he nonetheless hewed much closer to the position of the eighteenth-century *philosophes* Helvétius, Turgot, and Condillac in his attempt to overcome the apparent conflict between genius and equality. Seeing in education the best means to mitigate natural difference, he looked forward to a day in the future when the "space that separates the two extremes of genius and stupidity" would be effaced by equal access to knowledge and the means to its cultivation. In the meantime, a genius like Descartes or Newton served as a beacon and an image of what all men—and in Condorcet's advanced opinion, all women, too—might one day strive to become.[11]

Condorcet's bracing vision of the future progress of the human mind was conceived at a fateful moment in the Revolution, when matters that divided republicans had begun to turn violent. Completed in hiding from Robespierre's political faction, the Jacobins, in the spring of 1794, on the brink of Condorcet's own death, the work is soaring in its rhetoric, sanguine in its hopes, and uplifting in its faith in humanity. Yet, as a practical response to the fear that genius might be at odds with republican equality, the work was not entirely convincing. For only in some distant future might the considerable natural differences that separated human beings be effaced. Until then, in Condorcet's view, men of exceptional genius would be the primary engines of human progress. How could one be sure that these geniuses would not exploit their inherent advantage, that those of greater natural intelligence would not benefit from their natural gift? It was exactly for this reason that Robespierre worried, with Rousseau, that what both men acknowledged were inborn inequalities of mind would only be exacerbated in civil society. The point of government, on their understanding, was to work to correct the intellectual inequality that nature had inscribed, imposing civil equality by means of virtue. Virtue, at least, could be taught and learned; Cato, to repeat, was of more value than any man of genius.

These republican debates had their analogues in Benjamin Franklin's native United States, where a language of merit tended to take precedence over one of natural worth. But they played out with greater ferocity in Europe, where both the assertion of human equality—and the inveterate resistance to it—were more violent and insistent than in the young United States. What opponents of the French Revolution soon described as Robespierre's "evil genius" (*génie infernale*)—and his monstrous facility with words—were put to the service of terrible crimes, with the guillotine giving chilling illustration, or so it seemed, to a point made by the great counterrevolutionary polemicist Joseph de Maistre. Maistre had said that "blood is the fertilizer of this plant called genius," but he also believed that genius was a kind of "grace." It followed that those who abused this divine gift were like fallen angels, satanic in their power.[12]

Maistre was hardly a disinterested observer. But his Christian iteration of the venerable fear that the possessor of genius might be tempted and led astray—that the possessor might prove a man possessed— accorded well, ironically, with Robespierre's more pagan concern that a man of genius like Caesar might challenge the republic and rule in corruption as a tyrant. The genius of France—like the modern genius himself—was suspended perilously between liberty and death. What powerful energy held it in place? What great life force would move it?

CHAPTER IV

ROMANTIC GENIUS

T HROUGHOUT THE REIGN OF Dionysius the Tyrant, the curious at
Syracuse had stared. No one had yet discovered the hidden meaning
of the design, and the inability to do so only compounded their amazement. They called it the "Rhodian Genius," or the "Genius of Rhodes,"
on account of the fact that the picture had been recovered from a shipwreck bearing the cargo of that ancient city-state. At its center presided
a *genius*, bathed in bright light, suspended between heaven and earth.
With soft features and a childlike face, the *genius* nonetheless commanded a "glance of celestial fire." A butterfly rested on his shoulder,
he held a lighted torch in his hand, and he looked down "as a master"
upon a group of garlanded youth, naked at his feet, commanding them
"to obey his laws without regard to their ancient rights." Wearing "purely
terrestrial expressions" of desire and sorrow, they stretched out their arms
to one another, as if to indicate their hope of union. But their troubled
looks turned toward the figure above them. What did the *genius* signify,
and what was its relation to the whole? Many wondered, but no one
with conviction could say.[1]

Set in the ancient Sicilian city-state of Syracuse in the fourth century BCE, "The Vital Force, or The Rhodian Genius," as this little tale is
known, is in fact a product of revolutionary Europe, the handiwork of
the young Prussian naturalist Alexander von Humboldt. Humboldt, who
would go on to become a celebrated scientist and explorer—a "genius"
himself, in the estimation of Goethe—was at the time little known. But
in the mid-1790s, he had fallen in with a group of Weimar intellectuals, including Goethe, the philosopher Johann von Herder, and the poet
Friedrich Schiller, who in 1795 launched the literary journal *Die Horen*,
where the "Rhodian Genius" first appeared. Devoted to an engagement

with classicism, the journal nonetheless boasted in its two-year run the participation of a number of figures who would emerge as prominent advocates of what contemporaries were soon calling the "Romantic sensibility" or the "Romantic school."

Humboldt's essay, like the journal in which it appeared, was written at a crossroads, mediating the ancient and the modern, the classical and the Romantic, the eighteenth and the nineteenth centuries. Returning to the ancients, Humboldt conjured a composite classical *genius*—a clean-shaven companion, "filled with celestial fire," who hovered between earth and sky. And yet, to this ancient figure and force, Humboldt posed a very modern question, one that had occupied Enlightened observers throughout the eighteenth century and that would continue to mystify the Romantics and their nineteenth-century heirs: What does genius signify? What does the genius mean? The very questions that perplexed the characters in his Rhodian fable were put to his contemporaries as well.

Humboldt's answer, elaborated in the remainder of the story, is that the *genius* of the tale could be explained as a kind of vital energy. Growing out of his scientific investigations into what Germans called the *Lebenskraft*, the source of life, his answer hints at what would prove to be a nineteenth-century preoccupation: the effort to isolate genius scientifically in the body. And yet, the idea that the man of genius might be "charged" with a superabundance of energy—and so able to store and communicate significant quanta of power—was widely communicated in literary circles as well, reminding us that in this "Age of Wonder" the search for the sublime was conducted across disciplinary as well as geographic frontiers. In the United States, the author and statesman Fisher Ames could observe that genius was "to the intellectual world what the electric fluid is to nature, diffused everywhere, yet almost everywhere hidden." The English Romantic William Hazlitt similarly described genius as a "pervading and elastic energy." And Mary Shelley, in one of the defining novels of her generation, recounted the quest of the "modern Prometheus," the demented Dr. Frankenstein, to capture this elusive force, employing his own evil genius to isolate the "principle of life." Well into the early twentieth century, scientific accounts made use of the terms "life force," "vital force," and "energy" to characterize genius as male charisma and power, often in explicitly sexualized terms.[2]

There is an irony to these descriptions. To characterize genius as vital energy was to return to the very oldest accounts of that enigmatic power, the elemental life force that coursed through the universe, the genetic, generative principle that expressed itself in the *lectus genialis* of the Roman patriarch and was present in the *numen* of the god. Humboldt was likely aware of that connection; others most certainly were, speaking, like Herder, of genius as *genius*, a modern instantiation of the ancient protector, or, like Goethe, of the mysterious "daemonic" force that took possession of the greatest men. To a much greater degree than their Enlightenment forebears, in fact, those who succeeded them in what is still called, for lack of a better term, the Age of Romanticism, were prepared to acknowledge the genius's enchanted lineage, celebrating it openly with references to the prophets and protectors, the saviors and apostles, the angels and *genii* who had formerly watched over human beings. That the genius was their heir—a modern hero in possession of superhuman powers—was made explicit. But that he might also possess in his quantum of energy something dangerous, something terrible, something that might well be abused, was also clearly faced. The hints of despotism in Humboldt's essay—set in Syracuse, the seat of the ancient tyrants—are telling. For his modern tale is a parable, if only an unwitting one, of the life-force genius that both dazzles with godlike powers and holds onlookers in thrall.

In this case, life proved true to art, for at the very moment that Humboldt was composing the "Rhodian Genius," a powerful life-force was taking shape to the west, preparing to vent his fury on Europe. In the person of Napoleon Bonaparte, Romantics would find a paragon of the genius of deeds. And in their speculation on the power that moved him and that coursed through the veins of men similarly endowed, commentators as diverse as Shelley and Byron, Coleridge and Blake, and Schopenhauer and Goethe would detect a force that could contain multitudes, with the capacity to shape the spirit of the age and to carry the many along.

N APOLEON. THE NAME ALONE provides a working definition of the "Romantic genius." He is a prime illustration of the type. Contemporaries may have chosen on occasion to consider others alongside him: Goethe, Byron, and Beethoven were legitimate pretenders. But Goethe himself deemed Napoleon a "genius" whose "destiny was more brilliant than any the world had seen before him, and perhaps ever would see again." Byron, to an even greater extent, was obsessed with the man, enraging classmates at Harrow by keeping a bust of England's scourge in his room. And though Beethoven famously turned against Napoleon after the general proclaimed himself emperor in 1804, the composer had once admired him enough to dedicate the so-called "Eroica Symphony" (Symphony No. 3 in E-flat Major) to Napoleon's genius. Few could resist the spell. The portrait common to virtually all Romantic reflection on Bonaparte was that of an omniscient and omnipotent genius.[3]

That such characterizations rested to a considerable degree on Napoleon's own prodigious talents is without question. Time and again, his admirers and detractors alike marveled at his vision, his intense focus, and his ability to master vast quantities of information with apparent ease. They were equally astounded by Napoleon's seemingly limitless energy, his capacity to work for great stretches of time while others ate, amused themselves, or simply collapsed in exhaustion. As a leader, and above all as a general, Napoleon possessed imposing psychological strengths, enabling him to marshal his personality to great effect. A master at gauging the mood of his troops or rallying it to suit his needs, he could at the same time impose his will at the negotiating table or in the drawing room, bringing the most powerful men in Europe to their knees. Finally, the vast range of his curiosity and knowledge—from his youthful dabbling as a writer and *philosophe* to his mature concern for science and support for the arts—meant that he could seduce across an astonishing array of interests. Goethe came away from his celebrated audience with the emperor in Erfurt in 1808 convinced that he had met a genius. Tsar Alexander felt the same. As the Comtesse de Rémusat grudgingly conceded (and as the bluest of blueblood aristocrats, she was not a woman to relish the ascent of an upstart), "To be truly a great man, in whatever field, you have to have genuinely made a part of your glory." That Napoleon had done so, she could scarcely deny.[4]

Napoleon's uncommon abilities, then, were widely attested. As one of his leading generals, Jean-Baptiste Kléber, was moved to remark during the campaign in Egypt, "General, you are great like the world, and the world is not great enough for you." Yet, as the quotation also illustrates, Napoleon's genius was mythic, and the cult around it myth-making. To interpret his status as the iconic genius of the age as a simple reflection of his gifts would be naive. For genius is invariably constructed, and geniuses themselves are often skilled in the art of assemblage. As we saw in Chapter 3, Newton was a shrewd publicist and self-promoter who consciously crafted his image, notwithstanding his undeniable gifts, and one could say the same of other geniuses of the eighteenth century, from Rousseau to Benjamin Franklin to Voltaire. In this sense, and however much advocates of original genius might protest the fact, genius was certainly "made" and not just born.[5]

Napoleon was no exception, and in fact he may be interestingly compared to other artistic virtuosi who emerged during this period, such as Franz Liszt, Niccolò Paganini, and Beethoven, who were similarly adept at performing their genius and creating a spectacle of themselves. But with the apparatus of an empire at his disposal, Napoleon could afford to do far more than gesticulate on stage. Indeed, like no other statesman before him, with the possible exception of Augustus, Napoleon used his genius to enhance his power and to impose his will on the age. Drawing self-consciously on the discourse of genius that had developed over the whole of the eighteenth century, Napoleon cultivated an image of himself as a man greater than man. An essential part of his genius, it may be said, was precisely his ability to assume it, and to use it to his further advantage. In this respect, Napoleon's timing, as on the battlefield, was superb. To an even greater extent than the infant Mozart and his calculating father, Napoleon marshaled the force of genius at the perfect moment, after a century had proclaimed its prodigious capacity, and after the upheavals of a revolutionary decade had primed Europe for a guardian and savior in the flesh. Building on the French Revolution's imperfect precedents and the cult of great men, Napoleon showed how genius might be put to the service of political ends.[6]

The groundwork for this strategic deployment was laid early on and sustained throughout his reign. As early as 1797, while Napoleon served as the commander of the French army in Italy, he used his propaganda organ there, the *Courrier de l'armée d'Italie*, to present himself as a man of the heavens who "flies like lightning and strikes like thunder," a man who is "everywhere and who sees everything," because he "unites the most sublime virtues to a vast genius" (*un vaste génie*). Napoleon, the journal stressed, was "one of those men for whom power has no limits save for his own will." With his rise to political office in 1799, followed by the promotion to life consul in 1802 and then to emperor in 1804, such representations only grew bolder and more frequent. An official biography lauded Napoleon typically as a visionary, ready to realize "grand conceptions of genius." Mayors, prefects, and even priests made use of their positions as representatives of the realm to laud the genius of the emperor, or the emperor as a genius. Thus did the new mayor of the city of Feurs in the Loire Valley see fit in 1801 to praise "the genius who presided over the happy day of the 18th Brumaire" and who now guided the "ship of state with such wisdom and assurance." Following Napoleon's crossing of the Rhine in 1805, a local priest back home explained enthusiastically to his parishioners that "fifteen days of Napoleon's genius had obtained more for Germany than Charlemagne had been able to accomplish—or had even dared to dream—in his entire life." At the same time, in theater productions and in the ubiquitous festivals held to celebrate military victories and national holidays, Napoleon was regularly addressed as "the genius," a title that served as one of the most common descriptions of the consul-cum-emperor in the formal speeches delivered on such occasions. In official art, busts, medals, and engravings, finally, a self-conscious effort was made to present a collective image of Napoleon in keeping with his increasingly inflated self-estimation as a man "who had proven that he sees farther than other men." "Omniscient, omnipotent, a prophet or oracle," Napoleon could boast of knowing "more in his little finger than all other heads combined." He was a master of fate, a controller of destiny, for whom the heavens had special regard, a point that Napoleon insisted on by a constant allusion to his star. If, as Horace had observed, the *genius* was the companion who controlled our birth star, governing the individual's fortune in the universe, Napoleon's genius was overseen by his own astral body, variously depicted as a comet, a meteor, or some other heavenly point of light. Like the *sidus Iulium* of Caesar, Napoleon's star was taken as a measure of his special favor and a symbol of Fate's alignment with his inexorable rule.[7]

Napoleon's self-conscious efforts to construct his genius are crucial to any full understanding of his role as the genius of the age. But to assume that he alone was responsible for creating that image would be to reproduce the myth of omnipotence that his propaganda aimed to impart. In the end, neither Napoleon himself nor his agents of publicity had the power to compel conviction, and belief in his genius was never simply inscribed in the soft wax of passive minds. The more interesting truth is that the cult of Napoleon's genius was often freely accepted and enthusiastically received, both within his lifetime and for generations thereafter, down to the present day. Not only did Napoleon play a role in fashioning his image, this image played a role in fashioning him.[8]

To come at the problem in this way is to acknowledge the importance of the social dimension of the construction of genius, to appreciate the ways in which shared categories of perception—common experiences, expectations, and beliefs—invariably affect the way messages and images are received. And to do that is to raise the question of which categories most influenced the reception of Napoleon's genius, and helped, in turn, to shape it. Or, to put the question another way, just what was it about genius that appealed to Europeans at the beginning of the nineteenth century? Why should Napoleon, a modern leader, choose to present himself in this way?

The questions, at first glance, may seem straightforward, even self-evident. But they become less so when one considers just how unprecedented it was for a cult of genius to form around a living political leader. In the eighteenth century, genius was associated predominantly with scientists, artists, and men of letters, the better part of whom were dead. And although Napoleon's contemporaries did speak on occasion of Richelieu or Frederick the Great, or George Washington or William Pitt, as statesmen of genius—and geniuses themselves—no modern European leader (and certainly no French monarch) had ever justified his rule by an explicit appeal to genius as such. A cynic might reply that Napoleon did so out of necessity, given that he lacked the luxury of a formal accession, a long lineage, or divine right, and that is undoubtedly true. It is also true that from at least the fourth century BCE, when Plato dreamed in the *Republic* of an ideal state governed by a philosopher-king, Europeans had flirted intermittently with the fantasy of marrying brilliance to power, combining, as Machiavelli put it in the *Prince*, the strength of the lion with the cunning of the fox. In the Old Regime, that fantasy had taken the form of the "wise legislator" imagined by Rousseau, or the "enlightened despot" who employed gentle force to effect a program of reason and reform. Napoleon was undoubtedly received through both of these categories. Yet it was above all the experience of the French Revolution that created the conditions for a genuine departure. For, by linking the cult of genius explicitly to politics and revolutionary change, and by allowing for the emergence of a new type of leader, the Revolution made possible the rule of genius in the flesh, a rule based largely on the force of character and on the force of word and deed. Already, in the fleeting success of a Mirabeau or Lafayette, a Georges Danton or Robespierre, one catches a glimpse of this possibility, as well as an attendant longing for a new type of hero to rival the ancients, a god-man who would save. And though the pretenders to that role had turned out to be traitors, tyrants, or dwarves, they did not eradicate the desire to fuse genius to power. In this respect, as in others, Napoleon was the Revolution's child.

When Napoleon's contemporaries gazed at this novel figure, then, they saw a figure cloaked in genius—a genius—who was the living heir to the revolutionary cult and a century's reflection on the meaning of the term and the type. Again, the point may seem obvious, but it needs to be made, because there is a long tradition of exaggerating the degree to which the Romantic generation cast off the beliefs of the previous age, rejecting Enlightened principles and doctrines outright. A strong case can be made for disagreement, even divergence, in certain domains. But in matters of genius it makes more sense to speak of continuity and evolution, as opposed to rupture or a parting of ways. Gradually deepening, expanding, and extending positions that had been worked out over the course of the eighteenth century, the Romantic generation embraced and exaggerated notions of original genius developed by their predecessors. Certainly, they innovated in important ways, bringing to the genius a style and a flair all their own, introducing new accents and associations while pushing eighteenth-century conceptions to their extreme. Yet the figure was a recognizable type. The Romantic genius was a direct heir to the genius of the Enlightenment, and Napoleon a critical figure in effecting the bequest.

This is not to say that Napoleon's contemporaries beheld only a genius as the eighteenth century understood the term. They could not help but view him through the prism of a number of other established archetypes and forms. Before all else, Napoleon was a soldier, a general and conqueror of "greatness" and "glory," *grandeur et gloire*. Those ancient epithets, so admired in the eighteenth century, called to mind a host of virtues incarnate in the famed commanders and statesmen who people the pages of Plutarch's *Lives*: courage and self-possession, fortitude and self-sacrifice, magnanimity and love of the fatherland. Anyone with an education in Napoleon's time knew that venerable work, and so they "knew" that the Corsican was also a great-souled man, whose many virtues and the stunning victories that confirmed them bestowed *grandeur* and *gloire* in quantities that no other modern possessed. In the eyes of his contemporaries, Napoleon became Hannibal crossing the Alps, striking fear into enemy legions. He was Caesar, the emperor who rescued the republic from itself, his destiny similarly guided by a comet and a star. He was Alexander, pacifier of Egypt, conqueror of the world. He was Augustus, founder of a great empire. And finally, he was Charlemagne, who would reunite Europe and make the empire anew. Napoleon assumed each one of these forms, and others besides. But if his contemporaries thus viewed him—as he frequently viewed himself—in parallel with ancient lives, his image blurred quickly into that of another form, which was considerably less distinct. Napoleon resembled, in this view, not only the generals and statesmen of the ancient world, but also the legendary heroes and demigods of myth. Already in life, if far more so in death, Napoleon the man of action became Hercules, laboring to fulfill the dictates of the gods. He was Prometheus, who challenged the heavens in deliverance of the people, who saved and redeemed. And he was Solon, legendary lawgiver of Athens, a founder and father of renown.

In all these ways, Napoleon appeared to be an "epiphany of the ancients," an incarnation of the classical heroes they so revered and for whom they so clearly longed. Yet at the same time he was undeniably modern. Like Michelangelo in the celebrated description of Vasari, Napoleon not only rivaled the ancients, but surpassed them, and he did so in large part by breaking out of the mold of all previous forms. That was genius. At a time when individuality and uniqueness were coming to be valued as qualities in themselves, Napoleon was the consummate individual, who broke precedents and shattered norms. As a general, a statesman, a leader, a *grand homme*, Napoleon was a man of immense attractive force. He was a man of charisma, and charisma of a particularly modern type.[9]

The word itself is ancient, from the Greek *kharis*, meaning divine favor or grace. Homer used the term to connote a "gift of the gods," and Saint Paul did the same, writing in his epistles of *kharisma* as a sacred bestowal or heavenly gift. A long line of theologians developed the concept thereafter, but in modern parlance, the word immediately calls to mind the work of its most famous analyst and interpreter, the sociologist Max Weber, who made charisma a key notion in his description of religious and political authority. Charisma, Weber explained, is a "certain quality of an individual personality by virtue of which he is considered extraordinary and treated as endowed with supernatural, superhuman, or at least specifically exceptional powers or qualities." These powers "are not accessible to the ordinary person, but are regarded as of divine origin or as exemplary," and it was on their basis that charismatic leaders throughout history—whether prophets, shamans, warlords, or some other type—had drawn their legitimacy. Infused with a strong religious or magical quality, charismatic leadership was "a revolutionary force" that repudiated the past and assailed the status quo, whether this be the time-bound inertia of "traditional authority," on the one hand, or the impersonal legalism of modern "bureaucratic authority," on the other.[10]

Although Weber regarded charismatic leadership as an "ideal type," a tool of sociological analysis applicable across cultures and time, he was not insensitive to its historical development, a point that scholars have emphasized more recently, showing how charisma was constructed in late eighteenth-and nineteenth-century Europe in creative tension with the kindred notions of celebrity and fame. It is significant in this connection that Weber singled out Napoleon as a new form of charismatic leader, referring specifically to his "rule of genius." The reference is fleeting, though suggestive, for in fact there are close parallels between the mysterious force of genius and that of charisma. Both were conceived as gifts that, as Weber said of charisma, could be "'awakened' and 'tested'" but never "'learned' or 'taught.'" Both assailed tradition and rules, creating originally, revolutionarily, in new forms. And both bathed their possessors in an aura of magic, mystery, and fate that somehow connected them to the world beyond. As Goethe said of the rising Napoleon, he seems to have been "in a state of continued illumination[;] . . . indeed we see at his side divine protection and a constant fortune," the certainty of his "star." He was, Goethe concluded, the very model of the "dae-monic man."[11]

In Napoleon, then, charisma and genius were one. Viewing him simultaneously through the category of genius as this had evolved in the eighteenth century, as a hero—a soldier of glory—and a *grand homme*, his contemporaries endowed his genius with charisma, and his charisma with genius. It was an unprecedented combination, as the visionary and social theorist Henri de Saint-Simon observed in contemplating the con-struction of a vast monument to the emperor Napoleon in 1807. History had "written in golden letters the names of five heroic geniuses and five scientific geniuses of the highest order," Saint-Simon affirmed, singling out Alexander, Hannibal, Julius Caesar, the prophet Mohammed, and Charlemagne, on the one hand, and Socrates, Plato, Aristotle, Bacon, and Descartes, on the other. But until the present moment, no man had succeeded in entering the Temple of Glory "by both doors." Napo-leon alone had accomplished this feat, combining heroic with scientific genius in a completely original and explosive combination.[12]

Saint-Simon based his praise of Napoleon's scientific and philosoph-ical genius, which he likened to that of Newton, largely on his capacity to organize and set in motion the intellectual forces of his time. It is true that Napoleon was talented in mathematics as a schoolboy, and that his support of the sciences and the arts—from the scientific dele-gations he brought to Egypt to the founding of France's great universi-ties, the *grandes écoles*—was considerable. Still, the analogy to Newton will strike most observers today as far-fetched, though it was not at all uncommon at the time. Napoleon himself reportedly dreamed in his youth of becoming another Newton, a Newton of "small bodies" and minute details, the master of finite, if not infinite, space. And as an adult he gave some indication of having attained his goal. The naturalist Étienne Geoffroy Saint-Hilaire, for example, who accompanied Napo-leon to Egypt, described in awe how, in the midst of preparing for his departure, directing orderlies and aides, and saying goodbye to a for-lorn mistress, Napoleon simultaneously debated with Gaspard Monge, the leading mathematical physicist of France, regarding the question of whether Newton had "answered everything." Napoleon maintained that he hadn't, and then proceeded to show where the genius of Newton was wanting, apparently trumping the Englishman's with his own, or at least so it seemed to the astonished Saint-Hilaire. Somewhat later, in a substantial chapter of his classic *On War* devoted to the novel subject of "military genius," the military theorist Carl von Clausewitz emphasized how Napoleon repeatedly performed calculations on the battlefield worthy of the "gifts of a Newton or an Euler," easily grasping and dismissing "a thousand remote possibilities which an ordinary mind would labor to identify and wear itself out in so doing." Such an intuitive capacity— to find order where others saw chaos or chance, to anticipate movements dependent on infinitely complex variables, and "to perceive the truth at every moment"—could never be learned, Clausewitz said. It required "higher intellectual gifts" and an innate "sense of unity and power of judgment raised to a marvelous pitch of vision." When this supreme power of divination, "the sovereign eye of genius itself," was joined to the strengths of character required of the greatest commanders— firmness, staunchness, and sangfroid—the resulting blend of intellect and volition was of truly "historical significance."[13]

Napoleon was, then, as his many German admirers in the nineteenth century came to describe him, a *Taten-Genie*, a genius of deeds, who held out the immense possibilities of genius to alter human existence and transform the face of the globe. As such, he was an original type. For though, as Saint-Simon and Clausewitz took pains to emphasize, Napoleon possessed many of the same gifts as earlier men of genius— gifts of intellect, creativity, imagination, and will—he added to them a powerful capacity for action. The vital force that moved him propelled him from the study and the studio into the palace and the stateroom, sent him sweeping across battlefields into the very maelstrom of life. Earlier geniuses had created chiefly with canvas and words. Napoleon created with kingdoms. Human beings were his clay. And whereas earlier geniuses had challenged prevailing norms in art or science, spurning established rules, Napoleon overthrew centuries-old customs, traditions, and laws. A destroyer, he abolished kingdoms. A creator, he made them anew. Here was the basis of a powerful Romantic myth that was at once heir to the original genius of the eighteenth century and a genuine original. Combining creativity with action, originality with deeds, the genius could be a poet of the political, remaking the world in his image. The genius could be a legislator of the world.

The acknowledgment of Napoleon's legislative power proved more fleeting than the emperor had hoped. Yet even as his kingdom crumbled, and Europeans weighed its tremendous cost in blood, the example of his genius proved fertile, as creative in captivity and death as in life. "World-historical individuals are those who [are] the first to formulate the desires of their fellows explicitly," the German philosopher Georg Wilhelm Friedrich Hegel would famously declare in the year following

Napoleon's death, his example very much in mind. "When their ends are achieved, they fall aside like empty husks." Yet their spirit endured. "There is a power within them which is stronger than they are," and a power that moves through them, and so appears as "something external and alien."[14]

Just what that power was—the *divinum quiddam* of special men— constituted a venerable question that continued to exercise Napoleon's contemporaries while focusing attention on an apparent paradox that his case brought to the fore. How was it that the extraordinary individual— the genius—could be at once the great exception and a representative man, an oracle who spoke like no other and a paragon who spoke for all? On the coast across the sea, within sight of the island of Elba where Napoleon was once a captive, a gathering of mourners scoured the sand in search of answers to such questions. And in the circle of Romantic poets that surrounded them, they helped to formulate an answer, imagining the genius as a prophet, one who legislated for the people even when his authority was denied.

A FIRE BURNS ON THE TUSCAN COAST, defying the morning heat. Wood-smoke, pine and lime, incense and decaying flesh. The fierce pop and crackle of flames: a splinter or a shard of bone? Watery eyes wonder in silence, before the hands go in, plunging, amid ash and embers and smoke. A poet is dead. A genius has fallen. May the gods take him . . . all but his heart.

The story of Percy Bysshe Shelley's seaside cremation at the ancient Italian city of Viareggio in 1822—and of the dramatic rescue of his smoldering heart from the bier—might well have been scripted, and in a certain sense it was, presented from the time of his death as a Romantic set-piece, and embellished ever since. The young poet, not yet thirty years old, had disappeared five weeks earlier in the shipwreck of his schooner, the *Ariel*, also named the *Don Juan*, evoking the masterpiece of Shelley's intimate rival, Lord Byron. Drowned in the Ligurian sea and washed up on the beach, Shelley's body was discovered by his friend Edward John Trelawny, the Romantic adventurer who would later join Byron on his doomed journey to Messolonghi to fight in the Greek War of Independence, a self-conscious attempt to wed genius to action in the Napoleonic mode. It was Trelawny who rescued Shelley's heart from the fire—badly burning his hand in the process—and it was Trelawny who had arranged the seaside cremation, which local authorities demanded for reasons of health.[15]

Yet the group in attendance that day—including Byron and Tre-lawny, the poet Leigh Hunt, and Shelley's wife, Mary Wollstonecraft Shelley—ensured that the cremation would be read ever after as much more than a precautionary measure of public sanitation. Bringing wine and oil and incense, they doused the flames as if Shelley were an ancient hero, giving the avowed atheist a fittingly pagan end. Byron swam in the sea afterward in full view of the island of Elba. And they transformed with their pens and their presence a place of death into a Romantic *genius loci*, with Shelley as the guardian of the place.

Indeed, in snatching Shelley's heart from the fire, Trelawny and his friends were initiating a process of consecration, like that which attends all geniuses who speak beyond the grave, endowing this "relic," as they later called it, with sacred significance. "What surprised us all, was that the heart remained entire," Trelawny marveled. And so it remained, entire, if not intact, taken by Hunt and then guarded by Mary for years, enclosed, the legend goes, within a copy of Shelley's "Adonais," an elegy on the death of Keats.

> *. . . his fate and fame shall be*
> *An echo and a light unto eternity!"*

Bits of skull and jawbone were also spirited away from the cremation pit, or so it was claimed by the many who proudly displayed such fragments in their Victorian cabinets of curiosity. Others cherished them more inti-mately in small blue opaque jars, or kept strands of Shelley's hair in lock-ets, close to the breast. *Cor cordium* reads the Latin inscription on the tombstone in Rome where some of his ashes were eventually laid. "Heart of hearts."[16]

What Shelley himself would have thought of this corporeal traffic is impossible to know. Certainly, he appreciated the celebrity of great achievement—the "Poet's food is love and fame," he once wrote in his poem "An Exhortation." Given that he died starved of the one, though not the other, as his brilliant wife, Mary, ensured, he likely would have been gratified by the many memorials and shrines later erected in his honor—at Viareggio, in Rome, at University College, Oxford, and in the Speaker's Corner at Westminster Cathedral. It is also true that he shared with his circle a Gothic taste for the morbid and maca-bre. Byron himself, whose own heart and brain would be removed and preserved against his wishes, reportedly requested Shelley's skull at the cremation, and Mary showed no aversion to harboring his heart. Even so, an atheist might be supposed to frown at the veneration of relics, especially his own.[17]

Whether or not Shelley would have approved the practice, it is safe to say that he would have understood it—understood the lingering impulse to search for something extraordinary—something sacred even—in the remains of the special dead. Both he and Byron, after all, possessed extensive collections of Napoleonic memorabilia, including a snuffbox of the emperor's and an assortment of commemorative medals that Shelley presented to Byron for his thirty-fourth birthday. A similar impulse had moved the followers of Descartes to hallow his bones, even to carve rings from the recovered bits that turned up during the French Revolution. And a similar impulse summoned pilgrims well into the twentieth century to gaze in wonder at appendages as strange and diverse as Napoleon's purported penis, Kant's skull, Galileo's finger, and both Lenin's and Einstein's brains. But what beyond titillation and frisson did these onlookers hope to experience? Just what, if anything, did they hope to see?[18]

Shelley himself provides an important clue in a celebrated passage of his *Defence of Poetry* (1821), calling attention to a mysterious power, a "power of communicating and receiving intense and impassioned conceptions," that is detectable in special men. The "person in whom this power resides," Shelley insists, is compelled to serve it, for it is "seated on the throne of their own soul." And though often hidden, this vital force is made manifest when it is released and discharged, above all into works of creation.

> It is impossible to read the compositions of the most celebrated writers of the present day without being startled with the electric life which burns within their words. They measure the circumference and sound the depths of human nature with a comprehensive and all penetrating spirit, and they are themselves perhaps the most sincerely astonished at its manifestations; for it is less their spirit than the spirit of the age. Poets are the hierophants of an unapprehended inspiration; the mirrors of the gigantic shadows which futurity casts upon the present. . . . Poets are the unacknowledged legislators of the world.

As the oft-cited last line of the passage makes clear, Shelley located this special power to channel and capture the spirit of the age in "poets," a term that he uses broadly, like others of the day, to refer to rarefied creators across a variety of media. Shelley's poets are not only philosophers and artists in the broadest sense of the word, they are also "the institutors of laws & the founders of civil society," as well as holy men and religious figures who attempt to articulate the "agencies of the invisible world." The work of poets can thus assume many forms, and the terms Shelley used to describe their power are similarly eclectic. His references to mirrors and electric life, spirit and the invisible world, echo terms regularly employed to describe genius and great men. Here was the *furor poeticus* moving through man, Shaftesbury's vocal looking glass, surveying the world and human nature, reflecting truth back onto the self. Here was the vital energy, the flash of inspiration, the sweep of sublime imagination, and the two-way traffic ("communicating and receiving") that had long governed the conception of those special beings who traffic between the gods and men. Here, finally, was Hegel's world-historical individual who at once possesses and is possessed by the spirit of the times. The poet, like the genius, is what Shelley calls a "hierophant," one who, as the Greek etymology of the word suggests, "shows" or "reveals" the "sacred." And though, strictly speaking, that function does not render the poet sacred himself—an object of worship or a harvest site for relics—the confusion may be forgiven. For, in truth, Shelley's poet, like the Romantic genius of which he forms a type, is an exalted man, a privileged being, charged with a special mission and power. He is, Shelley says, a "prophet."[19]

Derived from the Greek *prophētēs*, and used in scripture as the translation of the Hebrew *nabi*, a mouthpiece or spokesman of God, the word is rich in religious resonance and commands an important place in Romantic discourse. In the Judeo-Christian context, it had been most often employed in reference to the prophets of scripture, such as the lawgiver Moses, the visionary Ezekiel, or Jeremiah or John the Baptist, who preached repentance and prepared the way of the Lord. But there was also a long tradition in the classical and pagan world of thinking of the poet as a prophetic being—an oracle, seer, or shaman. Over the course of the eighteenth century, those two traditions drew closer together. Seminal poets such as William Blake and the German author of *Der Messias* (The Messiah), Friedrich Gottlieb Klopstock, spoke ecstatically in prophetic tongues, while biblical and literary scholars cultivated an enhanced appreciation for the purely poetic qualities of scripture, emphasizing its genius and original power. The celebrated Anglican bishop and Oxford professor of poetry Robert Lowth, for example, insisted in his influential studies of the Old Testament that the prophetic and the poetic were one. At the same time, influential critics, such as the German philosophers Hamann and Herder, called attention to the sublimity and imaginative force of the prophetic language of scripture. Such work paved the way for reconceiving the ancient correspondence between prophecy and poetry. Its echoes can be heard in a range of Romantic pronouncements, from Samuel Taylor Coleridge's celebrated observation that "sublimity is Hebrew by birth" to the German critic Friedrich Schlegel's dictum that "no one is a poet but the prophet" to the short-lived Romantic author Novalis's reflection that the poetic sense "has a close kinship with the sense of prophecy and for the religious, oracular sense in general." Yet it was ultimately the shock of the French Revolution and its convulsive Napoleonic aftermath that brought out the augur in observers, who strained to see the future's horizon through the dust of crashing altars and toppled thrones. The period is well named. It was, indeed, the "time of the prophets."[20]

But what did a "prophet" mean to someone like Shelley, who no longer believed in God? And on what grounds did he and others claim prophetic powers? Shelley took pains to emphasize that poets were not simple fortunetellers, prophets "in the grossest sense of the word." Rather, he insisted on the older and weightier meaning, stressing the prophet's role as a lawgiver and legislator, a voice speaking truth to power and calling the times to account, renewing and revealing insights that the present age had forgotten or had yet to discern. The prophet "beholds intensely the present as it is, and discovers those laws according to which present things ought to be ordered." Then, by dint of his superior imagination, he is able to see the future inchoate in the present and to sow the seeds of its evolution and growth. "His thoughts are the germs of the flower and the fruit of latest time," Shelley wrote.[21]

Yet, if the future grows organically in the soil of the poet's mind, the fertilizing source of the poet-prophet's power comes from somewhere outside of himself. The true poet, Shelley contended, "participates in the eternal, the infinite and the one," but his participation is largely passive, unconscious, and unwilled. The poet, in other words, acts like a kind of transistor, conducting the energy coursing through the universe while amplifying the spirit of the age. To invoke a different metaphor of which Shelley himself was fond, the poet-prophet is like a musical instrument, an Aeolian lyre, on which a divine melody is harmonized and played.[22]

Shelley's emphasis on the passive and involuntary character of poetic creation, and his readiness to discount the role of the will in shaping the imaginative process, places him at one end of a spectrum distinguishing those who regard artistic capacity as inherent in the "possessor" from those who regard it as infused in the "possessed." The lines of the spectrum, first sketched in antiquity, were redrawn by the Renaissance consideration of *ingenium* and the *furor poeticus*, and frequently blurred. But though the modern insistence that genius was born, not made, tended to undercut the rationale for thinking of the poet as an empty vessel filled from the outside, the language of possession and inspiration proved resilient. Enduring throughout the eighteenth century and into the Romantic period, it was given new impetus by the likes of Shelley, who was by no means alone in emphasizing the way in which creative or imaginative genius might take possession of the mind, seizing it unawares. As Shelley's friend, the critic William Hazlitt, could declare, "the definition of genius is that it acts unconsciously." He added that "those who have produced immortal works have done so without knowing how or why." Germans, too, were quick to defend this position, often, like the philosopher Johann Gottlieb Fichte, by drawing on Kant, who had famously defined artistic genius as a force that "cannot describe or indicate scientifically how it brings about its products." It was nature that gave the rule to art, by working through its chosen. Thus does Fichte's erstwhile student Friedrich Schelling conceive of the "obscure concept of genius" as a movement akin to destiny by which a "dark unknown force" and "incomprehensible agency" realizes, through us, "goals that we did not envisage."[23]

It is worth emphasizing the heightened mystery of such talk in a post-Enlightened age. For without *genii* and angels, the Muses and the gods, to blow into our souls, where did the breath come from? Who or what did the blowing? Shelley's poet-prophet somehow intuits the spirit of the age, tapping into the pervasive energy of a "universal mind." Wordsworth, similarly, writes of the "impulse of a vernal wood" that might teach us more of "man / Of moral evil and of good / Than all the sages can." But among those who doubted the existence of beings able to take possession of the mind, it was far from clear how that impulse was to be conveyed. Talk of possession and inspiration, as a consequence, tended to be even more enigmatic than it had been in a fully enchanted world.[24]

Which is why even those, such as Shelley, who spoke of poetic creation as predominately passive were generally still inclined to acknowledge at least some role for the mind in actively shaping the imagination. The mind's constitutive role in shaping the categories of thought was, in fact, a commonplace of post-Kantian philosophy, with commentators frequently describing the mind not as a "blank slate," as the epistemology of John Locke would have it, but as a "lamp" that radiated outward, shining its light onto the world and imposing its own coherence and color on the raw data of perception. It followed naturally enough from this conception that only those of lofty mind could be genuinely inspired: the "possessed" were in some measure "possessors," drawing to themselves flashes of creative insight as a magnet drew shards of iron. The poet and critic August Wilhelm Schlegel, the brother of Friedrich and Germany's leading translator of Shakespeare, captured some of this when he pointed out, in a discussion of inspiration in his influential *Lectures on Dramatic Art and Literature* (1809–1811), that "the activity of genius" is "in a certain sense, unconscious; and consequently, the person who possesses it is not always able to render an account of the course he may have pursued; but it by no means follows that the thinking power has not a great share in it." Notions of the inspired poet—possessed, like the "Pythia," the priestess of the Delphic oracle, by an ecstatic fury—applied still less in arenas such as the theater, where inspiration, conscious reflection, and determination of the will worked together in the process of creation. Few in the nineteenth century conceived of the poet—as Plato had done disparagingly—as a mere empty vessel, contributing nothing of his own.[25]

But while positions varied on the extent of the individual's role in consciously cultivating genius, Romantics tended to agree with Shelley that the individual's power—whether subterranean or conscious, received or willed—derived from the ability to "participate" in "the eternal, the infinite, and the one." The terms they used to describe this enchanted realm differed. Shelley referred to it with Neo-Platonic overtones as "universal mind," a consciousness that permeated the universe and connected all living souls. Others opted for "world soul" or "world consciousness," "absolute Being," or "the Will," or borrowed Hegel's terminology of "Idea" and "Spirit" (*Geist*). Still others equated the divine directly with "Nature" in a form of pantheism indebted to Spinoza, while some continued to speak of "God," as in days of old. The welter of terms, however, hid a basic and common assumption that behind (or beyond) the prosaic realm in which we dwell from day to day lay another, deeper realm that structured all creation. In the influential terms of the philosophy of Kant, behind the "phenomena" of appearance lay the objective realm of "noumena" (derived from the ancient Greek *nous*, for intellect or mind), the ground of objective meaning and truth.

Here was the elusive source of an inspired revelation that for many could connect the individual genius to something greater, what the poet and draftsman William Blake described strikingly in a brief reflection as a "universal Poetic Genius," an all-encompassing spirit that permeated the world. Active throughout humanity, the Poetic Genius was like a universal soul, but was also a power and principle of individual creation.

And so Blake can observe that "the forms of all things are derived from their Genius, which by the Ancients was call'd an Angel & Spirit & Demon." The Poetic Genius, "which is everywhere call'd the Spirit of Prophecy," is also a principle of truth from which all sects of philosophy and all religions are derived. The Poetic Genius, finally, is like God, "for all similars have one source," and the source of all creation is the true Man, "he being the Poetic Genius."[26]

The title of this obscure and difficult work is "All Religions Are One," and Blake prefaced it with the words of the prophet Isaiah (and in turn John the Baptist): "the voice of one crying in the wilderness," preparing the way of the Lord. In so doing, he opened the text to a Christian interpretation. Given Blake's lifelong fascination with scripture, a Christian interpretation is certainly warranted, even if Blake does present major challenges to orthodoxy. But if the work can be read as preparing the way for the God-man Christ, who is at once the "true Man," the Creator and Spirit of all things, it also prepares the way for a latter-day apostle or saint similar to the one Shelley describes, the genius as poet, prophet, and hierophant. For the Poetic Genius, in Blake's cryptic formulation, is not only the "true Man" and the spirit of all things, but also a "faculty" akin to imagination, the human *vis activa*, which Blake and his fellows repeatedly insist helps to reveal the divine. It is imagination that allows the poet to create, and imagination that allows the prophet to conceive what is yet to be born. And although all human beings possess this faculty to some extent, only the poetic genius, in the sense of a single individual who taps into the Poetic Genius writ large, possesses (or is possessed by) an imagination of such power as to be able to see into the future and conjure another world. As the philosopher Schelling would put it, speaking also of art, every genius, so to speak, is *ein Stück aus der Absolutheit Gottes*, "a piece of the totality of God." It is the individual genius who reveals the genius of the world.[27]

Blake's use of the word "genius" in this latter sense—as a synonym for a broader informing spirit or soul—harkens back to the Roman belief that places, peoples, even the entire universe, might have a genius, a guardian keeper or soul. Such usage survived the fall of Rome in locutions such as *genius loci* or *génie de la langue française*, which authors invoked in the early modern period in reference to the distinctive character and spirit of a language or a place. In the eighteenth century, "genius" was used increasingly in reference to the distinct character of a time or country. Thus does Montesquieu speak of the "genius of the nation" in reference to its "morals and character," while others, such as the Scottish historian William Robertson, used the phrase to describe a country's peculiar "taste and spirit." Similarly, the German philologist Christian Adolph Klotz entitled a book in 1760 *Genius seculi*, in reference to the "genius of the century," prompting Herder to coin the term "Zeitgeist" in critical response; it was, in his view, a more felicitous phrase. Blake's use of "genius" echoed such precedents. But his linking of the individual poetic genius to the Poetic Genius writ large is characteristic of what would prove a widespread Romantic contention: namely, that true individuality reveals the universal, and that the universal is itself composed of a rich and diverse array of individual forms. Genuine originality, in other words, provided an authentic glimpse of something larger, a particular revelation of the whole.[28]

This paradoxical belief that the true original opened a window onto the universal helped to sustain a distinctly Romantic curiosity in the singular, exotic, and strange. But where genius was concerned, it also generated a curious article of faith: the belief that the exceptional individual—wholly other, alien, and unique—could somehow embody and represent the whole. Just as Napoleon, a man like no other, became the oracle of his people, the incarnation of France, the great exception of genius might serve as the rule. Through the alchemy of genius, the singular man became the representative man, the incarnation of all.

As it developed in the nineteenth century, this paradoxical belief took two principal forms. On the one hand, it became possible to claim that despite the great variety—and even apparent contradiction—of their interests and views, individual geniuses were ultimately united like saints before God, reconciled in a "brotherhood of genius" that represented the kinship of humanity in its many different expressions. Wordsworth called this "the animating faith" that linked "Poets, even as Prophets, each with each . . . in a mighty scheme of truth," despite each one having his "own peculiar faculty" or "Heaven's gift" that allowed him to see the world uniquely, in a way in which no one else before him had glimpsed. The German philosopher Arthur Schopenhauer defended a related point, emphasizing that "genius can find its use only by being employed on the universal of existence," and hence was of service to the "whole human race." Somewhat later, another German philosopher, the phenomenologist Max Scheler, captured this belief nicely when he observed that "the works of geniuses as a whole . . . 'grow' in history in the sense that all new works are created and add to the older ones, but without loss of any specific value of the earlier and older works." The "masterpiece of a genius," Scheler maintained, "offers us a vista into a microcosm," which is itself part of a totality (a macrocosm) united by a common soul. Like so many sides of a diamond, each successive work of genius was a further "revelation" that deepened and enriched the appearance of the whole.[29]

Scheler wrote these words in the early twentieth century while in the grip of his own philosophical concerns—and partially under the spell of what analysts were then openly calling the "religion of genius." But he entered into dialogue with early nineteenth-century authors to make the thoroughly Romantic point that in works of genius the particular and the universal were one. For Scheler, as for Blake, that identity made for an expansive and inclusive vision. All religions were one in the common human family, and all true geniuses were alike in their capacity to provide new "revelations"—a particular "disclosure of things, a welling up of their mysterious richness"—that allowed others to appreciate the profundity of the "being and essence of the world." Indeed, "for a genius it is his love of the world that becomes creative for his given view of the world." This love could set us free, providing "redemption from angst in life." Citing the great German poet Schiller, Scheler maintained that "it is only in a genius" that our "earthly angst" is dispelled.[30]

Some, on the other hand, construed the individual genius's capacity to incarnate and give voice to the whole in another, narrower way, and it was Herder who first articulated the conception most clearly. The genius, he insisted, could not be conceived apart from the people or nation in which he was rooted, for the genius was like a plant that grew in the soil of a particular culture and place. And given that individual poetic genius was, above all, a genius for language, it followed that the poet spoke not as a prophet for all places and times, but in the specific native tongue of his *Volk*. Shakespeare was the English genius par excellence precisely because he channeled the genius of the English people, capturing its cadences and rendering its idiom distinct. Homer did the same for the wild peoples of ancient Greece, while Ossian was the oracle of the ancient Scots, literally speaking for the people by committing their ballads to verse. In transcribing their genius, he assumed and became their voice.[31]

Herder, it should be stressed, was a pluralist by temperament, little inclined to rank peoples on the strength of their own particular genius. Nor did he conceive of peoples in racial terms. His own understanding of genius was conceived largely in response to what he regarded as the universal pretensions of French civilization and art, which imposed, with uniform standards of taste and aesthetic laws, an artificial formality on sincere and unaffected expression. True genius was spontaneous, Herder believed, natural and wild, and indeed, civilization was most often its enemy, killing off its vital source. The genius of the people would spend itself unless it was continually replenished and renewed.

But if Herder's own historicist vision was tolerant, self-consciously celebrating difference, his insistence that genius was embedded in the soil in which it grew begged the question of how to properly nourish the seed. If the genius was a product of the people, and if genius was born, not made, then did it not follow that it was bred in bloodlines and nourished by race? Though Herder did not pose this question, later observers did, analyzing the genius and the genius of the people according to hereditary laws that seemed to mandate struggle, domination, and control. Would the individual genius summon the collective power of the genius of the people to dominate other nations, even as he dominated his own? The example of Napoleon, on this view, was as terrifying as it was inspiring, recalling the ancient truth that creation and destruction were one.

There was another concern as well, with a history similarly ancient. For if the power that found a place at the throne of the poet's soul could turn him to despotism and oppression, it could also make him mad. "It is a great thing for a nation that it gets an articulate voice," Thomas Carlyle would later claim in the context of poetic and prophetic genius. But the prophet who gestured to the promised land might lead his people astray, veering into the wilderness where they were prey to demons, ending not in deliverance but in bondage and sin. To a much greater degree than their predecessors in the eighteenth century, the Romantics contemplated those specters, and in so doing they gave new voice to a set of old associations, linking genius further to madness and alienation, anguish and anomie, transgression and crime. The voice of one crying out in the wilderness, in thrall to a force that possessed it, could be both frightening and tragic in its despair.[32]

As early as 1819, the Romantic painter Eugène Delacroix was contemplating the fate of the Renaissance poet Torquato Tasso, who had been confined to an asylum against his will, mocked and abandoned in his madness, and tragically misunderstood. "What tears of rage and indignation he must have shed!" Delacroix wrote to a friend. "How his days must have dragged by, with the added pain of seeing them wasted in a lunatic's cell! One weeps for him; one moves restlessly in one's chair while reading his story; one's eyes gleam threatening, one clenches one's teeth." Delacroix conceived a painting of the subject to provoke a similar response, and the final version of 1839 aims to do just that. Confined to a madhouse and pining for a love he cannot have,

Tasso sits alone in his cell. His gaze is at once distracted and intense, suggesting inner isolation and withdrawal, a man seeking refuge in his mind. Manuscript pages are strewn about the floor. The poet pulls at one, absentmindedly, with his foot. Three intruders gawk at him from beyond the bars of the cell; one of them points to loose pages on the couch. A gesture of mockery and derision, or the misplaced homage of a "fan"? In either case, persecution and torment are the apparent consequence, and Tasso, bathed in celestial light in an otherwise dark space, suffers like a saint, or even Christ. His luminescent limbs and exposed chest recall the holy passions of the figures of El Greco. Driven to madness, a man abused and profoundly misunderstood, Tasso is a martyr—a martyr to genius, who must bear the cross of his own imagination.[33]

Such, at least, was the vision of Delacroix, the great French artist who has been described as the "Prince of Romanticism." And insofar as his painting captures a uniquely Romantic vision, it was true to its times, if not to Tasso's own. The poet himself, we can be sure, was never the perfect victim of Romantic legend. A pampered courtier whose brilliance was celebrated throughout his life, Tasso suffered all the same—from schizophrenia, some modern critics have speculated—and his spell in an asylum from 1579 to 1586 was no myth. Of his "genius" (*genio*) there can be little doubt— he was, in fact, among the very first men to use that term in the sense of a unique individual character or spirit, and he certainly possessed a genius of his own. The package proved hard for Romantics to resist. Hazlitt deemed Tasso's life "one of the most interesting in the world." Goethe wrote a play about him, *Torquato Tasso*, chronicling his persecution and creative struggles. Shelley wrestled with a tragedy of his own "on the subject of Tasso's madness," though he left behind only a few fragments. Byron, for his part, made a pilgrimage to the cell where Tasso was held and penned a lament in his honor, citing in the first of nine stanzas the

> *Long years of outrage, calumny, and wrong;*
> *Imputed madness, prison'd solitude,*
> *And the mind's canker in its savage mood.*

The poem, read in French translation, moved Delacroix deeply. The story of the poet's plight had a similar effect on the woman of letters Madame de Staël, who viewed Tasso, "persecuted, crowned, and dying of grief while still young on the eve of triumph," as a "superb example of all the splendors and of all the misfortunes of a great talent."[34]

Delacroix's painting, accordingly, was a perfect rendering of a Romantic archetype, the suffering genius, maligned and misunderstood, haunted to the point of madness by his creative gifts. The archetype was not without its precedents. The connection to melancholy and madness, after all, was as old as Plato's *furor poeticus* and the writings of Pseudo-Aristotle, and that connection had been reestablished and reinvigorated since the Renaissance. In the eighteenth century, too, an age well familiar with the classics, it was not uncommon to cite Democritus or Seneca, Horace or Longinus, on the mania that moved the poet, a practice that continued even after the language of the humors was abandoned in favor of new medical models that focused on the nerves as the source of mental instability. But if there was ever a touch of madness in the enthusiasm of genius, it was precisely the fear of an unrestrained enthusiasm—of the imagination run amok—that prompted Enlightenment authors to seek to contain it by means of judgment, reason, and taste. As the Scottish critic Alexander Gerard observed, making a point that was repeated time and again in the eighteenth century, natural genius "needs the assistance of taste to guide and moderate its exertions."[35]

The Romantics, it is true, did not do away with such talk entirely. But to a greater extent than their Enlightenment predecessors, they were comfortable with genius's natural wildness and enthusiasm, ready to countenance—even to celebrate—the potentially dangerous sources of creative power. "This is the beginning of all poetry," Friedrich Schlegel maintained, "to cancel the progression and laws of rationally thinking reason, to transplant us once again into the beautiful confusion of imagination and the primitive chaos of human nature. . . . The free-will of the poet submits to no law." Schiller echoed the sentiment, observing in his *Letters on the Aesthetic Education of Man* that "we know [genius] to border very closely on savagery." Genius was less a force to be contained than a power to be set free, and just as creativity and imagination could all too easily be suppressed by stultifying rules, the genius himself was forever threatened by those who lacked it. On this view, social convention, prevailing taste, and considered judgment were more apt to serve as shackles than as wise restraints. To be truly original, Romantic genius must liberate itself, laying down a law of its own, even at the risk of one's sanity.[36]

That, at any rate, was the pose. Very often it was nothing more. But even when such statements were merely rhetorical, they dramatized the creator's potential for conflict, for struggle with others and with himself. Beyond the ramparts of the self stalked philistines of the sort who had imprisoned Tasso, uncreative and unimaginative minds, slaves to convention who were hostile to greatness and who taunted, gawked,

FIGURE DI.₁. Mirabeau arriving at the Elysian Fields, greeted by Benjamin Franklin, Rousseau, Voltaire, and a host of ancient and modern geniuses. Engraving after Jean Michel Moreau le Jeune, 1792. *Copyright © RMN–Grand Palais / Art Resource, New York.*

FIGURE DI.₂. "I-doll-ization." A French representation of Benjamin Franklin from the eighteenth century, one of countless contemporary models, figurines, and images that responded to and fed the cult of genius. *Bridgeman-Giraudon / Art Resource, New York.*

FIGURE DI.₃. An image of Voltaire's sarcophagus and the cart used to "translate" his remains (minus his brain and heart) to the Panthéon in 1791. Voltaire's *genius* presides over him with a garland in hand, a symbol of his immortal genius. *Bibliothèque nationale de France.*

FIGURE DI.4. Genius leading genius. A *genius* burning with celestial fire leads Voltaire and Rousseau to the temple of glory and immortality, c. 1794. *Bibliothèque nationale de France.*

FIGURE DI.5. Genius trumps all. A French revolutionary playing card on which genius has assumed the place of kings, c. 1794. *Bibliothèque nationale de France.*

FIGURE DI.6. François Rude, *The Genius of the People*, early nineteenth century. The plaster model was likely a study for Rude's masterpiece *La Marseillaise* that now adorns the Arc de Triomphe in Paris, an image of the people triumphant. *Copyright © RMN–Grand Palais / Art Resource, New York.*

FIGURE D1.7. Jean-Baptiste Regnault, *Liberty or Death*, 1795. The "Genius of France" is suspended perilously between liberty and death. *Bpk, Berlin / Hamburger Kunsthalle, Hamburg / Hanne Moschkowitz / Art Resource, New York.*

FIGURE 4.1. Jean-Léon Gérôme, *Napoleon Before the Sphinx*, 1866. This celebration of Napoleon's ill-fated Egyptian campaign becomes a metaphor for the enigma of genius. *Courtesy Hearst Castle® / California State Parks.*

FIGURE 4.2. Antoine Aubert (*left*), *L'astre brillant*, 1813. Napoleon as master of the universe. The caption reads: "Brilliant and immense star, he enlightens, he enriches, and alone fashions, according to his will, the destinies of the world." *Copyright ©* *RMN–Grand Palais / Art Resource, New York.* FIGURE 4.3. The middle finger of Galileo's right hand. Galileo's body was exhumed in 1737, and three fingers, along with a vertebra and a tooth, were removed by admirers. The middle finger has been housed since 1927 at the Istituto e Museo di Storia della Scienza, Florence, which provided permission to use this picture.

FIGURE 4.4. Louis Édouard Fournier, *The Funeral of Shelley*, 1889. In this rendering of the 1822 cremation, Edward John Trelawny, the poet Leigh Hunt, and Byron are pictured from left to right. *Courtesy National Museums Liverpool.*

FIGURE 4.5. Eugène Delacroix, *Tasso in the Madhouse*, 1839. The martyrdom of genius. *Collection Oskar Reinhart "Am Römerholz," Winterthur, Switzerland.*

FIGURE 4.6. Caspar David Friedrich, *Wanderer Above a Sea of Fog*, c. 1816. The vision of Romantic genius: solitude and transcendence, individuality and mystical communion with nature, spirit, or "the one." *Bpk, Berlin / Hamburger Kunsthalle, Hamburg / Elke Walford / Art Resource, New York.*

Das ift mein lieber Sohn an dem ich Wohlgefallen habe

FIGURE 4.7. Evil genius. The German caption to this anonymous caricature of Napoleon is a dark play on Martin Luther's translation of Matthew 17:5: "This is my beloved son, with whom I am well pleased." *Napoleonmuseum, Thurgau, Switzerland.*

FIGURE 4.8. Dante Gabriel Rossetti, *How They Met Themselves*, 1851–1860. The theme of the doppelgänger, which fascinated Rossetti and many others of the age, was a nineteenth-century iteration of the venerable notion of the spiritual double. *Copyright © Fitzwilliam Museum, Cambridge / Art Resource, New York.*

FIGURE 4.9. Josef Danhauser, *Franz Liszt at the Piano*, 1840. Genius worshipping genius. Liszt, Alexandre Dumas, George Sand, and the Countess Marie d'Agoult (all seated) are joined by Hector Berlioz, Niccolò Paganini, and Gioachino Rossini (all standing) in reverent homage before the bust of Beethoven. A painting of Byron on the wall completes the image of what Germans would later describe as the "brotherhood of genius" (notwithstanding the two women depicted here), the universal fellowship of the saints. *Bpk, Berlin / Nationalgalerie, Staatliche Museen, Berlin, Germany / Jürgen Liepe / Art Resource, New York.*

and persecuted deviation from the norm. These were the figures who gave weight to Christ's words that a prophet was honored everywhere except in his own country and house. Many failed to recognize genius even in their midst. Was not Mozart buried in a pauper's grave? Did not the English poet Thomas Chatterton die, neglected, in a garret? Tasso was hardly alone. "The history of great men is always a martyrology: when they are not sufferers from the great human race, they suffer for their own greatness," the German critic Heinrich Heine declared. He was echoing a line of the French poet Lamartine: "Every genius is a martyr."[37]

Schopenhauer developed that same contention at length in an influential account, describing "suffering" as the "essential martyrdom of genius." Geniuses were often regarded as "useless" and "unprofitable" in the eyes of the world, he claimed, and they were subject themselves to "violent emotions and irrational passions" that rendered them unfit for normal human dealings." Geniuses felt too much, they saw too much, and they saw what others did not. As Schopenhauer added later in developing the point, "the genius perceives a world different from [ordinary men], though only by looking more deeply into the world that lies before them also." It was that very capacity of penetration and insight that allowed the genius to expose hidden truths in his creation, and in so revealing, to redeem. The genius suffered, like all martyrs, so that others could be healed. He sacrificed himself so that those, now blind, could see. Through the soothing balm of his creation, men and women could suspend the restless cravings of the will-to-life that moves through us all and know a measure of transcendence and peace.[38]

The martyrdom of genius necessarily entailed rejection. Even Christ had been denied and had perished on the cross, believing himself forsaken by his Father. In the genius's alienation and the alleged miscomprehension of his contemporaries lay the basis for a powerful trope—the Romantic trope of the misunderstood genius, unappreciated or undervalued in his—or her—own lifetime. This trope, in fact, lent itself particularly well to the case of women, who could complain with justice that their merits were undervalued, where not entirely ignored. The heroine of Madame de Staël's novel *Corinne* (1807), a genius who bears a distinct resemblance to Staël herself, dramatizes the plight of the brilliant woman in an uncomprehending world. It was, regardless of sex, a general Romantic theme. As Isaac Disraeli, the father of future British prime minister Benjamin Disraeli and author of an important book on the character of men of genius, declared, "the occupations, the amusements, and the ardour of the man of genius are at discord with the artificial habits of life," with the result that "the genius in society is often in a state of suffering." Such suffering was painful in itself, but it could also have the effect of precluding geniuses from fully realizing their gifts. The Scottish poet Robert Burns was one such figure, at least in the reckoning of Thomas Carlyle, whose own influential *On Heroes, Hero-Worship and the Heroic in History* played a crucial role in popularizing the Romantic cult of genius in the nineteenth century. Despite being "a giant Original Man" and "the most gifted British soul" of his age, Burns's tragically short life was lived largely in penury and oblivion. And in his final years, when he received a modicum of the recognition he deserved, things were no better. Disturbing Burns's tranquility and disrupting his work, "Lion-hunters" stalked the literary lion. They were, Carlyle alleged, "the ruin and the death" of him.[39]

Carlyle's complaint that Burns was first underappreciated and then appreciated too much speaks to the dilemma of the modern celebrity, who is forever in the public eye, but never really seen. Rousseau, a Romantic hero, had nursed a similar complaint, and in the nineteenth century both Byron and Beethoven did, too. On one level, theirs was a perfectly natural response to the unprecedented pressures of acclaim—pressures that those who were deemed geniuses within their lifetimes, such as Byron and Beethoven, experienced with a particular intensity. For the very definition of the original genius was that the genius was original—unique, singular, one of a kind. It was a priceless quality in an economy of fame, as Beethoven cheekily explained to his patron, Prince Lichnowsky, in asserting the rights of the new aristocracy of genius: "Prince! What you are, you are by circumstance and birth. What I am, I am through myself. Of princes there have been and will be thousands. Of Beethovens there is only one." But although such singularity was precious, it could make for dramatic isolation, a position highlighted in Romantic painting, where the "lonely genius" is often set apart, portrayed as solitary and distinct. And it could also make for prying eyes, which peered into the private lives of geniuses as they were exposed in a flourishing literary press. The revelation of Byron's originality—which included sleeping with his half-sister and a gaggle of other people's wives—got him hounded out of London; scandal and celebrity followed him across Europe in a way that slowly took its toll. As Byron himself observed, after invoking the Pseudo-Aristotelian association of melancholy with men of eminence: "Whether I am a Genius or not, I have been called such by my friends as well as enemies, and in more countries and languages than one, and also within a not very long period of existence. Of my Genius, I can say nothing, but of my melancholy that it is 'increasing and ought to be diminished.' But how?"[40]

Byron was aware that his own melancholy was a product, in part, of his celebrity. But that awareness did not prevent him from universalizing his particular condition. Geniuses were inherently prone to madness and despair, he said, and poets, especially, were a "marked race," destined for disappointment, misunderstanding, and neglect, regardless of whether they were discovered or not. The simultaneous complaint that geniuses were both underappreciated and appreciated too much was, in part, an authentic response to the dilemma of nascent celebrity. But it was also a paradox and a pose, an unresolved contradiction. Was the genius a martyr, or the master of humanity? An individual alienated from the many, or the apple of their eyes? A legislator of the world, or a hero unacknowledged and brought to despair? The Romantics could never really say for sure, because they wanted it both ways.

Which is only fitting: genius, like the "self" of the poet Walt Whitman, contained multitudes—contrasting and at times conflicting voices. As Carlyle affirmed, that worked to the genius's advantage. "It is the first property of genius to grow in spite of contradiction," he noted. "The vital germ pushes itself through the dull soil." Romantic genius nourished itself in this way, working through contradictions both external and internal. Externally, a variety of impediments—from the pressures of social conformity to public incomprehension and alienation—were ready to divert the shoots of the Romantic self, but internally, dangerous cankers and diseases threatened to attack the stalk at its root. Madness was the most common of these threats, treated as all but inseparable from genius itself. The "constant transition into madness" from the suffering of genius, Schopenhauer explained, was not only apparent from the "biographies of great men" (he cited Rousseau and Byron as examples), but also put on display in institutional settings. "I must mention having found, on frequent visits to lunatic asylums, individual subjects endowed with unmistakable gifts," he wrote. It was evidence, he believed, of the "direct contact between genius and madness." More to the point, it was a sign of the times, for pathological genius was becoming an important subject of medical and psychological investigation. And though the language of the laboratory and the asylum did not always register in a Romantic key, it tended nonetheless to reaffirm a common assertion: genius and madness shared a necessary connection. Mental instability was an essential aspect of the martyrdom of genius. If genius was a gift, it was also a curse.[41]

In accentuating and bringing to the fore the long-standing association between genius and mental affliction, the Romantics updated its
image, giving it a new style and "look." An intensely brooding Beethoven, wild-eyed with wild hair, replaced the dreamy melancholia of the
Renaissance sage, just as the tortured, restless striving of a Byron could
stand in for the fury of the *furor poeticus*. Romantics were quick to trace
their own associations onto the past (as their use of the image of Tasso
nicely conveys), finding persecuted geniuses throughout human history.
But at the same time, they partook of history's bequests, enhancing their
own image, if only indirectly, by reference to a venerable association. The
ancient link between genius and madness hinted at a connection to the
specially chosen one, the poet or prophet or ecstatic seer who channeled
the voice of the divine. Madness continued to hint at a form of possession, suggesting that those in thrall to genius were in the grip of a greater
power.[42]

Yet the contradictions of madness were such that it was never easy to
distinguish the devil from the divine. In the ranting of one's own mind,
a ghost might be taken for an angel, a demon for a genius, the voice of
Satan for the voice of God. The Romantics faced that possibility head on.
Gazing fixedly at Delacroix's painting of Tasso, the French poet Charles
Baudelaire glimpsed something of this confusion, seeing a "genius,
imprisoned in an unhealthy hovel," haunted by "swarms of ghosts,"
intoxicating laughter, doubts and fear, and strange cries that reverberated
from the walls of his dungeon. Well acquainted with hallucinations and
the seductions of evil, Baudelaire interpreted the painting as a struggle of
the soul, the imagination's battle with reality. The great Italian Romantic
poet Giacomo Leopardi also detected genius—and a *genius*—in Tasso's
plight. In his *Dialogo di Torquato Tasso e del suo genio familiare*, Leopardi
presents a dialogue between the imprisoned bard and his tutelary spirit
(*suo genio familiare*) as a metaphor for a man who is tormented by delusions. It is a Romantic rendering of the temptations of the saint in his
cell. Tasso conceives initially of his *genius* as a source of comfort. "My
mind has grown accustomed to talking to itself," he confesses during
the course of a long conversation. "I almost feel as though there were
people in my head arguing with one another." But when Tasso inquires
where the *genius* normally resides so that he may summon him again, the
spirit reveals that he is a figment of his mind. "You have not found out
yet?" "In qualche liquore generoso," comes the answer: "In some robust
drink." A spirit who dwells in strong spirits—or a vile of opium—this is
a genie in a bottle of a different kind, a dark *genius* who preys on genius
in place of granting a wish, disturbing the creative mind.[43]

Leopardi's conjuring, like Baudelaire's poetic sighting of ghosts, was by no means an isolated occurrence. With their penchant for the Gothic and ghoulish, Romantic artists frequently summoned spirits, and their indulgence in mind-altering drugs, such as opium and hashish, meant that they occasionally saw them. Many also evinced a strong interest in esoterism and the occult. But even when they summoned spirits only as a literary device, they gestured at something putatively real, a world of forces that lurked about us and in us, too, forces sinister, frightening, and portentous, beckoning and tempting with not just madness, but perversion, death, and crime. Close to genius hovered evil genius, his ominous brother and twin.

The Romantics, in fact, rediscovered that ancient creature. Calling him in from the dark night of the past, they gave him a new name. Critics have tended to overlook the point, but the Romantic doppel-gänger is an evil demon in modern dress, a more recent iteration of a fig-ure who had haunted humanity for centuries. The word, first coined in German in 1796 by the poet Jean Paul, literally means a "double-goer," and soon it was being used to signify a ghostly double who shadows the self. Heinrich Heine's poem of that name—hauntingly set to music by Franz Schubert in 1828, the year of the composer's death—is perhaps the best-known example of a Romantic work using this concept, with its dark account of a man who encounters his double writhing in the still of night before the house of a departed lover. But it is a common device of the period. E. T. A. Hoffmann, for example, employs a doppelgänger in his novel *The Devil's Elixir* (1815–1816) to symbolize the evil, madness, and sinister fate that plagues the work's protagonist, a Capuchin monk gone astray. Goethe writes in his autobiography *Dichtung und Wahrheit* of encountering his doppelgänger riding toward him on horseback. Shelley, too, makes use of the figure, writing in *Prometheus Unbound* of the magus Zoroaster, who "met his own image walking in the garden." Through him Zoroaster catches a glimpse of the other world beyond our own, a sinister world that

> *Is underneath the grave, where do inhabit*
> *The shadows of all forms that think and live*
> *Till death unite them and they part no more.*
> (ACT I.197–199)

And in Mary Shelley's masterpiece, *Frankenstein, Or the Modern Prometheus*—written in partial collaboration with Shelley himself—the theme of the doppelgänger is central to the text, with the monster serving as Dr. Frankenstein's alter ego and second self, a creation of his mind run amok.[44]

It is significant that Frankenstein's progeny is born of his "monstrous imagination," the product of an "enthusiastic frenzy" coupled with a deep interest in science and knowledge of the occult. For though the doppelgänger might in principle appear to anyone, Romantic authors were particularly sensitive to the threat that the evil genius posed to geniuses themselves. The very powers of creativity, imagination, and insight that could endow a genius with prophetic skills could also lead him astray. So does Viktor Frankenstein fall prey to what he describes as an "evil influence, the angel of destruction, which asserted omnipotent sway over me," cowing his more benevolent "guardian angel." Intrigued as a child by the works of occult philosophers (Agrippa, Albertus Magnus, Paracelsus), Frankenstein's incipient interest is later encouraged as a young man at the University of Ingolstadt in Bavaria, where he pursues research into the life force, the *Lebenskraft* that many Germans associated with the vital force of genius. "Whence, I often asked myself, did the principle of life proceed? It was a bold question, and one which has ever been considered as a mystery; yet with how many things are we upon the brink of becoming acquainted, if cowardice or carelessness did not restrain our inquiries." Undaunted, Frankenstein succeeds in harnessing the vital power of genius, loosing on the world the terrible creature of his own creation.[45]

A parable of the dangers of the misdirected mind, *Frankenstein* is thus a rumination on the potentially destructive power of genius. It was, in fact, one of a number of works taking up the theme in the aftermath of the French Revolution, an event that could be made to underscore the urgency of the point. The German novelist Carl Grosse's aptly titled *Der Genius*, for example, written between 1791 and 1795 and translated into English as the *Horrid Mysteries*, describes a lurid plot by conspirators who traffic with a supernatural being (the *Genius* of the title) to bring about a violent revolution of the sort that Maistre attributed to the "infernal genius" of Robespierre. Grosse's novel, like the conspiracy theories favored by Maistre, played on the fact that in the 1770s an actual conspiracy of Enlightenment radicals—the so-called Bavarian Illuminati—had been exposed in the German university town of Ingolstadt with the goal of toppling thrones and altars across Europe, unleashing the monster of revolution. Ingolstadt, not coincidentally, was the very town where Shelley's Dr. Frankenstein gave birth to his monster. The association in all of these cases was clear. Genius—evil genius—had called to life a raging, ravaging beast. The power of the creator was also the power to destroy.[46]

Napoleon served a similarly cautionary purpose. In England, especially—France's archrival throughout the Napoleonic Wars—the Corsican general was regularly denigrated as an evil genius and despot who showed just how far a man could fall from great heights. Coleridge considered him to be the perfect illustration of his celebrated assertion, in the *Biographia Literaria* (1817), that in "times of tumult," men of "commanding genius" are "destined to come forth as the shaping spirit of ruin, to destroy the wisdom of ages in order to substitute the fancies of a day, and to change kings and kingdoms, as the wind shifts and shapes the clouds." Napoleon was one of those "mighty hunters of Mankind" who had stalked the world since Nimrod. Coleridge continually likened him to Satan. Others were more forgiving. "Angel or Devil, what does it matter!" Victor Hugo demanded. The genius of Napoleon transcended such opposition. Napoleon was an artist, Hugo ventured, a Michelangelo of war, a man of imagination and creativity forced to contend with the same inertia, misunderstanding, and mediocrity that plagued other Romantic geniuses. Nor was the thought confined to his admirers. François-René de Chateaubriand, long an opponent, described Napoleon as "a poet in action," sublime in his imagination, tragic in his downfall. Even Coleridge could hail the "Poet Bonaparte" early in his rule.[47]

The image of Napoleon as a Promethean artist—one who struggled to realize a grand vision, only to be foiled by fate and those around him—was widely received in the aftermath of his defeat, when he became, for many, a symbol of noble striving and shattered dreams. The association was flattering to artists—Napoleon, it seemed, was one of them!—but it also served to dramatize on a grand scale what both the Romantics and many of their critics were inclined to believe about the fortunes of genius itself. To be an original involved breaking rules and flouting norms, legislating for oneself in ways that, as Diderot had observed in *Rameau's Nephew*, invariably put the genius at odds with the world around him. The power that moved through the person of vision and foresight, like a dark *genius*, a doppelgänger, or an ill-fated star, might lead him to places others dared not go. That was the privilege of genius, but also its perdition.

The thought expressed itself in various forms, from the world-historical heights of Napoleon's streaking comet down to the more intimate nether-regions of the soul. If geniuses were "originals," they were also "freaks," deviants, monsters, departures from the norm. Byron's congenital clubfoot called attention to that dubious distinction, as did the scandals of his sexual life, which seemed to lay bare a dark inner energy. A man who slept repeatedly with other men's wives, with relatives, and, it was whispered, with other men, was not like others. He violated taboos and crossed lines that nature kept distinct. He was strange, peculiar, queer. Historians of gender and sexuality, in fact, have noted that even as the genius was conceived as a predominately male ideal, coursing with virile energy, geniuses were often credited with a number of "feminine" traits. Their alleged volatility and lack of self-control, their "enthusiastic" or hysterical fits, their capacity for heightened sensitivity and feelings, were qualities commonly attributed to women, who likewise shared an essential fecundity, fertility, and active imagination. Coleridge's claim that "a great mind must be androgynous" thus reflected a sense of the genius's peculiar place between the sexes, a position that could be used to accentuate difference and also highlight a propensity for "deviance." In this same set of associations one finds the seeds of a suspicion that would later be voiced more openly: that geniuses—whether effeminate dandies, such as Oscar Wilde and Marcel Proust, or masculine women, such as George Sand and Gertrude Stein—displayed a particular tendency to homosexuality or the overt crossing of gender lines.[48]

The claim that geniuses were inclined to contest gender and sexual norms was an iteration of a more general theme. The same boldness and originality that led them to challenge conventional thinking in art and science might entail a broader rebelliousness against established authorities of all kinds. This antisocial propensity could take relatively benign forms—from mild eccentricity to outlandish dress to the innocuous flamboyance of the dandy. But more deviant behavior was ever a temptation. The genius's inherent tendency to mental instability could advance more dangerously from mild neurosis or obsession to "moral insanity," a condition whose ultimate expression was crime. Madness, deviance, and criminality, in fact, would come to be understood in medical accounts as specific symptoms of genius. Those same links were further elaborated in a flourishing nineteenth-century crime literature that glorified the criminal mastermind and aestheticized criminal activity. Villainy, in such writing, became a form of art, and crime more generally a privilege of the great. The criminal mastermind in Honoré de Balzac's *Père Goriot*, for example, is a genius who thinks of himself as a "poet," and Sherlock Holmes's archnemesis, Professor Moriarty, is the "Napoleon of Crime," a "genius, a philosopher, an abstract thinker."[49]

Yet even before such intriguing clues turned up at fictional crime scenes or surfaced in the formal diagnoses of physicians, the connection between genius and transgression was being explored by the poets, philosophers, and artists of the Romantic generation. Together, they gave credence to the claim in *Rameau's Nephew* that "it is impossible to refuse a certain consideration to the great criminal." Goethe, who oversaw the first translation and publication of that work, made precisely such consideration the main theme of his rewriting of *Faust*, a tale whose titular protagonist moves from science to magic to Mephistopheles in order to satisfy his craving for total knowledge. Mephistopheles is an incarnation of the devil, of course, and he gives Faust what he wants, but at the cost of the mortal's soul and innocent lives. The wager dramatizes a line attributed to Goethe about himself: "There is no crime of which I cannot imagine myself the author." Evil may lurk in every man, but the genius was more fertile in his imaginings, and more creative in his license. As the fellow-traveling Romantic Ralph Waldo Emerson declared with the example of Napoleon at hand, "There is no crime to the intellect." All might be justified by the rational and rationalizing mind.[50]

In the case of genius, however, there was more at stake than simply a creative conscience. For geniuses were exceptional men, and exceptional men were by definition exceptions—in morality as in art. As Hegel put it, towering from his philosophical heights, "a mighty figure must trample many an innocent flower under foot, and destroy much that lies in its path." What would seem like crime to some was in truth the privilege and duty of the great; the violence of destruction but the precondition of higher creation for which the ends absolved the means. Geniuses, self-legislating, were above the laws that governed ordinary men. They followed a law of their own.[51]

Such exceptional privilege entailed exceptional burdens and pains. It is a point that the dramas of Napoleon and Faust underscored. Life and art blurred in their work, and in the continual reenactment and retelling, both figures achieved a mythic status and the status of myth, becoming archetypes like Prometheus, whose superhuman strivings they shared. For Prometheus, too, was a criminal, and no less a Romantic hero, breaking the law to serve another. Stealing from the gods in the service of mankind, he was all the more noble for the suffering he endured in punishment for his audacity. He should, in justice, be absolved. Prometheus unbound. Shelley, who wrote a play of that name, said much the same of Satan, as John Milton had in *Paradise Lost*. The greatest of the fallen angels, Satan, "as a moral being," was "far superior to his God," Shelley claimed. He was a moving case of one who "perseveres in some purpose which he has conceived to be excellent in spite of adversity and torture." If even Satan should be forgiven his crimes, surely Faust must be saved as well, and so, too, Napoleon, who, in Byron's phrase, "strew'd our earth with hostile bones," and then languished in the island captivity of genius. Napoleon became a figure of pity and fascination, with millions of bodies still fresh in their graves—a tragic case of the genius thwarted, who yearned, it was said, only to save his people, only to redeem.[52]

B UT HOW AGAIN TO ACCOUNT for this contradictory force that could make of Satan a saint? This peculiar power that transformed men into prophets and crime into art, that ruled in rejection, and triumphed in despair? What was it, finally, that men of genius possessed? What possessed them? What devil could it be? The ancients had broached these questions, and Christians had followed them, likewise seeking answers in the divine. And though moderns tended to obscure the fact, they, too, sought recourse in a sacred language, redolent of enthusiasm and awe. What was true of the Age of Enlightenment was even truer of the poets and artists of the first third of the nineteenth century, who, to a greater and more self-conscious extent than their predecessors, charged the language of genius with a religious resonance and elemental power, multiplying its sublime mysteries.

Goethe provides a perfect example, for, looking back at the end of his long life in the 1830s, and attempting to answer the question of what it was that moved the greatest men, he thought he could detect in nature, in both the animate and the inanimate, in beings and objects with souls and without, "something which manifests itself only in contradictions, and which, therefore, could not be comprehended under any idea, still less under one word. It was not godlike, for it seemed unreasonable; not human, for it had no understanding; nor devilish, for it was beneficent; nor angelic, for it often betrayed a malicious pleasure. It resembled chance, for it evolved no consequences; it was like Providence, for it hinted at connexion." Even a man with the verbal skills of Goethe found it difficult to describe this mysterious force—a force that "contracted time and extended space," mediated opposites, and conflated the sacred and the profane. Yet the name he gave it was familiar. "To this principle, which seemed to come in between all other principles to separate them, and yet to link them together, I gave the name of Daemonic (*Dämonisch*), after the example of the ancients and of those who, at any rate, had perceptions of the same kind."[53]

By invoking the ancients and settling on the name that he did, Goethe entered into a conversation that was as old as speculation about Socrates's *daimonion*. That conversation had long focused on a central question—What was the nature of the force that attended extraordinary individuals?—and in the eighteenth century, Goethe's friends, the philosophers Hamann and Herder, had posed the question in the case of Socrates and arrived at competing answers. For Hamann, Socrates's *daimonion* was the voice of divinatory power and the sign of a man possessed. Socrates was a Christian prophet *avant la lettre*, a vessel who spoke the word of God. Herder, by contrast, preferred to think of the Socratic *daimonion* as a possession, an indwelling power or *Kraft* akin to the vital force present in men of genius. In Herder's lexicon, *Dämon* and *Dämonisch* were often used synonymously with genius (*Genie*), implying gifts of nature rather than gifts of heaven (*Himmelsgabe*). But whether Socrates was a possessor or a man possessed, he lay claim to a power that made him a marked man, a being chosen by nature or nature's God who was fundamentally different and distinct. To have what Socrates had was to be like no other. In this he was a model of a kind.[54]

Goethe was profoundly influenced by this dialogue, taking from it something from both his friends. And so it is hardly surprising that elsewhere he relates the "Daemonic" to genius and geniuses, raising the subject in several important conversations with his amanuensis Johann Peter Eckermann in the final years of his life. "The Daemonic," he insists, is "that which cannot be explained by Reason or Understanding; it lies not in my nature, but I am subject to it." It is a force, he says, that "manifests itself in the most varied manner throughout nature—in the visible and in the invisible." It is often present in the arts, in poetry, especially, and music too, and is evident in religious worship, where it is "one of the chief means of working upon men miraculously." Finally, and most importantly, the "Daemonic loves to throw itself into significant individuals," who possess and are possessed by this mysterious force. Goethe speaks of the Daemonic in both modes, emphasizing its bodily presence—as in Byron's magnetic, sexual attraction, or Napoleon's physical robustness, his ability to work at great length without food or sleep—and also its "out of body" origins. "No productiveness of the highest kind," he insists, "no remarkable discovery, no great thought that bears fruits and has results, is in the power of anyone; such things are above earthly control. Man must consider them an unexpected gift from above." Genius is "like the daemon, which does with [an individual] what it pleases," and "in such cases, man may often be considered an instrument in the higher government of the world—a vessel worthy to contain the influence of the divine."[55]

With his vague suggestion that genius was, as he put it, "something divine," Goethe not only echoed Cicero's definition of the elusive *divinum quiddam* but also summarized several decades of Romantic speculation. Goethe himself was never a Romantic, strictly speaking. A genuine original, he resists easy classification. Yet as an oracle and observer of his age, few possessed a keener sense of the vital forces that moved it, and here he channeled one of its most vital. Genius was something divine, and the genius, as its bearer, might be considered an instrument of providence—a prophet, an apostle, a hierophant. These were the terms in which Germans, especially, had spoken of the genius for decades, and in the remainder of the nineteenth century, the category would take on enormous popular influence there, emanating outward from art and philosophy to become a key concept in the culture as a whole. But its impact was felt everywhere that Romanticism had a voice. In the genius's person, something sacred moved and spoke, disclosing itself through him. Geniuses created, revealed, and redeemed, providing salvation and new life. Geniuses forged a link to something beyond themselves—to the eternal, the meaningful, the transcendent, the true.[56]

In such widespread Romantic convictions lay the basis of what later commentators would call explicitly the "religion of genius," a religion in which—as one of its most zealous proselytizers, Thomas Carlyle, put it with an annoying contempt for the standard rules of capitalization—"Great Men are the inspired (speaking and acting) Texts of that divine BOOK OF REVELATIONS, whereof a Chapter is completed from epoch to epoch, and by some named HISTORY." David Friedrich Strauss, a theologian and biographer of Jesus, was less cryptic when he observed, in 1838, that "the only cult which is left over from the religious debris of the preceding cults for the educated of our time is the cult of genius." The religion of genius was a religion for those who were departing from religion, a replacement and response, though it proved to be accepting of the old believers. A few Christians might still protest when, in the same year that Strauss wrote, church bells were rung at the unveiling of a statue of Friedrich Schiller in Stuttgart during a festival celebrating his life. Others muttered complaints of "idol worship." But many would make a place for the new faith, in time. As Strauss himself alleged, Jesus, too, was a genius.[57]

Yet if genius was a conduit for the divine, it expressed itself in bodies. Goethe's ruminations on this aspect of the vital force—its Daemonic bursts of productivity, its vigor in youth—echoed the interests of Humboldt and Herder in the *Lebenskraft* while gesturing toward a pressing question and concern. Just what sort of bodies did the Daemonic deign to inhabit? What kind of vessels could contain it? And where might these vessels appear? The religious devotion to genius begged the scientific question of what conditioned and determined its nature. In theory, the power might reveal itself anywhere, and among many different kinds of men. As Goethe explained, "whether a man shows himself a genius in science, like Oken and Humboldt, or in war and statesmanship, like Frederick and Peter the Great and Napoleon, or whether he composes a song like Béranger—it all comes to the same thing." Genius was a force common to all these individuals, and a range of others besides: Byron, Raphael, Mozart, Shakespeare, Dürer, Holbein, and the unnamed architects of the Strasbourg and Cologne cathedrals. And yet, as Goethe's examples illustrate, genius seemed to have a fetish for the bodies of European men, born in advanced European states. That "fact" was at odds with the theory of natural genius, according to which the power had little to do with place. If anything, genius ought to favor cultures in their infancy—states wild, rough, and rude, the primitive, unspoiled places like that which gave birth to Homer. Herder had made this point in the eighteenth century, as did others, concurring with the English critic William Jackson, who claimed that "the early stage of society . . . is most favorable to Genius." William Duff, who believed that original genius would "in general be displayed in its utmost vigour in the early and uncultivated periods of Society," was even so broadminded as to look to the East for examples. But in the nineteenth century, such breadth of vision was increasingly rare. The religion of genius was a European faith, and the science that evolved to explain it would confirm its myth of origins and primacy of place.[58]

CHAPTER V

GENIOLOGY

Ｈow can we detect the presence of genius? Do we know it when we see it? Or is it a secret of those in the know? The eighteenth century offered conflicting answers to these questions. The Romantics added to the confusion, conceiving of genius both as an unmistakable fact—as overwhelming as a Beethoven symphony or a Napoleonic frontal assault—and as a subtle nod to the knowing, missed by the many, acknowledged by the few. True, neither conception did justice to the complexity of the process by which genius is made—a process involving promoters and critics, publicists and the public at large. And appearances could be deceiving. What looked like the lightning strike of genius today might prove in time to be a flash in the pan. Or authentic genius might hide itself, assuming shapes that the genius's contemporaries failed to perceive. The undiscovered genius—the genius unacknowledged—was both a Romantic fantasy and a Romantic fear. Fed by tales of martyrs allegedly spurned in their lifetime, or driven to the margins, like Van Gogh, the fantasy (and fear) persisted well into the twentieth century. The contrasting myth of the epiphany of genius—genius that imposes itself with a force impossible to deny—also endured, and together these two ways of seeing played a powerful role in maintaining the mystery of a being who was at once hidden and manifest, difficult to detect and everywhere to see.[1]

Yet at the same time that artists and writers were generating these cultural perspectives, natural scientists in Europe and the New World were straining to see genius in different ways, identifying its presence and cataloging its traits. Rejecting the conceit that true genius was invisible to the many, as well as the view that it was plain for all to see, many sought instead to isolate genius in scientific criteria—criteria that could

be located in the body and described objectively in medical, psychological, and statistical terms. These researchers and theorists included physiognomists and phrenologists, such as the Swiss pastor Johann Caspar
Lavater and the German-born Franz Joseph Gall; doctors and physicians,
including the Frenchman Jacques-Joseph Moreau and the Italian Cesare
Lombroso; and experts in the measurement of achievement and intelligence, such as the Englishman Francis Galton, the Frenchman Alfred
Binet, and the American Lewis Terman. Genius must not be a mystery,
they contended, but a fact, a "thing," whose features could be measured,
whose symptoms could be diagnosed, whose incidence could be charted
and graphed. Granting scientific authority to the belief that the genius
was a wondrous exception to the rules, they further consecrated the
inequality and privilege of genius in the modern world. Paradoxically,
however, in pursuing research to this end, they contributed more to their
subject's mystification than to its unveiling or disenchantment. In seeking to free the genius from superstition, they succeeded in enchanting
him to a greater extent than ever before.

I F ASKED TO DESCRIBE what a genius looks like, most of us would
probably respond by way of a tautology. Genius looks like genius, we
believe, or at least like one of its well-known exemplars: a bust of Beethoven atop a Steinway, an Einstein with his shock of white hair, a Jackson Pollock dancing over a splattered canvas. At the time of the genius's
birth in the eighteenth century, the response would have been much the
same. For although insiders, such as Rousseau, might profess a gnostic
belief in the mystic communion of the saints—"Don't ask, young artist,
what genius is . . . either you have it or you don't"—the *grand public* was
generally more inclined to take genius at face value. In the images that
adorned the age—of Newton, Shakespeare, Franklin, or Rousseau—
eighteenth-century men and women did so literally, confronting genius
head-on.

What did they see? It helps to bear in mind that in the days before
photography, it was not easy to establish a certain likeness, and even
now, it remains impossible to know for sure what Newton, Shakespeare,
Franklin, or Rousseau really looked like. The fact calls attention to the
art of crafting an image, an art that was cultivated quite self-consciously
by portrait painters and draftsmen well into the nineteenth century.
Such artists delighted in representing genius in a variety of stylized
poses modeled on the iconography of religious painting. But what if one
looked more closely? Might it be possible to discern, captured in the
canvas or directly in the flesh, genius's objective features? Or to make

out its common characteristics and traits? Perhaps the features of genius could be isolated with precision, or made to yield a composite sketch. Perhaps the face of genius might be rendered by science in all its glorious perfection.²

That, in effect, was the aim of Johann Caspar Lavater, the Swiss Protestant minister and genius enthusiast who, in addition to his other talents, was the founder of physiognomy, the art of reading the face. We are quick to dismiss physiognomy today as an outmoded method of inquiry, a primitive and vaguely amusing relic of the past. But it exerted an important influence on nineteenth-century culture and, in particular, on the search for a science of genius. Indeed, in his multivolume *Physiognomische fragmente*, published between 1775 and 1778, Lavater followed up an ecstatic paean to genius as "prophet, priest, and king" with an attempt to sketch its contours and shapes. In his view, a power of such radiance could not help but reveal itself in the flesh. The face of genius would be marked by signs.³

Of course, it took a special eye to read the revelations, a "physiognomic genius" most subtle.⁴ Lavater quoted Rousseau to suggest, none-too-subtly, that he himself had what it took to know. When in possession of such a gift, cultivated by the appropriate training, a physiognomist of genius such as Lavater could readily single out the features and discern the signs. He focused, fittingly, on the lamp of the soul. "Geniuses have stars of order (*Ordenstern*) in their eyes," Lavater declared cryptically, emphasizing that the eyes of geniuses were distinct, set apart not only by their "glance, fire, light, and juice" but also by their "outer shape." That last feature was "essential for genius," though it was subtle and difficult to detect. Even painters of quality overlooked it. Other features were easier to see. "Intensive geniuses" (those who focused on one subject) were strong-boned, with "firm flesh"; they were also "slower and heavier in their movements" and had more pronounced foreheads than "extensive geniuses," who tended to have elongated faces, and were by comparison delicate, light, and loosely built. Then again, "there are many kinds of foreheads and shapes," Lavater observed, "of which you can say for sure that they are not built for genius." He illustrated the point with a series of sketches revealing "stupidity in a high degree," facial "flabbiness without any tension," and other deficiencies. A pair of drawings of Voltaire, by contrast, was supplied to illustrate how a genius should appear.

Lavater's two major treatises on physiognomy are filled with such musings. The face of Descartes, for example, clearly reveals his universal genius. "A physiognomy like his cannot possibly be misunderstood," Lavater writes. Similarly, "in all the works of Rubens, you feel the spirit

of his own physiognomy piercing through," whereas "the vast and powerful genius of Shakespeare" is "reproduced in characters perfectly legible
in each of the four parts of his face." Had Newton never written a single
equation, "we should want nothing now but his portrait, to assure us of
his deserving to be ranked among the greatest geniuses."[5]

Observations of this kind make clear that Lavater's own "genius" lay
in his ability to tell people what they thought they already knew. Like
a skilled astrologist or fortuneteller, he knew what they wanted to hear.
To fail to recognize signs of genius even after they had been pointed
out was to confess to one's blindness. Genius looked like genius, after
all. The truths of physiognomy were self-confirming, made manifest in
a simple wrinkle or a line. That said, Lavater was prepared to acknowledge in his more candid moments that it was easy to be fooled. "The
most transcendent physiognomic genius will be frequently in danger
of deceiving himself, and of misleading those who implicitly confide in
him," he confessed. The same charge was leveled often enough in the
nineteenth century by those who came to dominate the scientific study
of genius, forgoing the face to focus on the brain and the skull. Dismissing Lavater's subjective methods, they vaunted their own, allegedly
more objective, approach. Yet the truth is that their methods were not all
that different. Whereas Lavater believed in a one-to-one correspondence
between inner force (genius) and outer expression (the face), scientists in
the nineteenth century simply shifted the focal point of privilege, seeing
in the size, shape, and distinctiveness of the skull and brain the outward
expressions of inner power. Like Lavater, they focused on the exceptional
and the distinct, seeing departures from the norm as worthy of the closest scrutiny, discovering genius in genius. And also like Lavater, who
trained his acolytes to pay minute attention to the endless variations
of the human countenance, those who succeeded him pored over their
specimens with assiduous care.[6]

The similarity is easiest to detect in the German-born Franz Joseph
Gall, the founder of "cranioscopy," or what his student and collaborator
Johann Caspar Spurzheim redubbed "phrenology," from the Greek *phren*
(mind), and *logos*—the knowledge of the mind. Given that phrenology,
like physiognomy, would come in the second half of the nineteenth century to be judged of dubious merit by the majority of practicing scientists (despite, or perhaps because of, its tremendous popular success),
Gall may seem like an easy target, and in some respects he is. Yet Gall's
foundational role in the development of subsequent research on the
skulls and brains of geniuses was crucial. For although Europeans had
suspected since the time of the ancients that the head might be the locus

of intelligence and the generative life-force of genius, Gall did more than anyone before him to establish its privileged place. As a medical student in Vienna in the 1780s, he had been impressed by the capacity of certain fellow students to retain large quantities of information. They seemed to him to share a common feature: large eyes. But after initially entertaining this physiognomic hypothesis, he abandoned it in favor of another correspondence. Individual differences in the composition of the brain, he came to believe, explained differences in aptitude, character, faculties, and traits. What the ancients had called *ingenium*, and what many into the eighteenth century continued to attribute to the confluence of the bodily humors, Gall attributed to the sticky matter housed within our skulls.[7]

It was that attribution, made publicly with increasing fanfare in the 1790s, that earned Gall the wrath of the Catholic Church and a subsequent expulsion from Vienna. His theories smacked of materialism. In a revealing early hypothesis—suggested in part by his autopsies of prison inmates and residents of asylums—Gall speculated that there was such a thing as a faculty of murder or theft. Later, he elaborated a whole series of attributes that corresponded to what he identified as the twenty-seven "organs" or modules of the brain, enumerating faculties such as a sense for sounds and music; a sense for mechanics, construction, and architecture; a "moral sense"; parental love; and "the instinct of self-defence" and courage, to name only a few. The particular configuration of one's organs, he argued, left traceable impressions on the skull, and the nature, size, and shape of the skull, in turn, down to the narrowest crevice or ridge, could be read as a key to the contents within. The skull was the map of the brain, and the brain a map of individual character, a belief that later phrenologists put to dramatic effect, claiming to be able to read the mind according to the "bumps" or impressions made on an individual's (living) human head.

Gall maintained a distance from his more enthusiastic proponents, who went on to establish movements of great popularity on the Continent, in Great Britain, and in the United States. Notwithstanding its bizarre expressions in practice, his theory of localized brain function—whereby individual regions of the brain correspond to particular faculties of the mind—was prescient, anticipating contemporary psychological and neurological accounts of cerebral compartmentalization. In a further irony, however, it was this aspect of Gall's theory that most scientists who studied genius in the nineteenth and early twentieth centuries chose to reject. Whereas Gall's theory made room for multiple intelligences—a different genius for different kinds of things—his successors increasingly regarded intelligence as a reified unitary constant, capable of different applications, certainly, but fundamentally alike across types. A gifted artist shared the same "thing" as a gifted scientist, philosopher, statesman, or general. And this "thing"—call it genius or call it intelligence, for gradually the two were conflated—could be located, described, and measured with precision.[8]

It was that conviction—that genius could be precisely located and accurately described through study of the skull and brain—that owed most to Gall. For although most nineteenth-century scientists rejected his view of the mind, they borrowed heavily from his methods of investigation. Gall's deep conviction that intellectual and creative capacity was innate—inscribed in the brain, and recorded in the skull—served as the point of departure for subsequent craniometry. And his practices of collection and observation—closely studying brains and skulls, recording their dimensions, noting their similarities, and taking account of their differences—were the sine qua non of subsequent research. Gall in fact was a skilled (if largely self-taught) anatomist, and he developed important new techniques for the brain's dissection. As a collector of skulls and casts of heads, he set a precedent for the whole of the century.

From very early on, Gall perceived the value—as well as the utility, from a public relations standpoint—of amassing a collection of notable heads. He had begun to collect them himself in the early 1790s, and in one of his first formal reflections on his work—a private letter that was later edited and published in a prominent Weimar journal by the noted German poet Christoph Martin Wieland—Gall called attention to his cranial needs as well as the prejudices that stood in the way of their satisfaction. Long-standing taboos against the desecration of the body were still in place, and although it might be permissible to pilfer the corpse of a common criminal or an idiot from the madhouse, what Gall desired were the heads of celebrated men. "If only you could make it fashionable for geniuses of every kind to make me the heir of their heads," he observed, "then within ten years I would erect a splendid building, for which I have at present only a few exhibits." Gall joked that it "would be dangerous" for geniuses like Kant or Wieland if he had the means to quickly dispatch with their heads, though he offered to contribute his own in recompense ("like a good Christ"). In the meantime, he looked forward to a future when one might bring together in a kind of cranial museum the "elect of the human race." He regretted that past ages had not had similar foresight, preserving for posterity the skulls of Homer, Ovid, Virgil, Cicero, Hippocrates, Alexander, Frederick, Joseph II, Catherine, Voltaire, Rousseau, Locke, Bacon, Newton, and the like.[9]

As it turned out, Gall did leave his own head to posterity, and although it took somewhat longer than ten years to construct the kind of splendid building of which he dreamed in 1798, such buildings would, in fact, be built. Already by the time Gall was chased out of Vienna in 1805, he had established an informal museum of sorts, consisting of several hundred human skulls and plaster casts. When, after a hugely popular lecture tour through the German lands, he relocated to Paris, he began amassing new specimens. By the time of his death in 1828, his famed collection included busts and plaster casts of brains as well as the skulls of 103 notable men, 69 criminals, 67 mental patients, 25 pathological cases, and 25 "exotics" (non-European races).[10]

The inclusion of the skulls of so-called exotics in Gall's collection, along with those of criminals and the mentally ill, is an important reminder that research on the brains and skulls of persons of eminence was conducted from the beginning in a context of comparison. "Average" individuals, as well as women, non-Europeans, and pathological outliers (criminals and the insane) provided a continuum on which geniuses were placed. As Gall and his student and collaborator Johann Caspar Spurzheim observed in 1812, "there is an important difference between three sorts of skulls: the skulls of idiots; the skulls of those humans who are mediocre; and the skulls of those outstanding humans who are great geniuses. The former ones are characterized by their small size, the latter ones are characterized by their magnitude." The two organologists did not mention in this instance the non-European races, although already in the eighteenth century European scientists were judging the brains of Africans and others to be smaller than those of their allegedly more developed counterparts—a prejudice that would then be "confirmed" by countless studies in the nineteenth century. It is likewise true that Gall and his contemporaries (unlike their successors in the second half of the nineteenth century) generally did not compare the various specimens on their continuum directly, but chose instead to focus explicitly on single outstanding examples. It was largely for this reason that the skulls of known geniuses were so prized. Surely they would offer infallible signs of their singularity, revealing to science the secret of genius's special election. Gall salivated at the prospect of acquiring a genuine relic of this type, actively making inquiries until his death in 1828. Only the year before, upon receiving a new plaster bust of the head of Goethe by the German philosopher and psychologist Franz Brentano, he wrote back to say that such materials were invaluable "for a researcher of the organ of the brain." "I implore you to bribe the relatives of this unique genius to preserve his head in nature for the world," he told Brentano. Gall, to his consternation, never secured this prize; when Goethe died in 1832, his skull and body were safely sealed in the crypt of the Duke of Weimar.[11]

Not all geniuses were so lucky. Indeed, in what has been described as a European-wide wave of "cranioklepty" inspired by the very studies that Gall did so much to promote, geniuses throughout Europe lost their heads. In 1809, at the death of Haydn, an admirer of the "Gall system" bribed a funeral worker to remove the skull, which he venerated privately in a handsome glass case until his own earthly departure. The skull was bequeathed, in turn, to the Viennese Society of the Friends of Music, where it was finally received in 1895 after a circuitous translation. There it was housed until after World War II, when it was at long last reunited with the rest of Haydn's remains at the crypt of his patron, the prince of Esterházy, in Eisenstadt. The skulls of the Spanish Romantic painter Francisco Goya and of the Swedish scientist and mystic Emanuel Swedenborg were similarly pilfered intact; Beethoven's was picked over in parts. The composer may have vowed, famously, in a letter of 1801, that fate shall not "bend and crush me completely," but fate had considerable success with his skull, which was broken into fragments in a crude autopsy performed in 1827. Several pieces were chipped away then, never to be seen again, and several more went missing at an exhumation in 1863. The latter "miraculously" resurfaced in San Jose, California, only recently. Their authenticity confirmed by DNA analysis, the bones were duly put up for sale.[12]

Such traffic testifies to the still-extant market for the body parts and personal effects of celebrated individuals. Such a trade had flourished in the Middle Ages, when the relics of saints were bought and sold as precious commodities. It reemerged in the nineteenth century, sustained by the new cult of genius and celebrity. Consider the example of Napoleon. Even before his remains were repatriated to France in 1840, to be sealed amid great fanfare in the crypt of Les Invalides in Paris, admirers and erstwhile enemies alike clamored to get their hands on anything the *grand homme* might have touched. Traders in London snatched up personal possessions, cameos, paintings, articles of clothing, and autographed letters. And, in what was certainly the most amusing purchase of its kind, a British collector lay claim to a trove of Napoleon's heirlooms that were once owned by the Abbé Vignali, the young priest who had officiated at the emperor's death. Included in the collection was a shriveled piece of tissue purported to be a penis. The authenticity of the relic remains very much in doubt, but that didn't prevent the trader from flogging it off in 1924 to an American bibliophile and collector, Dr. A. L. Rosenbach, who proudly put his prize possession on display, exposing it publicly in 1927 at the Museum of French Art in New York in a glass case atop blue morocco and velvet. By the early twentieth century, the demand for relics of the modern sort had grown so intense that it prompted explicit comparisons with the cult of the saints.[13]

What did onlookers see in these objects? And why did they long to possess them? No doubt some were drawn by financial speculation, others by simple curiosity or the collector's urge, still others by the same prurient interest that carried crowds to the penny arcades to gawk at monsters and freaks. But that something else might have been involved has already been suggested by the example of Percy Bysshe Shelley, whose telltale heart and poetically charged remains were likewise spirited away and venerated after his death. Did something of the genius's power linger in his flesh and bones? Did it rub off, somehow, on the things that he wore and touched? A desire to confront—and capture—the mystery of genius was a factor in the preservation of these sacred remains.

But if the aura of genius might be detected in any old extremity or bit, its presence was undoubtedly greatest in the skull and what it housed, the brain. For the nineteenth century, the skull continued to serve, as it had for Hamlet and countless monks in their cells, as a spur to reflection on the human condition. In the special case of genius, however, this *memento mori* was a vivid reminder not only of humanity's mortal fate, but also of the genius's transcendence of that fate, of his capacity to live on through his work. The skull of a genius, accordingly, must be approached with special reverence, as Goethe reminded those privileged pilgrims who were afforded a glimpse of the cranium of the poet Friedrich Schiller, which was restored to Weimar, along with his other remains, in 1826. Placed on a pedestal in a fitting temple—the Duke of Weimar's private library, with Goethe serving as the priest of the inner sanctum—the skull was shown only to those who would "not [be] governed by [mere] curiosity but by a feeling, a knowledge of what that great man achieved for Germany, for Europe, and for the whole civilized world." Here was a particularly striking instance of genius keeping the vigil of genius, in the presence, no less, of the daemonly spirit! A privileged object in the economy of modern relics, the skull must be approached with reverence.[14]

Sustained by devotion, that privilege was conferred by the speculations of nineteenth-century science. As Hegel pointed out in the midst an extended, critical discussion of phrenology in his *Phenomenology of Spirit*, "when anyone thinks of the proper location of Spirit's outer existence, it is not the back that comes to mind," or any other part of the body, "but only the head." There, atop the shoulders, Hegel insisted, one confronted the "indwelling seat of Spirit"; the "skull-bone" was the locus of its "immediate actuality." The site of a great universal dialectic between matter and mind, the particular and the universal, the head was a sacred place. An arch-idealist himself, Hegel had nothing but contempt for what he regarded as the crude materialism of Gall and his successors. When a man is told "'You are this kind of person because your skull-bone is constituted in such and such a way,'" he quipped, the best reply would be to bash in the person's head in order to demonstrate "that for a man, a bone is nothing in itself, much less his true reality." And yet, what Hegel rightly perceived with his dialectical gaze was that even the phrenologists' most reductive attempts to reduce mind to matter had the paradoxical effect of endowing matter with a strangely spiritual significance. By isolating genius above the shoulders, they made a totem of the skull. And by concentrating genius's power in the brain, they made of its flesh a fetish that radiated with powerful allure. Behold the mystery of genius made manifest. Behold the secret of genius revealed.[15]

The observation holds for virtually the whole of nineteenth-century craniometry. For whether they were entrenched materialists or qualified idealists, Gall's scientific successors sought out the skulls of geniuses with all the avidity of collectors of relics, generating public excitement and interest in the hagiographic descriptions of prodigious specimens. News that Immanuel Kant's celebrated head had been investigated at his death in the spirit of Gall's system prompted considerable enthusiasm, and accounts of the autopsy were read closely. In 1880, more than seventy-five years after Kant's death, the skull was finally disinterred, reexamined, and put on display. Well after Gall's organology was abandoned in favor of different criteria from bumps, craniometrists competed to secure the very best heads in order to precisely calculate the brain's mass, study its convolutions and folds, and estimate its volume and size from measurements taken of the interior of the skull. The Göttingen anatomist Rudolf Wagner achieved a coup in 1855 when he secured the brain of one of the century's greatest mathematicians, Karl Friedrich Gauss. Not to be outdone, the Frenchman Paul Broca, the most celebrated brain anatomist of the century, went to considerable lengths to surpass German rivals, such as Wagner and the illustrious materialist Carl Vogt. Securing valued specimens of his own, Broca amassed the world's largest collection of brains and skulls to that point (more than 7,000 at his death in 1880), and called attention to weighty examples, including that of the French scientific genius George Cuvier, whose brain topped the French charts at 1,830 grams. In 1876, Broca helped to found the Society of Mutual Autopsy, in which eminent French men pledged their own heads to posterity, declaring their willingness to subject them to the scientific examination of their colleagues. Militantly atheist, the project was nonetheless religious, with Broca and his followers establishing a memorial system and liturgical rites to accompany the ritual of the autopsy. Modeled explicitly on religious practices, these rites represented a self-conscious effort to replace a spurned Catholicism. In the United States, where work on cranial capacity had long centered on demonstrating the inferiority of nonwhites, researchers such as E. A. Spitzka turned their attention to studying the brains and skulls of eminent men with similar zeal, amassing collections and compiling detailed descriptions of "remarkable heads." By the end of the nineteenth century, in fact, investigation of this kind was extensive, permitting proponents to boast, in a development that would have pleased Gall, of the establishment of substantial brain collections in cities as far afield as Göttingen, Munich, Berlin, Paris, Stockholm, Philadelphia, and Ithaca, New York.[16]

Regularly carried out in a context of explicit comparison with women and "inferior races," the craniometry and brain research of the second half of the nineteenth century went some way toward answering the question of what genius looked like. As Broca observed in 1862, in general the brain was larger "in men than in women, in eminent men than in men of mediocre talent, in superior races than in inferior races." Spitzka, for his part, concurred, noting that "the jump from a Cuvier or a Thackeray to a Zulu or a Bushman is not greater than from the latter to the gorilla or the orang." Geniuses, it followed, were white, were of "advanced" European stock, and were men—indeed, they were white men of large brains, such as Cuvier or the Russian novelist Ivan Turgenev, whose contemporaries marveled upon learning that his brain had broken the 2,000-gram threshold. Genius, lo and behold, looked like genius.[17]

Except when it didn't. Walt Whitman, who was partial to phrenology himself, weighed in at a disappointing 1,282 grams. And although Gall's detractors may have chuckled at his own measly 1,198 grams, how to account for the fact that Broca, so lovingly dissected by his friends, could muster just 1,424 grams, only slightly above average? Such anomalies were adeptly, if tortuously, explained away, though in the end the theories faltered in the face of carefully accumulated observations and common sense. Brain mass, after all, varies with body size (bigger people have bigger brains). And if it were really true that size alone mattered in questions of intelligence, then the whale would be lord of us all. "Must we suspect the great beast of genius?" one French scientist mused. "No, the size of the brain is not, in and of itself, a sign of intellectual superiority." By the early twentieth century, many researchers had come to share that opinion. Turning their attention from the crudities of the cranial index, some looked in the direction of what their colleagues in medicine and psychology had been saying for decades: the body of the genius revealed more interesting stigmata and signs.[18]

Τ HERE WERE OTHER TOOLS with which to probe genius besides calipers, scalpels, and scales. The medically trained physician and pioneering student of psychology Louis-Francisque Lélut made use of them all. Early in his career, Lélut conducted autopsies and experiments on skulls and brains. But he quickly abandoned the quest to discover genius in shape or size, pouring scorn on those who continued the effort, while attacking phrenology with particular ire. His own work with mental patients in asylums suggested that pathology—not morphology—held the key to the scientific study of genius. In 1836 he gave an indication of how, publishing a work that helped to drive a European-wide research effort into the following century.[19]

The title of Lélut's book, *Du démon de Socrate*, was familiar to the classically trained, mirroring precisely the French translation of Plutarch's *De Genio Socratis*. Its thesis was simple, though no less shocking for that: the father of philosophy, the paragon of reason and virtue, had lived his life on the edge of insanity, a fact that previous commentators had apparently failed to see. Now, in the light of medical science, Lélut affirmed, Socrates's diagnosis was clear. What had long been described as his "demon" or "genius" was but the specter of a morbid imagination. The inner promptings of his "celestial voice" were voices in his head, and the *daimonion* itself was a hallucination. Socrates, in short, was a madman (*un fou*), his vaunted "divine sign" a symptom of progressive disease.[20]

Conceived as a case study in the "application of psychological science to history," and expounded with impressive classical erudition, Lélut's text was among the earliest examples of "pathography," a term coined later in the nineteenth century by the German neurologist Paul Julius Möbius (he of the famed strip) to describe what was by then a flourishing genre. Cultivated into the twentieth century by prominent scientists, including Möbius's acolyte, the German psychiatrist Wilhem Lange-Eichbaum, pathographies were medical biographies that chronicled the maladies of geniuses and other great men. Lélut's work helped to launch the genre, even though its central thesis was not entirely new. The general association between genius and madness, after all, traced back as far as the ancients. It had been revived most recently by the Romantics, who dramatized (and even celebrated) the connection between mental prowess and mental disease. The specific belief in Socrates's madness also had precedents, especially in the eighteenth century, when Enlightenment authors speculated widely as to what the genius of Socrates might be. The most daring among them even suggested that the demon was but a figment of an unsettled mind.

Lélut candidly acknowledged this earlier discussion. Indeed, he saw his own efforts in part as a continuation of the skeptical tradition of the eighteenth century, an attempt to demystify what superstition had long obscured. Yet what distinguished his own work was its more rigorous scientific pretensions—its self-conscious effort to diagnose in clinical terms a condition that Lélut insisted had afflicted other men of genius. "There are names—great names—of artists, poets, scientists, and philosophers, whose psychology is the same . . . as what I attribute to Socrates." The diagnosis was apparent: genius was a mental affliction, a kind of illness, a symptom of underlying disease.[21]

Bearing as it did on the much-revered figure of Socrates, Lélut's book generated considerable controversy, prompting the poet Charles Baudelaire, among others, to mock him. Baudelaire, too, had a guardian demon that whispered in his ear. "Why then," he demanded, "shouldn't I, like Socrates, have the honor of obtaining my own certificate of insanity, signed by the subtle Lélut?" The good doctor was undeterred. In 1846 he published another study, which argued that the French mathematician and religious writer Blaise Pascal had suffered from similar hallucinations. And from a position of social and professional eminence, he continued to press his case. When, in 1856, Lélut appended a long preface to the second edition of *Du démon de Socrate*, he took satisfaction in the knowledge that his once controversial views were being credited by colleagues. As a fellow physician remarked just three years later, "how far behind us now are the days when the fact of the hallucinations of Socrates could be regarded as the most extravagant claim."[22]

The fellow physician, Jacques-Joseph Moreau, who was also a psychologist—and had extensive experience in the asylums of Paris and in his native Tours—did as much as anyone in the nineteenth century to develop Lélut's insights. He hailed Lélut as a pioneer and comrade-in-arms, and he shared Lélut's antipathy toward the fetish for skulls. "We doubt whether a single person working today with even a basic knowledge of physiology," he affirmed in his landmark work, *La psychologie morbide dans ses rapports avec la philosophie de l'histoire* (1859), "believes that genius can be determined by the weight of the brain or the size of the head." To be sure, that view continued to be "widely accredited" outside of medical circles and among the public at large. Nor had Moreau completely abandoned the prejudices of his adversaries. Acknowledging that "all is not completely false in the doctrine we combat," he conceded that there were real differences in brain size between races ("as, for example, between the European race and the black race"), where the one stood in relation to the other as did the "idiot" to the normal man. And yet, as far as differences between individuals within the same race were concerned, it would be easy to disprove the notion that the size or shape of the skull was a determining factor in genius. Gather together a group of so-called specialists, Moreau challenged, and ask them to distinguish between the skulls of those celebrated for their accomplishments and those of ordinary men. It would soon become clear that there were no essential differences in the "form or configuration" of the assembled heads. The origins of genius lay elsewhere, he contended—in the physiology of the human body, and, more importantly, in its pathology. Like Lélut, Moreau considered genius a disease.[23]

Moreau came to that conclusion through his work with mental patients and his intimate knowledge of the literature of the nascent (and largely French) field of medical psychology. But he also breathed deeply of the sickly sweet Romantic scent of the times. Following an extended trip to the Middle East in the 1830s, he began to experiment extensively with hashish, using it to treat patients and observing its effects on friends. He published a treatise on the subject, *Du Hachisch et de l'alienation mentale* (1845), and founded, with the celebrated Romantic writer Théophile Gautier, the "Club des Hachichins," an informal gathering that brought together a cross-section of bohemian Paris for monthly "smoke-outs" (*séances*, in the more elevated argot of the time). The club's members included Baudelaire, Victor Hugo, and the notoriously eccentric poet Gérard de Nerval, whose bouts of mental illness ended tragically in suicide in 1855. They gave Moreau a glimpse of the peculiarities of Romantic genius firsthand, and also impressed on him how seemingly healthy individuals could experience altered states of consciousness— trances, hallucinations, and dreams—remarkably similar to those of the insane. If a substance like hashish could bring about such dramatic changes, prompting creative and original thoughts, might not a foreign agent introduced into the body by illness do the same?[24]

Glimpsed through the iron bars of asylum windows and the smoky haze of drawing rooms, Moreau's suspicions crystallized in the contention that heredity and degeneration played crucial roles in producing what he described, in a nice coinage, as *pathogénie* (pathological genius).

The idea that mental illness might be congenital—a sort of family affliction or curse—was itself already common currency in medical circles,
and the concept of degeneration, bandied about since the eighteenth
century, had been given new articulation in the French-trained psychiatrist Bénédict Auguste Morel's *Traité sur les dégénérescences physiques,
intellectuels et morales de l'espèce humaine* (1857), from which Moreau
borrowed freely. Morel's work reflected on the causes of hereditary illness in human beings. Written prior to the publication of Darwin's *Origin of Species* (1859), it employed a crude and now discredited theory of
acquired characteristics to explain how the effects of unhealthy behaviors
and conditions could be passed from generation to generation via diseased and damaged "seed." Alcoholism, for example, social squalor, sexual
deviance, or crime could induce physical changes in an organism that
were then passed on to one's offspring, leading to further "degeneration"
over time in a kind of pathological devolution. Complete mental retardation or total insanity were the end results of this process, but, as Moreau
insisted in his own writing on the subject, there was an extensive range of
intervening disorders governed by the same "law of heredity." Genius, he
argued, was one such special case, a particular branch on a tree of pathological illness, whose main trunk extended outward into a great number
of neurotic afflictions.

Moreau, then, brought a new kind of scientific authority to the belief
that genius was born, not made. Invoking a distinction familiar since the
eighteenth century, he argued that although will, passion, and hard work
might produce talent, only a relatively rare set of pathological conditions, the result of a long process of hereditary incubation and decay,
could result in true genius. And though he was not always perfectly precise in tracing the etiological pathways of the affliction, he was adamant
in insisting that his scientific account superseded all previous explanations. Whereas craniometrists and phrenologists had drawn attention to
the form of the brain—emphasizing its size and shape—Moreau stressed
instead its (mal)function under the rarefied conditions of degenerative
disease. "Whenever one observes intellectual faculties that rise above the
common level," he insisted, "and above all in cases where they attain an
exceptional degree of energy, then one can be sure that a neurotic condition of some kind is acting on the organ of thought." Genius, in short,
was a "semi-morbid state of the brain."[25]

That insight, in Moreau's opinion, not only made sense of a mass of
clinical data, but also opened up new perspectives on genius and geniuses
in the past. For if his central thesis was true—namely, that hereditary
afflictions of the nervous system were favorable to the development of

the intellectual faculties—then traces of those same afflictions should show up in the case histories of men of genius. Moreau bemoaned the fact that, notwithstanding the efforts of Lélut, conventional biographers had paid scant attention to these unseemly details in their subjects. But through patient labor of his own, Moreau was able to provide brief sketches of the case histories of some 180 men of genius, beginning with Socrates in the ancient world and ending, in his own century, with Beethoven, Cuvier, and Hegel. He not only noted signs of pathology in the geniuses themselves—he cited, for example, Napoleon's belief in his star as an indication of the emperor's hallucinatory insanity—but also pointed out symptoms of mental illness or of physical infirmities in members of the geniuses' families. Instances of alcoholism, suicide, and epilepsy caught Moreau's eye, along with other indications of abnormal behavior—strange work habits, distractions, obsessions, and *idées fixes*—that might provide a clue to incipient *dégénérescence*. At the same time, he emphasized geniuses' all-engrossing passion for work and the fits of enthusiasm that overcame them in their inspiration:

> An impetuous current of arterial blood, saturated with oxygen, calories, and electricity, carries with it a tremendous heat. The face takes on color, the eyes grow animated, scintillating, the forehead burns— all announcing that a great work is taking place within. In effect, the brain, in a state of extreme vitality, is reacting with force against the perceptions and the ideas it receives: stirring them up, combining and putting them together[;] . . . the breath of inspiration spreads throughout the soul, *en Deus! Ecce Deus!* And so are produced great works of art. . . . So are opened up new and penetrating vistas, those sudden illuminations, the prophetic intuitions of genius, the gift that is received in order to discover the possible and invent the truth.[26]

Here was a naturalized account of the creative process, reminiscent of Diderot's descriptions of the enthusiasm of genius. Moreau actually cited one of Diderot's descriptions at length later in the work, noting how his own thinking further confirmed the "real nature" of the *divinum quiddam* evident in genial "enthusiasm, inspiration, ecstasy, and the hallucinatory state." The affinity is revealing. For like Diderot before him, Moreau sought to provide a thoroughly rational explanation of a process that others, in their superstition, had explained by recourse to the gods or God. "How have these psychological phenomena been interpreted before?" Moreau asked. Some had spoken of "metaphysical intervention into the human mind," others of a "freeing of the soul from the material ties that bind them to earth." Such explanations were perfectly understandable: men of genius themselves had accounted for their powers in these terms, often believing, like Socrates, that they lived in the special protection of the divine. But now that the phenomenon could be viewed in the light of science, it must be conceded that "between the man of genius who asks himself if the ideas flowering in his enthusiasm-heated brain are really his own, and the *aliéné* who believes that they come from a superior power, a familiar *genius*, or God himself, there is no difference, psychologically-speaking." It was simply a matter of degree.[27]

In blurring the lines between madness and mental prowess, and insisting on the hereditary pathology of both, Moreau intended to provide a purely scientific account of the phenomenon of genius. Yet what is striking in his description is the degree to which it repeats and reifies earlier claims. In many ways, Moreau simply lent scientific credence to the Romantic construction of the mad genius, a construction that itself drew on themes stretching all the way back to Plato's *furor divinus* and the long line of subsequent development. Lélut and Moreau may have exorcized the demons, but did not something of the *daimonic* linger in the elusive pathogens they put in their place? It is significant that later psychologists writing in the degenerationist tradition sometimes reverted to that older language, troubled, as they were, by the same inability to put their finger on the something that men of genius possessed. As the noted German psychologist Ernst Kretschmer observed in his *Psychology of Men of Genius*, first published in 1929: "To straightforward talent there must be added, to make genius, this 'daemon,' and it seems that the daemon, the inner voice, is founded in the psychopathic element. For the daemonical, which is the essence of genius, embraces the inexplicable, the spiritually creative and original and the whole gamut of strange passions and uncommon ideas."[28]

Kretschmer was nominated for a Nobel Prize in the same year this study appeared (he also believed, in a modern form of physiognomy, that genius could be detected in facial features). But his argument draws out a point that is already clear in the context of Moreau's writings: the genius remained a man possessed, an exalted seer endowed with a special capacity to envision truth and to disclose it. His genius was a "thing" that was common to all who suffered its burdens and drew on its intuitions. And even though the thing itself was difficult to detect, one could be sure of its presence by its symptoms and signs as well as by its tremendous discharge of power. The genius's sudden illuminations and prophetic epiphanies, his ecstatic visions and convulsive energy, continued to wrap him in the mystery and charisma that once had given the prophets their power. Just as Diderot had adopted, despite himself, the terms of an older discourse of enthusiasm to explain the quandary of genius, Moreau, for all his science, echoed earlier religious claims.

Not that the genius was meant to be saintly. On the contrary, in appropriating Morel's language of degeneration, Moreau placed geniuses in the proximity of prostitutes, criminals, and the "morally insane." As a character in the French novelist Émile Zola's *Dr. Pascal* explains, heredity "produces imbeciles, madmen, criminals, and great men. Certain cells collapse, others take their place, and a rascal or a raving lunatic appears instead of a genius or a mere honest man." That difference, too, was a matter of degree; Zola knew of what he wrote. Not only did he share many of the assumptions of men like Morel and Moreau, but in the 1890s he consented to an examination by fifteen psychiatrists, who sought to diagnose his own degenerative condition. That Zola was a genius, the doctors agreed, concluding that he had been fortunate in managing to escape the affliction's more sinister effects. Zola got off with a diagnosis of mild neurosis. But not all geniuses could be so lucky. They risked madness or incarceration. For although Moreau did not insist on the fact, his theory clearly predicted that the insanity of genius could lead naturally enough to moral insanity. The distance separating eccentricity and odd behavior from the rejection of social norms and outright crime was likewise a matter of degree. It took a man with a deep interest in criminals—one of Moreau's great admirers and, in the end, one of his greatest proponents—to develop that connection.[29]

Born in Verona to a wealthy Jewish family, Cesare Lombroso is most often remembered today as a criminologist and criminal anthropologist. But he was also a medically trained psychologist who served as an army surgeon, and then directed an insane asylum, before occupying a prestigious chair at the University of Turin. From early in his career he expressed a deep interest in genius. One of his first books— *Genio e follia* (1864)—was devoted to the subject, investigating how genius, madness, and degenerative disease were interrelated, a theme to which he returned throughout his career. A substantially revised version of the book, republished in 1889 as the *L'uomo di genio* (1889), was quickly translated into a great many languages, including English in 1891, as part of the prestigious Contemporary Science Series edited by the British psychologist and sex researcher Havelock Ellis. Heavily influenced by Moreau and the French school of degeneration, Lombroso also drew vulgarly on Darwin and other evolutionary thinkers to fashion his own version of what might be termed "devolutionism." Put simply, Lombroso held not only that human beings were susceptible to moral and physical degeneration as the result of hereditary pathology, but that in degenerating, they reverted to earlier, less developed human types. Degenerates, in other words, were human atavisms, harboring in their persons characteristics of more primitive species. In criminals, this degenerative tendency expressed itself in a reversion to violence and bloodlust—a propensity for the alleged aggression of primitive man— whereas in "higher degenerates" (geniuses), emotional instability, impulsiveness, egoism, and a decrease in the sense of morality were common.

But degeneration could be detected in more than just behavioral traits. In Lombroso's lurid vision, it was inscribed physically (anatomically) on the body in what he referred to as "stigmata," the outward signs of inward decay. He cataloged a great many such signs in criminals— from long arms and greater skull thickness to precocious wrinkles and dark skin—and also described the stigmata of the "higher degenerates," using a kind of genial profiling that responded directly to the question of just how a genius might look. Geniuses, it seemed, were short of stature, small of body, and frequently emaciated. Geniuses were men: "In the history of genius women have but a small place," he wrote. They were generally sallow, generally pale—indeed, generally white. More often than not they were left-handed. They were sickly in childhood, and frequently of a "cretin-like appearance" as adults. Many had rickets. Many stammered. Very few looked like their parents. And that was only on the outside. "Lesions of the head and brain are frequent among men of genius," Lombroso further proclaimed, and he cited research to show that Petrarch, among others, had a sloping forehead, while Byron and Humboldt displayed "solidification" of the cranial sutures. To a far greater extent than Moreau, Lombroso was prepared to draw on the craniometrical literature when it suited his purposes. And so, after acknowledging that "the capacity of the skull in men of genius is, as is natural, above the average," he proceeded to cite various studies that pointed out their cranial flaws: a "bony crest between the sphenoid and the basilar apophysis" in the composer Gaetano Donizetti; a "hydrocephalus" in Milton, Cuvier, Carl Linnaeus, and Edward Gibbon; and numerous other abnormalities in the brains of eminent men. Within as without, the genius was, quite literally, a marked man.[30]

To the question of what genius looked like, then, Lombroso offered a vivid response. The picture he painted was not pretty, and he made sure to present it in all its ugly detail. Noting, like Moreau before him, that biographers had too often ignored signs of pathology in their subjects, he aimed to make amends for this past neglect by combing through historical sources and summoning recorded examples with an impressive, if manic, erudition, and an amusing taste for the piquant detail. Lombroso happily repeated the story that the Italian philosopher Giambattista Vico had derived his genius from a childhood fall, later observing that "it has frequently happened that injuries to the head and acute diseases . . . have changed a very ordinary individual into a man of genius." Freely mixing together scientists, artists, poets, philosophers, musicians, and statesmen as examples of geniuses, Lombroso also drew extensively from contemporary data when he could, making use of copious lists and detailed charts and graphs. Thus, to "prove" his assertion that genius was generally undersized, Lombroso mustered a historical roster of those "famous" for their "short stature"—which ran three-quarters of a page in minuscule type—while at the same time providing statistical data from modern surveys, including an elaborate "Diagram of the Relation of Genius and Stature in France."[31]

Wherever he could, in fact, Lombroso sought to quantify his claims. This practice reflected his belief that numbers and numerical precision distinguished the modern era from the vague opinions and prejudices of the past. Like others of a positivist bent, newly discovering the power of statistics, Lombroso regarded numbers as oracular forces that could speak for themselves. Numbers revealed facts, facts revealed truths, and the man of science must heed their call, wherever they might lead. The intrepid Lombroso was not afraid to follow them in contradictory directions. Despite his insistence on the diseased and degenerative character of genius, for instance, Lombroso offered up reams of data to affirm the longevity of men of genius, their higher than average lifespans. Similarly, although the thrust of his degenerative argument aimed to illustrate the influence of heredity on character, he freely admitted the role of environmental conditions, drawing particular attention to the importance of geography and climate. "All flat countries—Belgium, Holland, Egypt—are deficient of men of genius," it seemed. But "so also were those, like Switzerland and Savoy, which, being enclosed between very high mountains, are endemically afflicted with cretinism." Not too low, and not too high, small rolling hills were just right, providing the optimal environment to produce genius. Climatic and meteorological conditions were even more important. "It is evident," Lombroso concluded, "that the first warm months distinctly predominate in the creation of genius." April, it might be said, was the smartest of months.[32]

Such pronouncements are strangely reminiscent of the work of another Italian, Marsilio Ficino, whose *Three Books on Life* abound in similarly surprising assertions regarding the strange habits and habitus of men of genius. But though it is easy, and perhaps necessary, in Lombroso's case, to laugh at such pronouncements, doing so should not allow one to lose sight of the extent of their influence, or their sinister implications. It is certainly true that Lombroso's theories were never uncontested. In England, America, and on the Continent, strong voices rose at the end of the nineteenth century to affirm what George Bernard Shaw called, in a work of that name, the "Sanity of Genius." The American psychologist William James (brother of the novelist Henry James and a man much interested in genius himself) penned several devastating reviews in 1894 and 1895 of a number of the leading theorists of degeneration, Lombroso included. And a good many other scientists and men of letters on both sides of the Atlantic protested what they saw as Lombroso's facile conclusions and shoddy science. And yet, such reaction is itself an indication of how seriously even Lombroso's opponents took his work. On the Continent, especially, where the degenerationist position was always strongest, Lombroso enjoyed considerable influence and strong networks of support among a motley array of allies, advocates, and fellow travelers, who continued to assert the connection between genius and madness, heredity and crime, up until World War II. Even in a country like Great Britain, which tended on the whole to equate genius with progress, degenerationists could call on the qualified support of influential advocates, such as Havelock Ellis and the prominent psychiatrist Henry Maudsley, or unrestrained popularizers, such as the journalist John Nisbet, author of *The Insanity of Genius* (1891).[33]

The belief in an inherent link between genius and madness, then, did not go unchallenged. Moreover, those who accepted it employed the discourse of degeneration in different ways. In Russia, for example, nineteenth-century radicals, and later their Soviet successors, used pathographies and degeneration theories to explain away the aberrations of otherwise admirable writers of genius, such as Nikolai Gogol, Fyodor Dostoyevsky, and Leo Tolstoy, who had turned to religion later in life—a clear sign of dementia! Morel himself came to see the conditions of modern industrial society as the cause of *dégénérescence*, and so used the rhetoric of degeneration theory to indict capitalism. Lombroso and his admiring acolyte Max Nordau, a leading European Zionist, tended to take much more conservative social positions, equating degeneration with decadence, moral license, and social decline. Finally, in a terrible irony, Hitler and the Nazis would expropriate this rhetoric for their own purposes, linking degeneration to much of modern art and the pollution introduced by "diseased" races, particularly the Jews.[34]

Yet whatever the range of specific uses to which the discourse of degeneration was put, it bequeathed, where genius was concerned, a number of collective judgments. Most importantly, it tended to reaffirm the view that genius was inscribed on the body, which, under close examination, would reveal its stigmata and signs. Whereas craniometrists equated genius with the size or peculiarity of the brain, degenerationists linked genius to pathology's effects on the brain's function. The end result was the same—a tendency to reify genius as a meaningful and measurable condition that was traceable to specific organic functions (or the organs themselves) that inhered in the flesh by nature's command. This belief, in turn, further strengthened the hereditarian assumptions that had risen to prominence in the eighteenth century, the conviction that genius was born and not made. Lombroso and others might concede that certain social conditions—not to mention the right climate or a timely bump on the head—could influence genius for better or for worse. But without the right stock, the right "predisposition," as Moreau put it, nurture could, at best, produce talent, never genius. The true genius was something exalted, a freak of nature, a man set apart. He was, to use a word first invoked by Diderot in this connection (and employed commonly throughout the nineteenth century), a "monster."[35]

And therein lies a final collective judgment of the degenerationist account. For not only did it lend scientific authority to the Romantic construction of the mad genius, it also gave further credence to the specific connection between genius and moral transgression or evil. As one contemporary observed, "genius carries in itself the principle of destruction, of death, of madness, like a fruit carries a worm." Pathological genius was pathological in the extreme; criminal behavior was a natural consequence of the diseased mind. Lombroso developed this connection at length, asserting that it was not uncommon for geniuses to be born of criminal parents, or for criminals themselves to display signs of genius. The criminal masterminds who fascinated the nineteenth century were at once a source and a reflection of this belief. And yet, the genius as criminal might do more than steal a cache of diamonds or crack a safe. In the lurid imagination of Lombroso, Nordau, and their sundry admirers, the mad genius could exercise his dominion, like Napoleon, over empires and states. "The frequency of genius among lunatics and of madmen among men of genius, explains the fact that the destiny of nations has often been in the hands of the insane," Lombroso observed. It was not intended as a comforting thought. In their relentless search for novelty and their hostility to established tradition, geniuses were inherent enemies of order, natural-born rebels and revolutionaries, who spurned established rules and laws. The British criminologist H. T. F. Rhodes summarized this line of thought in his fittingly entitled *Genius and Criminal: A Study in Rebellion*, in 1932, arguing that "it is the aim of the genius, to overthrow society and rebuild it upon lines that would bring it into harmony with him." Citing Napoleon, Nietzsche, and Lenin as cases in point, Rhodes emphasized that in their "sublime hatred" of the status quo, geniuses of this type would stop at nothing to realize their ends. "Everything is permitted to genius," Lombroso concurred, summing up their "special morality," as demonstrated by their actions in the past. Exceptions, outliers, and extremes, geniuses were laws unto themselves. It was a judgment, ironically, with which those who saw the genius not as a degenerate, but as the highest human type, could agree.[36]

FRANCIS GALTON WAS NOT MUCH interested in madness, and he was only tangentially concerned with questions of degeneration and congenital crime. He did flirt with a curiosity in brain size and the circumference of the head, overseeing in the 1880s an "anthropometric laboratory," where he took precise measurements of physical features in relation to "mental capacity," including those of the "beautifully shaped . . . though rather low" noggin of British Prime Minister William Ewart Gladstone. By and large, however, the Victorian polymath preferred to look for genius in places his predecessors had not, pioneering methods that are still in use today. An intrepid explorer and travel writer, an accomplished anthropologist and mathematician, and an innovative psychologist and inventor, who perfected the use of the fingerprint to fight the criminal geniuses that eluded Scotland Yard, Galton was also the cousin of Charles Darwin and, notoriously, the founding father of eugenics. The subject that drew together all of these concerns was genius—"hereditary genius," to be precise. It served as the crux of his landmark 1869 study, *Hereditary Genius: An Inquiry into Its Laws and Consequences.*[37]

The idea of the link between genius and heredity first occurred to him, Galton reports, "during the course of a purely ethnological inquiry, into the mental peculiarities of different races." His final study did not lack for such peculiarities. Galton recorded them in depressing detail, adding his own scientific authority to prejudices that were widely shared by his contemporaries. "The average intellectual standard of the negro race," he told his fellow Anglo-Saxons, "is some two grades below our own," whereas the "Australian type" of aboriginal was "one grade below the African negro." Galton was more upbeat about Italians and Jews, "both of whom appear to be rich in families of high intellectual breeds," and expressed curiosity in Germany and America, which were "also full of interest." It was "a little less so with respect to France," alas, as the "Revolution and the guillotine [had] made sad havoc among the progeny of her abler races."[38]

Notwithstanding such sweeping assertions, Galton's greatest concern in *Hereditary Genius* was less the relationship between peoples than the variation within them. Drawing largely on data gathered from the United Kingdom, he sought to prove that genius was inherited, passed on in familial lines. Moreover, he attempted to show that its distribution could be explained according to the statistical law of the "deviation from an average." Here he invoked the work of the respected Belgian mathematician and astronomer Alphonse Quételet. Quételet had been among the first to demonstrate the power of quantitative statistical methods for analyzing social phenomena. In a famous study, he showed how the chest sizes of Scottish soldiers varied according to a law of deviation from an average that, when plotted on a graph, resembled a "Gaussian" curve, named in honor of the mathematician whose brain weighed 1,492 grams. Today we usually call this a "bell curve" on account of its clarion shape. But by whatever name, it suggested to Quételet and Galton alike that nature clustered around a mean, with symmetrical distribution on either side. What was true of chest size was true of height and other physical features, and so, Galton reasoned, it must be true with respect to mental capacity. "What I am driving at," he wrote, is that "analogy clearly shows that there must be a fairly constant average mental capacity in the inhabitants of the British Isles, and that the deviation from that average— upwards toward genius, and downwards towards stupidity—must follow the law that governs deviations from all true averages."[39]

Like Quételet before him, then, Galton concluded that there was such a thing as an "average man." But whereas the Belgian tended to think of averages in positive terms, as nature's ideal and mean, Galton conceived of it disparagingly as "mediocrity." Impressed by the "enormous" range of mental powers between the "greatest and least of intellects," Galton was drawn to the upper end of the scale. He focused his attention on those "grand human animals, of natures preeminently noble, born to be kings of men." These were the exceedingly rare "prodigies of genius," the "illustrious men" on whose thoughts depended the course of human events. "Scattered throughout the whole historical period of human existence, their number does not amount to more than 400," Galton judged at one point. The somewhat less exalted number he arrived at elsewhere is more familiar: geniuses, he calculated, were "like one to a million."[40]

This was, ironically, the very same ratio cited by Lavater, who maintained that the "the proportion of genius to the vulgar is like one to a million." There is no indication that Galton took his calculations from his Swiss predecessor. And yet, far from instilling confidence, the coincidence suggests that the number reflected more than just the iron law of statistics. Nor is that the only similarity between Galton's science of genius and that of earlier practitioners. Indeed, just as physiognomists and craniometrists had detected the presence of genius only in bodies already classified as such, Galton derived his conclusions about genius's origins in reference to opinions long conferred. He was, to be sure, straightforward about his method, calling attention to his central assumption that "high reputation is a pretty accurate test of high ability." Genius, he reasoned, would always "out," disclosing itself in a record of achieved distinction that could be evaluated statistically. By looking at indicators of public and professional esteem—entries in dictionaries of national biography, references in newspapers, the conferral of prizes and awards—Galton believed he could arrive at an accurate portrait of the geniuses of an age. Built into his definition of genius, in fact, was the assumption not only of ability, but of an "inherent stimulus [to] climb the path that leads to eminence, [and] the strength to reach the summit." This was what Galton described as the "concrete triple event"—ability, zeal, and a capacity for hard labor—that was the necessary precondition of a type who, far from being an outcast or a degenerate, was conceived as the fittest of the species, robust in body as well as in mind. However much Romantics might piffle on about undiscovered genius, a man who didn't produce, and through that production achieve a place of eminence in society, leaving behind a clear record of distinction, simply wasn't a genius.[41]

Despite Galton's overly facile assumption regarding the direct correspondence between achievement and recognition, there is undoubtedly something to his method; indeed, it continues to serve as the basis of an ongoing branch of psychological investigation known as "historimetrics." But what made the assumption particularly problematic was Galton's further insistence that reputation reflected *hereditary* genius. His use of indices of achievement, in other words, was not meant to suggest that fame played a part in creating genius; fame, in Galton's view, reflected what was already there. Genius was inherent, the product of natural gifts. And although many since the eighteenth century have shared that view, Galton rightly claimed to be the first to treat the subject statistically. Marshaling an impressive array of data, he provided statistics on a vast range of outstanding individuals, from musicians, poets, and scientists to judges, statesmen, and even wrestlers and rowers. In doing so, he emphasized time and again how often these high performers were related by ancestry and birth. The conclusion to be drawn, Galton stressed, was that "natural abilities," like anything else in the organic world, were derived from inheritance. Nature trumped nurture. Genes alone, as we would say, were the source of genius.[42]

Few today would doubt that inheritance plays some role in shaping human capacities, although whether it should be treated as the dominant factor remains a hotly contested point. Galton assumed that it was the dominant factor, but his data did not prove it, and the reasons should be clear. To treat reputation alone as the sign of genius was to completely ignore those structures of power that conferred it, evaluating success and dictating admission to the competition in the first place. Should the absence of women on Galton's lists, or the virtual lack of all save white Europeans, be taken as a sign of their natural inferiority? Of course not, though Galton himself concluded as much. And should the interrelatedness of Galton's families of English genius be read first and foremost as the predictable consequence of a system that confined privilege and opportunity to very small circles? Of course, though the thought seems not to have occurred to him, or if it did, Galton dismissed it as unimportant.

The thought did, however, occur to others. In an explicit response to Galton, the eminent Swiss botanist Alphonse de Candolle, for example (who himself showed up in Galton's detailed family trees), took pains to press the importance of environmental factors in influencing achievement in his 1873 study, *Histoire des sciences et savants depuis deux siècles*. Others responded similarly, keeping alive an argument that had been cultivated (if only in the minority) since the eighteenth century, when the likes of William Sharpe and Claude Adrien Helvétius had made a concerted case for nurture over nature in the production of genius. But although the reception of Galton's work was by no means uniformly positive, generating among religious observers, especially, a strongly negative response, it did enjoy extensive support, particularly in those quarters of the scientific community where the prestige of Darwin had already rendered many amenable to arguments based on the laws of inheritance. Darwin himself wrote to his cousin after the publication of his work in strongly congratulatory terms, and he later reaffirmed his endorsement in print on numerous occasions, noting in one such instance that "some writers have doubted whether those complex mental attributes, on which genius and talent depend, are inherited. . . . But he who will study Mr. Galton's able work on 'Hereditary Genius' will have his doubts allayed."[43]

Yet the success of Galton's work owed to much more than Darwin's stamp of approval, or even to the force of its own arguments. Equally important was the fact that Galton said what students of genius were prepared to hear. Since the eighteenth century, they had been told repeatedly that genius was born, not made. Philosophers and poets, no less than anatomists and criminologists, shared that assumption, and by the second half of the nineteenth century it had become a default assumption. It is revealing that even the self-help author Samuel Smiles, who was committed to the proposition that individuals could pull themselves up by their bootstraps by dint of hard work, conceded that genius was another matter. "It is not, however, through the preparatory efforts of labour and talent, however persevering," he said, "that [the greatest works] are conceived and perfected, but through the influence of what we call Genius." Galton provided yet another scientific iteration of a well-established claim. His numbers dazzled. His statistics impressed. And they put into quantifiable terms the belief that genius was genuinely precious, one in a million. His work inspired a range of ambitious studies modeled on his methods, including Havelock Ellis's *A Study of British Genius* (1904) and James McKeen Cattell's *American Men of Science* (1906). But what such studies could not do was test for the presence of the very thing they claimed to reveal.[44]

Galton was aware of this shortcoming—aware, that is, that his statistical studies of past achievement could no more detect genius in our midst than could the craniometrical studies of the dead and departed. At the very best, his statistical methods confirmed the presence of what was known to have been there already. Like the studies by craniometrists, moreover, Galton's investigations dealt only with the past, not with living geniuses. Investigation of the dead was insufficient. For as Galton suggested in *Hereditary Genius*, and then advocated more boldly as his interest in eugenics increased, if one could identify genius in living human beings, singling out the one in a million, then, "just as a new race" could be obtained in animals and plants by selective breeding, so "a race of gifted men might be obtained, under exactly similar conditions." It was for this reason that Galton was drawn to anthropomorphic studies focusing on living subjects. He measured heads, like Gladstone's, which were still attached. And he gathered data on a range of indicators—from reaction time to the strength of the handshake to the color sense—hoping to discover some characteristic that would indicate the presence of genius among the living. Such faltering attempts on Galton's part, however, ended in failure. And so it was left to two of his great admirers—one French, the other American—to complete his work, devising a test that could be used to reveal genius in the flesh.[45]

T HE STORY OF THE GENESIS of the "intelligence quotient," commonly known as "IQ," is a story that has been told often and well. And yet part of that story has received insufficient emphasis: the degree to which the IQ exam emerged directly out of—and intersected directly with—the "geniological" investigations examined in this chapter, the long search for a science of genius that captivated researchers throughout the nineteenth and early twentieth centuries. Alfred Binet, it is true, first developed the initial version of the exam in order to screen for the presence, not of genius, but of mental retardation. A professor of psychology at the Sorbonne, he had been asked by the French government in 1904 to devise a reliable means to assess students suffering from mental disabilities, so-called *anormaux*. Together with his colleague Théodore Simon, Binet produced a diagnostic tool the following year that aimed to do just that, seeking to classify subjects on a scale descending from "normalcy" to "idiocy," "imbecility," and *débilité* (moronity), in the brutal categorical language of the time. Prescribing a series of tests designed to calculate the mental age of the subject in relation to his or her actual age, the exam worked by assigning groups of tasks that in theory a normal child of a given age could perform with ease. All normal seven-year-olds, Binet reckoned, would be able to distinguish between a butterfly and a fly, a piece of a wood and a piece of glass, and paper and cardboard, distinctions that would be less apparent to normal five-year-olds. Organized accordingly, the exam as a whole was conceived as a series of barriers of increasing difficulty that could be used to classify subjects in relation to what was deemed "normal" for any given stage of development. The immediate goal was to classify those falling below normalcy, but it was readily apparent that an exam of this sort could be used to do the opposite, too—identifying and ranking individuals whose mental ages were above average.[46]

Binet, in fact, like Galton before him, had long been intrigued by individuals who departed from the mean at the other end of the Gaussian curve, pointing out that "people of talent or genius serve better than average examples for making us understand the laws of character, because they present more extreme traits." Over the course of two years, he had studied the case of Jacques Inaudi, a young man from Piedmont who could perform extraordinary feats of mathematical calculation in

his head. Chess players and other "great calculators" drew Binet's attention, along with subjects of prodigious memory, whom he examined
with clinical methods not unlike those employed by Edouard Toulouse,
the physician who had investigated the neurotic genius of Émile Zola.[47]

Nor was that his only debt to an earlier form of research devoted to
the study of genius. At the same time that he was pursuing case studies of extraordinary minds, Binet was aggressively pursuing craniometric research along the lines laid out by Paul Broca, taking calipers to
the heads of subjects both living and dead. In 1898, with his colleague
Nicolas Vaschide, Binet published an extensive historical review of the
literature on craniometric and brain research, paying close attention
to the work of Gall, Broca, and a host of others. And in the following
six years he published close to a dozen more articles on craniometric
themes, searching, like Galton, for evidence of a physical sign that could
be used to identify genius within. By 1904, Binet had grown increasingly
skeptical of craniometry's ability to provide actionable results, but he
refused to abandon the search for some kind of objective indicator. The
potential benefits were enormous. As Vaschide explained in 1904, "if it
were possible to recognize from infancy, by means of special signs, those
of superior intelligence, one could push their education much further,
prepare them specially for high culture, to the end that, on becoming
adults, they would be an intellectual elite capable of advancing society in
all branches of its activity."[48]

It should come as no surprise, then, that an exam initially intended
to identify *anormaux* on one end of the scale was quickly applied to those
on the other—conceived as a powerful means to identify individuals of
extraordinary ability. A revised 1908 version of Binet's scale provided
explicitly for this possibility. And when, in 1912, the German psychologist William Stern proposed that mental age be divided by actual age,
and then multiplied by a 100, to yield an intelligence *quotient*, IQ, in
much the form that we know it today, was born. With it came the tantalizing prospect that the living sign for which Galton and others had
searched was now within science's grasp.

Binet, it should be emphasized, was never comfortable with the hard
hereditarian position advocated by Galton (still less so with eugenics),
and in the years before his premature death in 1911 he showed himself
acutely aware of the possibility that his research might be abused. The
man most responsible for refining his work and putting it into practice, however, showed fewer such compunctions. Also a professor of psychology, Lewis Terman hailed from a Midwestern farming family in the
United States, the twelfth of fourteen children. In a delicious irony, he

later attributed his lifelong interest in intelligence to the early visit of an itinerant phrenologist, who felt the bumps on the young boy's head and concluded that a big brain lay below. Whether or not the bumps played any part in the process, Terman did manage to overcome his immediate circumstances. He attended college and then graduate school, earning a PhD from Clark University in 1905. Several years later, he took up a position at Stanford, where he spent the remainder of his long career. It was there in 1916 that he published the Stanford Revision of the Binet-Simon Scale, which he continued to refine throughout his life. Significantly updated, the Stanford-Binet Intelligence Scales remain a paradigm to this day, a primary tool for measuring IQ.

Terman was ideally placed to appreciate Binet's contribution, the value of which, he judged, "can hardly be overestimated," even if it had not received "the attention that it deserved." As a graduate student, Terman had studied intelligence testing in children, publishing the findings of his dissertation research in 1906 as *Genius and Stupidity: A Study of Some of the Intellectual Processes of Seven "Bright" and Seven "Stupid" Boys*. The title alone is revealing, pointing to the trademark fascination with deviation from the norm. Like his geniological predecessors, Terman marveled at the vast gulf that separated the best and the brightest from the dim and the dull. Such differences, he concluded, could never be explained by environmental factors, but must be based in heredity. It was of the utmost importance, as a consequence, that educators be equipped with the means to identify genius at an early age, so that they might nurture it accordingly. In Terman's view, nothing less than the future of civilization was at stake. As he stressed in his guidelines for administering his revision of the Binet-Simon exam, "whether civilization moves on and up depends most on the advances made by creative thinkers and leaders in science, politics, art, morality, and religion. Moderate ability can follow or imitate, but genius must show the way."[49]

Terman's vision of the heroic natural genius leading the way of humanity is reminiscent of Galton's own perorations to those "grand human animals" destined to be "kings of men." The similarity is no coincidence. For although Terman admired Binet, he admired Galton even more. "The publication of Galton's *Hereditary Genius*, in 1869, marks the beginning of a new era," he declared. In his own landmark work, *Genetic Studies of Genius*, he sought to realize Galton's dream of identifying genius in the flesh. The work, the first volume of which was published in 1925, summarized the initial findings of a vast human experiment begun in 1911 and made feasible by "the entirely new situation" created by Binet. "It was at last possible to determine with some degree of proximation the brightness of a given child," Terman recalled. Armed with their instruments and scales, he and his assistants set about scouring the school districts around Stanford and San Francisco to locate little geniuses. In succeeding years, the study was formalized and expanded, permitting Terman's team, with the aid of a sizable grant from the Commonwealth Fund for the study of "genius in the making," to administer the Stanford-Binet test to a large number of children. The result was the identification of some 1,000 gifted boys and girls ("Termites"), defined as those with an IQ of over 140, who were then followed in regular intervals throughout the course of their lives.[50]

A longitudinal study of this ambition and scope necessarily pointed toward the future. As Terman emphasized in the opening lines of the study's initial volume, "It should go without saying that a nation's resources of intellectual talent are among the most precious it will ever have. The origins of genius, the natural laws of its development, and the environmental influences by which it may be affected for good or ill are scientific problems of almost unequaled importance for human welfare." The study undoubtedly gestured toward a brave new world, already getting under way, in which governments as far afield as South America, Europe, Russia, and Japan would pursue the hunt for national genius (and the attendant filtering of the intellectually undesirable) in standardized tests like those that Terman helped to develop for widespread consumption in the United States. Terman himself played a key role in helping to design the notorious battery of mental tests administered to 1.75 million recruits to the US Army in World War I, sorting "morons" from the fit. Meanwhile, racist popularizers, such as H. H. Goddard, brought Terman's methods to Ellis Island and the schools, using the Stanford-Binet scale to call attention to the danger that "feeble-minded" immigrants and blacks would poison the pool of American genius and so weaken the "natural aristocracy" fit by birth to lead. That said, Terman's own study undoubtedly furnished a wealth of data that has continued to yield useful information, paying dividends long after his Termites had grown and left the nest. Yet his instruments proved less successful as a means of detecting genius. Not only did comparatively few of the Termites go on to national or international renown, but the study famously failed to detect two men—Luis Alvarez and William Shockley—who would later be awarded Nobel Prizes in Physics. Their tested IQs failed to meet the cut-off of 140, and they were weeded out and discarded accordingly.[51]

Such oversights pale in significance alongside those of the countless men and women who were wrongly classified at an early age as genetically inferior and tracked accordingly. The result was a tragic waste of human resources, and in many cases worse. Yet they do serve nicely to highlight the question of just what it was that Terman and his IQ exam were really measuring. The stated aim, of course, was to isolate genius, but what Terman's instruments were really designed to detect was something else: intelligence. The word was an old one, having long been used in theological parlance to distinguish between the material and immaterial realms. "Intelligences" belonged primarily to the latter along the scale of the Great Chain of Being: they were angels, souls, *genii*, minds. Gradually, beginning in the eighteenth century, intelligence was extended to animals in a number of taxonomic schemes, which were used to distinguish hierarchically between creatures said to have more of it, and those who had less or none at all. In a further extension, nineteenth-century anthropologists expropriated this zoological category, using it as a principle of difference to distinguish between "lower" and "higher" races. Intelligence, in the crude conceptions of craniometrists, was supposed to reside in greater quantity in bigger and whiter brains than in smaller brains or the brains of people of color. The term was applied in other ways as well, but the point is that prior to Binet, it was seldom used outside of anthropology as a criterion to evaluate genius or to distinguish individuals or groups.[52]

The adoption of the category of intelligence by Binet and Terman thus marks an important shift of emphasis. Downplaying the vital, pathological, and even creative elements of genius in favor of something apparently more rational and stable, Binet and Terman hoped to identify an attribute that would be more useful in meeting the demands of complex societies, in which the general capacity to acquire knowledge was of immense value. Tellingly, Terman gradually abandoned the word "genius" in his public comments on his work after 1945. And although that development reflected the changed circumstances of the postwar discussion, it also reflected Terman's tacit acknowledgment—based on the less-than-spectacular findings of his study—that intelligence and the elusive thing called "genius" were not the same thing. As Terman confessed in the fourth volume of *Genetic Studies of Genius*, published in 1947, "we have seen that intellect and achievement are far from perfectly correlated."[53]

Be that as it may, Terman's entire enterprise was heir to the centuries-long search to isolate genius in the flesh, and that search continued to shape his findings, beginning with the category of "intelligence" itself.

For Terman's intelligence was, in truth, "general intelligence," a notion that had been developed independently by the British psychologist and statistician Charles Spearman—another of Galton's admirers—at the beginning of the twentieth century. Using a complex statistical technique known as factor analysis, Spearman had concluded that a single factor—he called it g (general intelligence)—must govern an individual's scores in different sections of exams, like those administered by Binet, that measured different mental abilities (spatial analysis, abstract reasoning, verbal ability, and so forth) in a single sitting. Rather than conceive of intelligence as multiple and varied—as critics of Spearman, including L. L. Thurstone, did at the time, and as more recent observers, such as Howard Gardner, do still—Spearman, and with him Terman, thought of general intelligence in the same way that geniologists thought of genius, as a single, unitary, measurable "thing" given at birth, rooted in biological nature, and constant over a lifetime, though protean in its powers. G was the mental energy that governed performance where matters of the intellect were concerned. G was the "mental power" (on the analogy of horsepower) that ran the machine. What Goethe had said of genius—whether a man distinguished himself in science, war, statecraft, or music, "it all comes to the same thing"—was said by Spearman and Terman of general intelligence. The category continued to belie its past.[54]

The same was true of other aspects of Terman's findings, which gave, he claimed, "considerable support to Galton's theory as to the hereditary nature of genius." Terman noted the "very great deficiency of Latin and negro ancestry" among his gifted subjects, for example, and the "100 per cent excess of Jewish blood." Women scored highly on his exam, it is true, and he even called attention to the injustice of denying them fuller access to professional life. But that didn't prevent him from asserting that women still fell behind men at the very highest levels. Terman noted that "the facts we have presented are in harmony with the hypothesis that exceptionally superior intelligence occurs with greater frequency among boys than among girls." And in another nod to Galton, and in a challenge to those inclined to link genius to madness and degeneration, Terman took pains to point out that his exceptional subjects were, on the whole, healthier, more robust, and better adjusted psychologically than were average individuals.[55]

In all of these ways, Terman's research reflected the concerns, and frequently the conclusions, of his predecessors. His greatest debt to the past, however, was more explicit. The entire second volume of *Genetic Studies of Genius* was devoted to measuring the IQs not of the living, but of the dead. Terman's assistant, Catharine Morris Cox, served as the primary author of the study, but it was Terman who oversaw the work and developed the method by which it was carried out. In a 1917 paper, he had attempted to estimate the IQ of none other than Francis Galton. Administering an exam to a corpse, it might be thought, would be even trickier than locating clues of incipient pathology in the dead or taking the measure of the brains of the departed. Terman was undeterred, confident that reports of Galton's childhood activities, pastimes, and accomplishments could furnish the necessary information. "From the evidence given," he observed, "one is justified in concluding that between the ages of three and eight years . . . Francis Galton must have had an intelligence quotient not far from 200." As he hastened to point out, none of the children encountered in his study at Stanford could approach such a number, with the best among them topping out at 170. Galton, it followed, was no ordinary genius.[56]

Cox proceeded along similar lines, starting from a list of 1,000 eminent individuals, based on entries in biographical dictionaries compiled by the American psychologist James McKeen Cattell, yet another acolyte of Galton. Cox winnowed the list down according to the availability of information on each candidate's childhood, excluding for this reason all individuals who lived prior to the mid-fifteenth century. The remaining 301 people on the list were drawn almost exclusively from Europe and America and included notable figures in the sciences, arts, letters, statecraft, and military professions up to 1850. John Stuart Mill topped the charts, with an estimated IQ of 190, and Goethe, the mathematician Gottfried Wilhelm Leibniz, and the Dutch political theorist Hugo Grotius followed closely at 185. Voltaire recorded a respectable 170, whereas Newton (130), Napoleon (135), and Beethoven (135) were given less impressive marks. Napoleon's great general André Massena claimed the lowest recorded entry, a measly 100 IQ, making it something of a miracle that French armies held out as long as they did.[57]

The Cox study is still described by reputable psychologists as a "classic work," which "has been cited more frequently perhaps than any other book on genius." As an attempt to apply a new method to an old problem, it was undoubtedly innovative, even if its conclusions were in many cases laughably speculative. And yet, it is striking how much it shared with earlier efforts to isolate, quantify, and calculate this thing called genius. Cox herself grounded the study in this age-old effort, noting in her opening line that "the factors which determine the appearance and development of geniuses have presented a persistent problem ever since man, in his earliest study of man, began to take account of individual differences." But the similarities were most striking with respect to the history of the preceding 150 years. Whereas Lavater, Gall, and Broca had searched in vain for the stigmata of genius above the neck; whereas Moreau and Lombroso had hunted for telltale signs of incipient pathology in the case histories of the dead; and whereas Galton had looked to eminence as an indicator that the best men were best, Cox crunched the numbers of IQ in search of a single revealing sign of the presence of the ghost that had been sighted long before she even began. Genius looked like genius. Except when it didn't. But precisely what genius looked like remained difficult to say.[58]

"AMONG MANY PROBLEMS hitherto unsolved in the Mystery of the Mind stands the prominent question of genius," Helena Blavatsky observed in 1889. The Russian-born American citizen was the founder of the Theosophical Society, which was devoted to exploring the occult mysteries of the universe. She considered genius a fitting subject for exploration. "Whence, and what is genius?" she asked in an essay devoted to the subject, what was "its *raison d'être*, and what were the causes of its excessive rarity?" Was genius a "gift of heaven," and if so, why did it descend on some, while others languished in "dullness of intellect or even idiocy"? Was it the product of "blind chance," dependent, as the materialists would have it, "on physical causes alone"? Perhaps genius was an "abnormal aptitude of the mind," or a growth of the "physical brain"? Or perhaps, as the Romantics maintained, it was the faculty of growth itself, a vital power that could take one beyond oneself?[59]

In entertaining these speculations, Blavatsky demonstrated an impressive familiarity with the authoritative positions on genius of her age. But to these she offered her own, rather surprising, suggestion: "Perchance, in their unsophisticated wisdom," she ventured, "the philosophers of old were nearer the truth than our modern wiseacres, when they endowed man with a tutelary Deity, a spirit whom they called genius." Here, in the belief in a personal spirit that outlived the physical self, unique to each and common to the universal all, interceding on high and conveying messages from the beyond, was a doctrine closer to the truth, Blavatsky believed, than anything the moderns could muster. To be sure, she hastened to qualify the point in keeping with the particulars of her own esoteric philosophy, which drew eclectically on Buddhism and Indian religion to posit a belief in the reincarnation of the ego and its karmic movement toward (or away from) an all-encompassing "Oversoul." Still, the central belief of the ancients, Blavatsky maintained, and the key to understanding their hero worship, was the notion that what distinguished the greatest men "was the imprisoned Spirit, the exiled 'god' within." That notion, she insisted, retained its basic truth. In "every manifestation of genius," Blavatsky continued, "in the warrior or the Bard, the great painter, artist, statesman or man of Science," one could discern "the undeniable presence of the celestial exile, the divine Ego whose jailor thou art, Oh man of matter!" What was called "deification" applied to the "immortal God within."

Blavatsky was well aware that most scientists would dismiss her ecstatic musings. "The very idea that every man with a 'soul' in him is the vehicle of (a) genius will appear supremely absurd, even to [religious] believers, while the materialist will fall foul of it as 'crass superstition.'" Yet, lest we grant our assent too readily, it is well to bear in mind that her invocation of the occult was far from an aberration, and her theosophical teaching hardly an isolated phenomenon. A number of scholars have argued recently that theosophy and spiritualism were central to modern culture. Certainly, theosophy interested a great number of eminent writers, artists, and intellectuals, including, to name only a few, William Butler Yeats, Rudolf Steiner, Igor Stravinsky, Arthur Conan Doyle, and even Thomas Edison. Fascination with spiritual forces turned up in surprising places. The great French writer Victor Hugo, for example, experimented throughout his life with the occult, holding séances and invoking the spirits of the dead. During one such session, he and friends managed to contact the *genius* of Shakespeare, who kindly dictated the first act of a new play, in French! Other encounters led to conversations with the spirits of Dante, Racine, and Molière. In Germany and England, those who ventured into occult worlds, flirting with theosophy, hypnotism, mesmerism, and alchemy, could readily conceive, like the leaders of the Hermetic Order of the Golden Dawn in London, of a higher, angelic, or godlike self—a "Genius"—who acted as an intercessor to the divine.[60]

Whether beliefs of this type, which enjoyed an undeniable vogue toward the end of the nineteenth and the beginning of the twentieth century, represent truly modern creations, or illustrate instead the tenacious persistence of the past, is a debatable question. But what is clear, at least where matters of genius are concerned, is their continued resonance. Blavatsky's general claim that the phenomenon of genius entailed something like the *divinum quiddam* of the ancients—a piece of the divine in us—could readily appeal to men and women who would not have shared other aspects of her esoteric philosophy, with its Eastern allusions and proto–New Age language. The theosophist's contention that genius involved a connection between the individual (Ego) and a transcendent "over-soul," in fact, was not far removed from the Romantic belief that the genius participated in what German idealists conceived as the noumenal realm of Idea or Spirit, what Shelley called the "eternal, the infinite, and the one." Christians, too, could recognize in the ancient idea of a *genius*, or its modern incarnation in man, a connection to the demons, spirits, and angels that had long attended human beings or the eternal souls that animated their flesh, raising them to God. The phenomenon of genius, in short, seemed to underscore the point that there was more to the world than positivists could explain, defying the desacralizing efforts of modern science. Call it superstition, but it remained the case that the "unsophisticated" and "uneducated masses" registered a truth nonetheless in their confrontations with genius, Blavatsky wrote. "Feeling themselves in the presence of that which in the enormous majority is ever hidden, of something incomprehensible to their matter-of-fact minds, they experience the same awe that popular masses felt in days of old when their fancy, often more unerring than cultured reason, created of their heroes gods." The genius made manifest the marvelous, and so the masses made of the genius an exalted being who was more than a man.[61]

Despite the exorcizing efforts of the science of genius throughout the whole of the nineteenth century, then, *genii* continued to haunt the genius; *daimones* were still detectable in daemonic man. Nor was this lingering presence simply the consequence of the failure of science to penetrate down to men and women on the streets. On the contrary, the magical and mystical aura that continued to surround the genius was the product, in part, of that science itself. Exorcisms, no less than incantations, are religious rites, and in their efforts to perform them, men as varied as Gall and Galton, Moreau and Broca, and Lombroso and Lélut succeeded, in spite of themselves, in further enchanting the creature whose demons they intended to purge.

Admittedly, the genius, in their reckoning, was a natural creation, but in his singularity and election he resembled a variation of the genius of Kant, through whom nature spoke its truth to art, providing epiphanies of a more beautiful world. The genius, in other words, continued to be conceived as a medium, an oracle who channeled nature's revelations, disclosing its truths, revealing its wonders, and laying down its laws—and not only in art. For genius was a power, like *g*, common to eminence in many domains. Those chosen creatures who possessed it remained creatures apart, marked by stigmata, as Lombroso contended, or stigmatized by signs, singled out by virtue of their madness, disease, or exalted physique. One in a million, one in ten million, the genius was like no other, the exception who defied the rule(s).

How ironic, then, that Terman could declare, in announcing the advent of the science of genius, that its inception had been long retarded by the "influence of current beliefs, partaking of the nature of superstitions, regarding the essential nature of the Great Man, who has commonly been regarded by the masses as qualitatively set off from the rest of mankind, the product of supernatural causes." For the science that he and others advocated did as much to qualitatively set the Great Man apart as any received superstition. By substituting natural for supernatural causes, they granted the imprimatur of science to what remained, fundamentally, a myth regarding the right and capacity of higher beings to rule the world. Further enhancing the genius's favored inequality and exceptional status, they objectified his difference from ordinary human beings. And yet the pathogens and pieces of brain, the hereditary intelligence and genetic force that scientists of genius discovered in the places where the *genii* once roamed, could not succeed in entirely displacing them. The very effort to purge the body of spirits was in some sense to credit their existence.[62]

Indeed, that the genius might still be haunted by demons was a prospect on which both advocates of science and their more spiritual detractors could frequently, if surprisingly, agree. While Lombroso and his followers speculated openly about the genius's potential for madness, revolution, and crime, Blavatsky observed that, "like the good and bad *genii* of old with whom human genius is made so appropriately to share the name, it takes its helpless possessor by the hand and leads him, one day to the pinnacles of fame, fortune, and glory, but to plunge him on the following day into an abyss of shame, despair, often of crime." Even the acolytes of Galton, though denying genius's inherent pathology, might agree that, were one of these grand human animals to catch an evil scent, he might ravage the world with catastrophic results, like a terrible, prowling beast. To a recovering Romantic like Friedrich Nietzsche, that was not an altogether unpleasant thought. Men of genius, he observed, "were like explosives," the danger in them "extraordinary." The power of destruction was the natural counterpart to the power of creation. When that power, legitimated by science and consecrated by a militant religion, was put to the service of politics, the consequences proved truly apocalyptic.[63]

CHAPTER VI

THE RELIGION
OF GENIUS

I N THE MID-NINETEENTH CENTURY, the Danish philosopher Søren
Kierkegaard published a short essay with an intriguing title, "On the
Difference Between a Genius and an Apostle." Like so many of Kierkegaard's occasional writings, the essay called attention to what he regarded
as a disturbing tendency of the present age. Science and learning had
confused Christianity, he charged, with the result that religious discourse
was adopting science's terms. Pastors now described the likes of Saint
Paul as a "genius," hailing his brilliance and lauding his style. The praise
was well intentioned, but the consequence was a fatal conflation: "Esprit
and the Spirit, revelation and originality, a call from God and genius,
all end by meaning more or less the same thing." In truth, Kierkegaard
insisted, a "genius and an Apostle are qualitatively different." A man like
St. Paul "has no connection whatsoever with Plato or Shakespeare."[1]

Kierkegaard's essay was prompted by the case of the contemporary Danish pastor and philosopher Adolph Peter Adler, who claimed
to have received a new revelation from God, and then amended the
account under scrutiny, explaining it as a revelation of genius instead.
But as Kierkegaard well knew, confusion of this kind was by no means
an isolated occurrence: across Europe in the nineteenth century, Christian apologists lauded the heroes of their faith in similar terms, concurring with the abbé Louis Bautain, who observed that "it is by men of
genius, prophets, poets, apostles . . . that the life of heaven has been
communicated to humanity since the beginning." Among Protestants,
Martin Luther emerged in the nineteenth century as a robust example
of the Christian genius. At the same time, Catholics redefined their own
prophets and saints, calling attention on occasion, in a pious nod to the

science of the time, to signs of holy madness and enthusiasm as symptoms of an underlying genius. True, only skeptics dared suggest that Jesus himself suffered from a morbid pathology. But disciples and disbelievers alike could agree that Jesus was a "great man" and an "original genius," a claim that was increasingly common in the nineteenth and early twentieth centuries (to say nothing of our own). When Ernest Renan penned his controversial biography of Jesus, *La vie de Jésus*, in 1863, he followed David Friedrich Strauss in making that claim central to his account, prompting the withering scorn of Nietzsche, who later observed that the "concept of genius" was completely inappropriate when applied to the "Jesus type."[2]

With that much, at least, Kierkegaard would have agreed, for as he rightly appreciated, to apply the label "genius" to an apostle of God was to recognize a standard of authority that was human, not divine. Just as it would be treason "to ask whether a king is a genius" as a condition of loyalty, or it would be an act of filial rebellion to maintain that "I obey my father, not because he is my father but because he is a genius," it was misconceived to base the divinely conferred power of an apostle on aesthetic or intellectual grounds. "To ask whether Christ is profound is blasphemy," Kierkegaard maintained. Genius and divine authority were entirely different things.[3]

The blurring of that distinction concerned Kierkegaard primarily insofar as it weakened and humanized Christianity, tacitly recognizing the genius as the highest human type. But there was a related consequence that the Danish philosopher hinted at with his examples of filial rebellion and *lèse-majesté*. Genius was becoming a criterion of political authority, assuming the awe and aura once reserved for divinely conferred majesty. Just as the apostle could be confused with the genius, the genius could be confused with the apostle and hailed as a prophet, a redeemer, a savior, and ruler of men.

That process of conflation had been underway since the birth of the genius in the eighteenth century, and it was given further impetus during the French Revolution and the reign of Napoleon—the period of "the dawn of the idols"—when genius was invoked self-consciously as a criterion of political legitimacy. The Romantics and others in the nineteenth century reinforced the conflation, repeatedly describing the genius as a redemptive figure, a lawgiver and prophet, who could embody the national spirit, while science gave credence to the genius's special election. But it was ultimately only in the first decades of the twentieth century—ironically, at the very moment that Kierkegaard's work was experiencing an important revival—that the genius's political power was fully realized and revealed as part of what insightful contemporaries labeled the "religion of genius" or the "genius cult." Flourishing across Europe between the wars, the cult was put to the service of even larger faiths, co-opted and instrumentalized by the two main "political religions" of the twentieth century, communism and fascism. Marxists employed the cult of genius in the Soviet Union to bolster the legitimacy of Lenin and Stalin, and leading scientists, such as the German neurologist Oskar Vogt, traveled to Moscow to dissect Lenin's brain in the quest to engineer the perfect man. In the German-speaking lands in the aftermath of World War I, the religion of genius flourished even more spectacularly, achieving its terrible apotheosis in the genius-cult of the Nazis. A key factor in shaping the self-conception of Adolf Hitler, the religion of genius proved crucial to preparing and consolidating his public image and mystique. Yet genius was also the category through which the world imagined his rival and avenger, the good genius Albert Einstein, who would triumph over evil and do his best to rid the world of genius's power by taking it upon himself.[4]

THERE WERE OTHERS BEFORE him who proclaimed it, and many more who practiced its rituals and followed its rites. But the Jewish historian Edgar Zilsel was the first to devote an explicit, critical analysis to what he termed, in his seminal 1918 work of that name, *die Geniereligion*, the "religion of genius." Originally published in Vienna, where Zilsel made his home until 1938, the work called attention to a cult then flourishing across the German-speaking world. The appreciation of genius, Zilsel aptly observed, had been on the rise since the seventeenth century, achieving prominence during the Age of Enlightenment and the German *Sturm und Drang* before the Romantics and Arthur Schopenhauer further enhanced its aura. Numerous others had cultivated the faith in the nineteenth century, preparing the way for a formidable array of apostles and "genius enthusiasts," including the composer Richard Wagner, the man of letters Otto Weininger, and the author and critic Houston Stewart Chamberlain, who zealously preached "Genius worship as a religion." The signs of their proselytism were now everywhere apparent. "In the windows of our bookstores we see biographies and letters of Goethe, Beethoven, Schopenhauer, Wagner," Zilsel wrote. "Our novelists write stories about the lives of Leonardo da Vinci, Schiller, Spinoza, Schubert, Tycho Brahe, Frederick the Great, Goethe, and Paracelsus. Our musicians show us on stage how Schubert and Palestrina lived and composed. And our souvenir shops offer for pennies the pictures of our great men." The full array of modern mass media had been put to the service of the cult. Theater pieces, color prints, busts, and death masks vied for attention with illustrated newspapers and magazine features that gathered the sayings of departed geniuses while providing countless commemorations of their lives and works. "We worship the relics of our great men," Zilsel further observed, "their autographs and locks of hair, their quill pens and tobacco cases, like the Catholic Church worships the bones, implements and robes of the saints." So, too, had the resting places of geniuses been transformed in the shadow of Westminster and the Pantheon from simple graves to elaborate tombs, modern Valhallas that drew adoring crowds of pilgrims, who also flocked to birthplaces and monumental sites—Weimar, Stratford-upon-Avon, Bayreuth—as Catholics journeyed to Lourdes. Indeed, for all its scientific and medical pretensions, the primary attraction of the genius religion was its emotional appeal. Zilsel coined a new word to describe it: *Abfärben*, the "rubbing off" or "bleeding into" of feelings that passed from the genius to the genius enthusiast by way of all with which the great man had come into contact. To be in the space a genius had inhabited, or in the presence of an object he had touched, was to experience a feeling akin to religious awe.[5]

Although Zilsel focused overwhelmingly on Austria and Germany in his description of the genius religion, his knowledge of its wider European cultural foundations was extensive. In 1926, in fact, Zilsel published a history of the development of the genius concept from antiquity to the Renaissance that remains a useful resource. And though he never finished a projected second volume bringing the story up to the present, he was well aware that the genius religion drew on articles of faith that had been elaborated throughout Europe since the eighteenth century. Chief among them was the belief, clearly articulated by the Romantics, and stressed above all by Schopenhauer, that the true genius occupied a salvific role, serving to overcome human alienation through his vision, life, and work. A central feature of what has been described as an "ideology of genius" evident in nineteenth and early twentieth century literary culture, this belief emphasized the genius's indispensable role as a savior who healed and redeemed. Germans described this capacity of genius as an *Erlösungskraft*, a power of deliverance or redemption, and they emphasized that it might be either terrible or sweet. The scholar Hermann Türck, for example, in his tremendously popular *Der geniale Mensch* (1899), first published in English as *The Man of Genius* in 1914, treated the unlikely pairing of Jesus and Napoleon to illustrate the point that the savior and the conqueror were "alike in their striving after the highest, eternal state of being." Like Alexander and Julius Caesar, both Jesus and Napoleon felt themselves in the grip of a higher power—God, Fate, the *daimonic* pull of their stars—and both worked to sweep away the old in the creation of the new, delivering their subjects from bondage and realizing their visions in the world. The point in Türck's handling was self-consciously Hegelian: creation and destruction were closely allied, deliverance and death united in a common cause. But it serves nicely to illustrate a sentiment shared by those of other philosophical persuasions. Even if the genius as redeemer was most often conceived as an artist in the broadest sense—a "poet," in Shelley's parlance—he could easily be imagined as a ruler of men like Jesus or Napoleon, Alexander or Caesar, a *Tatengenie* (a "genius of deeds") who created in flesh. Above all, the spellbinding example of Napoleon kept alive the possibility and hope that the genius and the statesman-creator might again someday be one.[6]

The power to redeem, and potentially to rule, was enhanced by the genius's privileged position "midway" between ordinary humanity and whatever might transcend it. As Thomas Carlyle, one of Zilsel's primary "genius enthusiasts," had observed in preaching the virtues of "hero-worship" in the nineteenth century, the genius or hero as man of letters "must be regarded as our most important modern person," for he performed "the same function which the old generations named a man Prophet, Priest, Divinity for doing," teaching all men that "a God is still present in their life." There was a "sacredness" to genius, Carlyle affirmed, and in a skeptical age, the genius's role was to call attention to the "True, Divine, and Eternal," which always exists behind the ephemera of life, but is rarely glimpsed by the many until it is revealed. Ralph Waldo Emerson, Carlyle's friend, preached a similar faith in the United States. "Genius is religious," he assured, adding elsewhere that "when nature has work to be done, she creates a genius to do it." The bearer of natural providence, the genius was a mediating force who "should occupy the whole space between God or pure mind, and the multitude of uneducated men," continually negotiating between the real and the apparent, the many and the one. It was a point that the German philosopher Herder and his admirers were concerned to make in a different register: the genius spoke for the nation, articulating the spirit—the genius—of the *Volk*.[7]

This special role put the genius in an inherently ambiguous relationship vis à vis the people, a point that Zilsel, a man of the Left, stressed with particular insistence. The religion of genius fostered a "salvation addiction" (*Erlösungssucht*) among the masses, he claimed, causing them to alienate and relinquish their power. It is true that the relationship need not be conceived solely in coercive terms. The nineteenth-century liberal

Benedetto Croce observed that "great geniuses reveal to us ourselves," and implicit in this widely repeated notion was a prospect that could captivate liberal minds: the possibility of individual empowerment and democratic awakening. Emerson, for one, developed the thought. Yet, more often, the relationship between the genius and the many was conceived to be fraught. The tension was apparent in the Romantics' ambiguous stance toward the people, whom they simultaneously praised as bearers of the *genius populi* and scorned as ingrates who stifled originality and made martyrs of genial men. Ambiguity of this kind showed up in the nineteenth century even among those who were otherwise well-disposed toward the people. John Stuart Mill, to take one salient example, insisted "emphatically on the importance of genius" and geniuses, judging these special creatures to be indispensable to the progress of humanity. And yet, because "persons of genius" were a "small minority," and "*ex vi termini*, more individual than any other," they were uniquely threatened by the power of the majority and the expanding equality of modern societies. Like Tocqueville, Mill worried that the "general tendency of things throughout the world is to render mediocrity the ascendant power among mankind." The tyranny of the majority was a greater threat to the genius than to anyone else.[8]

Attitudes of this kind were given further impetus by the advent of aesthetic modernism, which to an even greater extent than Romanticism was deeply conflicted in its attitudes toward the masses. On the one hand, modernists frequently pretended to a salvific role: they dreamed of transforming society in the image of art and believed earnestly that their work could set the people free. Yet, on the other hand, their work was often so arcane as to make it inaccessible to all but the discerning few. Those who failed to grasp its significance or even to try were dismissed as "philistines," a common term of contempt for the barbarians who willfully refused to acknowledge genius's authority. The term was evidence in itself of modernism's ambivalence toward the masses, part of its broader "trouble with genius" that took the form of an alternate longing and loathing, a desire to lead the people as an "avant-garde" and a contempt for those left behind. Seeking refuge in a fantasy of future fulfillment, the unacknowledged genius would be redeemed by posterity, taking up his place in the "brotherhood of genius" that united true greatness in the timeless and universal fellowship of death.[9]

In developing these points—the core of what he termed the "dogma" of the religion of genius—Zilsel called attention to the irony of a cult that lavished appreciation on the "unappreciated genius," pointing out ruefully how the frequent invocation of posterity justified a pose of suffering and martyrdom in the here and now. But there was even more to this dogma than Zilsel revealed, for, in effect, the genius had occupied a special stance toward the future since the eighteenth century, when he was presented to the world as a beacon of the new. Charged with creating the unprecedented, the genius displaced an older mimetic ideal that aimed, it was said, only to replicate what already was. To create originally, by contrast, was to bring into being what had yet to be, which meant that the creator of genius must be gifted with the foresight to see beyond the horizon of the times. It was in part for this reason that the Romantics had emphasized the genius's prophetic and visionary power. Members of the avant-garde stressed the point even more deliberately with their frequent injunction to "make it new." As the great French poet Arthur Rimbaud put it, "one must be absolutely modern." The religion of genius consecrated that commandment. And as the English physician (and degeneration theorist) Henry Maudsley insisted, the man of genius thrilled with the "prophetic pulse of an unknown future." He was pregnant with the new.[10]

In looking toward the future, the genius was ruled by an inherently hostile attitude toward established authority, an attitude that Zilsel found particularly troubling in light of the fact that the genius religion possessed no stable moral ground. The genius was revered for the alleged "depth" of his person and the profundity of his work, regardless of its content or moral consequences. Zilsel was no conservative, intent on justifying the status quo. Yet he rightly detected in the genius religion's cult of personality a disturbing tendency not only to accept moral transgression, but to praise it as necessary and natural. In the religion of genius, one confronted a faith that knew no rules, save the right of the genius to make them for himself and to legislate, accordingly, to others.[11]

It is curious in this connection that Zilsel made almost no mention of Friedrich Nietzsche, who had himself declared, "My religion . . . lies in working for the production of genius," and whose own cult had already achieved prominence in Germanic culture. It is true that Nietzsche's thinking about genius and geniuses was complicated. The term *das Genie*, rather surprisingly, is not crucial to his vocabulary, giving rise to the speculation that perhaps Nietzsche's own early intimacy with a genuine genius, in the person of Richard Wagner, and their subsequent bitter break cured him of the tendency to embrace the notion without reserve. Be that as it may, Nietzsche's importance in this connection lies less in his specific thoughts about geniuses than in his broader contention, continuously reaffirmed, that creativity was the highest human calling, one that necessarily involved conflict, domination, and even violence. Creation was amoral, beyond good and evil, and morality itself a creation, the product of creators, who alone could see what lay on the human horizon. As Nietzsche put it in *Thus Spoke Zarathustra*, his most widely read work: "What is good and evil, no one knows yet, unless it be he who creates. He, however, creates man's goal and gives the earth its meaning and its future. That anything at all is good and evil—that is his creation."[12]

The creative man was the constructor of values, the self-legislating being who in following the higher law of his own making might well look like "evil" in a more conventional sense. In a revealing passage of his *Human, All Too Human*, Nietzsche poses a question: What would be the nature of a "genius of culture"? "He would manipulate falsehood, force, the most ruthless self-interest as his instruments so skillfully he could only be called an evil, demonic being," even though his ultimate goals would be "great and good." Such cryptic statements were open to a variety of interpretations and appropriations. But despite the fact that Nietzsche himself could be insightful about the psychological processes at work in the creation of the genius as a "miraculous" being, he contributed enormously to the resonance and reception of the genius cult. Above all, his frequent coupling of creativity and cruelty, and his oracular pronouncements about the higher men of the future who would redeem through their creation, gave sanction to key tenets of the genius religion, for which Nietzsche himself became an object of reverence and veneration at the end of his life. Was he not a prophet of redemption and renewal? A martyr to his own creation? A man who, unappreciated in his career, was driven to insanity by the great burden of his mind? These, at least, were the enthusiastic claims, and they were given credence by Nietzsche's genuine descent into madness in the 1890s. Incoherent and incapacitated by strokes, the prophet spent his final years in the house of his sister in Weimar, which served simultaneously as the site of the Nietzsche Archive and a place of pilgrimage, replete with votive offerings, icons, and an altar to the great man and his work. Here was the place where genius had suffered for the creation of genius. Amply justifying Nietzsche's own fear that "one day I shall be pronounced 'holy,'" the site continued to function as a shrine after his death in 1900, in counterpoint to the residence of Wagner in Bayreuth, and in complement to the houses of Goethe and Schiller just down the road. Whatever the reasons for Zilsel's neglect of the burgeoning cult of Nietzsche, it only confirmed his larger point regarding the special prominence of the genius religion in the German-speaking lands and his concerns about the uses to which it might be put there.[13]

    The extraordinary importance of *Kultur* in the creation of German
identity is a phenomenon well-attested. But although commentators have
not insisted on the point as often as they might, the genius, as *Kultur's*
bearer and embodiment, played a critical role in the process of imagining the German nation. Already in 1839, the composer Robert Schumann
captured this nascent role nicely when he observed that Beethoven was
to German culture what Napoleon was to France. "With Beethoven," he
claimed, "every German imagines that he has reversed the fortunes of
the battles that he lost to Napoleon." The music of Beethoven justified
the past and beckoned to the possibilities of the future, highlighting the
unique place of music and musicians in the genesis of the genius cult
in Germany and their role in the creation of German national identity.
Schumann, whose unhappy descent into madness only enhanced his own
"genial" reputation, contributed to this union in his own right. But after
Beethoven, it was undoubtedly Wagner, another of Zilsel's central "genius
enthusiasts" and "priests," who did the most to couple genius and German nationalism in the nineteenth century. For the degeneration theorist Max Nordau, Wagner was the very embodiment of the degenerate
genius, and the "Wagner cult" a sign that modern society was in thrall to
its disease. But to the composer's countless admirers, he was the annunciation of new life, a German savior, whose art promised to fulfill the task
of redemption demanded of the true genius. When the genius enthusiast Houston Stewart Chamberlain—British by birth but German by
election—married Wagner's daughter, Eva, in 1908, he not only assumed
a leading role among the guardians of the temple at Bayreuth, but also
effected a proximity to genius that he preached in his many popular writings on the subject. Chamberlain's tremendously influential *Die Grund-
lagen des neunzehnten Jahrhunderts* (*The Foundations of the Nineteenth
Century*), first published in German in 1899 but reprinted extensively in
the first third of the twentieth century, selling nearly a quarter of a million
copies by 1938, was among the genius religion's most important tracts.
"Genius is like God," Chamberlain enthused, "in its essence it is free from
conditions; . . . it rises out of time and time's death-shadow, and passes
in all the glow of life into eternity." He suggested giving thanks of praise,
"thanks above all to the advent of men of great genius who alone give life."
Chamberlain's book was itself a hymn and a prayer, drawing attention to
the special connection "between the lonely genius and the masses," and
asserting, like Carlyle, the genius's privileged place as the great mover of
peoples. "With what reverence must we look up to the greatest phenomenon that nature presents to us—Genius!"[14]

The critic and writer Otto Weininger, the third of Zilsel's central genius enthusiasts, wholeheartedly agreed with that sentiment. Jewish born (though he converted to Christianity in the year before his death), Weininger shared Chamberlain's passion for Wagner and even made a pilgrimage to Bayreuth. But when he sought his own proximity to genius, he preferred Beethoven, taking his own life in 1903 in the house in Vienna where the German composer had died. In doing so, the man Hitler later infamously described as "the only good Jew" transformed himself into a martyr to the genius faith at the age of twenty-three, while transforming his sole published work, the sprawling *Sex and Character*, into an instant cult-classic. Preaching a deeply misogynist reverence for the emphatically male genius, the work went through eighteen editions in German alone by 1919. In it, Weininger insisted, like Chamberlain in the *Foundations*, that the great man could gather in himself the many, and make of them one. "A man is to be called all the more of a genius the more people he unites in himself," Weininger stressed. It was the "very ideal of the artistic genius" to live in the plurality, to lose himself in others, and to reabsorb them in his expansive personality in a unity of his own making. The true genius fashioned his original vision through the medium of other human beings.[15]

Wagner, Chamberlain, and Weininger were all anti-Semites—in Weininger's case of the Jewish variety. Anti-Semitism would prove of crucial significance to the subsequent development of the genius religion. But what is striking is just how widely received that religion was at the time of Zilsel's writing. Zilsel surely exaggerated when he claimed that virtually no one in the German-speaking world perceived the genius religion as a threat. And yet it was undeniably the case that the genius religion extended far beyond the sect of anti-Semites and right-wing nationalists who sought to make it their own. The critic and cabaret performer Egon Friedell provides an instructive example. Like Zilsel a left-leaning humanist and an Austrian of Jewish descent, Friedell cultivated the genius religion with an enthusiasm that knew few restraints. As he argued in his *Cultural History of the Modern Age*, a popular three-volume work published between 1927 and 1931, the genius embodied the spirit of the times, both shaping his epoch and speaking for it. Socrates in Greece, Voltaire in France, the philosopher Gotthold Ephraim Lessing in Germany, Shakespeare in Renaissance England, "in our time Nietzsche"—in such men "the whole age became objective in itself." The genius was the "intensified expression of each nation," the "concentrated formula" revealing the "desires and achievements of all his contemporaries." But at the same time, the genius was the "great solitary," a "completely unrelated and unrepeated singular," part of the "particular race of men who differ from the rest of their species in being creative." "No-one can resist these wizards," Friedell insisted. "They give us wings and they cripple us, intoxicate and sober us." They move mountains; they stir up "wars, revolutions, social earthquakes"; and they "behead kings, prepare battlefields, and sting nations to duels." At once beautiful and majestic, terrible and sublime, geniuses revealed the awesome power of God. "The genius makes it visible—that is the function of genius," Friedell wrote. To draw forth the divinity and the devil that "every man bears within him" was the genius's special calling.[16]

The fervency of Friedell's faith did not save him in the end from those fanatics who shared a surprising number of its tenets. He committed suicide in Vienna in 1938 rather than fall into the Gestapo's hands, making him, no less than Weininger, though for very different reasons, a martyr to the genius cult. That odd concurrence highlights just how catholic the religion of genius could be—in Germany and Austria, especially, but elsewhere, too. "It has been forgotten," Croce lamented in his native Italy, that genius is "not fallen from heaven." The noted Spanish philosopher José Ortega y Gasset made a similar point, warning in the 1920s that "one should beware of notions like genius and inspiration," for they were a sort of "magic wand" that mystified more than they made clear. From Germany, finally, the psychiatrist Wilhelm Lange-Eichbaum explained in *The Problem of Genius* in 1931, "among modern civilized beings a reverence for genius has become a substitute for the lost dogmatic religions of the past." Lange-Eichbaum regretted the fact, but he was insistent that "the notion, or rather the emotionally-tinged conviction, that genius has a peculiar sanctity is widely diffused throughout the modern world." The claim held even to the East, where at the very moment that Zilsel was publishing his account of the religion of genius, the Russian Revolution was giving rise to a heterodox faith of its own.[17]

IN FEBRUARY 1925, THE GERMAN neurologist Oskar Vogt traveled to Moscow with his French wife and research partner, Cécile, at the invitation of the Soviet government. Vogt was a world-renowned brain specialist, the founding director of the prestigious Kaiser Wilhelm Institute of Brain Research in Berlin, and an expert in the evaluation of elite brains. He was also a eugenicist, believing that his research could be used to establish criteria for the breeding of superior brains. Though he had been to the Soviet Union before, continuing a long tradition of German-Russian collaboration in the sciences, the circumstances of his visit on this occasion were unique. Vogt had been asked to confirm, on neuro-anatomical grounds, the "genius" of Vladimir Ilyich Lenin, who had died the previous month. After a preliminary meeting with a high-ranking commission of Soviet physicians, Vogt and his Russian colleagues agreed that, by employing Vogt's techniques, it would be possible to "provide information on the material substrate of Lenin's genius."[18]

Just why the representatives of the newly constituted Soviet Union should entrust this delicate task to a foreigner, seeking scientific confirmation of what, to their comrades in Russia, was already palpably clear, is not immediately apparent. Vogt was a recognized expert, the "best and only possible choice," in the opinion of the committee that recommended him. And though Vogt was not a member of the Communist Party, he was broadly sympathetic to the Left and had been active in the German Independent Social Democratic Party of the Weimar Republic, which had replaced the Hohenzollern monarchy at the end of World War I. But the most important reason for Vogt's invitation was likely his personal connections to important party officials, and, in particular, to the social hygienist Nikolai Alexandrovich Semashko, the "people's commissar for health" and one of the Soviet Union's leading advocates of eugenics. Semashko had met, and had been impressed by, Vogt on an earlier visit, and part of the lure in attracting him to Russia was the prospect not only of studying a brain of Lenin's stature, but, more ambitiously, of heading a brain institute with the explicit design of furthering the eugenic understanding of genius.[19]

Eugenicists had long found important advocates among utopians of the Left, who looked forward to building better human beings to inhabit better human worlds. The French utopian socialist Charles Fourier, for example, waxed ecstatic in the nineteenth century about the untapped potential of the human mind, looking forward to a future when the earth would teem with "37 million poets equal to Homer, 37 million geometricians equal to Newton, 37 million dramatists equal to Molière, and so on through all the talents imaginable." Although Fourier placed greater emphasis on social conditioning than he did upon altering human biology, his belief that knowledge of the "seeds" of human talent might be of service to those who would develop it along socialist lines was indicative of a basic willingness to put science to the task of improving humanity. In the Russian case, that willingness was very much a part of a broader fascination with genius that the educated population shared with (and frequently borrowed from) its counterparts in Europe. A subject of intense public interest—with leading exemplars, such as Alexander Pushkin, memorialized as national heroes, and others, such as Leo Tolstoy, sought out in their homes—genius was

FIGURE 5.1. Jean Honoré Fragonard, *Inspiration*, 1769. This stylized rendering of the inspired artist recalls a common motif of religious painting, in which the saint is startled by an epiphany or divine voice. *Copyright © RMN–Grand Palais / Art Resource, New York.*

FIGURE 5.2. Paul Cézanne, *The Poet's Dream*, c. 1858–1860. Despite modern skepticism toward *genii*, angels, and demons, the divine fury of inspiration continued to be represented as if creators were mysteriously possessed, perpetuating a sense that geniuses could connect with forces beyond the self. *Copyright © RMN–Grand Palais / Art Resource, New York.*

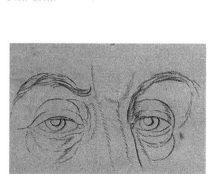

FIGURE 5.3. The eyes of a genius, from Lavater's *Physiognomische Fragmente*, 1775–1778. *Wellcome Library, London.*

FIGURE 5.4. The silhouettes of "four great men" displaying the traits of "superiority of genius." From Lavater's *Physiognomische Fragmente*, 1775–1778. *Wellcome Library, London.*

FIGURE 5.5. Jewish genius (*Spinoza left, Mendelssohn right*). Two images from the German psychologist Ernst Kretschmer's *Geniale Menschen* (1929), translated into English as *Psychology of Men of Genius*. Kretschmer, who was nominated for a Nobel Prize in 1930, illustrated his book with dozens of examples displaying the facial features of geniuses, testimony to the lasting influence of physiognomy. *Wellcome Library, London.*

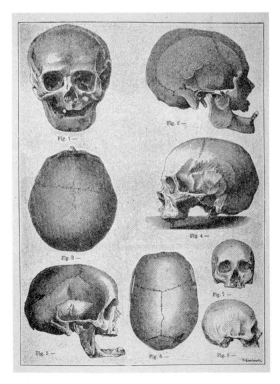

FIGURE 5.6. An image from the third English edition of Cesare Lombroso's *The Man of Genius*, originally published in Italian as *L'uomo di genio* (1889). Three views of the skull of Immanuel Kant are compared to those of three Italian geniuses. Kant's skull was disinterred and studied closely in 1880, eliciting widespread public commentary. *Yale University Library, Harvey Cushing / John Hay Whitney Medical Library.*

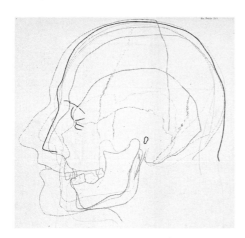

FIGURE 5.7. Bigger is better. A design by the respected German anatomist Johann Christian Gustav Lucae for Wilhelm Gwinner's 1862 hagiography of the philosopher Arthur Schopenhauer. The size of Schopenhauer's skull (the largest) is plotted in comparison to that of six others, including Immanuel Kant, Friedrich Schiller, Charles Maurice de Talleyrand, Napoleon, the German poet Christoph August Tiedge, and a "cretin." *Image courtesy of John M. Merriman.*

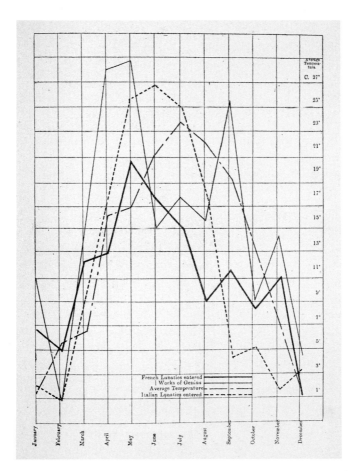

FIGURE 5.8. "The Relation of Average Monthly Temperature to Admission of Lunatics to Asylum, and to Productions of Works of Genius." One of many such graphs in Cesare Lombroso's *The Man of Genius* purporting to demonstrate, with the power of modern statistics, the "stigmata" of genius and the correlations between genius and insanity, illness, and other aberrations. *Yale University Library, Harvey Cushing / John Hay Whitney Medical Library.*

FIGURE 5.9. A hereditary "tree" of idiosyncratic nervous illness included in Jacques-Joseph Moreau's *La psychologie morbide* (*Morbid Psychology*) of 1859. In the upper right, just a branch above that containing criminals and prostitutes, is the branch of "exceptional intelligence," which leads to offshoots of genius in the arts, letters, music, painting, and the sciences. *Yale University Library, Harvey Cushing / John Hay Whitney Medical Library.*

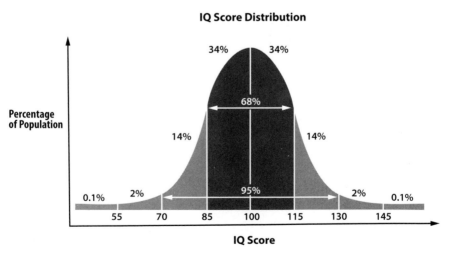

FIGURE 5.10. The IQ scale. Extrapolating from the work of earlier statisticians, Francis Galton suggested that intelligence, like other characteristics in a population pool, should follow the contours of a Gaussian distribution, or "bell curve," an insight that was critical to the later elaboration of the intelligence quotient (IQ). Here, IQ is plotted to show its natural variation, with only 2 percent of populations achieving scores over 130, and only 0.1 percent over 145.

Figure 5.11. Auguste Joliet, *The Genius of Destruction*, 1872, after a design by François Nicolas Chifflart. The nineteenth century gave new sanction to the old links between genius, evil, destruction, and crime. *Bibliothèque nationale de France.*

FIGURE 6.1. Wilhelm Lehmbruck, *Ode to the Genius*, 1917. A fallen angel, or *genius*, is prostrate before a work of art, in search of redemption. Note the streaking comet, symbol of genius, in the background. *Erich Lessing / Art Resource, New York.*

FIGURE 6.2. The genius as leader. A writer and chairman of the Dusseldorf Society for Culture, Lamoen argued in this short work that "the genius is the highest form of humankind and his destiny is to lead the people." *Bpk / Staatsbibliothek zu Berlin / Dietmar Katz / Art Resource, New York.*

FIGURE 6.3. Genius by association. As part of his effort to present himself in the "brotherhood of genius," Hitler made strategic pilgrimages to key German sites. Here, he contemplates Fritz Röll's bust of Nietzsche at the Nietzsche Archives, the house in Weimar where the German philosopher died. When Hitler visited in 1934, he was greeted by the philosopher's eighty-eight-year-old sister, Elizabeth Förster Nietzsche, an ardent Nazi supporter. *Klassik Stiftung, Weimar, Goethe-Schiller Archiv 101/239.*

FIGURE 6.4. Hitler, high above the angels, paying homage with his staff to the genius of Napoleon at his tomb in Paris, June 1, 1940. *Keystone / Hulton Archives / Getty Images.*

FIGURE 6.5. The cover of a film program of one of the Nazis' many "genius films," *Friedrich Schiller: The Triumph of a Genius* (1940), which celebrated the German poet's refusal to submit to ordinary laws. The film contains the line "The Genius . . . is not just born of his mother, but of his whole people." *Bundesarchiv, FILMSSG 1/4782.*

FIGURE 7.1. A piece of genius. A microscopic slice of Einstein's brain. *Miguel Medina / AFP / Getty Images.*

FIGURE 7.2. The marriage of business and genius. Henry Ford and his friend Thomas Edison. *Culver Pictures / Art Archive at Art Resource, New York.*

FIGURE 7.3. A contemporary religion of genius. The twentieth-century Vietnamese religion Cao Dai venerates the French writer Victor Hugo as one of its three founding fathers. Other revered figures include Napoleon, Shakespeare, Descartes, Tolstoy, Julius Caesar, and Thomas Jefferson. Hugo is shown here (center) in a painting at the Great Temple at Tay Ninh, Vietnam. *Jean-Pierre Dalbera.*

also the object of scientific scrutiny. Russian psychologists and physicians read widely in the works of their European colleagues, absorbing the teachings of Moreau and Lombroso, while noting the use they made of Russian examples of genius in their case studies of *dégénérescence*. Crafting their own pathographies, in turn, Russians detailed the manias of Gogol, the epileptic fits of Dostoyevsky, and the neuroses of Tolstoy while debating the extent to which genius was the consequence of a broader degeneration, whose adverse effects might be treated and cured. Others argued that, far from being the product of illness, genius was the sign of robust health, biological evidence of what the noted psychiatrist Nikolai Bazhenov described at the very end of the nineteenth century as "progeneration." In this conception, the genius was the prototype of the perfect man of the future, an early annunciation of a higher human being, whose biological mysteries scientists would one day solve. By the time of the Russian Revolution, such hopes were perfectly explicit. Leon Trotsky looked forward in the year of Lenin's death to a future in which "the average human type will rise to the heights of an Aristotle, a Goethe, or a Marx." The new communist man would be a "super human," and all might be geniuses, bred to a "higher social-biological" type. The physician G. V. Segalin even proposed establishing an "Institute of Genius" to carry out research on the bodies and brains of deceased men of talent, who would be required by law to donate their remains for dissection. His aim was the cultivation of geniuses through eugenics and what he termed "ingeniology" (the study of creative work). Segalin claimed to have detected a "gene" for creativity, and, in what he described as the "biogenetic law of genius," explained how this gene required illness for its full expression. It was thus incumbent on the state, he argued, to establish clinics to provide special care for geniuses and *Wunderkinder*, alleviating their adverse symptoms while harnessing their power.[20]

Segalin's utopian scheme to establish an Institute of Genius was never realized. But even though Vogt would have somewhat better success as an institutional founder, it was the same deep interest in the eugenic improvement of humanity and the related fascination with genius that best explains Vogt's invitation to Russia in the early, heady days of the Revolution. Lenin's brain was a prize specimen in itself, but it also had the potential (or so it seemed) to reveal mysteries about genius that would be crucial to the advance of human progress. Vogt wasted no time. In February 1925, he, his wife, and a small team of assistants began the arduous process of analyzing and dissecting the brain, which they eventually sliced into more than 30,000 specimens. Meanwhile, Vogt set to work drafting a proposal, with Semashko's support, for the establishment of a brain research institute with a much wider mandate to study cerebral architectonics in conjunction with human race biology. Created and granted funding in 1926 on the personal approval of Stalin, the V. I. Lenin Institute for Brain Research, or, as it was more commonly known, the "Moscow Brain Institute" (Institute Mozga), was officially opened the following year in a lavish mansion expropriated from an American businessman. Under Vogt's directorship, the institute continued work on Lenin's brain as well as on the brains of "renowned revolutionaries" and other "significant Russian public figures." It also served as the site of an extraordinary collection, the so-called Pantheon of Brains, which gathered together the vital organs of prominent Soviet artists, scientists, and politicians. Part museum and part "Bolshevik Valhalla," the pantheon was a public attraction, displaying replicas, casts, and photographs of the brains of leading revolutionaries along with detailed descriptions of their achievements. In the very same building, technicians worked diligently on the actual brains themselves, ensuring that in death, as in life, these highly evolved organs would continue to serve the revolutionary cause.[21]

Conceived partly on the example of the French Panthéon, the Pantheon of Brains was intended as a resting place for the genius of *grands hommes*. Lenin's brain was the chief attraction—a complement to his body, which was preserved not far away on Red Square—even if only half of it was displayed. The left side, which was severely damaged by the strokes that preceded his death, was hardly presentable as a model of Bolshevik perfection. Still, onlookers would doubtless have been able to detect what Vogt himself, in a preliminary report of 1929, claimed to have seen. "Our anatomical results," he affirmed, "show Lenin to have been a mental athlete (*Assoziationsathlet*)." Long before the examination was complete, its findings were clear.[22]

In light of the extraordinary cult of genius that had grown up around Lenin even before his death, Vogt's verdict is hardly surprising. It was in perfect harmony with popular sentiment and the party line. Grigory Evdokimov, deputy chair of the Leningrad Soviet, declared in his eulogy in 1924, "The world's greatest genius has left us, this giant of thought, of will, of work, has died." The chief mourner of the state funeral, Grigory Zinoviev, went so far as to claim that the "genius of Lenin" flew "with wings" over his own interment. Lenin was a "prophet of genius," others maintained, whose insight had long foreseen the coming of the Revolution of 1917, and whose superhuman powers had achieved it. Peasants wrote in spontaneously, declaring their departed leader "the great genius of mankind, such as is hardly born once in a thousand years." Artists and intellectuals also did their part. The modernist poet Vladimir Maya-kovsky outdid his comrades in drawing an extended, if unlikely, parallel between Lenin and Christ. "Lenin lived! Lenin lives! Lenin will live!" Mayakovsky wrote, in imitation of the memorial acclamation of the Eucharistic prayer, "Christ has died, Christ is risen, Christ will come again." The lines were purposely blasphemous, but they articulated nicely what was (and what still is) plainly visible in the mausoleum on Red Square: a once deeply Christian culture would find its redeemers and saints even in the midst of a materialist revolution. In Russia, as else-where, the genius served a religious role.[23]

Some made this role explicit. In his first book, *The Meaning of the Creative Act* (1916), the Russian philosopher Nikolai Berdyaev explained how the "cult of genius" would complement "the cult of saints" in the kingdom of tomorrow. "Genius is another kind of sainthood," Berdy-aev insisted, a sainthood of daring rather than obedience. But make no mistake. In his sacrifice and perfection, in his universality and appeal to a better world, the "genius is religious in nature," Berdyaev noted, the harbinger of a more perfect human being and a more perfect world. Berdyaev, who was sympathetic to Marxism in his youth, later turned in the direction of an idiosyncratic Christianity pleasing neither to church nor state. The Russian Orthodox Church banished him, and then, in 1922, the Bolsheviks expelled him from the country. Both parties made their point. The worship of genius may be akin to a religious act, but such things should not be said aloud.[24]

Indeed, the question of religion in a state without religion was a deli-cate one for the Soviets, as it had been for previous revolutionary regimes and the theorists who imagined them. The French Revolution altered its calendar to culminate in festivals of genius, and bowed down before its Panthéon of great men. But its fledgling efforts to establish a civil reli-gion to replace the one it swept away never took hold, leaving visionaries to ponder the question in the nineteenth century. The attempt by the French sociologist and founder of positivism Auguste Comte to sketch the outlines of a "Religion of Humanity" is the best known of these mus-ings, and is altogether revealing of the role of genius in a world without God. In place of the *deus creator omnium*, Comte's religion worshipped *homo creator*, or rather, the great creative geniuses and discoverers who had furthered human progress throughout history. The thirteen months of Comte's liturgical calendar were named after pioneering individuals—Homer, Aristotle, Archimedes, Shakespeare, Gutenberg, Descartes—as were the days of the week. And so in the month of Shakespeare, one might say a prayer on Voltaire day, or perform a good deed on the day of Lessing, Beethoven, Mozart, or Schiller. Genius would be worshipped throughout the year.[25]

However outlandish Comte's Religion of Humanity might now seem, its readiness to replace the Creator God with the creative genius as an object of veneration was symptomatic of a wider tendency in European culture. But in the Marxist context, there was a problem with this type of transmutation, and Lenin himself addressed it explicitly. When the news that the good leader had miraculously survived a second assassination attempt in 1918 provoked an outpouring of acclaim for the people's "dear father," "savior," and "enlightened genius," Lenin was reportedly indignant. "It is shameful to read," he said from his hospital bed. "They exaggerate everything, call me a genius, some kind of special person. . . . All our lives we have waged an ideological struggle against the glorification of the personality of the individual; long ago we settled the problem of heroes." The comments were reported secondhand, and Lenin may never actually have said them. But they were in perfect keeping with the right principles of Marxist doctrine. Marx himself ridiculed the practice of "bowing to nature's noble and wise: the cult of genius," as he described it in a scathing review of the writings of Thomas Carlyle. And although it might be possible to talk of "social genius"—the creative strength that arose from collective endeavor—to idealize the individual as a being apart was to slip into a reactionary bourgeois rhetoric. Classes made history, not great men, and social forces shaped the ideas and events of any given epoch, not heroic individuals.[26]

If Marxist doctrine was thus in inherent tension with the cult of genius, this was even more the case with respect to the eugenically inflected brain science promoted by the circle around Vogt. For, in effect, such men sought to reduce human ability to innate biological difference, separating geniuses from all others on the basis of qualities that were inborn. The fact that even those sympathetic to Marxism could continue to sustain such claims testifies to the power and prevalence of the belief in original genius—a belief that since the eighteenth century had militated against explanations that placed a greater emphasis on human conditioning and environment. But the contradiction with basic Marxist tenets of human equality and the primacy of the social was too great to sustain. Increasingly the eugenics movement in Russia came under attack. Had not conservatives always explained human differences on the basis of biology in order to avoid addressing social conditions? It was a question raised by a critic in the main Bolshevik journal of Marxist theory in 1925. The article, entitled "Human Heredity and Selection: On the Theoretical Premises of Eugenics," made clear that these premises were not at all consistent with the teachings of Marx, who held that "people are the product of conditions and education." Such voices steadily grew bolder, and although some Russian eugenicists sought refuge in a form of Lamarckian environmentalism, arguing that social conditions shaped acquired characteristics that were then passed on through the genes, the science was already dated outside the USSR. Rather than compromise their core beliefs, most eugenicists simply ceded, in the end, to public and party pressure.[27]

Those who didn't risked disfavor. When the American eugenicist Hermann J. Muller suggested to Stalin in 1936 that "it would be possible within only a few generations to bestow the gift even of so-called 'genius' upon practically every individual in the population," Stalin ordered an attack on his work. Muller, resident at the Academy of Sciences in Moscow as a communist sympathizer since 1933, was lucky to escape with his life. He had spent a year at the Kaiser Wilhelm Institute of the Brain in Berlin prior to his arrival in the Soviet Union. But he returned now to Columbia University in the United States, where, improbably, he was awarded a Nobel Prize in 1946. The fate of genius in the USSR, however, was different. By 1930, the eugenics movement there was all but finished, ceding its place to the Neo-Lamarckian theories favored by the notorious Trofim Lysenko, who would emerge as Stalin's most influential biologist. The *Great Soviet Encyclopedia* wrote the epitaph of the movement the following year. Eugenics, it noted damningly, was a "bourgeois doctrine."[28]

As with eugenics, so with Dr. Vogt and the Pantheon of Brains, which closed to the public in 1930. Vogt's Moscow Brain Institute was taken over by the Communist Academy in March of that year, depriving the German scientist of any further influence over its direction. Although Vogt himself continued to counsel his Russian colleagues from abroad, he no longer traveled to the Soviet Union, and with Hitler's rise, he was barred from doing so. Stripped of his directorship of the Kaiser Wilhelm Institute in 1935 on account of his political sympathies, he was forced to join the German Army as a private in his sixties.

Yet research on Lenin's brain continued, and in 1936, the committee of scientists, now headed by Vogt's onetime Russian assistant Semion Aleksandrovich Sarkisov, delivered its final report. Lenin's brain had been studied in comparison with those of other prominent Soviet citizens collected by the Moscow Brain Institute, including the great novelist Maxim Gorky, the physiologist and Nobel Prize winner Ivan Petrovich Pavlov, and Mayakovsky. Mayakovsky, disillusioned by the course of the revolution, shot himself in April 1930, before Lenin could rise from the dead and come again. Not surprisingly, Lenin's brain bested them all, showing extremely "high organization" and topping the charts on a number of indices associated with "speech, recognition, action," and other "processes requiring great diversity and richness of cognitive powers," including an "exceptionally high functioning of the higher nervous system." Lenin, party officials could rest assured, was a genius.[29]

But what really had been revealed? When Vogt and Semashko had begun their venture in 1924, they had hoped, as Semashko had declared in an article published in Berlin's Communist Party newspaper, the *Red Flag*, that their research would hasten the victory of materialism "in the area where metaphysics and dualism are still strong," the study of genius. But their research in fact yielded a strikingly different conclusion, one highlighted by Stalin's decision not to publicize any of the study's findings, and to shroud both the study and the work of the Moscow Brain Institute in total secrecy. At first glance, the decision is puzzling. Why not proclaim Lenin's genius as a "scientific" fact? It is true that the science could be contested—if not in the Soviet Union, then by researchers working abroad—and that was an eventuality that secrecy foreclosed. Secrecy, by this stage, moreover, had become an end in itself. But even more dangerously, the study made plain what the Pantheon of Brains had also (briefly) exposed: at the very highest levels of the Communist Party, apparatchiks harbored the belief that not all men were alike, that some were constitutionally better than others, that geniuses were a breed apart. Whatever Marx's strictures regarding the "cult of genius," a good many Bolsheviks shared that "bourgeois" faith. As Trotsky revealed to the party in a speech delivered in 1923 as Lenin lay on death's door, "Lenin was a genius, a genius is born once in a century, and the history of the world knows only two geniuses as leaders of the working class: Marx and Lenin. No genius can be created even by the decree of the strongest and most disciplined party, but the party can try as far as possible to make up for the genius as long as he is missing, by doubling its collective exertions."[30]

Trotsky, in the end, underestimated the power of the party. But he correctly identified the belief in genius that helped to sustain it, a belief that, however contradictory to Marx's principles, was evident from the very moment of Marx's death. Marx himself, in this respect, as in others, constituted the best refutation of his own beliefs. For just as the spectacular influence of his doctrines gave the lie to his assertion that social forces, not ideas, were the true movers of humanity, his own vast creative output summoned a label that few in the nineteenth century could refuse. "Marx was a genius; we others were at best talented," Friedrich

Engels confessed, in downplaying the importance of his own efforts in their mutual labors. "What I contributed, Marx could very well have done without me." Or, as Engels observed famously in delivering the funeral oration at Marx's burial at London's Highgate Cemetery on March 17, 1883, Marx was "to the laws of Human history what Darwin was to organic nature." He had been "the greatest living thinker." Even to a man who had spurned the cult, the title of genius could not be denied.[31]

Nor was it. In a wave of encomia and hagiographic literature, Marx's genius was affirmed again and again, and Lenin was the direct heir to that praise. If Marx was the genius of theory, Lenin was the genius of praxis, the "genius of revolution," as Stalin affirmed in *Pravda* following the Russian leader's death. It was to that title that Stalin himself lay claim. Marx's devoted servant, Lenin's watchful keeper, Stalin, too, would be a creator of history, "the wisest man of the century," the "genius of the age." As the Kazakh poet Dzhambul Dzhabaev declared, "the genius of Lenin burns on in Stalin."[32]

Stalin's success in keeping that flame alive had nothing to do with the materialist science of the brain. But the Moscow Brain Institute continued to do its work in secrecy, nonetheless, and in fact long outlived the supreme leader and the genius of the age. It was collecting notable specimens into the 1980s, when it acquired the brain of A. D. Sakharov, the once-loyal nuclear physicist who later became a dissident and human rights activist and who was awarded the Nobel Peace Prize in 1975. Even today, the work of the Moscow Brain Institute remains a closely kept secret. Access to its collections is denied to Western researchers, including the author of this book. But then, as Zilsel aptly perceived, the cult of genius, whatever its pretensions to the contrary, was never about science, but rather about filling the emotional needs of the people in ways that religion had long supplied. Rather than draw the people's gaze to a place in the brain that reminded them of what they could never be, far better to raise their eyes aloft to a living genius who was their perfect expression and keeper. Where neither God nor kings nor democratic mandate could confer legitimacy, genius would take its place.

To be sure, the widespread assertion of Stalin's genius—an assertion that flooded Soviet propaganda in the 1930s, and an assertion that Stalin himself sincerely believed—rested on the ruthlessness and repression of a man who did not shy from murdering millions of his own subjects. He who would create must destroy. Genius, clearly, was above all law. And yet, if Stalin used genius largely to consolidate a power already procured by force, we should not underestimate the extent of its acceptance. "After all," the Soviet statesman Mikhail Gorbachev later recalled, "the Stalin 'personality cult' had essentially consisted in the myth that Stalin was a man of genius, the leader and follower of all the peoples. This myth had been instilled in people's minds by an all-powerful propaganda machine with no alternative sources of information. The effectiveness of this propaganda, backed up by repression, the reality of a deeply rooted delusion bordering on mass psychosis—these were impressively confirmed by the feelings of shock that affected millions of people when Stalin died." Millions had mistaken evil genius for something else. To Russia's West, that same mistake was made on an equally horrendous scale. But there, in Adolf Hitler's Nazi Germany, the cult of genius did not simply sanction a tyranny already established by force. It helped put one in place.[33]

Hitler's *Mein Kampf* is many things: a confession, a programmatic statement of goals, a hate-filled and disturbing rant. It is also a series of revelations, and one in particular is of special interest to anyone who would attempt to fathom Hitler's understanding of himself and his subsequent embrace by large segments of the German population. "In the monotony of everyday life," Hitler explains, "even important people often seem unimportant and hardly stand out above the average." But when called by some special circumstance, they reveal, to the astonishment of the world, that they are fundamentally different from the great mass of average men and have always been this way. True, "an inventor establishes his fame only on the day of his invention," yet "one must not think that genius [*die Genialität*] entered the man only at this hour. The spark of genius [*der Funke des Genies*] will be present in the forehead of the truly creatively gifted man from the hour of his birth, although for many years in a smoldering condition and therefore invisible to the rest of the world." For "true genius is always inborn and never acquired by education or, still less, by learning." At some crucial moment, however, "through an external cause or impetus of some kind, the spark becomes fire, something that only then begins to stir the attention of other people." And although there may be any number of such external causes, Hitler singled out war as the perfect catalyst needed "to call genius into action." In his hour of trial, the beardless boy is revealed as a hero. And through a "hammer-stroke of Fate," the outer shell of everyday life is broken, revealing to the eyes of an astonished world his true inner kernel and core. At first the people are incredulous, refusing to believe that a being who had seemed so much like them is in truth of another kind. But that is "a process which repeats itself with every eminent human being."[34]

Although Hitler here mentions no names, there can be little doubt that he saw himself as a perfect illustration of what he describes. His revelation was the revelation of genius. A fledgling bohemian artist in Vienna from the early part of the century, Hitler was famously denied admission to both the academy of painting and the academy of architecture there, living down and out and even for a while spending time in a homeless shelter before a small inheritance allowed him to pursue *la bohème* on slightly more comfortable terms. He copied paintings from postcards to sell in the street, indulged his long-standing passion for Wagner, and whiled away mornings in the public library, reading without structure or aim, dreaming of himself as a future artistic genius. In 1913, in large part to avoid the Austro-Hungarian draft, he exchanged the cafés of Vienna for the beer halls of Munich. The Habsburg Empire was corrupt, he believed. He would fight for Germany. And so the beardless boy of twenty-five went away to war in 1914, unremarkable and unremarked, average only in a generous estimation. But war's "hammer-stroke" revealed something beneath the shell, a "heroism" that prompted him to risk his life again and again. Wounded seriously on several occasions and highly decorated for his service, Hitler received the news of Germany's capitulation in 1918 as a summons to politics and a call for redemption. His own interest in political affairs had long paled before his affections for art. But Germany had been denied and betrayed, and she must be redeemed. Throwing himself into the morass of Munich's right-wing fringe, Hitler quickly discovered a skill for speechmaking in a virulent, anti-Semitic mode. He took a prominent role in the failed right-wing coup attempt of November 1923, the so-called Beer Hall Putsch, that led to his incarceration in Bavaria. And it was there, in the Landsberg Prison in 1924, that he wrote *Mein Kampf*, the first part of which was published the following year.

These details are common knowledge. But what is less well known, and what professional historians themselves have only recently begun to appreciate, is how the before and after of Hitler's life—that of the would-be artist in Vienna and Munich and the improbably successful politician on the world stage—fit together. It was long customary to treat the two apart, as if they were essentially unrelated. Hitler's failures as an artist were read as confirmation of his own basic mediocrity, or the source, perhaps, of his festering resentment. But his early aesthetic interests were treated as little more than that. Recently, however, a number of scholars have begun to appreciate what Hitler himself tells us clearly in *Mein Kampf*: the man before and the man after were one and the same. Far from abandoning his interest in art, Hitler, via politics, pursued aesthetics by other means. The evidence is considerable, ranging from his abiding interest in architecture to the lavish attention he devoted to collecting art and his intimate involvement in the staging of Nazi festivals, rallies, exhibitions, and processions. But the most direct link is his deep fascination with Wagner, a fascination that began in his youth and endured until the very end.[35]

One may debate whether "there was a good deal of 'Hitler' in Wagner," as Thomas Mann later provocatively declared. But there was undoubtedly a good deal of Wagner in Hitler, a point that the latter, as Führer, emphasized again and again. He saw *Lohengrin* at thirteen, and *Rienzi* at fifteen. The story of the last Roman tribune, a populist who rallies the people, *Rienzi* was based on a novel by Bulwer Lytton that was dear to Benito Mussolini; Hitler was moved by the music. After seeing the opera for the first time at the Landestheater in Linz in 1905, he allegedly declared, "I want to become a tribune of the people." He later spoke of the experience as life-changing, claiming, "In that hour it all began." These were admittedly recollections, and likely projections. But the feeling of continuity is important all the same. There is a reason why the overture to *Rienzi* served from early on as a signature tune to the Hitler movement and an unofficial Nazi anthem: it connected Hitler emotively to the Wagnerian passions that stirred him in his youth and later moved him to dream of German redemption. That dream, so widely shared, was central to Wagner's entire project, which sought, on the shoulders of Schopenhauer, to create a religion of art, conceiving shared aesthetic experience as a way to overcome modern disenchantment and transform the *Volk* through myth. Revealing the riches of Germany's mythical creative past, Wagner's music simultaneously opened up a future in which the German people might achieve a kind of salvation through art. In his "Wagnerian self-fashioning," Hitler aimed for a similar effect, seeking to reproduce the same transports of feeling on the political stage that he himself experienced in Wagner's music. Before the podium, Hitler became the heroic artist he couldn't be before the easel. He was the people's tribune, its savior, its redeemer—Rienzi, Parsifal, and Siegfried all in one. As he made clear in 1924, "the spiritual sword that we wield was forged in Bayreuth, first by the Master himself [Wagner], then by [Houston Stewart] Chamberlain."[36]

Hitler's invocation of the critic Chamberlain, Wagner's son-in-law (who had married Eva von Bülow, Wagner's daughter with Cosima von Bülow), and Bayreuth, Wagner's musical and spiritual home, in the context of a discussion of the values that fired the sword of national redemption hints at the indispensable quality of the man who would wield it:

genius. As early as 1920, in a speech delivered on April 27 of that year, Hitler began insisting that Germany needed a "dictator who is a genius." He was, as of yet, unwilling to audition for the role, but he received a critical endorsement just two years later, when he traveled to visit the Chamberlains at their home in Bayreuth at the invitation of Winifred Wagner, who was married to Wagner's son, Siegfried. Winifred would become one of Hitler's closest admirers and friends, frequently hosting him in Wahnfried, Wagner's home, sparking rumors of an affair. But in 1923, just weeks before the Beer Hall Putsch, the most meaningful support came from Chamberlain, who wrote to Hitler shortly after their meeting in glowing terms, describing him as a "true awakener" and a man with "immense achievements" ahead of him. Invoking Goethe's distinction in *Faust* between *Gewalt und Gewalt*—chaotic violence and the ordering force that shapes the universe—Chamberlain observed in Hitler the latter. He was, in "a creative and universal sense" (*in solchem kosmosbildenden Sinne*), a constructive man. "That Germany in its hour of greatest need has given birth to a Hitler," Chamberlain enthused, "was a testament to its vitality."[37]

To receive this "blessing" from the greatest genius enthusiast in Germany, who was himself a living link to the man whom Hitler regarded as the archetypal German genius of the nineteenth century, was a major endorsement. In practical terms, it meant that Hitler could publicize his ties to Chamberlain and the Wagner family as proof of his status as heir to the Wagnerian *Kampf*. He wasted no time in having Chamberlain's letter published in a party newspaper and did the same with subsequent correspondence. But, just as importantly, if less tangibly, the letter could only have confirmed Hitler's intuitive sense that he himself possessed the precious spark. Doubts engendered by his earlier failures could be dispelled, and those "failures" themselves could be transformed by a curious Romantic/modernist logic as further confirmation of his special status. For the true genius was always ahead of his time—a man of the future whose creative energy and vision would be greeted initially with miscomprehension, if not outright denial. As Hitler maintained in *Mein Kampf*, this was the way of all great men. By a similar reasoning—one reinforced by the whole of nineteenth-century *Geniegedanke* (thought about genius) and the scientific study of eminent men—genius could be understood as an adaptive power and transferable "skill." The same spark that had burned in the young artist could quite naturally take flame in the political man without a corresponding loss of heat.

The thinly veiled allusions in *Mein Kampf* indicate that Hitler was already applying this law of the conservation of genius to himself. Others certainly were. The author Georg Schott's *Das Volksbuch vom Hitler*, for example, the first biography of the young leader, published in Munich in 1924 and reprinted throughout the Nazi era, aimed to present Hitler to the people as he really was. That Hitler was a genius, Schott maintained, and to what extent, had recently been proclaimed by an "outstanding personality." He called attention to the letters of Chamberlain as proof. To ask whether Hitler was a genius was to find the answer in the question. The subheadings of the book spoke for themselves. Hitler was the "prophetic man," the "religious person," the "man of will," categories that were subsumed in the key chapter, "The Genius," which left no doubt as to Hitler's exalted status as a being apart. Hitler's future minister of propaganda, Joseph Goebbels, himself a frustrated man of letters despite a doctorate in literature from the University of Heidelberg, hailed Hitler not long after their first meeting as a "genius" and the "natural, creative instrument of divine fate." Early disagreements did not alter the impression, with Goebbels bending to what he regarded as the "political genius" of the "greater one." Few would show themselves more effective in sustaining Hitler's view that, as Hitler himself explained in a speech in the mid-1920s, the people formed a pyramid with "the great man, the genius," at its head.[38]

It was here that Hitler's own delusions, wedded to a ruthless strategic acumen and a gift for impassioned oratory, merged with a current of millennial expectation that flowed through the religion of genius. In the uncertain climate of Weimar Germany, with its weak republic and economic malaise, Hitler's call for a "dictator who is a genius" was echoed widely. Thus did the Tübingen historian Joseph Haller implore Germans, in his *Die Epochen der deutchen Geschichte* of 1922, to hope for the coming of the "right man at the right time," who would restore Germany's greatness and enable it to overcome its afflictions with the "miraculous powers of a genius." The epigraph on the title page, a line from Homer's *Iliad*, reaffirmed the point, declaring prophetically, "The Day Shall Come." The sentiment enjoyed surprising currency among intellectuals and university elites, where political messianism and the cult of heroic genius found important bases of support. As the historian Karl Alexander von Müller declared in a speech in Munich in 1924, "the hour will come in which the lightning of the genius shall flash through the dark clouds of our confusion and burn out the mountains of our shame." Of course, it was impossible to know what form the rescuing genius would take. As the literary scholar and acting vice chancellor of the University of Berlin, Gustav Roethe, mused rhetorically as early as 1919, who can say whether he would be a "king, military commander, statesman, poet, or an economist? We do not see him, nor is he far away. But he will come as the great individual. The true birth of German yearning and singularity."[39]

That Hitler was able to assume his role convincingly owed as much to the reception of his audience as it did to his skills on the stage. The religion of genius was a precondition of Hitler's acceptance, the legitimating ground of the Führer cult. But he was undeniably a master at playing to the crowd, and his understanding of genius made full allotment for the people's participation. True, Hitler was perfectly clear that the motor of human history was the outstanding individual: "Progress and the culture of mankind," he observed in *Mein Kampf*, "are not products of the majority, but they rest exclusively on the genius and the energy of the personality." And yet he emphasized again and again that the relationship was symbiotic. Immediately following his account of the awakening of the individual genius by the "hammer-stroke of Fate," and his assertion that true genius is "always inborn" and never learned, Hitler hastened to add that what was true "for the individual" was also true for the "race." "Creatively gifted" peoples were so from their inception, and his Aryan followers, Hitler insisted, were uniquely gifted. The Aryan was the "prototype" of mankind, the "founder of higher humanity as a whole," and the true mover of history. "What we see before us of human culture today," Hitler wrote, "the results of art, science, and technical achievements, is almost exclusively the creative product of the Aryan." The Aryans were a race of "culture founders," "the 'Prometheus of mankind,' from whose shining brow the divine spark of genius has at all times flashed forth."[40]

In emphasizing the uniquely creative capacity of the "Aryans," a term that in his vocabulary was all but synonymous with the "Germans," Hitler was repeating a widely held claim of nineteenth- and early twentieth-century race theorists. The claim was by no means exclusive to Germany. The French historian and cultural critic Hippolyte Taine, for example, made much of the distinction between "Germanic" peoples—who he said were visionary, intuitive, artistic, and creative—and "Latin" peoples, who in his considered judgment (he himself was a Latin!) tended to be logical and methodical, yet imitative and sterile. Oppositions of the sort were central to a wide variety of influential European commentators on race, from Arthur de Gobineau, Georges Vacher de Lapouge, and Ernest Renan to Charles Maurras and Gustave Le Bon. Le Bon, in addition to making cranial studies of genius, was interested in how the genius of the race expressed itself in the mass gatherings of crowds. Hitler may well have been familiar with his work, and that of several of the others, besides. But his primary source for his discussion of German creative capacity was Chamberlain, whom he invoked directly, and who dwelled on the theme in *The Foundations of the Nineteenth Century* at length. Chamberlain, in this respect, was undoubtedly Hitler's "spiritual sword," and in so arming him Chamberlain dispatched another powerful weapon that could be used to effect the union between the genius of the individual and the genius of the race: anti-Semitism. The Jews, both Hitler and Chamberlain agreed, were the anti-creative people par excellence. "The Jew possesses no culture-creating energy whatsoever," Hitler maintained. He was an "outward imitator" rather than an "ingenious creator," and for that reason there had never been, and could never be, a true "Jewish art." Forever aping and mimicking the cultures in which they lived as foreign bodies, the Jews had no culture of their own.[41]

This perverse opposition between the inherently creative German *Volk* and a Jewish *Gegen Volk* that was devoid of all creative capacity played on a central distinction that had characterized the discussion of original genius since the eighteenth century. To create was to bring into being all that was new and unprecedented; to imitate was to copy and render what others had done. Creation required genius; imitation drew on talent, at best. It was a distinction that Wagner himself had made in his anti-Semitic essay of 1850, "On Jewishness in Music," a work that was all the more repugnant for the fact that Wagner borrowed liberally from Jewish composers in crafting his own distinctive style. Chamberlain showed his fidelity to his master by surpassing him in vehemence. To imitate was not simply to plagiarize or steal, he deemed, but to corrupt the source of creativity itself. The Jewish imitator, Chamberlain alleged, was in truth a parasite, who in sucking the blood of its host, sapped and poisoned the creative energies of the body that fed it.

Faithfully recycled by Hitler, this discourse presented the Jews as the greatest threat to the creative genius of the German people. On the one hand, Jews (and other non-Aryans) allegedly polluted German blood, weakening German genius biologically through racial intermingling, a point that Hans F. K. Günther, a leading German racial theorist and eugenicist, emphasized in one of the many works by him that Hitler owned and recommended to the Nazi faithful. "What is at stake," Günther insisted, "is the unhindered development of the bearers of the highest culture of mankind, who, if the process of amalgamation with [the Jews] goes further, run the risk in mind and body of wandering off those paths which their own genius has marked out for them." Hitler shared this view wholeheartedly, but he also stressed, on the other hand, that the Jews undermined the very foundations of genius worship intellectually by casting the Germans' healthy "admiration for their own geniuses" as a kind of "idolatrous admiration." As soon as a people succumbed to this "Jewish arrogance and impudence," Hitler warned, it renounced its own powerful energy, which is "based on the veneration of the genius and the elation and the devotion brought about by him." The Jews, in other words, sowed doubts among the faithful and skepticism among the followers of the genius religion in a manner that required a diabolical skill. Hitler freely admitted as much. "Today the Jew is looked upon as 'clever,'" he acknowledged, "and in a certain sense he has been so at all times." The Jew's "intellectual abilities [had been] schooled in the course of centuries."[42]

Such concessions reflected the currency of an image of "smart Jews," a stereotype of superior Jewish aptitude and ability that fed its own cult of the Jewish genius, and that competed and at times intersected with anti-Semitism. Already in *Hereditary Genius*, Galton had called attention (despite his own anti-Semitic views) to what he suspected was the peculiar eminence of the Jewish people, who were uncommonly "rich in families of high intellectual breeds." The degeneration theorists Max Nordau and Cesare Lombroso emphasized this point as well, the latter by singling out what he called the Jewish "neurotic tendency." The "Jewish elements in the population furnish four and even six times as many lunatics as the rest of the population," he maintained, a point that rendered Jews especially susceptible to the genius of *dégénérescence*! Critics and anti-Semites, of course, could point out that Nordau and Lombroso were Jews themselves, casting doubt on their assertions, or question the results of other Jewish researchers such as the historian and folklorist Joseph Jacobs, whose *Studies in Jewish Statistics* (1891) found that in conditions of relative freedom, the Jews produced more geniuses and men of eminence, on average, than other peoples. It was harder, however, to deny the host of apparently more objective studies carried out in the aftermath of World War I that demonstrated the superior performance of Jews on intelligence tests and IQ exams. As one of the exam's key architects, Lewis Terman, put it, the Jews filled their quota of "gifted children" at a factor of roughly twice what would be expected on the basis of their presence in the population. At the very highest levels, too, they far surpassed the mean. Between 1905 and 1930, men of Jewish ancestry claimed 20 of the 153 Nobel Prizes awarded to individuals, an impressive 13 percent. At the very least, the image of the smart Jew had data to back it up.[43]

Without seeking to deny (or even to acknowledge) such assertions outright, Hitler simply worked around them, emphasizing the gulf that separated creativity and original genius from mere intelligence and imitative cleverness. In calling attention to the Jews' singular capacity to dissemble, deceive, and destroy, however, he granted them a certain "genius" of their own. Hitler, in fact, referred to the Jews as the "evil genius" of the German people, "whose great men are only great in the destruction of mankind and its culture." Chamberlain developed the same point, insisting, "We cannot understand Judaism and its power . . . cannot form a just and proper estimate of the Jew among ourselves, until we have recognized his demoniacal genius." Here were the makings of a terrible metaphysical clash. For whereas the Jew represented the evil genius of humanity, the pure-blooded Aryan constituted its good genius, an opposition that Chamberlain highlighted in a particularly striking way. "The man who belongs to a distinct, pure race, never loses the sense [of this powerful presence]," he claimed. "The guardian angel of his lineage is ever at his side, supporting him where he loses his foothold, warning him like the Socratic *Daemon* where he is in danger of going astray." Race, then, was the genius of the people, humanity's *daimonic* power, which in its purity "lifts a man above himself," said Chamberlain: "It endows him with extraordinary—I might almost say supernatural—powers, so entirely does it distinguish him from the individual who springs from the chaotic jumble of peoples drawn from all parts of the world. And should this man of pure origin be perchance gifted above his fellows, then the fact of Race strengthens and elevates him on every hand, and he becomes a genius towering over the rest of mankind." The genius of the race could only fully express itself in and through the genius of the great man, whose highest task was to revive, resuscitate, and reawaken the people's creative spirit. The genius incarnated the highest aspirations and striving of the *Volk*.[44]

Here, in summary, was Hitler's own view of his relationship to the German people. It was a view that in certain respects could call upon a venerable line of development, stretching back at least as far as the eighteenth century, and arguably well before, to the moment when Augustus Caesar first sought to conflate his own *genius* with the *genius populi Romani*, linking its fortune and fate to his star. In the eighteenth century, thinkers from Montesquieu to Herder began to theorize an explicit relationship between the genius of the people and the genius who could articulate, capture, or express the people's spirit in a striking way. The Romantics consolidated these thoughts, seeing in outstanding individuals, such as Beethoven or Napoleon, the oracles and incarnations of peoples. Hitler was aware of most of these precedents. He, too, claimed to have a star, and in the "comet-path of genius" of Napoleon and his German counterpart, Frederick the Great, he claimed to find explicit models to help guide its trajectory. But where Hitler broke definitively from such precedents was in racializing the relationship between the genius and the *Volk*, claiming that the connection was in the genes. That imagined connection was largely the product of the science of the nineteenth and early twentieth centuries, and when combined with the religion of genius, it made for a sinister concoction. For if the evil genius of the Jewish people corrupted the creative genius of the Germans, must not the Jewish presence be removed? At a minimum, the Jews must be prevented from breeding with Germans and further polluting their hereditary genius and blood.[45]

And so a program of eugenics followed logically, if not inexorably, from Hitler's *Geniegedanke*. It was, above all, a negative eugenics: the uncreative, unproductive elements must be prevented from poisoning the truly creative race. As Hitler put it in a 1938 speech justifying the expulsion of "degenerated elements" and "Neanderthal culture" from German soil, "whether or not we can today call geniuses of eternal standing our own is as always difficult to judge, but in the end it is of little consequence for our actions. What is of great consequence, however, is the preservation of an environment in which true genius can be nurtured." Genius, in other words, might be fostered, but the laws of its creation were mysterious. It was arguably for this reason that Hitler never pursued the eugenics of genius with the same zeal as his early Soviet counterparts. "Only a genius can turn himself into a genius," he would comment in 1942. Only a genius can create genius; only a genius can bring genius into being through an act of will. The genius of eternal standing was an enigma and a lonely exception. He could never be the norm, and perhaps could never be bred at all, a point on which eugenicists themselves sometimes insisted, despite Galton's earlier robust hopes. As the Norwegian racial hygienist Jon A. Moejn argued in the pages of the international *Eugenics Review* in 1926, the answer to why the "great genius disappears in the next generation" was simple: "because every child has two parents," one of whom invariably weakened the stock. Others pointed out that geniuses, as nature's exceptions, displayed a tendency to sterility. But whatever the specific views of Hitler's racial scientists, who continued to measure heads and dissect brains at the Kaiser Wilhelm Institute for Brain Research in Berlin, his own focus was on providing the conditions in which true genius could flourish. That meant, in practice, creating a racial pool of "pure" Aryan stock, from which the genius and the genius of the people could spontaneously emerge.[46]

That horrific goal was the stated aim of Hitler's self-described "dicta-torship of genius," which he theorized about long before assuming power in 1933. The artist-führer, the Genius as Führer, would serve as a sav-ior and redeemer, an embodiment of the German *Volksgeist* who would restore and recall its creative potential. As the new Nazi minister of cul-ture in Bavaria, Hans Schemm, declared in 1933, Hitler was the "German artist," who embodied the "totality of the artistic and political genius of the German people." A front-page story in the leading Nazi newspaper, the *Völkischer Beobachter*, two years later reaffirmed the point. Announc-ing an exhibition of Hitler's watercolors, the article's subtitle proclaimed "Art as the Basis of Political Creativity." That Hitler did not become a student at the Academy of Vienna was an act of fate, the article alleged, for "he was destined for greater things than simply becoming a good painter or perhaps a great architect." Still, art was fundamental to who he was—it touched the "very core of his being," and there was an "indis-soluble link" between the "Führer's artistic works and his great political undertaking." For once, the Nazi mouthpiece approximated the truth, for Hitler's self-understanding as an artist of genius was crucial both to his project and to his reception. Politics, he stressed, was an art. And the "true artist," Goebbels confirmed, "was a genius," capable of molding the people to his will, giving it shape and releasing its inner creativity.[47]

That this belief approximated a kind of religious faith was a point that many, then as now, have appreciated. The Protestant theologian Dietrich Bonhoeffer observed, just days after Hitler came to power, "The moment the *Volksgeist* is considered to be a divine metaphysical entity, the Führer who embodies the *Geist* assumes a religious function. . . . He is the messiah, and with his appearance the ultimate hope of every individual begins to come true." Bonhoeffer would later earn fame as a Christian martyr. He was an apt and early critic of the Nazi regime, and he correctly identified how it distorted and made use of Christian symbolism to suit its ends. Hitler the "king" became a perverted incar-nation of the *corpus mysticum*, gathering and redeeming the people in his person for resurrection and rebirth. And yet there was another, and in the end more important, precedent for his redemptive faith: the religion of genius, which prepared the German people for Hitler's coming and endowed him with the certainty of redemptive power. As Goebbels put it, "genius is drawn from grace." Such grace could set one free, liberat-ing the chosen from the moral restraints and norms that bound mere mortals. That, too, was a central tenet of the faith as it had evolved since the eighteenth century, and in Germany, in particular, the notion that creativity was by its very nature amoral—even immoral—could draw on strong roots. As Nietzsche insisted over and over again, true creativity and morality were incompatible: "good" people, he claimed, were "incapable of creating." And although there is no strong evidence that Hitler ever studied Nietzsche's writings with particular care, this general sentiment was widely received. Hitler echoed it in *Mein Kampf:* "Geniuses of an extraordinary kind do not admit consideration of normal humanity." Or, as Goebbels observed in his novel *Michael,* written in the early 1920s but first published in 1929, "the people are for the statesman what stone is for the sculptor." He added, shortly thereafter, that "Genies verbrauchen Menschen. Das ist nun einmal so" (Geniuses use up people, that is just the way it is). The creation of genius was beyond good and evil. It would involve, of necessity, domination, subjugation, sacrifice, and force.[48]

It was in part for that very reason that the legal scholar Hermann Heller observed, in an essay on the subject that he first published in 1931, that "the political genius religion must necessarily be a religion of violence." Heller was, as it happens, an Austrian of Jewish descent, like Edgar Zilsel, and an equally inveterate opponent of fascism. Neither man would survive the war: Heller died in exile in Spain in 1933 after the Nazis came to power, and Zilsel took his own life in Oakland, California, in 1944 after much of his family was murdered in the Shoah. But they were equally astute in their lifetimes in seeing where the religion of genius could lead. As Heller affirmed, using Fascist Italy as a precedent, the political genius religion could only be constructed in one direction, from the top down. The "genius" was a strong man, independent of all social rules, who would impose his will on the people using any means he could. That was just the way it was.[49]

There were others who, in contemplating the dogma of the religion of genius, accurately predicted its fate. One of the most insightful was Thomas Mann. In his novel *Lotte in Weimar* (1940), and then in the remarkable essay "Bruder Hitler" (Brother Hitler), published in English translation in *Esquire* magazine in March 1939, Mann took up the subject that he would later explore at length in his great novel *Doctor Faustus* (1947): the corrupting power of genius. The essay makes difficult reading still. Hitler was a "brother," Mann confessed, an "unpleasant and mortifying brother," a "catastrophe," but a brother nonetheless, a fellow "artist phenomenon," a dark and evil twin. It was an iteration of an insight that Mann developed at greater length in *Lotte in Weimar,* his rumination on the moral impact of the genius of Goethe: that good and evil in the theology of art were but common expressions of the divine. "If God is All, then he is also the Devil," Mann wrote. In the gaze of art, the two were conflated, producing that "horrifying approach to the godlike-diabolic which we call genius." Mann discerned that same gaze in Hitler and the flock that sustained him. "Our notion of genius has always been shrouded in a superstitious haze," he confessed. But now it was time to see clearly, "for today it is our fate to encounter genius in this one particular phase," genius as madness tempered by calculation and driven by sadism and revenge. It was a penetrating analysis, yet written in exile and too late to do much good. As Zilsel had complained as early as 1918, there were far too few in the German-speaking world who saw the religion of genius as a cause for concern.[50]

That fact—that faith—and the blindness it entailed helps to explain what are otherwise striking contradictions: that a man whose entire political regime represented "an organized contempt for the mind" could be taken as a great thinker; that an individual whose artistic tastes were conventional, even kitsch to the extreme, could understand himself, and be understood, as a heroic creator; that a person of seething and unfathomable hatred could be received as a savior and redeemer; that the face of genius could be imagined ranting and demented, twisted up in ire. But then, the religion of genius never claimed to be a purely rational faith, a religion of reason. Through enthusiasm, ecstasy, and transport before the sublime, it honored a higher power. The very irrationalism of Hitler's vision constituted, in this light, a further confirmation of his genius. His fury was furor, the possession of a daemonic man. Could there be great genius without some touch of madness?[51]

And so Adolf Hitler was admitted to the brotherhood of genius, and throughout the Nazi regime every effort was made to picture him in that place. Propaganda posters, photographs, and popular tracts depicted him in the company of geniuses of the past, while an entire genre of "genius films" sought to Nazify the dead in order to draw continuities with Hitler's present. Schiller, Mozart, Michelangelo, and Frederick the Great, among others, were subjected to cinematic makeovers; Leni Riefenstahl's *Triumph of the Will* presented Hitler as a genius for all eternity, descending to earth like an avenging angel on a Wagner score to merge with the genius of the people. The German genius, too—the genius of the *Volk*—was continually represented to itself in books, pageantry, mass rallies, and art. And all the while, Hitler imagined himself in the company of his true brethren. He strategized alongside Napoleon, Julius Caesar, and Frederick the Great, using his genius to impose on the more considered judgments of his generals. He designed sets for the productions of Wagner operas. He founded cities like Alexander had in ancient times. And he kept alive a vision of the great work that would guarantee his immortality. As he told a group of his confidants in 1942, politics was only a "means to an end." When the war was over and his duties fulfilled, he confessed, "then I would like to devote five or ten years to clarifying my thought and setting it down on paper. Wars pass by. The only things that exist are the works of human genius. This is the explanation of my love of art." Hitler singled out "music and architecture" in the same conversation as the disciplines in which "we find the recorded path of history's ascent." Of Wagner, he noted, "When I hear [him], it seems to me that I hear rhythms of a bygone world." And he hinted, vaguely, at the physics and metaphysics of architecture, commenting on the elusive dimensions of space and the "infinity of the cosmos," which was "infinitely great" and "infinitely small," but that should "always be expressed in an accessible fashion."[52]

Such fantasies were sustained until the very end. In his final days in the underground bunker in Berlin, Hitler busied himself with the vast architectural model that he and the architect Hermann Giesler had designed for his native city of Linz. It was there that he had first seen Wagner's *Rienzi* as a young man, and he had with him until he died the signed manuscript of the original score, a gift for his fiftieth birthday. Like Hitler's genius, it went missing in the flames and has never been seen again.

BEHOLD THE MAN. He is "shy, almost saintly," with wild hair, wide eyes, and a whimsical air, if perfectly respectable in coat and tie. And yet behind him looms a terrible symbol of his force: a mushroom cloud emblazoned with the equation the whole world now recognizes, $E = mc^2$, energy equals mass times the speed of light squared. The war is over, ended by a man who discovered the hidden laws of the universe and then used them to unleash an apocalyptic power. Einstein is Prometheus, a new titan, who has stolen atomic fire from the gods and bestowed it upon mortals, but now must watch as those same mortals make use of it as they will. The balance of the universe has been irrevocably altered. As the cover of *Time* magazine declared in 1946, Albert Einstein was a "cosmoclast," literally, "a destroyer of order."[53]

In truth, he had long upset the heavens. Einstein's *annus mirabilis* had arrived more than four decades earlier, in 1905, when, as an obscure twenty-six-year-old patent clerk working in the cobbled Swiss capital of Bern, he had produced four papers on four separate subjects, any one of which would have represented a significant lifetime's achievement. Here was pioneering work further explaining the existence and behavior of atoms. Here was the theory of special relativity, which posited the constancy of the speed of light and the dilation of time. Here was work on the photoelectric effect, analyzing light as both particle and wave, for which he would be awarded a Nobel Prize in 1921. And here, finally, was the paper detailing the equivalence of energy and matter, which contained the basis (though not the derivation itself) of the famous equation. This astounding body of work quickly earned Einstein the recognition of colleagues and a string of professorships, culminating in a prestigious appointment at the University of Berlin in 1914. Yet it was only with the elaboration of the theory of general relativity in 1916, and its apparent empirical confirmation three years later by a team of British astronomers working in northern Brazil, that Einstein was transformed into a living genius on a truly international scale. "Lights All Askew in the Heavens: Einstein's Theory Triumphs," a headline in the *New York Times* proclaimed. As J. J. Thomson, the discoverer of the electron and the president of the British Royal Society, observed in a special meeting convened to report the findings to the world, Einstein's work was epoch-making, on a par with that of Newton, Copernicus, and Galileo, "one of the greatest achievements of human thought."[54]

It does nothing to detract from that genuine achievement to observe that the cult of genius that followed in its wake was largely constructed. The world, wearied by World War I and eager for some display of human transcendence, transformed Einstein overnight into an international celebrity, rendering his name what it remains today, a synonym for genius. Einstein had altered the image of the heavens, and like Newton before him, he was hailed in spiritual terms. In England, he was the "greatest Jew since Jesus." In Palestine, a "Jewish saint." And in Austria, as an eyewitness reported, audiences greeted him "in a curious state of excitement": "It no longer matters what one understands," said the observer, "but only that one is in the immediate neighborhood of a place where miracles happen." Einstein's fame recalled perfectly the response to Einstein's favorite composer, Mozart. Both were wonders, who made a wonder of the world.[55]

Einstein was alternately pleased and perturbed by such reverence, complaining that the burden of fame interrupted his work, while at the same time basking in the limelight. Yet he had no illusion that the cult of his genius was based on any real comprehension of his work, "about which," he pointed out laconically, "[the public] cannot understand a word. I am sure that it is the mystery of non-understanding that appeals to them." It was a perceptive remark. Traveling in the United States, where he met often with such credulous incredulity, he noted that "the cult of individual personalities is always, in my view, unjustified. . . . It strikes me as unfair, and even in bad taste, to select a few individuals for boundless admiration and to attribute superhuman powers of mind and of character to them. This has been my fate." But he added that this "extraordinary state of affairs" offered one consoling thought: "It is a welcome symptom in an age, which is commonly denounced as materialist, that it makes heroes of men whose ambitions lie wholly in the intellectual and moral sphere."[56]

With his references to the appeal of the "mystery of non-understanding" and the "superhuman" powers accorded to extraordinary individuals like himself, Einstein hinted at the way in which his own personality was being recruited for service in the religion of genius. Published just the year before Einstein was canonized in 1919, Edgar Zilsel's *Die Genie-religion* makes no mention of the physicist in the context of the religion of genius; nor, indeed (with the partial exceptions of Tycho Brahe, Descartes, and Leibniz), does it refer to any modern scientist or mathematician at all. There is no reference to Galileo, Newton, or Darwin; no discussion of Euler, Riemann, or Gauss. The omissions likely reflect Zilsel's own prejudices as a teacher and historian of science. He was loath to equate religion with men whom he regarded as disinterested seekers of truth. But the oversight points to more than just Zilsel's predilections. For despite a repeated insistence since the eighteenth century that genius was a protean power—whose empire, in the Scottish writer William Duff's words, was "unbounded"—many followed Kant in seeing science and genius as realms apart.

There were numerous exceptions that might complicate this perception, Newton most notably, though it is revealing that Newton was regularly praised in language that related his genius to that of men of letters or the arts. Newton was not simply a natural philosopher, he was an original genius, later a man inspired, who glimpsed the workings of the universe in the falling of an apple and who could read the mind of God. In the nineteenth century, the English chemist Humphry Davy sought self-consciously to present himself as a Romantic genius (with some success), and there were more than a few mathematicians who did the same.[57]

Still, when "scientists" called attention to the greatest of their own, they were generally more restrained. A "genius of observation" was the eighteenth century's term of praise, used to describe not visionaries and seers of tomorrow, but men with "well-stocked memories" and piercing eyes who looked carefully at what was close at hand—men, such as Carl Linnaeus or Georges-Louis Leclerc, the count of Buffon, who were particularly adept at recognizing recondite details and discerning patterns. In the nineteenth century, the presentation of the "scientific self" was similarly understated, conceived as the product of due diligence, patience, exacting method, and the sweat of one's brow. Scientists, in short, were less inclined than their counterparts in other domains to imagine themselves as revolutionaries, prophets, or legislators of the world. Such self-appraisals ran in counterpoint to more extravagant popular imaginings—whether the fantasy of Mary Shelley's Victor Frankenstein or the musings of a Jules Verne or an H. G. Wells. They also run in counterpoint to our conceptions today: Was there a more revolutionary figure in the nineteenth century than Darwin? Still, the fact remains that when the people of the nineteenth and early twentieth centuries imagined the pantheon of genius, they were usually inclined to give scientists a secondary place.[58]

Einstein changed that. More than any other figure, he is responsible for making science the default domain of genius. His timing, like Mozart's (like that of all geniuses?), was perfect in this respect. Working at a period and in a place in which the power of science was increasingly apparent, he benefited from the enhanced visibility and prestige of both the applied and the natural sciences (*Naturwissenschaften*), which, in prewar Germany, especially, earned scientists such as Fritz Haber and Max Planck great wealth and acclaim. Such men rubbed elbows with aristocrats and the rich and famous in Wilhelmine Berlin, just as in the United States, a practical inventor, such as Thomas Edison, could schmooze with senators and captains of industry, earning accolades and front-page celebrity. Yet Einstein was more than a *Wissenschaftler*, an inventor, an entrepreneur—he was a genius, or so he became, according to the terms of the time.

A revolutionary, Einstein upended the rules of Newtonian physics and rewrote its laws. A visionary, he saw into the most remote workings of the universe, bending time itself. A wondrous being, he made the world wondrous, mysterious, even as he revealed. And although his labors were painstaking in their rigor, his approach to problem-solving was mystical, intuitive, inspirational. Like Planck, who was keenly aware of what he described as the "divine mysteries" of the creative process and of the close relationship between science and art, Einstein made plain that science could be as imaginative as any painting or poem, a disclosure that was further reaffirmed by the seeming consonance between his own theories and contemporary metaphysics and art. So all-encompassing were Einstein's revelations that they seemed to his contemporaries to capture perfectly the spirit of the age. The theory of relativity described the perspectivism of Nietzsche's philosophy or the fractured space of

Cubist painting. Einstein's understanding of time confirmed the subjective chronology of Virginia Woolf, James Joyce, or Marcel Proust. Like Newton, he struck his contemporaries not only as a scientist, but as a man in possession of something more, and that *divinum quiddam* was central to his appeal. Einstein was never a conventionally religious man. But he had a deep religious streak. Here was an individual whose soul was spiritual and profound, who could stand between mortal men and the infinity of space. He even looked the part. Rumpled and unkempt, Einstein was an eccentric, an original, an embodiment of genius.[59]

He was also a Jew, a fact that ensured a clash with a regime that conceived of Jews as the anti-creative people par excellence, though the conflict was more personal than that. Einstein, from very early on, had been clear-eyed and outspoken about the looming Nazi threat and the danger of the "cold, barbaric, animalistic resoluteness" of Hitler. He used his genius to denounce the regime, giving targeted vent to a general feeling he had evinced since youth. "The foolish faith in authority," he observed when still in his twenties, was "the worst enemy of truth," and Hitler and the Nazis were truth's antithesis. Right-wing extremists responded in kind throughout the 1920s, denouncing relativity as a "Jewish fraud" and attacking Einstein himself as a pacifist, a communist, and an enemy of the German people. So virulent were these attacks that Einstein feared assassination, and with good reason, though he rarely held his tongue. He continued to warn of the dangers of German nationalism while preaching pacifism, internationalism, and Zionism in turn. Hitler, for his part, told a journalist as early as 1931 that Einstein would have to go. "Everything [Jewish scientists] have created they have stolen from us," he observed. "We do not need them."[60]

When Hitler came to power, then, the groundwork for a dramatic clash had already been laid. Einstein was abroad at the time, and he condemned the Nazis immediately from California. But he waited until he set foot again on European soil to formally withdraw his membership from the Prussian Academy of Science, sending a letter to that effect as he disembarked in Ostende, Belgium, on March 28, 1933. The Nazis blasted him in return, with Goebbels, among others, personally denouncing his "agitation." Confiscating his property, they burned his books and revoked his citizenship, and later placed a bounty on his head. In the press and in official pamphlets and propaganda, Einstein was repeatedly vilified as a "Jewish criminal." "I am now," he was able to boast, "one of the people they [the Nazis] most love to hate."[61]

Was the reason for this hatred the fact, as one historian judges, that Einstein was among "Hitler's greatest antagonists"? Undoubtedly,

Einstein was untiring in his opposition to Hitler, but it was less his actions that generated the animus than who he was: a Jew, yes, but also a widely regarded "genius," and as such a man who exposed through his very being the fraudulence of the Hitler myth, predicated as it was on the essential and exclusive nature of Aryan creativity. In that sense, Einstein was indeed a major antagonist, for he represented a rival myth of genius that challenged Hitler's own. Whereas Hitler put his genius at the service of a narrow nationalism and xenophobic hatred, Einstein harnessed his to the vastness of the cosmos and the fellowship of all. Hitler was a maker of empires, Einstein a "maker of universes" without blood on his hands. Hitler was a genius of the *Volk*; Einstein a genius for humanity. The two were mutually exclusive. But they were products, in part, of the same nexus of forces. Mass media, the culture of celebrity, and the religion of genius that flourished between the wars gave rise to the genius of each, and they faced each other on far-flung and at times unlikely terrain. A 1939 survey at Princeton University asked incoming freshman to list the greatest living people. Adolf Hitler ranked first, and Einstein, who had been resident there since 1935, second. The majority of Princetonians came to see things differently, as would, in time, the majority of the citizens of the world. Perhaps, as Einstein himself is said to have remarked, "the world needs heroes, and it is better that they be harmless men like me than villains like Hitler."[62]

That may well be true, but it was not at all apparent to many in 1946 that Einstein was in fact a harmless man. Former Nazis, readers of *Time* magazine, and agents of J. Edgar Hoover's Federal Bureau of Investigation might well have disagreed. A man who could discern the secrets of the universe was at once an asset and a risk. Would he sell those secrets to the Soviets? Could he devise something even more horrible than the bomb? Enough of the *genius* lurked in the genius to make of even this pacifist soul a threat.[63]

Einstein prevailed over such doubts. But his victory had less to do with his own actions and beliefs than with those of countless other men and women, whose names are now forgotten. The same is true of the war, where Einstein's achievements, however noble, highlight, if anything, the impotence of the individual before ideologically driven masses and the organized violence of states. Though Einstein certainly played a small role in urging the Roosevelt administration to pursue a policy of atomic weapons research—famously signing a letter to that effect penned by the Hungarian physicists Edward Teller and Leo Szilard in 1939—he took no part in the bomb's construction, and his science was of little value to its development. Einstein was not, it is clear, "the father of the bomb," any more than it was he who defeated Hitler or terminated the war. What he did help to end, and what would settle in time from the fallout of the destruction, was the idolatry of genius itself. Einstein, in this respect, was an iconoclast, not a cosmoclast—a genius who contributed to dismantling a faith in which he himself could be imagined as both savior and destroyer.

CONCLUSION

The Genius of the People

B Y THE TIME THOMAS HARVEY was finished, there were close to
240 pieces of Einstein's brain, carefully sliced, labeled, and preserved. Harvey was the medical examiner of Princeton Hospital, and he
had been asked to perform a routine autopsy. But the corpse that lay
before him on the 18th of April, 1955, was hardly routine. Once before,
he had encountered Albert Einstein in the flesh. Performing a house call,
Harvey had gathered a specimen of the great man's urine, and it induced
a special thrill. But this was an opportunity even more thrilling. Unaware
of the clause in Einstein's will stipulating that his body be cremated on
the day of his death, and his ashes scattered in a secret location, Harvey removed the brain and spirited it away. The ophthalmologist Henry
Abrams, Einstein's friend, took the eyeballs, which are locked in a safe
deposit box to this day. But Harvey kept the best bits for himself.[1]

Men of more delicate conscience might have paused at the thought
of sawing into a Jewish skull in the wake of the Nuremberg trials, when
the world first learned of the sinister "experiments" of Joseph Mengele
and the Nazi effort to demonstrate the physical inferiority of the Jewish
brain. Yet Harvey's intentions were avowedly more pure. As a medical
student, studying pathology, he had been intrigued by the work of Paul
Broca, and would later claim that his decision to take Einstein's prized
possession was inspired by the example of Oskar Vogt and his quest to
solve the mystery of genius through an analysis of the brain of Lenin.
Had not Einstein himself allowed his head to be wired to electrodes at
the Massachusetts General Hospital in 1951, while the needle of an elec-
troencephalogram (EEG) rode the waves of his mind? Surely scientists
in the West could not pass on the prospect of studying the brain of the
greatest genius the world had known.

Others agreed. When Lieutenant Colonel Webb Haymaker of the United States Armed Forces Institute of Pathology learned of the bountiful harvest, he summoned Harvey to Washington, in full cognizance of the fact that the Soviets were busy studying their own elite brains. Haymaker himself had worked on the brain of Benito Mussolini after US soldiers had recovered the dictator's battered corpse in 1945. He had hoped to find a sign—of genius, madness, or degenerative disease—that would explain Mussolini's power. He held out similar hope that the study of the brain of Einstein would reveal, as he told the press, "a general pattern for the brain of a genius." But despite Haymaker's plea, he could not induce Harvey to surrender the relic in his keeping.[2]

The legal status of corpses is complicated, and like so many of the grave robbers who pilfered the skulls of geniuses in the nineteenth century, Harvey was never prosecuted for his theft. And even though he lacked the training and expertise to study the specimens on his own, he was never forced to hand them over. Princeton Hospital eventually dismissed him for his failure to exploit the scientific possibilities of the specimens, and, as Harvey's life and career headed south, so did Einstein's brain. Their subsequent peregrinations are a tale in themselves: driven across the country in the trunk of Harvey's car, stored in a cardboard box behind a beer cooler in Kansas, stamped and posted via US Mail, Einstein's brain got around. But Harvey had grown attached to his relics, and he found it difficult to give them up. Inquiring here, and soliciting there, he eventually provided four small samples to a group of neuroanatomists working in California. In a study published in 1985, they concluded that Einstein's brain exhibited a higher-than-average concentration of "glial" cells that aid neurons in the processes of neurotransmission. A later study—published in 1999 in the British medical journal *Lancet*, but based on a different sample of fourteen pieces of the brain—noted irregularities in the Sylvian fissure and concluded that Einstein's parietal lobe (associated with language, spatial understanding, and mathematics processing) was 15 percent wider than normal. These studies generated a great deal of publicity, although their scientific value is questionable. But today interested observers can scrutinize Einstein's brain for themselves. Bequeathed to the National Museum of Health and Medicine in Silver Spring, Maryland, following Thomas Harvey's death in 2007, Einstein's brain has since been digitized and is now available as an iPad app in 350 microscopic slides. For a mere $9.99, genius may be downloaded to your touchscreen and venerated in your home.[3]

The posthumous journey of Einstein's brain—from absconded relic to downloadable app—says more about the fate of genius in the postwar world than it ever will about the physiology of creative intelligence. In effect, it traces the arc of the genius's decline and even death, marking out a trajectory of devolution to the people. For the same forces that would bring genius to every screen and put a piece of it in every home have shattered the aura of the genius's sanctity, divesting him of his special significance and rarefied power. That process, moreover, has been willed. Just as the citizens of Athens saw fit to banish Socrates and his demon from the polis, we have felt the need to exclude the genius and his exception from the public square.

That may seem a surprising claim. Was not Einstein the "person of the century," the "genius among geniuses," as *Time* magazine declared in 1999? And surely the continuing effort to locate the stigmata of Einstein's genius confirms that old habits die hard. The methods may no longer be those of Broca or Vogt. But the search to isolate genius—to pinpoint it in the body, to confirm it in the flesh—is similar all the same. So is the yearning that lies behind it. The need to establish the genius's fundamental difference is stubborn, and the human desire for the transcendent and the extraordinary is great, no less now than when Socrates's contemporaries first marveled at his *daimonion*.[4]

All that is true. It is no less true that even today, in the liquid crystal light of a computer-generated image, one may still detect a faint glow of the sacred. The French critic Roland Barthes called attention to the familiar *numen* in 1957. "Paradoxically," he observed, "the more the genius of [Einstein] was materialized under the guise of his brain, the more the product of his inventiveness came to acquire a magical dimension." Einstein's brain had become a "mythical object," and Einstein's genius a myth, which served to mediate the secrets of the universe and to comfort us in our darkness and insecurity. The genius of Einstein resembles even now what the ancients once called a "middle term" of the universe, shuttling between ordinary human beings and the heavens. The *divinum quiddam* of his brain provides a glimpse of another dimension; it is a portal to a mysterious realm.[5]

Yet, at the same time that Barthes was describing the brain of Einstein as a totem of genius in ways that recalled the rites and rituals of old, others were calling attention to a development that worked against the familiar process of sacralization. The German Jewish philosopher Hannah Arendt in 1958 wrote of the "commercialization and vulgarization of genius," a process that was gradually dissipating the "great reverence the modern age [had] so willingly paid to genius, so frequently bordering on idolatry." This was a process, Arendt appreciated, evident from even before the war. As the Austrian novelist Robert Musil observed in the first volume of his modernist classic, *The Man Without Qualities*, written in the 1930s, "the time had come when people were starting to speak of genius on the soccer field or in the boxing ring." The widening of the field was already apparent, and to the dismay of Musil's narrator, even made room for "a racehorse of genius," which, chomping on celebrity's bit, sped by his rivals on the outside. Galton had included oarsmen in his surveys of hereditary genius. But what caught the eye of Musil's protagonist was the burst of movement and surge of activity in the stables of popular culture. Genius was no longer confined to the artists, statesmen, and scientists who had long commanded pride of place.[6]

This trickling down (or welling up) of genius along the vertical axis leading from high culture to low was accompanied, as well, by a horizontal expansion, a pushing outward of gender boundaries and geographical frontiers. If even a horse could be a genius, then surely men and women beyond Europe and the United States might qualify for the title? That acknowledgment was often grudging. But genius had a way of imposing itself. The eminent English mathematician G. H. Hardy modestly denied that he himself was a genius. But in the Indian autodidact Srinivasa Ramanujan, whom he brought to Cambridge in the summer of 1913, Hardy was humbled to confront a person he was convinced was "in the class of Gauss and Euler," a true "*natural* mathematical genius," among the greatest of the greats. Others saw a similar creative prowess in the Indian poet Rabindranath Tagore, catching a glimpse of what still other observers would discern in the flash of Pablo Neruda or Charlie Parker, Jorge Luis Borges or Naguib Mahfouz: creative originality of the very highest order. As the doyen of American anthropology, Alfred Kroeber, argued in a seminal study in 1944, genius was less a function of blood than of environment and culture. Taking aim at the eugenics of Galton and the Nazis, Kroeber included in his study data from the great civilizations of China and India, Mesopotamia, and the Arab world, making clear that genius might come from anywhere, as long as the conditions were right. Feminists of the avant-garde, meanwhile, were quick to make a similar point with respect to women, taking courage in Gertrude Stein's bold avowal that "I am a genius." Not all were so forthright. But most shared the conviction that the empire of genius knew no sex.[7]

This gradual expansion of genius—in effect, its democratization and globalization—gathered momentum in the aftermath of 1945. The development marked, in some sense, a return to an older understanding of genius as a faculty possessed by all. That understanding, it is true, had never been entirely abandoned. Although men and women had spoken for centuries of genius as a general disposition or trait, Europeans, and especially Americans, continued long after the eighteenth century to acknowledge that different people might have *a* genius for different things. As even Charles Spearman, the analyst of the all-governing *g*, was prepared to admit, "every normal man, woman, and child is . . . a genius at something." By the same logic, Spearman added, everyone was "an idiot at something," perhaps a less surprising revelation. But he was far from alone in harboring the suspicion that there might be a bit of genius in us all.[8]

In the decades since World War II, that thought has become commonplace—so much so that some critics have described it as "our genius problem." Genius is now everywhere. A 1993 cover story in *Newsweek* magazine, for example, observed that "judging by the hundreds to the thousands of newspaper references to 'geniuses' every month, we're overrun with them." Not to be outdone, *Esquire* boldly declared in its end-of-the-millennium "Genius Issue" that we are "living in an age of genius." Proof of the assertion was forthcoming in the names of those who at that very moment were enjoying their fifteen minutes of genius-fame, including the fashion designer Tom Ford, the Amazon executive Jeff Bezos, the Broadway musical singer Audra McDonald, the basketball star Allen Iverson, and the actor Leonardo DiCaprio. More recently, the well-regarded German newspaper *Die Zeit* devoted a special issue to "geniuses who have changed our life," profiling such modern incarnations of the type as Howard Schultz, the CEO of Starbucks; Mark Zuckerberg, the founder of Facebook; Miuccia Prada, the Italian designer; Ingvar Kamprad, the founder of Ikea; and, of course, Steve Jobs, widely hailed at the time of his death in 2011 as a departed "genius." There is irony in this description of Jobs, insofar as the genius historically has been regarded as an original creator, and Jobs, by his own admission (more or less), did not create, but rather tinkered and tweaked, adapting the ideas of others for sleek and widespread consumption. Undoubtedly there is brilliance in such "tweaking," and in other ways Jobs fit the part, embodying the image of the eccentric rebel and temperamental sage, prone to fits of anger and not averse to trying LSD. Yet, judged in historical terms, this master of marketing and mimesis was the very opposite of the genius ideal, who created from nothing, ex nihilo, drawing on no example but his own.[9]

Not that we should be surprised by the description of Jobs, or by the appearance of the other names on these lists. The blurring of the lines between genius and celebrity has been under way since the eighteenth century. In America, especially, where the business of the country is business, to think of individuals in the vanguard of the digital age, such as Steve Jobs or Bill Gates, as geniuses is even less of a surprise. With their historical suspicion of theory and their predilection for practical application and common sense, Americans have long treated applied genius with special reverence. If Benjamin Franklin, the first genius of the United States, was a tinkerer and entrepreneur par excellence, Thomas Edison was his fitting heir, the archetypal American genius, for whom usefulness and utility were the ultimate tests. Edison was "the greatest inventive genius in the world," in the opinion of Henry Ford, and widely regarded as a "wizard." Yet he worked hard to dispel the illusion that his powers were magical, claiming, famously, that "genius is 1% inspiration, and 99% perspiration," the consequence of dogged persistence and good old-fashioned elbow grease. Fittingly, Ford was among Edison's closest friends. The two together represented the perfect coupling of ingenuity and application, and the attendant financial rewards. Genius, in the American way, was not just thinking new thoughts and creating new things, but finding a use for them, and then using them to make a buck.[10]

It is little wonder, then, that as genius attended the rich and famous, it hovered—and hovers still—before those who yearn to be both. Once genius was born, now it is (self)-made. That, at least, is the claim of a flourishing self-help literature that offers genius as a lifestyle and aspiration. Have a look at *How to Be a Genius: Your Brain and How to Train It*. Or set your imagination on fire in *Ignite the Genius Within*. For those who prefer fewer flames, there are *Sparks of Genius: The Thirteen Thinking Tools of the World's Most Creative People*, or the "30 Ways to Spark Your Inner Genius" in *Everyday Smart*. *Becoming a Problem Solving Genius* is within your grasp, as is *Uncommon Genius: How Great Ideas Are Born*, or even *Ordinary Genius: A Guide for the Poet Within*. "You can "unlock your inner genius" in *Thought Revolution*. Or learn how to think like "history's ten most revolutionary minds" in *Discover Your Genius*. Stumble upon "your best ideas" in *Accidental Genius*. *Cracking Creativity*, according to its subtitle, discloses *The Secrets of Creative Genius*, and *Practical Genius* provides, as its subtitle proclaims, *The Real Smarts You Need to Get Your Talents and Passions Working for You*. You can learn *How to Think Like Leonardo Da Vinci* in a book of that title, poke around in *Pocket Genius*, or rummage through *Junk Genius*. There is *Football Genius, Negotiation Genius*, and *A Genius for Deception*, which recounts *How Cunning Helped the British Win Two World Wars*. And, if you have done all of that and want something more, consult *So, You're a Creative Genius . . . Now What?* Or put a little spice in your life with *Penis Genius: The Best Tips and Tricks for Working His Stick*. There is genius in just about everything these days. As one recent bestseller sums it up, there is *Genius in All of Us*.[11]

But if genius is everywhere, the genius is nowhere, or at least harder than ever to see. The same forces that have democratized and expanded genius's kingdom have sent the genius into exile or to an early grave. That curious fact will become apparent if one tries to name a genius in the postwar world. Einstein comes immediately to mind, of course. But he is the exception who proves the rule. And though there are others—including artists, such as Pablo Picasso and Jackson Pollock, or scientists, such as J. Robert Oppenheimer and Richard Feynman—they tend either to be holdovers from an earlier age or fail to command common and overwhelming assent. The truth is that we live at a time when there is genius in all of us, but very few geniuses to be found.

What does that paradox say? Was Einstein not only the genius of geniuses, but the last of the geniuses? It is possible that it is simply too early to tell. Just as the genius of Shakespeare was only recognized after the fact, it may be that the geniuses of today will only be discovered tomorrow. Still, even if they now walk among us, we no longer regard geniuses as we once did; nor do we look to them for the same things that we did in the past. The religion of genius is a moribund faith: the genius is all but disenchanted.

The defeat of Hitler marked a turning point in this respect, largely putting an end to the formal rites of the genius cult in Europe while putting the people on guard against investing human idols with such power. True, the cult lingered on in the Soviet Union and China, and some far-flung redoubts. And something of the sacred continued to lurk about Einstein, and continues still (if his eyeballs ever go on sale, they will no doubt fetch a pretty price). But he himself did his best to discourage such veneration. It is telling that when Israeli Prime Minister David Ben-Gurion inquired whether Einstein would be willing to accept the presidency of Israel in 1952, Einstein politely refused. The post was largely ceremonial, and Einstein was deeply sympathetic to Israel's fate. But, as he pointed out in his official response, he lacked the "natural aptitude" and the requisite "experience" necessary "to exercise official functions." Genius was not a transferable skill; genius in science did not a genius in politics make. Einstein was hardly above using his celebrity to enhance his support for a variety of political causes. But his refusal to be enshrined as a genius in an official capacity is in keeping with his resistance to a world that would allow the many to relinquish their power to the few. By making of some men more than men, the many made less of themselves.[12]

Notwithstanding the faint glow of the sacred that continued to attend Einstein the victor, the defeat of the evil genius Hitler served to expose the idolatry of the genius religion, providing an answer of sorts to the petition and prayer of the Yiddish poet Kadya Molodovsky. "God of Mercy," reads the last line of her haunting 1945 poem of that name, "deliver us from the spirit of genius." The blood of the Gulag and the Great Cultural Revolution in time did the same, disabusing all save the zealous and the blind of the illusion that the dear leader, the genius of the people, was any such thing. Even the all-powerful Chairman Mao came to deny the label that both he and Comrade Stalin had once so freely claimed. "I am no genius," he told a group of "responsible comrades" in 1971. The responsible comrades must have been surprised: they had heard the opposite for years. No matter. Genius did not depend "on one person or a few people," Mao insisted. The product of "collective wisdom," genius was built by the masses. Although Mao was simply reverting to an older and purer Marxist line, he nonetheless correctly identified the collective force—the *genius populi*, the genius of the people—that was working to topple the idol and destroy the altar on which the people had sacrificed so much.[13]

Revulsion against the excesses of evil genius in the twentieth century, in both its fascist and communist forms, thus played a crucial part in precipitating the general demise of the genius and the genius religion. But another factor was also involved: the simple recognition of the group dynamics at play in all creative endeavor. That recognition, ironically, emerged more clearly amid the conditions of capitalism than it did in the communist republics. It was of a piece with the broader democratization of genius, and those working in the natural sciences were among the first to make it explicit. As a research director at the storied management-consulting firm of Arthur D. Little, Inc., observed in the early twentieth century, "organized research does not depend upon individual genius; it is group activity. . . . Supermen are not required." With the development of large-scale industrial research and development (R&D), that perspective gained broad adherence, reflecting the changed (and changing) nature of the scientific workplace. Individuals were now urged to work together in teams to obtain better results, like the celebrated scientists in the "idea factory" of Bell Labs, which employed at its height close to 1200 PhDs. Producing one stunning innovation after the next, Bell scientists would go on to amass no fewer than thirteen Nobel Prizes. Such integrated efforts underscored the point that in many cases, many heads were better than one.[14]

Scientists themselves registered the development, downplaying the mythology of individual genius. *They* knew that the vast majority of scientific work was laborious and matter-of-fact. True, an outsider might still suggest that the genius of science channeled a kind of magical force, as the celebrated economist John Maynard Keynes did in a public lecture delivered shortly before his death in 1946. Newton, Keynes said, was a "magician" who had been "tempted by the Devil" to believe "that he could reach *all* the secrets of God and Nature by the pure power of mind." Insiders, however, were, increasingly more cautious. Some might still make an exception for Einstein, along with a handful of other greats. But among practicing scientists, the word "genius" largely fell out of favor after the war, its use treated as a professional and social faux pas.[15]

At roughly the same time, genius fell out of favor among scholars of the humanities as well. Motivated by Marxian analysis in many cases, and in turn by the literary currents of poststructuralism and deconstruction, scholars exposed the "fiction" of agency, pronounced the "death" of the author, and emphasized the social forces at work in literary and artistic production. Genius, in such accounts, functioned largely as a cipher, while geniuses themselves were widely dismissed as desiccated relics of the past, part of a mummified category and order of things that was likewise dead and gone.[16]

Finally, the role of genius in the social sciences, and even in psychology, the discipline that long claimed genius as its own, has changed considerably. There are still reputable psychologists who devote themselves to the study of genius, described as such. But many have altered the name to protect the innocent (or hide the guilty), studying, like Terman in his later years, the more limited "intelligence" and the ways to test it; or investigating "creativity" and its correlates; or isolating the characteristics of "outliers," high achievers, and expert performers. Moreover, there has been an effort to reexamine and rethink the very notion of a unitary intelligence on the model of genius and the IQ. The psychologist Daniel Goleman, for example, has spearheaded the study of what he calls "emotional intelligence," or EQ. In an enormously popular series of books on the subject, beginning with his 1996 bestseller *Emotional Intelligence: Why It Can Matter More Than IQ,* Goleman (along with a host of others since) has promoted the idea that emotional well-being and insight may be a better predictor of success than purely cognitive measures of the mind. The noted Harvard psychologist Howard Gardner, meanwhile, has reenergized a line of inquiry originally pursued by those, such as L. L. Thurstone, who argued in the early twentieth century that "intelligence" was in truth composed of a number of "primary mental abilities." In Gardner's influential formulation, crystallized in his 1983 *Frames of Mind: The Theory of Multiple Intelligences*, there are eight such primary abilities, including intelligence not only for language, logic and mathematics, and spatial awareness, but also for music, the body and its movement, interpersonal relations, and even for a relation to the natural environment and existence itself. Human beings, it follows, may be gifted in different ways. And though neither the theory of emotional intelligence nor that of multiple intelligences has been immune to criticism, they register perfectly the broader push to pluralize and democratize what once was called genius.

Such research is in high demand in education departments, the military, corporations, and other places where identifying and nurturing talent is placed at a premium. Yet, even there, a focus on the many has tended to crowd out concentration on the gifts of individuals or the singular attributes of the one. Borrowing a term from contemporary economics, analysts of innovation today stress the importance not just of multiple intelligences but of "collective intelligence," reaffirming the idea that the many know best. It follows that what matters most in furthering innovation is putting the many in touch with one another. Urban concentrations and markets, social media, and other networks of exchange have become the sites for creative investigation and the investigation of creativity, with the result that individual genius, by and large, no longer garners the attention of experts, presenting a "genius problem" of its own.[17]

There is considerable irony in the fact that genius has largely vanished as a category of academic research while exploding as a trope in popular culture. It wouldn't be the first time that academia and the world have missed each other. But, in truth, the two phenomena are related. For not only does the research emphasizing the social underpinnings of creativity track with the broader democratization of genius since World War II, but it also provides a foil. The more we learn about the collaborative nature of creativity in an increasingly complex and interconnected world, the more the myth of the lone genius becomes appealing. In societies that tend by their very nature to thwart it, an emphasis on individual agency is reassuring, if also a little bit quaint.[18]

There are probably other psychological forces that help keep alive a belief in genius and geniuses as special individuals whose natural endowments and inherent gifts seem to determine their success in advance. It may be that a belief in natural genius gives societies and parents an out: where time and resources are limited, the belief provides an excuse to focus intensely only on those who are "born" for success. It may be, too, that a belief in giftedness gets the rest of us off the hook, explaining our own shortcomings and failures as the result of genetic endowments (or the lack thereof) over which we have little control. Finally, as I have taken pains to show in this book, the human need for transcendence is great. Endowing others with genius still serves to satisfy a longing for the marvelous. It fills a need.[19]

For all of these reasons, genius continues to titillate, drawing steady interest and quixotic quests. The American optometrist and entrepreneur Robert K. Graham made headlines in the 1980s and 1990s with his attempt to establish a Nobel Prize sperm bank, the Repository of Germinal Choice. Graham gathered material that Terman had allowed to fall by the wayside, collecting the sperm of the Nobel Laureate in Physics William Shockley, the coinventor of the transistor whom the *Genetic Studies of Genius* had famously overlooked. Despite generous donations from Shockley and, presumably, other Nobel Prize winners—though none of these have been willing to come forward publicly—the bank closed its vaults in 1997. More recently, the neuroscientist Allan Snyder has garnered media attention for his attempts to develop a "creativity cap" at his lab at the University of Sydney. By applying an electrical current to targeted areas of the brain, Snyder hopes to mimic the capacities of savants, bringing out the inner Rain Man in everyone. The results so far are decidedly mixed. And for skeptics inclined to give up on the search for human genius altogether, there is the ongoing hope of artificial intelligence (AI). AI may be genius's final frontier, entailing an effort to build a machine that can go beyond human nature and do what human beings cannot. A computer, Deep Blue, succeeded in tying the grandmaster of chess, Garry Kasparov, in 1997. But successful efforts to build machines that genuinely create—composing a symphony or writing a poem—are still some ways off. In the meantime, continuing to think about genius in human beings is good press, and for many, good fun.[20]

But there is one other reason that helps account for our continued fascination with genius at the moment of the genius's demise: the long and complicated dance of equality, with which the genius has been locked in awkward embrace since birth. The cult of genius emerged in tension with the notion that all human beings are created equal, and it did so at the very moment in history when the notion of equality was on the rise as an organizing principle of society. Genius contested that principle for centuries, and in some ways, it contests it still. Yet equality may finally be having the last laugh, and it was equality's greatest student who predicted that this would be so. Alexis de Tocqueville made his name as an observer of democracy in America, as the title of his greatest work suggests. But he was just as much an observer of Europe, and his image of the American republic was colored by his hopes and fears of what Europe might become. Equality, Tocqueville believed, was a relentless force that leveled age-old hierarchies and swept all before it, leaving behind few distinctions with which to take the measure of man. "When there are no more hereditary riches, privileges of rank, and prerogatives of birth," he wrote, "it becomes clear that what makes the principal difference among the fortunes of men is intelligence." Some were quicker, others more creative, and still others worked harder to better themselves. Yet, on the horizon of the American republic, extreme differences flattened out. "Scientific and literary genius is as rare as ability is common" in the United States, Tocqueville observed. The country was conspicuous for the absence of minds that towered above the fray, and great writers, scientists, and thinkers played a much smaller role in the American republic than they did in Europe. That was a state of affairs that owed much to the exceptional history of the United States. But although Tocqueville did not rule out the possibility that in the future "some speculative genius" might emerge there, the thrust of his analysis aimed to show that under advanced conditions of democracy and equality, "genius becomes rarer and enlightenment more common." What in aristocratic societies was concentrated in the exceptional few would be "divided equally among all," and with tremendous possibilities, unleashing a combined creative ingenuity and capacity for application greater than anything the world had known. Long before the latest avatars of collective intelligence, Tocqueville understood that there was strength in numbers. In a land without geniuses, there would still be plenty of smarts to go around.[21]

Is this not the image of the United States today, and so, too, of Europe, where equality has moved farther and faster in recent years than in the land in which Tocqueville first read the future long ago? Great disparities continue to exist, of course, and an alarming (and expanding) inequality of wealth in the United States threatens to concentrate its creative capital and squander its human resources in ways that are far from maximally productive. And yet, when viewed historically over the *longue durée*, equality has undoubtedly flexed its muscles. Suspicious of authority of the mind, and wary of the brightest and the best, we bend no knee to greatness. All might be geniuses now; everyone has a genius for something. We have pulled the genius down to size, fitting him and shaping her to human, perhaps all-too-human, dimensions. The distrust is well earned, and the peoples' skepticism is useful, serving to protect us from the impulse to raise idols and to bow and scrape before them.

But if to proliferate genius so that the genius is lost in the crowd is an effective strategy against submission, it comes at a cost. Socrates may well have been a threat to the democracy of Athens, but when its citizens voted to convict him, they sullied themselves. And for all the abuse of genius since the presence of the *divinum quiddam* was first detected in the minds of special men, it long kept alive an exhilarating sense of the possibilities of being—and being transcendent—in the world. As Ralph Waldo Emerson acknowledged of "the excess of influence" of great men, their "attractions warp us from our place." But he also knew that it was natural to believe in them. "We feed on genius," he said, we need it as sustenance to survive.[22]

In an age as suspicious of "greatness" as our own, it is worth recalling that truth, and recalling that, although those who prostrate themselves before idols make themselves small, those who fail to take the measure of true stature are similarly diminished. Great men and great women still have their uses. As Emerson put it over a century and a half ago in a passage that serves as an epigraph to this book, the genius of humanity continues to be the right point of view of history. "Once you saw phoenixes: they are gone; the world is not therefore disenchanted." May it never be.[23]

ACKNOWLEDGMENTS

I HAVE UNDOUBTEDLY SUFFERED from many delusions in my life—and undoubtedly suffer from many still. But being a genius is not one of them. Exacting, if loving, parents saw to it that their son never "got too big for his britches," as my father liked to say, and an exacting, if loving, family does much the same today. Truth be told, I am far more likely to go through the week thinking of myself as an imbecile—unable to properly assemble my children's toys, baffled by modern technology, and forgetting (yet again) to take the laundry out of the dryer—than to suffer *la folie de la grandeur*. My own failings have much to answer for. But there may be an institutional explanation as well. For, in the early 1970s, as a child in the California public school system, I was administered an aptitude test for "Mentally Gifted Minors." It was, as I recall, somewhat akin to an IQ test, with shapes and pictures and the like, and although many of the specific details of this test have faded from my memory, I know for sure that I didn't pass. It hardly helped that I was told I *almost* passed. To be almost gifted is likely as satisfying as being almost pretty. As I watched my little friends trundle off each week to special classes for the specially endowed, the thought provided little consolation.

I recount the story here not only in an effort to combat (however imperfectly) my own sense of self-importance, but also because this book is in part about the power of labels and those who grant them, and the tremendous difficulty of measuring anything as elusive, as multicausal, and as complex as giftedness, creativity, or genius. When I recently spoke with a teacher who helped to oversee the administration of the test I took in California—one of the many fine teachers, I should add, who did their best with those of us who were apparently cheated at birth—she laughed as she recalled the students who had "passed," and those who had not, and how they eventually turned out. Suffice it to say that she didn't put much stock in the predictive value of this sort of exam.

Much of the material chronicled in this book would likely reaffirm that basic skepticism. And yet that doesn't mean that the impact of such tests—and the assumptions that tend to undergird them—are any less powerful or enduring than we typically assume. At an early age, I was told, with all the objectivity of science, that I was not the recipient of gifts. I might have just thrown in the towel then and there, but I am a stubborn sort, and I spent many years disputing the verdict, working away to prove to myself and to others, dammit, that I had not been slighted at birth. It was only much later that I realized that this little exam had unwittingly done me a favor—and not simply because intellectual self-doubt is an ideal disposition for writers and scholars. I had been freed at the outset from a burden that might well have been difficult to sustain. There is evidence to suggest that an exaggerated belief in the strength of one's innate capacities can actually harm a child's development, sapping motivation and initiative. And there is even more evidence to show how damaging it can be to tell young people that, according to the numbers, they just don't measure up.

Standardized tests have been with us since the early twentieth century, and they are here to stay. But at a time when they are assuming an ever greater importance in our educational system, it is worth thinking seriously about their impact, and about the assumptions they entail. For, as this book takes pains to show, despite our foundational belief in the self-evident truth that all are created equal by birth, we in the West (and elsewhere besides) have shown ourselves to be deeply invested in an antithetical proposition, continually reaffirming the natural and inherent superiority of the few.

Why this should be so is as much a question for psychologists, evolutionary biologists, and political philosophers as it is for historians, who might consider together why it is that human beings evince a need to draw hierarchical distinctions, even (or especially) in conditions of nominal equality. We might also ponder why it is that we show a propensity to base these distinctions in nature and the fatality of birth. By focusing on the tremendous fascination with genius and geniuses in the modern world, this book hopes to begin an answer.

IN WRITING THIS BOOK, I have benefited immensely from the kindness and expertise of others. If that is the case with all creative endeavors, it is especially so with this one, since genius touches on so many different domains. Science, psychology, sociology, historical aesthetics and the study of literature, music, art, and even theology and demonology all find their way into the study of genius, not to mention political history and the history of celebrity and fame.

For helping me to negotiate this varied and difficult terrain, I wish to thank, first of all, a number of institutions and individuals who helped me to organize conferences and symposia that were of great assistance in shaping my thinking. The ever-generous Martin Seligman and Angela Duckworth at the University of Pennsylvania helped bring together an extraordinary group of experts, including James Gleick, Douglas Hofstadter, Anders Ericcson, Rebecca Goldstein, Robert Scales, David Lubinski, Roy Baumeister, and Dean Keith Simonton, for two days of rewarding discussions in Philadelphia. Sarah Buck-Kachaluba, the humanities librarian at Florida State University, my own institution, along with the obliging staff at FSU's Strozier Library, have been of great service in a number of ways, most immediately by helping to organize a one-day symposium, "Facets of Genius," in February 2012, along with Professor Christian Weber and myself. Finally, the Huntington Library in Pasadena, California, generously allowed my friend and colleague Joyce Chaplin and me to bring together a dazzling array of scholars in May 2012 to consider genius for two days in the most congenial of settings.

Antoine Lilti graciously invited me to deliver a series of lectures and spend a month at the École Normale Supérieure in Paris in the spring of 2010, which proved of immense value (at least to me). David Armitage and Peter Gordon arranged for me to speak to an engaging audience at the Center for European Studies at Harvard University; Dan Edelstein and Keith Baker did the same at the French Culture Workshop at Stanford University; and Tony Judt, in the months before his death, had me one last time to the Remarque Institute at New York University to share my thoughts on genius before a stimulating group and to steal a precious moment with him. For much of my professional career, Tony served as a guardian angel and *genius bonus*. I am grateful to have known him, and I miss him every day.

I am also grateful to Carolina Armenteros for an invitation to deliver a key-note address at Jesus College, Cambridge, amid the Fifth International Collo-quium on Joseph de Maistre; to Annie Jourdan for her hospitality and invitation to speak about evil geniuses before the faculty of European Studies at Amster-dam University; to Ivo Cerman for a chance to consider the "religion of genius" at the Historical Institute of the Czech National Academy of Science in Prague; to Hans Stauffacher for the opportunity to speak on "geniology" at the Institut für Religionswissenschaft at the Freie Universität in Berlin; and to Steven Vin-cent, Tony La Vopa, Malachi Hacohen, and the gracious participants at the Tri-angle Intellectual History Seminar at the National Humanities Center in North Carolina for an invitation to present a chapter of my work and for their temerity in reading it, much to its improvement. I also delivered papers on the subject of genius at the Western Society for French Historical Studies, the Consortium on Revolutionary Europe, the American Historical Association, and Potsdam Uni-versity. I am grateful to the audiences at all of these places for their comments and consideration.

I am likewise grateful to my colleagues at Florida State, who provided a great deal of helpful feedback during the two work-in-progress talks I delivered at the Department of History. Rafe Blaufarb, Ron Doel, Charles Upchurch, George Williamson, Fritz Davis, Nathan Stoltzfus, and Robert Gellately kindly read individual chapters with particular care and offered much helpful advice. John Marincola in the Department of Classics did the same with his generous and discerning eyes, and François Dupuisgrenet Desroussilles brought his astound-ing erudition to bear on two chapters that eventually became one. Edward Gray heard me out on many occasions, lifting my spirits even as he did damage to my liver. And for professional assistance and personal relief, I must also thank the brothers of the Order of St. Walpurgis—John Corrigan, Thomas Joiner, Neil Jumonville, David Kirby, John Maner, Mark Petralunga, David Scott, and Mark Weingardner—for their robust courage in doing battle against the demons of academic pomposity, intellectual laziness, provincialism, boredom, and excessive sobriety. The three other members of the "4 D's Dining Club," who in the inter-est of discretion shall remain nameless, have done much the same.

Very special thanks are due to several individuals who read the draft man-uscript in its entirety. David Bell, whose insight and generosity is unsurpassed, has more to do with this project's improvement, and less to do with its short-comings, than anyone I know. *Merci, bonne étoile.* David Armitage, *copain* and comrade in arms, read through the draft with his characteristic brilliance and wit, keeping me laughing and enthused for great stretches of its composition; and Steven Englund, whose Paris drawing room is a rejuvenating place of sweetness and light, offered the wise judgments of a writer who is also a very fine historian.

A great many other individuals shared knowledge, references, insight, or unpublished work. A complete list would run to several pages, but let me at least express my gratitude to Kathleen Kete, John Carson, Adam Potkay, David Bates, Pascal Dupuy, Lauren Gray, Nathalie Heinich, April Shelford, Rob Riemen, Eric Eichman, Robert Folkenflik, Mark Juergensmeyer, Kent Wright, Jeremy Caradona, Daniel Roche, Jacques Revel, Eva Giloi, Laurel Fulkerson, Christine Zabel, Larry Fischer, Michael Carhart, Julianna Baggot, Danny Markel, Cyril Triolaire, Philippe de Carbonnières, Peter Hicks, Thierry Lentz, John Randoph, Rolf Reichardt, John Merriman, Eliyahu Stern, Mark Lilla, Stéphane Van Damme, Matthew Day, Will Hanley, Sophia Rosenfeld, Thomas Meyer, Sonja Asal, Shalyn Rae Claggett, W. Warner Burke, James Younger, Lynn Hunt, Irina Sirotkina, Margaret Jacob, and the late Frank Turner, who died too young, but taught me much.

Tarah Luke, Katherine Cox, Darren Darby, and Antje Meijners all assisted me with research and tracking down materials. In Berlin, Dorit Brixius was of invaluable assistance in helping me with German sources. And my doctoral students in Tallahassee, Joe Horan, Cindy Ermus, Shane Hockin, Bryan Banks, and Jonathan Deverse, were all pulled into the process at one stage or another and helped out with great efficiency and good cheer.

Much of this manuscript was written in Berlin, that remarkable city that has known so much suffering and inflicted so much pain, and yet has transformed itself into a capital of great enlightenment and pleasure. I am immensely grateful to the Alexander von Humboldt Stiftung for sponsoring my time there as well as to Günther Lottes, who was a model host, ever generous in his friendship, ideas, and wit. Iwan d'Aprile was similarly forthcoming, and the many wonderful graduate students at the University of Potsdam made this a lively and welcome retreat, just as Irmela Schautz, Christian Ridder, and their daughter, Salome, helped to make our rented flat in Prenzlauer Berg a genuine home. Finally, my professional residence, Florida State University, was no less generous in granting leave-time and resources, including a Council on Research and Creativity grant that helped get this project off the ground.

My wife, Courtney McMahon; my agent, Tina Bennett; and my editor and publisher, Lara Heimert, are a trio of Muses—strong, intelligent women who could inspire even the dullest of minds. They have inspired me. Courtney, above all, withstood my distractions to help create a space in which I could create in peace, at no small sacrifice to her own. By contrast, my children, Julien and Madeleine, to whom this book is dedicated, did everything they could to delay the project, and with some success, peering in my office door, jumping on my back, and waking me in the middle of the night. If only the book had taken longer.

NOTES

INTRODUCTION

1. See, typically, David Harris, *The Genius: How Bill Walsh Reinvented Football and Created an NFL Dynasty* (New York: Random House, 2008); Danny Goldberg, *Bumping into Geniuses: My Life Inside the Rock and Roll Business* (New York: Gotham Books, 2008). The BBC film led to a book, edited by the director Christopher Sykes, entitled *No Ordinary Genius: An Illustrated History of Richard Feynman* (New York: W. W. Norton, 1995). James Gleick's excellent biography of Feynman is entitled simply *Genius: The Life and Science of Richard Feynman* (New York: Vintage, 1992).

2. "Think Like a Genius: How Exceptional Intelligence and Creativity Arise," *Scientific American Mind*, special issue, November/December 2012. The title is also that of Todd Siler's *Think Like a Genius* (New York: Bantam Books, 1999).

3. Joyce Goldenstern, *Albert Einstein: Physicist and Genius* (Berkeley Heights, NJ: Enslow Publishers, 1995), 12.

4. On Einstein's "carefree manner of a child," see Howard Gardner, *Creating Minds: An Anatomy of Creativity as Seen Through the Lives of Freud, Einstein, Picasso, Stravinsky, Elliot, Graham, and Gandhi* (New York: Basic Books, 2011), 113. "Mystical, intuitive" is the characterization of Hans C. Ohanian, *Einstein's Mistakes: The Human Failings of Genius* (New York: W. W. Norton, 2008), 3, 215, 332. For the *Time* cover and quotation, see the July 1, 1946 issue. Einstein's actual role in warning President Franklin D. Roosevelt of the bomb and furthering the Manhattan Project in pursuit of an atomic weapon was comparatively small. See the discussion in Chapter 6 below.

5. Einstein is cited in Alice Calaprice, ed., *The New Quotable Einstein* (Princeton, NJ: Princeton University Press, 2005), 194.

6. I owe the phrase "history in ideas" (as opposed to a history *of* ideas) to my friend and colleague David Armitage, who develops the thought, along with the notion of "trans-temporal" history, in his "What's the Big Idea? Intellectual History and the Longue Durée," *History of European Ideas* 38, no. 4 (2012): 493–507. For further methodological reflection on this approach to the past, see my "The Return of the History of Ideas?" in *Rethinking Modern European Intellectual History*, eds. Darrin M. McMahon and Samuel Moyn (New York: Oxford University Press, 2014).

7. A notable exception to the general tendency to overlook the importance of religion to the study of genius is Edgar Zilsel's *Die Geniereligion: Ein kritischer*

Versuch über das moderne Persönlichkeitsideal, intro. Johann Dvorak (Frankfurt: Suhrkamp, 1990), originally published in 1918, as well as the more recent and penetrating work of the French sociologist Nathalie Heinich. See, for instance, her *The Glory of Van Gogh: An Anthropology of Admiration,* trans. Paul Leduc Browne (Princeton, NJ: Princeton University Press, 2006). A characteristic example of the scientific dismissal of religion is Hans Jürgen Eysenck, *Genius: The Natural History of Creativity* (Cambridge: Cambridge University Press, 1995). The impetus for the literary and critical assault on genius was provided by Roland Barthes and Michel Foucault, whose seminal work assailed the notion of the autonomous creative "author" as source of originality and genius. See Barthes's 1967 essay "La mort de l'auteur" and Foucault's 1973 rejoinder, "Qu'est-ce qu'un auteur?" Two more recent and fruitful engagements with the question of genius from a postmodern perspective are Julia Kristeva, "Female Genius: General Introduction," in *Hannah Arendt,* trans. Ross Guberman (New York: Columbia University Press, 2001), ix–xxi, vol. 1 of *Female Genius: Life, Madness, Words—Hannah Arendt, Melanie Klein, Collette; a Trilogy,* and Klaus Ottman, *The Genius Decision: The Extraordinary and the Postmodern Condition* (Putnam, CT: Spring Publications, 2004).

8. Will Durant, *Adventures in Genius* (New York: Simon and Schuster, 1931), xv; Harold Bloom, *Genius: A Mosaic of One Hundred Exemplary Creative Minds* (New York: Warner Books, 2002), 7.

9. Wilhelm Lange-Eichbaum, *The Problem of Genius,* trans. Eden and Cedar Paul (New York: Macmillan, 1932), 6, xvii–xviii. The original German edition was published in 1931, in part as an abbreviation of Lange-Eichbaum's much larger *Genie, Irrsinn, und Ruhm* (Munich: E. Reinhardt, 1928). On the developing sociological analysis of genius in this period, see, as well, Albert Solomon, "Zur Soziologie des Geniebegriffs," *Die Gesellschaft: Internationale Revue für Sozialismus und Politik* 3, no. 2 (1926):504–513.

10. Lange-Eichbaum, *Problem of Genius,* 49–51, 152–153, 156–159, 160–162.

11. Lange-Eichbaum was a key German proponent of the dubious, though popular, scientific belief that genius was a form of madness or degenerative disease. On this theory and its European proponents, see chap. 5 below. Lange-Eichbaum was also responsible for perpetuating the belief that Nietzsche's insanity (and hence his "genius") was a result of syphilis. See his *Nietzsche: Krankheit und Wirkung* (Hamburg: Lettenbauer, 1946). Hitler was featured on the cover of *Time* on January 2, 1939. On Hitler and the Nazis' enmity with Einstein, see Jürgen Neffe, *Einstein: A Biography,* trans. Shelley Frisch (New York: Farrar, Strauss, and Giroux, 2007), 284.

12. "Germany: Genius Hitler," *Time,* May 2, 1938. Hitler is cited in Ian Kershaw, *Hitler: 1889–1936* (London: Allen Lane, 1998), 151. For Hitler's autobiography, see Adolf Hitler, *Mein Kampf,* trans. Ralph Mannheim (London: Hutchinson, 1969), 266. Goebbels is cited in Jochen Schmidt, *Die Geschichte des Genie-Gedankens in der deutschen Literatur, Philosophie und Politik, 1750–1945,* 2 vols. (Heidelberg: Universitätsverlag, 2004), 2:207.

13. For the strong "constructivist" position, which minimizes the role of an individual's talent or gifts in making genius, see Tia De Nora, *Beethoven and the*

Construction of Genius: Musical Politics in Vienna, 1792–1803 (Berkeley: University of California Press, 2005). For a critique of this position, see Jean-Michael Menger's *Le travail créateur* (Paris: Gallimard, 2009).

14. On the genius as the "highest human type," see, for instance, Herbert Dieckmann, "Diderot's Conception of Genius," *Journal of the History of Ideas* 2, no. 2 (1941): 151–182.

15. On the "withdrawal of God," see Marcel Gauchet, *The Disenchantment of the World: A Political History of Religion*, trans. Oscar Burge (Princeton, NJ: Princeton University Press, 1997), as well as, from a different perspective, Charles Taylor, *A Secular Age* (Cambridge, MA: Belknap Press, 2007). Gauchet does not address the dismissal of spiritual mediators and companions, but that development is consistent with his account.

16. On re-enchantment, see Joshua Landy and Michael Saler, "Introduction" to Landy and Saler, eds., *The Re-Enchantment of the World* (Palo Alto, CA: Stanford University Press, 2009), 2. See also Saler's "Modernity and Enchantment: A Historiographic Review," *American Historical Review* 111, no. 3 (2006): 692–717.

17. Surprisingly little work has been done on the intellectual history of equality, though a notable exception is the scholarship of Siep Stuurman. See his *De Uitvinding van de Mensheid* (Amsterdam: Prometheus, 2010), the rationale of which is provided in English in his "How to Write the History of Equality," *Leidschrift* 19, no. 3 (2004): 23–38. On the denial of equality to targeted groups, see Uday S. Mehta, "Liberal Strategies of Exclusion," in *Tensions of Empire: Colonial Cultures in a Bourgeois World*, eds. Frederick Cooper and Ann Laura Stoler (Berkeley: University of California Press, 1997), 59–86. Jefferson is cited and discussed in John Carson, *The Measure of Merit: Talents, Intelligence, and Inequality in the French and American Republics, 1750–1940* (Princeton, NJ: Princeton University Press, 2007), 11. The phrase "shadow language of equality" is Carson's (xiii). On European artists as natural aristocrats, see Nathalie Heinich, *L'élite artiste: Excellence et singularité en régime démocratique* (Paris: Editions Gallimard, 2005). My own analysis of genius as an exception to the notion of equality concurs broadly with Carson's and Heinich's fine studies. I am indebted to both authors for their conversation and insight.

18. Edgar Zilsel's *Die Enstehung des Geniebegriffes: Ein Betrag zur Ideengeschichte der Antike und des Fruhkapitalismus*, intro. Heinz Maus (Hildesheim, Germany: Georg Olms, 1972 [1926]), traces the concept of genius from antiquity to the Renaissance by following both the genealogy of the word and early approximations of the type. Unlike Zilsel's earlier, critical analysis of the "genius religion" of Germany and Austria in the early twentieth century, cited in note 5 above, his historical work on genius shows almost no interest in religion as an explanatory factor in its development. On the distinction between words and things, see Quentin Skinner, "The Idea of a Cultural Lexicon," in Skinner, *Visions of Politics*, vol. 1, *Regarding Method* (Cambridge: Cambridge University Press, 2009), 158–175. The recent interest in the history of celebrity, charisma, and heroism provides a fresh take on the old question of "great" men. See, for example, Edward Berenson and Eva Giloi, eds., *Constructing Charisma: Celebrity, Fame,*

and Power in Nineteenth-Century Europe (Oxford, UK: Berghahn Books, 2010); Antoine Lilti, *Figures publiques: Aux origines de la célébrité (1750–1850)* (Paris: Fayard, forthcoming).

19. See the insightful reflections of Marjorie Garber, "Our Genius Problem," *The Atlantic*, December 2002, www.theatlantic.com/past/docs/issues/2002/12 /garber.htm.

CHAPTER 1

1. W. K. Simpson, ed., *The Literature of Ancient Egypt: An Anthology of Stories, Instructions, Stelae, Autobiography and Poetry*, 3rd ed. (New Haven, CT: Yale University Press, 2003); Benjamin A. Elman, *A Cultural History of Civil Examination in Late Imperial China* (Berkeley: University of California Press, 2000), 64; Jacqueline Ki-Zerbo and Joseph Ki-Zerbo, "The Living Tradition," in *Methodology and African Pre-History*, ed. Joseph Ki-Zerbo (Berkeley: University of California Press, 1989), 62–73.

2. For a recent articulation of the case for Western dominance of outstanding human achievement, see Charles Murray, *Human Accomplishment: The Pursuit of Excellence in the Arts and Sciences, 800 B.C. to 1950* (New York: HarperCollins, 2003), 245–383.

3. The story of Kakheperresenb's complaint and the example of the *Katha sarit sagara* are discussed by John Barth in his delightful essay, "Do I Repeat Myself? The Problem of the Already Said," *The Atlantic*, July 5, 2011, Fiction 2011 Special Issue.

4. The phrase "There is nothing new under the sun" is from Ecclesiastes 1:9. The phrase and concept "a time of origins" is that of Mircea Eliade and is central to all of his work, but see, in particular, *The Myth of the Eternal Return: Cosmos and History*, trans. Willard R. Trask (Princeton, NJ: Princeton University Press, 1991), first published in French in 1949. The conception of an "absolute past" governing the temporal orientation of religious societies until roughly the eighteenth century is that of Marcel Gauchet in his *The Disenchantment of the World: A Political History of Religion*, trans. Oscar Burge (Princeton, NJ: Princeton University Press, 1997), 23–33.

5. "Solus Deus creat," Aquinas affirms, adding that "Nullum corpus potest creare," that no other body—angelic or human—can bring something into existence out of nothing. See Aquinas, *Summa Theologica*, I, Q. 45, Art. 2, ad. 2 and 3; Q. 46, Art. 1, ad. 5. Saint Augustine similarly points out, in reference to man, that "creatura non potest creare" (the created thing cannot create) (*De Trinitate*, III, 9).

6. The potential danger and transgression of usurping creation is a point made with great erudition and insight in John Hope Mason's *The Value of Creativity: The Origins and Emergence of a Modern Belief* (Burlington, VT: Ashgate, 2003), on whose accounts of Prometheus and Enoch I draw here.

7. Mason, *Value of Creativity*, 30; Weihua Niu and Robert J. Sternberg, "The Philosophical Roots of Western and Eastern Conceptions of Creativity," *Journal of Theoretical and Philosophical Psychology* 16, nos. 1–2 (2006): 18–38. On the emergence of creativity, see, in addition to Mason's excellent study, Wladyslaw

Tatarkiewicz, "Creativity: History of the Concept," in his *A History of Six Ideas: An Essay in Aesthetics*, trans. Christopher Kasparek (The Hague: Nijhof, 1980), 244–265.

8. Plato, *Phaedrus*, 242b–c. The translation here and in all subsequent citations is that of Alexander Nehamas and Paul Woodruff in the Hackett edition of the *Phaedrus* (Indianapolis: Hackett, 1995). Revealing references to the *daimonion* may be found in the *Apology*, 31d, 40a–b; *Euthypro*, 3b; *Alcibiades*, I, 103a, 105a; *Euthydemus*, 272e; *Republic*, 496c; and *Theatetus*, 151a, among the canonical Platonic texts, and Xenophon, *Memorabilia*, 1.1.2. The translation here and below is that of E. C. Marchant in the Loeb Classical edition of the *Memorabilia* (Cambridge, MA: Harvard University Press, 2002 [1923]), 3. Socrates's comments on his trial are from Plato, *Apology*, 31c–d. The Pythia's line, widely repeated in the ancient world, is taken here from Diogenes Laertius's life of Socrates, 2.37–39, in the Loeb Classical edition of *The Lives of the Eminent Philosophers*, trans. R. D. Hicks (Cambridge, MA: Harvard University Press, 1972), 169; see also Plato, *Apology*, 40a–b.

9. Cicero, *De Divinatione*, 1.54.122; Paul Friedländer, *Plato*, trans. Hans Meyerhoff, 3 vols. (New York: Pantheon, 1958), 1:32. For recent scholarly views on the subject of Socrates's *daimonion*, see Pierre Destrée and Nicholas D. Smith, eds., *Divine Sign: Religion, Practice, and Value in Socratic Philosophy*, a special issue of *Apeiron: A Journal for Ancient Philosophy and Science* 38, no. 2 (Kelowna, British Columbia: Academic Printing and Publishing, 2005).

10. Walter Burkert, *Greek Religion*, trans. John Raffian (Cambridge, MA: Harvard University Press, 1985), 179–181. On the relationship between happiness (*eudaimonia*) and the "good *daimon*" (*eu daimon*), see my *Happiness: A History* (New York: Atlantic Monthly Press, 2006), 3–5.

11. Hesiod, *Work and Days*, 1.252; Xenophon, *Memorabilia*, 1.1.3.

12. Plato, *Republic*, 496c.

13. On Socrates's appearance, see Paul Zanker, *The Mask of Socrates: The Image of the Intellectual in Antiquity* (Berkeley: University of California Press, 1995), 32–39.

14. Plutarch, *On the Sign of Socrates*, 580c–d, in the Loeb Classical edition of vol. 7 of the *Moralia*, trans. Phillip H. de Lacy and Benedict Einarson (Cambridge, MA: Harvard University Press, 2000 [1959]). Immediately after discussing the *daimonion*, Socrates describes himself in *Phaedrus* 242c as a "prophet," though "not a very good one." That tenuous link was used by later commentators as a textual basis for establishing Socrates's powers of divination and prophecy by virtue of the *daimonion*. See John M. Rist, "Plotinus and the 'Daimonion' of Socrates," *Phoenix* 17, no. 1 (1963): 15–16; Cicero, *De Divinatione*, 1.54.123; Maximus of Tyre, *Orations*, 8.3, in *The Philosophical Orations*, trans. and intr. M. B. Trapp (Oxford: Clarendon Press, 1997), 71. Maximus uses the expression "middle term" in *Orations*, 9.2.

15. *Symposium*, 202e–203a. Plato says the *daimones* are a "kind of gods" in the *Apology*, 27d.

16. The different translation is that of Robert Fitzgerald. See his Homer, *The Odyssey*, trans. Robert Fitzgerald (New York: Farrar, Straus, and Giroux, 1998), 1 (emphasis added).

17. Homer, *Odyssey*, 8.51–53; Hesiod, *Theogony*, 30–34, as cited in Penelope Murray, "Poetic Genius and Its Classical Origins," in *Genius: The History of an Idea*, ed. Penelope Murray (Oxford: Blackwell, 1989), 12. The discussion of ancient conceptions of poetic genius that follows draws heavily on Murray's rich and concise article. See also her "Poetic Inspiration in Early Greece," *Journal of Hellenic Studies* 101 (1981): 87–100.

18. See, for example, John Harold Leavitt, ed., *Poetry and Prophecy: The Anthropology of Inspiration* (Ann Arbor: University of Michigan Press, 1997). In the Delphic model, the *prophētēs*, or spokesman who relayed the message of the oracle, was not understood to be possessed like the Pythian priestess, but merely someone who interpreted her words for the questioner.

19. Exodus 4:10–11. Unless otherwise stated, all scriptural references are taken from the New International Version of the Bible.

20. Plato, *Ion*, 534d.

21. Ibid., 534b. The critical discussion in the *Phaedrus* occurs in 244a–246a.

22. Plato, *Ion*, 533e.

23. Plato, *Phaedrus*, 244c–246e, 249c–249e, 238c.

24. Plato, *Republic*, 414b–415d. According to the influential reading of Leo Strauss and his acolytes, Plato intended his works for a "natural aristocracy determined neither by birth nor wealth." See, typically, Allan Bloom's preface to *The Republic of Plato*, trans. and intro. Allan Bloom (New York: Basic Books, 1991), xviii. I draw the general distinction between the possessor and the possessed from Peter Kivy, *The Possessor and the Possessed: Handel, Mozart, Beethoven, and the Idea of Musical Genius* (New Haven, CT: Yale University Press, 2001).

25. Plato, *Timaeus*, 90a–90c. See also Plato, *Laws*, 732c, 877a.

26. Heraclitus, DK 22 B 119. Democritus similarly observed that "the soul is the dwelling of the *daimon*" (DK 68 B 171). See Fritz-Gregor Herrmann, "Greek Religion and Philosophy: The God of the Philosopher," in *A Companion to Greek Religion*, ed. Daniel Ogden (Oxford: Blackwell, 2010), 385–398 (citations on 393); Apuleius, *On the God of Socrates* (*De Deo Socratis*), 150, in Apuleius, *Rhetorical Works*, trans. Stephen Harrison, John Hilton, and Vincent Hunink, ed. Stephen Harrison (Oxford: Oxford University Press, 2001), 206.

27. Pindar, *Olympian*, 9.100.

28. Murray, "Poetic Genius," 15.

29. Aristotle, *Poetics*, 17.2.

30. The *Problems* is often still included in editions of Aristotle's collected works, like the one I cite below. On the history of the text and attempts to ascertain its author, see Pieter de Leemans and Michèle de Goyens, eds., *Aristotle's Problemata in Different Times and Tongues* (Leuven, Belgium: Leuven University Press, 2006).

31. [Pseudo-Aristotle], *Problems,* 30.1, 30.26–28, 30.35, in *The Complete Works of Aristotle: The Revised Oxford Translation,* ed. Jonathan Barnes, 2 vols. (Princeton, NJ: Princeton University Press, 1984), 2:1498–1501.

32. Tibullus, *The Elegies,* 1.7.49–64; Ovid, *Tristia,* 3.13, addressing the "god of his birth," in *Ovid with an English Translation, Tristia, Ex Ponto,* trans. Arthur Leslie Wheelter (New York: G. P. Putnam's Sons, 1924), 151; Horace, *Odes,* 4.11.6–11. I am using here the bilingual edition and translation of David Ferry, *The Odes of Horace* (New York: Farrar, Strauss, and Giroux, 1997), 297.

33. Plautus, *Aulularia,* 724–725 ("Egomet me defraudavi animumque meum geniumque meum"); Plautus's *Truculentus,* 182; Persius, *Satira,* 5.151; Erasmus, "Indulgere genio," *Adagia,* 2.4.74. These and many other texts are discussed in Jane Chance Nitzsche, *The Genius Figure in Antiquity and the Middle Ages* (New York: Columbia University Press, 1975).

34. Ittai Gradel, *Emperor Worship and Roman Religion* (Oxford: Clarendon Press, 2002), 37; Georg Wissowa, *Religion und Kultus der Römer* (Munich: C. H. Beck, 1902), 182. On the vexed relationship between *genius, numen,* and *mana,* see Duncan Fishwick, "Genius and Numen," *Harvard Theological Review* 62, no. 3 (1969): 356–367. On the Etruscan connection, see Massimo Pallotino, *The Etruscans,* trans. J. Cremona (Bloomington: Indiana University Press, 1975), 158, 295. The artistic and iconographic depiction of Roman *genius* is treated thoroughly in Hille Kunckel, *Der Römische Genius* (Heidelberg: F. H. Kerle, 1974). On horns, horns of plenty, and *genius,* see R. B. Onians, *The Origins of European Thought About the Body, the Mind, the Soul, the World, Time, and Fate* (Cambridge: Cambridge University Press, 2000 [1951]), 238–245.

35. Plutarch recounts the tale of Alexander's conception and the sighting of a serpent in Olympia's bed in his life of Alexander in the *Lives,* 2.4. For Livy's discussion, see *Ab urbe condita,* 26.19.7. Except where noted, all subsequent English translations from this text are taken from the Loeb Classical edition, *Livy in Fourteen Volumes,* trans. B. O. Foster (Cambridge, MA: Harvard University Press, 1988 [1919]); Suetonius, "Divus Augustus," *De vita Caesarum,* 2.94.4.

36. Wissowa, *Religion und Kultus,* 176–178.

37. W. Warde Fowler, *Roman Ideas of Deity in the Last Century Before the Christian Era* (London: Macmillan, 1914), 19–22; Christine Battersby, *Gender and Genius: Towards a Feminist Aesthetics* (Bloomington: Indiana University Press, 1989), 52–70.

38. Horace, *Epistles,* 2.2.187–189, in *Epistles and Satires,* trans. John Davie (New York: Oxford University Press, 2011), 105; Nitzsche, *Genius Figure,* 22.

39. Seneca, *De tranquillitate animi,* 17.10 ("Nullum magnum ingenium sine dementiae fuit"); Longinus, *Peri hypsous,* 36.1–2.

40. Varro is cited in St. Augustine, *City of God,* 7.13. Varro also speaks, with Platonic and Stoic inflections, of the individual *genius* as a microcosm of the great universal *Genius* (the "god who controls all that is begotten"), a world soul or cosmic mind. See the discussion in Nitzsche, *Genius Figure,* 24–26. See also

Apuleius, *De Deo Socratis*, 15; Plutarch, "Marcus Brutus," in the Dryden translation of *Plutarch's Lives*, ed. Arthur Hugh Clough, 2 vols. (New York: Modern Library, 2001), 2:596–597; Servius, from his gloss on Virgil's *Aeneid*, 6.743, cited and translated in Nitzsche, *Genius Figure*, 33.

41. S. MacCormack, "Roma, Constantinopilis, the Emperor, and His Genius," *Classical Quarterly*, 25, no. 1 (1975): 135–150.

42. On Alexander as the first famous person and the line from Cicero, see Leo Braudy, *The Frenzy of Renown: Fame and Its History* (New York: Oxford University Press, 1986), 32, 77.

43. Max Weber, *Economy and Society: An Outline of Interpretive Sociology*, eds. Guenther Roth and Claus Wittich, 2 vols. (Berkeley: University of California Press, 1978), 1:241. Weber discusses charisma at length in vol. 2, chap. 3, section iv, "Charismatic Authority," and section v, "The Routinization of Authority."

44. Braudy, *The Frenzy of Renown*, 108.

45. Suetonius, *Divus Augustus*, 93. Here I have cited from "The Deified Augustus," in *Lives of the Caesars*, trans. Catharine Edwards (Oxford: Oxford University Press, 2000), 92.

46. Plutarch, "Antony," 33, in *Plutarch's Lives*, 2:500–501. Shakespeare makes use of the account in *Antony and Cleopatra*, Act I, Scene 3. On Augustus and the gods, see the discussion in Gradel, *Emperor Worship*, 112–114; Franz Altheim, *A History of Roman Religion*, trans. Harold Mattingly (New York: E. P. Dutton, 1938), 368–369.

47. Weber, *Economy and Society*, 1:243; Livy, *Ab urbe*, 21.62, in *Livy in Fourteen Volumes*, 5:186. Although Livy does not refer specifically in the cited passage to the Genius of the Roman People, writing only of a sacrifice to "Genius" ("et Genio maiores hostiae caesae quinque"), most scholars agree that he had one of these variously named collective *genii* of the Roman city in mind; see J. R. Fears, "Ho demos ho Romaion: Genius Populi Romani. A Note on the Origin of Dea Roma," *Mnemosyne* 31, no. 3 (1978): 274–286; Duncan Fishwick, *The Imperial Cult in the Latin West: Studies in the Ruler Cult of the Western Provinces of the Roman Empire* (New York: Brill, 1987), 1:52.

48. See the extensive discussion of the libation and swearing of oaths in Lily Ross Taylor, *The Divinity of the Roman Emperor* (Middletown, CT: American Philological Society, 1931), 151–152 and 181ff. The impact and significance of the compital cults is treated thoroughly in Gradel, *Emperor Worship*, 116–128.

49. On the debate over the existence of a state cult of the emperor during the reign of Augustus, see Gradel, *Emperor Worship*, chaps. 4–5; Taylor, *Divinity of the Roman Emperor*, 222–223; Ovid, *Fasti*, 5.145–146.

50. Weber, *Economy and Society*, 1:244. Echoes of the *genius* of the Roman emperors endure well into the Middle Ages in the medieval notion of the king's two bodies. See Ernst H. Kantorowicz, *The King's Two Bodies: A Study in Medieval Political Theology* (Princeton, NJ: Princeton University Press, 1997 [1957]), 80, 82, 501–504.

CHAPTER 2

1. Eusebius, *The Ecclesiastical History*, trans. Kirsopp Lake, 2 vols., Loeb Classical Edition (Cambridge, MA: Harvard University Press, 1949), 1:349.

2. On the oath, see Rhona Beare, "The Meaning of the Oath by the Safety of the Roman Emperor," *American Journal of Philology* 99, no. 1 (1978): 106–110; Fergus Millar, "The Imperial Cult and the Persecutions," in *Le Culte des souverains dans l'Empire romain*, ed. Willem den Boer (Geneva: Fondation Hardt, 1973), 145–165; Origen, *Contra Celsum*, 8.65, trans. Henry Chadwick (Cambridge: Cambridge University Press, 1965), 502. For Tertullian's comments on the *genius* of the emperor, see his *Apology for the Christians*, esp. chap. 32.

3. This account, and all direct citations, are taken from Ambrose's "Letter to Marcellina on Finding the Bodies of Sts. Gervasius and Protasius," trans. H. de Romestin and Thomas Head, in the *Library of Nicene and Post Nicene Fathers*, 2nd ser., vol. 10 (New York, 1896), accessed March 30, 2012, www.ccel.org/ccel/schaff/npnf210.v.viii.html.

4. Augustine, *Confessions*, 9.7, as translated by R. S. Pine-Coffin (Hammondsworth, UK: Penguin, 1961), 191. See also the brief account in *City of God*, 22.8.

5. Ambrose, "Letter to Marcellina on Finding the Bodies," 10. The line from the anniversary sermon is provided, along with an in-depth analysis on which I draw here, in Jean Doignon, "Perspectives ambrosiennes: SS. Gervais et Protais, génies de Milan," *Revue des études Augustiniennes* 2 (1956): 313–334.

6. The decree of November 8, 392, outlawing sacrifices to *genius* may be found in the *Codex Theodosianus*, 16.10.12pr. On the persistence of the cult of the *genius* and pagan practices more generally, see Claude Lecouteux, *Démons et génies du terroir au Moyen Age* (Paris: Editions Imago, 1995), 43–44; Ramsay MacMullen, *Christianity and Paganism in the Fourth to Eighth Centuries* (New Haven, CT: Yale University Press, 1997). The continuity between the cult of *genius* and the saint is analyzed in Peter Brown, *The Cult of the Saints: Its Rise and Function in Latin Christianity* (Chicago: University of Chicago Press, 1981), esp. chap. 3 ("The Invisible Companion").

7. The judgment on Moses is that of the noted first-century BCE philosopher Philo, cited in Louis H. Feldman, *Philo's Portrayal of Moses in the Context of Ancient Judaism* (South Bend, IN: University of Notre Dame Press, 2007), 3. On the general relationship between heroes, prophets, and saints, see Geoffrey Cubitt's concise and insightful "Introduction" to *Heroic Reputations and Exemplary Lives*, eds. Geoffrey Cubitt and Allen Warren (Manchester: Manchester University Press, 2000), 1–26; Peter Brown, "The Saint as Exemplar in Late Antiquity," *Representations* 1, no. 2 (1983): 1–25.

8. A classic sociological statement of the continuum binding together the hero, the prophet, and the saint is Max Scheler's *Vorbilder und Führer*, first published in 1933. On the classical and Christian ideal of the divine man, see Helmut Koester, "The Divine Human Being," *Harvard Theological Review* 78, nos. 3–4 (1985): 243–252.

9. On the uses of *daimon* and *daimonion* and their Hebrew equivalents in scripture, see the article "δαίμψν, δαίμόνιον," in *Theological Dictionary of the New Testament*, ed. Gerhard Kittel, trans. Geoffrey W. Bromiley, 10 vols. (Grand Rapids: Wm. B. Eerdmans, 1964–1976), 2:1–20; Tertullian, *Apology*, 22; Lacantius, *The Divine Institutes*, 2.15; Augustine, *City of God*, 8.16.

10. As Robin Lane Fox observes succinctly, "paganism was reclassified as a demonic system." See his *Pagans and Christians* (San Francisco: HarperCollins, 1988), 326.

11. Peter Brown, "The Rise and Function of the Holy Man in Late Antiquity," *Journal of Roman Studies* 61 (1971): 81; Eric Sorensen, *Possession and Exorcism in the New Testament and Christianity* (Tübingen, Germany: Mohr Siebeck, 2002); Augustine, *City of God*, 7.26.

12. Theresa and Catherine were not canonized as *doctores*, however, until the 1970s. On the process by which doctors are chosen, see Lawrence C. Cunningham, *A Brief History of Saints* (Oxford: Blackwell, 2005), 87–91; Jerome, *De viris illustribus*, "Introduction," available at www.newadvent.org/fathers/2708.htm.

13. Franz Cumont, "Les anges du paganisme," *Revue de l'histoire des religions* 72 (1915): 159–182; F. Sokolowski, "Sur le culte d'angelos dans le paganisme Grec et Romain," *Harvard Theological Review* 53, no. 4 (1960): 225–229. Of the vast literature on early Jewish conceptions of angels, W. G. Heidt's *Angelology of the Old Testament* (Washington, DC: Catholic University Press, 1949), Michael Mach's *Entwicklungstadien des judischen Engelsglauben in vorrabbinischer Zeit* (Tübingen, Germany: Mohr Siebeck, 1992), and Kevin P. Sullivan, *Wrestling with Angels: A Study of the Relationship Between Angels and Humans in Ancient Jewish Literature and the New Testament* (Leiden: Brill, 2004), provide useful introductions.

14. The precise number of the angels was a question that obsessed Christian and Jewish investigators, particularly during the Middle Ages. Talmudic scholars apparently taught that the number could be calculated at 301,655,172, but the seventeenth-century German Jesuit Gaspar Schott wins the prize for computational innovation. In his *Magia universalis naturae et artis* (1657), he places the number of angels in the universe at 297,814,995,628,536,548,496,165,479,368, 800,000,000,000,000,000,000,000! See H. Leclercq, "Anges," in *Dictionnnaire d'archéologie Chrétienne et de liturgie*, 15 vols. (Paris: Letouzey et Ané, 1907), vol. 1 (Part 2): 2154–2155. It is surprising that the relationship between the classical *genius* and Christian conceptions of angels has not been more fully explored. The most thorough study of the connection, to which I am indebted, is Robert Schilling, "Genius et anges," in his *Rites, cultes, dieux de Rome* (Paris: Éditions Kincksieck, 1979), 415–441.

15. Origen, *Homilies*, 12.4, in Origen, *Homilies on Luke; Fragments on Luke*, trans. Joseph T. Lienhard (Washington, DC: Catholic University of America Press, 1996), 49–50. On the persistence of a belief in a personal evil demon, see the entry "Diable," in *Dictionnaire raisonné de l'Occident medieval*, eds. Jacques Le Goff and Jean-Claude Schmitt (Paris: Fayard, 1999), 260–272. Jerome is cited in Hugh Pope, "Angels," in *The Catholic Encyclopedia* (New York: Robert Appleton, 1907), retrieved on July 18, 2011, from New Advent, www.newadvent.org

/cathen/01476d.htm. For Jerome's description of the angel as a *comes*, and on oaths and addresses, see Schilling, "Genius et anges," 432–435; Brown, *Cult of the Saints*, 51; Peter Brown, *The Making of Late Antiquity* (Cambridge, MA: Harvard University Press, 1993), 72, 121n64; H. Grégoire, "'Ton ange,' et les anges de Thera," *Byzantische Zeitschrift* 30 (1929–1930): 641–644.

16. Gunnar Berefelt, *A Study on the Winged Angel: The Origin of a Motif*, trans. Patrick Hort (Stockholm: Almqvist and Wiksell, 1968), 7. The line is that of Pseudo-Dionysius, cited in Jean Daniélou, *The Angels and Their Missions: According to the Fathers of the Church*, trans. David Heimann (Westminster, MD: Christian Classics, 1991), 16.

17. On the persistence of belief in guardian angels, see Carlo Ossalo, *Gli angeli custodi: Storia e figure dell' "Amico vero"* (Turin: Einaudi Editore, 2004); Jean-Patrice Boudet, Philippe Faure, and Christian Renoux, eds., *De Socrate à Tintin: Anges gardiens et démons familiers de l'Antiquité à nos jours* (Rennes, France: Presses Universitaires de Rennes, 2011). Marcellinus is cited in Brown, *Cult of the Saints*, 52–53. Gregory is cited in Brown, *Making of Late Antiquity*, 71–72.

18. Matthew 22:30; Mark 12:25; Luke 20:36; Hebrews 2:7.

19. David Keck, *Angels and Angelology in the Middle Ages* (New York: Oxford University Press, 1998), 44, 144.

20. Cited in Daniélou, *Angels and Their Mission*, 18.

21. Tertullian, *Apology*, chap. 22, Augustine discusses the derivation of "demon" in a chapter of the *City of God*, 9.20, fittingly entitled "The meaning of the word 'demon.'" Augustine may well have found this same derivation in Plato, who employs it in *Cratylus*, 398b. On Isidore and the broader medieval understanding of the connection between demons and knowledge, see Valerie J. Flint, *The Rise of Magic in Early Medieval Europe* (Princeton, NJ: Princeton University Press, 1991), 107.

22. A. L. Williams, "The Cult of Angels at Colossae," *Journal of Theological Studies* 10 (1909): 413–438; Council of Laodicea, Canon 35, cited in Glenn Peers, *Subtle Bodies: Representing Angels in Byzantium* (Berkeley: University of California Press, 2001), 10. The fifth-century council is described in MacMullen, *Christianity & Paganism*, 126.

23. On the distinction between natural and demonic magic, see the classic study by D. P. Walker, *Spiritual and Demonic Magic from Ficino to Campanella* (University Park: Pennsylvania State University Press, 2003), originally published in 1958 by the Warburg Institute in London. On attempts to contact angels, see Claire Fanger, ed., *Invoking Angels: Theurgic Ideas and Practices, Thirteenth to Sixteenth Centuries* (University Park: Pennsylvania State University Press, 2012).

24. On the Neo-Platonist revival and the critical influence of Bernardus Silvestris and Alain de Lille, see the extensive scholarly introduction to Bernardus Silvestris, *Cosmographia*, trans. and ed. Winthrop Wetherbee (New York: Columbia University Press, 1990), as well as Wetherbee's *Platonism and Poetry in the Twelfth Century: The Literary Influence of the School of Chartres* (Princeton, NJ: Princeton University Press, 1972). On the allegorical genius figure beginning with Alain de Lille's *Plaint of Nature* and Guillaume de Lorris and Jean de Meun's

Romance of the Rose, see Denis N. Baker, "The Priesthood of Genius: A Study of the Medieval Tradition," *Speculum* 51 (1976): 277–291; Donald G. Schueler, "Gower's Characterization of Genius in the *Confession Amantis*," *Modern Language Quarterly* 33 (1972): 240–256; George D. Economou, "The Character Genius in Alan de Lille, Jean de Meun, and John Gower," *Chaucer Review* 4 (1970): 203–210; D. T. Starnes, "The Figure of Genius in the Renaissance," *Studies in the Renaissance* 11 (1964): 233–244.

25. Noel L. Brann, *Trithemius and Magical Theology: A Chapter in the Controversy over Occult Studies in Early Modern Europe* (Albany: State University of New York, 1999); Frank I. Borchardt, "The *Magus* as Renaissance Man," *Sixteenth Century Journal* 21, no. 1 (1990): 57–76. Agrippa writes most explicitly about the Genius in chapters 20–22 of Book Three of *De occulta philosophia*. I cite here from the Llewellyn's Sourcebook Series' annotated edition of the *Three Books of Occult Philosophy*, ed. Donald Tyson, trans. James Freake (Woodbury, MN: Llewellyn Publications, 2006), 527–528, but I have consulted the Latin original and verified all passages using the fine critical edition *De occulta philosophia libri tres*, ed. V. Perroni Compagni (Leiden: Brill, 1992).

26. Borchardt, "The *Magus* as Renaissance Man," 69–72. On the curiosities of Dee and Bruno, among others, see Wayne Schumaker, *Renaissance Curiosa* (Binghamton, NY: Center for Medieval and Early Renaissance Studies, 1982).

27. Jerome Cardano, *The Book of My Life (De vita propria liber)* (New York: Dover Publications, 1962), 240–247 (Cardano discusses his *genius*, which he also refers to as an angel and *spiritus*, in chap. 47, "Guardian Angels"); Agrippa, *Three Books*, 525 (Book 3, chap. 21, "Of Obeying a Proper Genius, and of the Searching Out the Nature Thereof").

28. Marsilio Ficino, *Commentary on Plato's Symposium on Love*, trans. Sears Jayne (Dallas: Spring Publications, 1985), 171–172 (Speech 7, chap. 15). "No man has ever been great" is cited in Noel L. Brann, *The Debate over the Origin of Genius During the Italian Renaissance: The Theories of Supernatural Frenzy and Natural Melancholy in Accord and in Conflict on the Threshhold of the Scientific Revolution* (Leiden: Brill, 2002), 89.

29. Plotinus, *Enneads*, 3.4.5, in the Penguin Classics translation of Stephen MacKenna, intro. John Dillon (London: Penguin, 1991), 170–171.

30. Bruce Gordon, "The Renaissance Angel," in *Angels in the Early Modern World*, eds. Peter Marshall and Alexandra Walsham (Cambridge: Cambridge University Press, 2006), 51–52; Michael J. B. Allen, "The Absent Angel in Ficino's Philosophy," *Journal of the History of Ideas* 36, no. 2 (1975): 219–240.

31. Pico della Mirandola, "Oration on the Dignity of Man," trans. Charles Glenn Wallis, in *Oration on the Dignity of Man*, intro. Paul J. W. Miller (Indianapolis: Hackett, 1998), 3–5.

32. [Pseudo-Aristotle], *Problems*, 30.1, in *The Complete Works of Aristotle: The Revised Oxford Translation*, 2 vols., ed. Jonathan Barnes (Princeton, NJ: Princeton University Press, 1984), 2:1498. Charles B. Schmitt, *Aristotle and the Renaissance* (Cambridge, MA: Harvard University Press, 1983); Dennis Des Chene, *Life's*

Form: Late Aristotelian Conceptions of the Soul (Ithaca, NY: Cornell University Press, 2000).

33. Already in the *Platonic Theology*, Ficino devoted a brief reflection to a possible benefit of melancholy. Noting that the bodies of men so afflicted were unusually "dense," he speculated that this humoral configuration would allow them to become more excited when seized by divine force, burning more fervently. Citing directly from the *Problems*, he concurred with the view expressed there that Socrates had likely been a melancholic, and that this would have aided his prophetic communications with his *daimonion*. See Marsilio Ficino, *Theologica Platonica/Platonic Theology*, eds. James Hankins and William Bowen, trans. J. B. Allen and John Warden, 6 vols. (Cambridge, MA: Harvard University Press, 2001–2006), 4:163 (13.2.33).

34. Marsilio Ficino, *Three Books on Life: A Critical Edition and Translation with Introduction and Notes*, eds. Carol V. Kaske and John R. Clarke (Binghamton, NY: Medieval and Renaissance Texts and Studies, 1989), 117 (1.5), 121–129 (1.6–7).

35. On the "vogue" of melancholy and the Aristotelian and Platonic responses to Ficino's theory, see Brann, *Origin of Genius*, esp. chaps. 5 and 6, as well as Raymond Klibansky, Erwin Panofsky, and Fritz Saxl, *Saturn and Melancholy: Studies in the History of Natural Philosophy, Religion, and Art* (London: Thomas Nelson, 1964), 254–274. See also Winfried Schleiner, *Melancholy, Genius, and Utopia in the Renaissance* (Weisbaden, Germany: Otto Harrassowitz, 1991); Lawrence Babb, *The Elizabethan Malady: A Study of Melancholia in English Literature from 1580 to 1642* (East Lansing: Michigan State University Press, 1965); Pompanazzi, *De naturalium effectuum admirandorum causis sive de incatationibus*, cited in Brann, *Origin of Genius*, 170–171. "How Black Bile Makes People Intelligent" is the chapter title of Book 1, chap. 6, of Ficino's *Three Books on Life*. As one of the great pioneers in the study of magic long ago observed, "those who sought a natural explanation for what others regarded as possession by demons found it in an excess of melancholic humor." Lynn Thorndike, *A History of Magic and Experimental Science*, 8 vols. (New York: Macmillan, 1923–1958); 8:50. See also Stuart Clark, *Thinking with Demons: The Idea of Witchcraft in Early Modern Europe* (New York: Oxford University Press, 1999), 265.

36. On the uses of *ingenium*, see Harald Weinrich, "Ingenium," in *Historisches Wörterbuch der Philosophie*, ed. Joachim Ritter, 13 vols. (Basel: Schwabe, 1971–2007), 4:36–63; Edgar Zilsel, *Die Enstehung des Geniebegiffes: Ein Beitrag zur Ideengeschichte der Antike und des Frühkapitalismus*, intro. Heinz Maus (Hildesheim, Germany: Georg Olms, 1972), esp. 265–296; and the discussion in the text and appendix of Patricia Emison's *Creating the "Divine" Artist: From Dante to Michelangelo* (Leiden: Brill, 2004), which deals nicely with the concept in its application to the arts. Pompanazzi is cited in Brann, *Origin of Genius*, 171. Although Brann translates *ingenium* as "genius," I have left it in the original in order to avoid anachronism.

37. Carlos G. Noreña, "Juan Huarte's Naturalistic Humanism," *Journal of the History of Philosophy* 10, no. 1 (1972): 71–76. On Huarte's life and career, see

Malcolm K. Reade, *Juan Huarte de San Juan* (Boston: Twayne, 1981); Juan Huarte de San Juan, *Examen de ingenios para las ciencias*, ed. Esteban Torre (Madrid: Editora National, 1976), 117.

38. Huarte, *Examen de ingenios*, 370–374, 331. The discussion of Christ's brain was subsequently censored by the Inquisition. On the prevailing Galenic and Aristotelian assumptions, see Londa Schiebinger's masterful *The Mind Has No Sex? Women in the Origins of Modern Science* (Cambridge, MA: Harvard University Press, 1991), 160–170.

39. The rumination on the etymology of *ingenium* was included in a new first chapter added to the revised edition of 1594. I cite from the 1594 edition of Juan Huarte de San Juan, *Examen de ingenios*, ed. Guillermo Serés (Madrid: Ediciones Cátedra, 1989), 186–194.

40. Vives is cited in Emilio Hidalgo-Serna, "*Ingenium* and Rhetoric in the Work of Vives," *Philosophy and Rhetoric* 16, no. 4 (1983): 230–231. See also Noreña, "Juan Huarte's Naturalistic Humanism," 75; Reade, *Juan Huarte*, 58; C. M. Hutchings, "The *Examen de ingenios* and the Doctrine of Original Genius," *Hispania* 19, no. 2 (1936): 273–282.

41. Erwin Panofsky, "Artist, Scientist, Genius: Notes on the 'Renaissance-Dämmerung,'" in *The Renaissance: Six Essays* (New York: Harper and Row, 1972), 171–173; Huarte, *Examen de ingenios* (1594), 201–202. Huarte cites a Latin translation of Aristotle's *Nichomachean Ethics*, 1095 b 10, as follows: "Optimum ingenium est illud quod omnia per se intelligit." Needless to say, Aristotle did not employ the term *ingenium*, though he does observe, citing Hesiod, "Far best is he who knows all things himself" (*Nichomachean Ethics*, 1095 b 10, in *The Basic Works of Aristotle*, ed. Richard Mckeon, intro. C. D. C. Reeve (New York: Modern Library, 2001), 938). Huarte adds that Adam alone was born with "all sciences infused": "Sólo Adán (dicen los teólogos) nació enseñado y con todas las ciencias infusas" (201).

42. Huarte, *Examen de ingenios* (1594), 202–203; John Hope Mason, *The Value of Creativity: The Origins and Emergence of a Modern Belief* (Burlington, VT: Ashgate, 2003), 45–49.

43. Ficino is cited in Kaske and Clark, eds., "Introduction," *Three Books on Life*, 22; Alberti is cited in Emison, *Creating the "Divine" Artist*, 33.

44. Brann, *Origin of Genius*, chap. 6.

45. Calvin is cited in Peter Marshall and Alexandra Walsham, "Migrations of Angels in the Early Modern World," in *Angels in the Early Modern World*, eds. Peter Marshall and Alexandra Walsham (Cambridge: Cambridge University Press, 2006), 57.

46. Giovanni Mario Verdizotti, *Genius, sive de furore poetico* (Venice, 1575); Zilsel, *Enstehung des Geniebegriffes*, 288–299.

47. C. S. Lewis, "Wit (with Ingenium)," in his *Studies in Words* (Cambridge: Cambridge University Press, 1960), 86–111; Jean Nicot, *Thresor de la langue françoyse tant ancienne que moderne* (Paris: Editions A. et J. Picard, 1960), 313. This is a modern reprint edition of the 1621 version of Nicot's text, but the definition contained in the original 1606 edition is identical. The entry for "genius"

from Elisha Coles's *An English Dictionary* (1676) may be found in the Scolar Press facsimile edition (Menston, UK: Scolar Press, 1971); Henry Cockeram, *The English Dictionarie of 1623*, intro. Chauncey Brewster Tinker (New York: Huntington Press, 1930), 78; John Dryden, *A Parallel of Poetry and Painting* (1695), in *The Works of John Dryden*, eds. Edward Niles Hooker et al., 20 vols. (Berkeley: University of California Press, 1956–2000), 20:61.

48. Giorgio Vasari, "Michelangelo," in *The Lives of the Artists*, trans. and intro. Julia Conaway Bondanella and Peter Bondanella (Oxford: Oxford University Press, 1998), 415. "Saintly old man" is Vasari's description, cited in the "Introduction" to *The Divine Michelangelo: The Florentine Academy's Homage on His Death in 1564. A Facsimile Edition of the Esequie del Divino Michelagnolo Buanorriti*, trans. and intro. and annotated by Rudolf Wittkower and Margot Wittkower (London: Phaidon Press, 1964), 14. The text is a bilingual edition of Jacopo Giunti's *Esequie*, or "obequies," of 1564, a chronicle that draws heavily on contemporary sources and accounts of the funeral rites of Michelangelo. The description of the opening of the casket is that of Don Giovanni di Simone, from a letter dated March 18, 1564, cited in "Introduction," *Divine Michelangelo*, 16. Michelangelo died on February 18, 1564, and so, in truth, had been dead only twenty-two days. For descriptions of the "life-like" body, see Giunti, *Esequie*, in *Divine Michelangelo*, 74–77; Vasari, "Michelangelo," 486. The first edition of the *Lives* appeared in 1550, and the second, revised edition in 1568, four years after Michelangelo's death.

49. On the "incorruptibility" of the bodies of saints, see Michel Bouvier, "L'incorruptibilité des corps saints," in *Les miracles, miroirs des corps*, eds. Jacques Gélis and Odile Redon (Paris: Presses et Publications de l'Université de Paris-VIII, 1983), 193–221; Caroline Walker Bynum, "Bodily Miracles and the Resurrection of the Body in the High Middle Ages," in *Belief in History*, ed. Thomas Keselman (Notre Dame: University of Notre Dame Press, 1991), 68–106. On Michelangelo and Saturn, see Rudolph Wittkower and Margot Wittkower, *Born Under Saturn: The Character and Conduct of Artists* (New York: New York Review of Books Classics, 2006 [1963]), 104–106, though some scholars have questioned whether Michelangelo was in truth Saturnine. See Don Riggs, "Was Michelangelo Born Under Saturn?" *Sixteenth Century Journal* 26 (1995): 99–121, and the full consideration in Piers Britton, "'Mio malinchonico, o vero . . . mio pazzo': Michelangelo, Vasari, and the Problem of Artists' Melancholy in Sixteenth-Century Italy," *Sixteenth Century Journal* 34, no. 3 (2003): 653–675. The line on "living form" is that of the poet Bartolommeo Panciatichi, cited in *Divine Michelangelo*, 81. The string of wondrous contemporary adjectives evoked by Michelangelo's art is discussed in David Summers, *Michelangelo and the Language of Art* (Princeton, NJ: Princeton University Press, 1981), 171–176.

50. On the use of the adjective "divine," see Zilsel, *Enstehung des Geniebegriffes*, 276; Emison, *Creating the "Divine" Artist*, 288–289; Martin Kemp, "The 'Super-Artist' as Genius: The Sixteenth-Century View," in *Genius: The History of an Idea*, ed. Penelope Murray (Oxford: Blackwell, 1989), 32–53. Mourners are cited in *Divine Michelangelo*, 77, 85–86; Benedetto Varchi, *Orazione funerale di Messer*

Benedetto Varchi fatta, e recitata da lui pubblicamente nell'essequie di Michelagnolo Buonarroti in Firenze nella chiesa di San Lorenzo (Firenzi, 1564), published as e-text no. 3 in the series *Quellen und Dokumente zu Michelangelo Buonarroti*, ed. Charles Davis, accessed July 4, 2012, http://archiv.ub.uni-heidelberg.de/artdok /volltexte/2008/643/.

51. The anecdote of the bedknobs is in Emison, *Creating the "Divine" Artist*, 5. In addition to Emison's fine study, see A. Richard Turner's *Inventing Leonardo* (Berkeley: University of California Press, 1992), for a skillful example of this approach.

52. Vasari, "Michelangelo," *Lives*, 472.

53. Eugène Delacroix, *Journal (1822–1863)*, preface Hubert Damisch, intro. André Joubin (Paris: Librarie Plon, 1980), 43 (entry for Tuesday, December 30, 1823). On the Romantics' reading of the Renaissance and its long influence on scholarship, see the careful discussion in Emison, *Creating the "Divine" Artist*, esp. "Appendix: The Historiography of *Ingegno*," 321–349.

54. Vasari, "Leonardo," *Lives*, 284. I have altered the translation slightly here, substituting "makes himself known as a thing endowed by God" for "makes himself known as a genius endowed by God." This is a more literal rendering of "si fa conoscere per cosa (como ella è) largita da Dio" and also avoids the anachronistic use of "genius" referred to above.

55. On Vergil, see Brian Copenhaver's excellent introductory essay to Polydore Vergil, *On Discovery*, trans. and ed. Brian P. Copenhaver (Cambridge, MA: Harvard University Press, 2002), vi–xxx. Scaliger and Tasso are cited in William J. Bouwsma, *The Waning of the Renaissance, 1550–1640* (New Haven, CT: Yale University Press, 2000), 31. See also Vasari, "Preface," *Lives*, 3; Vasari, "Michelangelo," *Lives*, 472, 454. "Mortal God" is the sixteenth-century humanist Paulo Pino's expression for both Michelangelo and Titian, cited in Zilsel, *Enstehung des Geniebegriffes*, 277.

56. Vasari, "Michelangelo," *Lives*, 465; Ficino, *Platonic Theology*, 4:177 (13.3.6). This remarkable passage comes in the midst of a discussion of poetry and invention.

CHAPTER 3

1. René Descartes, *Meditations on First Philosophy*, in *Discourse on Method and Meditations on First Philosophy*, ed. David Weissman, trans. Elizabeth S. Haldane and G. R. T. Ross (New Haven, CT: Yale University Press, 1996), 62–65. The original Latin and French versions were accessed July 3, 2012, from *Descartes' Meditations*, A Trilingual HTML Edition, edited by David B. Manley and Charles S. Taylor, www.wright.edu/cola/descartes/.

2. Stuart Clark, *Thinking with Demons: The Idea of Witchcraft in Early Modern Europe* (New York: Oxford University Press, 1999), 174; Alice Browne, "Descartes's Dreams," *Journal of the Warburg and Courtauld Institutes* 40 (1977): 256–273; Michael H. Keefer, "The Dreamer's Path: Descartes and the Sixteenth Century," *Renaissance Quarterly* 49, no. 1 (1996): 30–76; Geoffrey Scarre, "Demons, Demonologists and Descartes," *The Heythrop Journal* 31, no. 1 (1990): 17–18.

3. Antoine Galland's French translation of the Arabic classic *Les mille et une nuits*, published in twelve volumes beginning in 1704, made frequent use of the word "*génie*," a convention that was subsequently adopted in English translations, where "genius" and "*genie*" remain commonplace to this day. See Voltaire, "Génies," *Dictionnaire philosophique*, in *Œuvres de Voltaire*, ed. Adrien-Jean-Quentin Beuchot, 72 vols. (Paris: J. Lefèvre, 1829–1840), 30:39–40.

4. Voltaire, "Ange," *Dictionnaire philosophique*, in *Œevres de Voltaire*, 26:383–384; J. G. A. Hamann, *Socratic Memorabilia*, trans. James C. O'Flaherty (Baltimore: Johns Hopkins University Press, 1967), 170–171.

5. [Antoine Furetière], "Génie," *Dictionnaire universel, contenant généralement tous les mots français tant vieux que modernes et les termes de toutes les sciences et des arts* (1690), Slatkine reprint edition, 2 vols. (Geneva, 1970), 2: n.p. Note that one may find even earlier instances of "genius" employed in this way. In 1662, for example, the English author John Evylen referred to the Dutch natural philosopher Christiaan Huygens as a "universal mathematical genius," though such examples are comparatively rare. See Giorgio Tonelli, "Genius from the Renaissance to 1770," in *The Dictionary of the History of Ideas*, ed. Philip P. Wiener, 4 vols. (New York: Charles Scribner's Sons, 1974), 2:293–297 (citation on 294).

6. Abbé Paul Tallemant, "Eloge funebre à Charles Perrault," *Recueil des harangues prononcées par Messieurs de l'Académie françoise, dans leurs réceptions, & en d'autres occasions differentes, depuis l'establissement de l'Académie jusqu'à présent*, 2 vols. (Amsterdam, 1709), 2:593. I am grateful to Oded Rabinovitch for bringing this reference to my attention. See also *Nouveau dictionnaire de l'Académie françoise*, 2 vols. (Paris, 1718), 1:754 (emphasis added); G. Matoré and A.-J. Greimas, "La naissance du 'génie' au dix-huitième siècle: Etude lexicologique," *Le Français Moderne* 25 (1957): 268.

7. Joseph Addison, *Spectator* 160 (September 3, 1711). Goethe, Justus Möser, and Herder all commented ironically in the 1770s on what Möser described as the "mania for genius" gripping his countrymen. See J. Ritter, "Genie," in *Historisches Wörterbuch der philosophie*, ed. Joachim Ritter, 13 vols. (Basel: Schwabe, 1971–2007), 3:279–309; Joyce E. Chaplin, *The First Scientific American: Benjamin Franklin and the Pursuit of Genius* (New York: Basic Books, 2006), 3.

8. On Shakespeare, see Jonathan Bate, *The Genius of Shakespeare* (New York: Oxford University Press, 1982), esp. chap. 6, "The Original Genius," 157–187; William L. Pressly, *The Artist as Original Genius: Shakespeare's "Fine Frenzy" in Late Eighteenth-Century British Art* (Cranbury, NJ: Associated University Presses, 2007). See also Kirsti Simonsuuri, *Homer's Original Genius: Eighteenth-Century Notions of the Early Greek Epic (1688–1798)* (Cambridge: Cambridge University Press, 1979). On the reception of Pindar, see Jochen Schmidt, *Die Geschichte des Genie-Gedankens in der deutschen Literatur, Philosophie und Politik, 1750–1945*, 2 vols. (Heidelberg: Universitätsverlag, 2004), 1:179–192. Scott is cited in Christine Battersby, *Gender and Genius: Towards a Feminist Aesthetics* (Bloomington: Indiana University Press, 1989), 83. See also *Biographium Fæmineum: The Female Worthies; or, Memoirs of the Most Illustrious Ladies, of*

All Ages and Nations, 2 vols. (London: J. Wilkie, 1766), 1:vii. The line from Staël, though almost certainly spurious, is cited in Maria Fairweather, *Madame de Staël* (New York: Carroll and Graf, 2005), 240. I am grateful to Kathleen Kete for drawing it to my attention, and for sharing her (then unpublished) manuscript, *Making Way for Genius: The Aspiring Self in France from the Old Regime to the New* (New Haven, CT: Yale University Press, 2012), which contains a detailed study of Staël's conception of genius. See also Bonnie G. Smith, "History and Genius: The Narcotic, Erotic, and Baroque Life of Germaine de Staël," *French Historical Studies* 19 (1996): 1059–1081; Johann Georg Hamann, *Briefwechsel*, eds. Walther Ziesemer and Arthur Henkel, 8 vols. (Wiesbaden, Germany: Insel, 1955–1979), 2:415.

9. On the genius as a new "privileged individual" in the age of Enlightenment and a model of the "highest human type," see Baldine Saint Girons, "Génie," in *Dictionnaire européen des lumières*, ed. Michel Delon (Paris: Presses Universitaires de la France, 1997), 496–499; Herbert Dieckmann, "Diderot's Conception of Genius," *Journal of the History of Ideas* 2, no. 2 (1941): 151–182.

10. For aesthetic explanations, see, for example, M. H. Abrams, *The Mirror and the Lamp: Romantic Theory and the Critical Tradition* (New York: Oxford University Press, 1953); James Engell, *The Creative Imagination: Enlightenment to Romanticism* (Cambridge, MA: Harvard University Press, 1981). For the Marxist argument, see Alfred Opitz, *Schriftsteller und Gesellschaft in der Literaturtheorie der französischen Enzyklopädie* (Frankfurt: Peter Lang, 1975), esp. 207–211. A critique and subtle consideration of this thesis is provided in Peter Bürger, "Some Reflections upon the Historico-Sociological Explanation of the Aesthetics of Genius in the Eighteenth Century," in *The Decline of Modernism*, trans. Nicholas Walker (University Park: Pennsylvania State University Press, 1992), 57–70. The scholarship on the author and copyright, originally indebted to the work of Michel Foucault, has developed in rich and independent ways. See Mark Rose, *Authors and Owners: The Invention of Copyright* (Cambridge, MA: Harvard University Press, 1983); Martha Woodmansee, "The Genius and the Copyright: Economic and Legal Conditions of the Emergence of the 'Author,'" *Eighteenth-Century Studies* 17, no. 4 (1984): 425–448; Zeynep Tenger and Paul Trolander, "Genius Versus Capital: Eighteenth-Century Theories of Genius and Adam Smith's *Wealth of Nations*," *Modern Language Quarterly* 55, no. 2 (1994): 169–189; Carla Hesse, "The Rise of Intellectual Property, 700 B.C.–A.D. 2000: An Idea in the Balance," *Daedalus* 131, no. 2 (2002): 26–45.

11. On creation, commerce, and genius, see John Hope Mason, *The Value of Creativity: The Origins and Emergence of a Modern Belief* (Burlington, VT: Ashgate, 2003), esp. chaps. 4–6; *Journal de commerce et d'agriculture* 19 (1762): 78. On the relationship of genius to engineering in the French case, see Janis Langins, *Conserving the Enlightenment: French Military Engineering from Vauban to the Revolution* (Cambridge, MA: MIT Press, 2004), 166, 179–180, 213–214. The rise of the inventor is treated nicely in Christine Macleod's *Heroes of Invention: Technology, Liberalism, and British Identity, 1750–1914* (Cambridge: Cambridge University Press, 2007).

12. My account of God's withdrawal draws on Marcel Gauchet, *The Disenchantment of the World: A Political History of Religion*, trans. Oscar Burge (Princeton, NJ: Princeton University Press, 1997), 53–57. See also Charles Taylor, *A Secular Age* (Cambridge, MA: Belknap Press, 2007), esp. chap. 6. Leading historians who have adapted Gauchet's insights include Keith Michael Baker, "Enlightenment and the Institution of Society: Notes for a Conceptual History," in *Civil Society: History and Possibilities*, eds. Sudipta Kavirag and Sunil Khilnani (Cambridge: Cambridge University Press, 2001), 84–105, and David A. Bell, *The Cult of the Nation in France: Inventing Nationalism, 1680–1800* (Cambridge, MA: Harvard University Press, 2003).

13. Gauchet, *Disenchantment of the World*, 10–11, 176–180; Reinhart Koselleck, *Futures Past: On the Semantics of Historical Time*, trans. Keith Tribe (New York: Columbia University Press, 2004).

14. See Christopher Hill's classic *The World Turned Upside Down: Radical Ideas During the English Revolution* (London: Maurice Temple Smith, 1972).

15. On the assertion of natural equality and the reactions to it, see the concise account in Lynn Hunt, *Inventing Human Rights: A History* (New York: Norton, 2007). On the way in which elite artists in the nineteenth century engaged in complex ways with both aristocratic values and a democratic culture emphasizing equality, see Nathalie Heinich, *L'élite artiste: Excellence et singularité en régime démocratique* (Paris: Editions Gallimard, 2005); Anthony Ashley Cooper, Third Earl of Shaftesbury, "Soliloquy, or Advice to an Author," *Characteristicks of Men, Manners, Opinions, Times*, foreword Douglas Den Uyl, 3 vols. (Indianapolis: Liberty Fund, 2001), 1:129. I have modernized the capitalization and spelling here and below.

16. Shaftesbury, "Soliloquy, or Advice to an Author," in *Characteristicks*, 1:106–108.

17. Ibid.

18. Johann Caspar Lavater, *Physiognomische Fragmente, zur Berförderung der Menschenkenntnis und Menschenliebe*, 4 vols. (Leipzig und Winterthur, 1775–1778), 4:80–83; Johann Gottfried Herder, *Über Genie, Geschmack und Kritik* (Mainz, Germany: Marxen, 1937), esp. chap. 1, "Genie."

19. William Belsham, "Observations on Genius," in *Essays, Philosophical, Historical and Literary*, 2 vols. (London: G. G. and J. Robinson, 1799), 2:457; Edward Young, *Conjectures on Original Composition*, ed. Edith J. Morley (Manchester: Manchester University Press, 1918), 13.

20. Young, *Conjectures*, 13, 15. The line by Cicero is from his *De natura deorum*, 2.66.167. I have been unable to locate the provenance of "Sacer nobis inest Deus" (Holy is the God within us) in Seneca's writings, though he does comment similarly in the *Epistulae morales*, 41.2, "Sacer intra nos spiritus sedet" (Holy is the spirit that dwells within). On the influence of ancient conceptions, see Penelope Murray, "Poetic Genius and Its Classical Origins," in *Genius: The History of an Idea*, ed. Penelope Murray (Oxford: Blackwell, 1989), 29; Peter Kivy, *The Possessor and the Possessed: Handel, Mozart, Beethoven, and the Idea of Musical Genius* (New Haven, CT: Yale University Press, 2001).

21. Joshua Landy and Michael Saler, "Introduction" to *The Re-Enchantment of the World*, eds. Landy and Saler (Palo Alto, CA: Stanford University Press, 2009), 2. See also Saler's "Modernity and Enchantment: A Historiographic Review," *American Historical Review* III, no. 3 (2006): 692–717.

22. Dieckmann, "Diderot's Conception of Genius," 157. On the "Je ne sais quoi," see Annie Becq, *Genèse de l'esthétique française moderne: De la raison classique à l'imagination créatrice, 1680–1814* (Pisa: Pacini, 1984), 1:701ff; Richard Scholar, *The Je-Ne-Sais-Quoi in Early Modern Europe: Encounters with a Certain Something* (Oxford: Oxford University Press, 2005); Thomas Hobbes, *The Answer of Mr. Hobbes to Sir William Davenant's Preface Before Gondibert*, in the *English Works of Thomas Hobbes of Malmesbury*, ed. Sir William Molesworth, 11 vols. (London: Bohn, 1839–1845), 4:448. On enthusiasm, see Michael Heyd, *"Be Sober and Reasonable": The Critique of Enthusiasm in the Seventeenth and Early Eighteenth Centuries* (Leiden: Brill, 1995); J. G. A. Pocock, "Enthusiasm: The Antiself of Enlightenment," in Lawrence E. Klein and Anthony J. La Vopa, *Enthusiasm and Enlightenment in Europe, 1650–1850* (Pasadena, CA: Huntington Library Press, 1998), esp. 9–14.

23. John Locke, *An Essay Concerning Human Understanding*, 4.19 ("Of Enthusiasm"); Jan Goldstein, "Enthusiasm or Imagination? Eighteenth-Century Smear Words in Comparative National Context," *Huntington Library Quarterly* 60 (1998): 29–49.

24. On the French debate, see Kineret S. Jaffe, "The Concept of Genius: Its Changing Role in Eighteenth-Century French Aesthetics," *Journal of the History of Ideas* 41, no. 4 (1980): 579–599. On the German staging of this debate, which borrowed heavily from France, see Pierre Grappin, *La théorie du génie dans le préclassicisme allemande* (Paris: Presses Universitaires de France, 1952), 117–121; Locke, *Some Thoughts Concerning Education*, Section 1; William Sharpe, *A Dissertation upon Genius: Or, an Attempt to Shew, That the Several Instances of Distinction, and Degrees of Superiority in the Human Genius Are Not, Fundamentally, the Result of Nature, but the Effect of Acquisition* (London: C. Bathurst, 1755), 6. For Helvétius, I have used a facsimile edition of the contemporary English translation, *De l'esprit, or Essays on the Mind and Its Several Faculties* (London: J. M. Richardson, 1809), published in the Elibron Classics Series by the Adamant Media Corporation (2005), 204 (Essay 3, chap. 3, "Of Memory"), and 365–366 (Essay 4, chap. 1, "Of Genius").

25. For an introduction to the extensive literature on deliberate practice, see K. Anders Ericsson, Neil Charness, Paul J. Feltovich, and Robert R. Hoffman, eds., *The Cambridge Handbook of Expertise and Expert Performance* (Cambridge: Cambridge University Press, 2006). The views of Ericsson have been developed and presented to a wide audience in Malcolm Gladwell's *Outliers: The Story of Success* (New York: Little, Brown, 2008). See also Hobbes, *Leviathan*, chap. 13 ("Of the Natural Condition of Mankind"), and chap. 8 ("Of the Virtues Commonly Called Intellectual"); Sharpe, *Dissertation upon Genius*, 48.

26. I take the modern discourse of genius, in this respect, to be an extreme case of what the historian of science John Carson has called a "shadow language

of inequality," an exception of inherent difference that accompanies societies that are at least nominally committed to human equality. See his *The Measure of Merit: Talents, Intelligence, and Inequality in the French and American Republics, 1750–1940* (Princeton, NJ: Princeton University Press, 2007), xiii. As the scholar Bernhard Fabian rightly concludes, an eighteenth-century author "may be said to qualify as a new theoretician of genius in proportion as he was anti-Sharpean or . . . anti-Hélvetian." See the excellent introductory essay to his edited edition of Alexander Gerard, *An Essay on Genius*, ed. and intro. Bernhard Fabian (Munich: Wilhelm Fink, 1966), xxi.

27. Addison, *Spectator*, No. 160, September 3, 1711.

28. On the "modernity" of the ancients, see Dan Edelstein, *The Enlightenment: A Genealogy* (Chicago: University of Chicago Press, 2009), 19–68; Larry F. Norman, *The Shock of the Ancient: Literature and History in Early Modern France* (Chicago: University of Chicago Press, 2011). I should stress that my use of "Moderns" in the title to this chapter refers *not* to the one side in the battle against the ancients, but rather to modernity and modern persons more generally. On the importance of originality, see, typically, William Duff, *Critical Observations on the Writings of the Most Celebrated Original Geniuses in Poetry: Being a Sequel to the Essay on Original Genius* (London: T. Becket, 1770), 2–3.

29. Young, *Conjectures*, 17. On the origins and endurance of the talent-genius distinction, see Reino Virtanen, "On the Dichotomy Between Genius and Talent," *Comparative Literary Studies* 18, no. 1 (1981): 69–91. Resewitz is cited in Grappin, *La théorie du génie*, 130; Arthur Schopenhauer, *The World as Will and Representation*, trans. E. F. J. Payne, 2 vols. (New York: Dover, 1958), 1:391. I have altered Payne's translation slightly, in keeping with the original.

30. Paul Kaufman, "Heralds of Original Genius," in *Essays in Memory of Barret Wendell by His Assistants*, eds. W. R. Castle Jr. and Paul Kaufman (Cambridge: Cambridge University Press, 1926), 201. On the reception of British concepts of genius in Germany, see Schmidt, *Die Geschichte des Genie-Gedankens*, 1:150–193; John Louis Kind, *Edward Young in Germany* (New York: AMS Press, 1966 [1906]); and J. Ritter, "Genie," in Ritter, ed., *Historisches Wörterbuch*, 3:285–296; Voltaire, *Lettres philosophiques, par M. de V . . .* (Amsterdam: E. Lucas, 1734), 211.

31. H. B. Nisbet, "Genius," in Alan Charles Kors, ed., *Encyclopedia of the Enlightenment*, 4 vols. (Oxford: Oxford University Press, 2003), 2:108–112. On painting, see R. Wittkower, "Imitation, Eclecticism, and Genius," in *Aspects of the Eighteenth Century*, ed. Earl R. Wasserman (Baltimore, MD: Johns Hopkins University Press, 1965), 143–161. Notwithstanding its age and teleological bias, Ernst Cassirer's chapter on the "Fundamental Problem of Aesthetics" in *The Philosophy of the Enlightenment*, trans. Fritz C. A. Koelln and James P. Pettegrove (Princeton, NJ: Princeton University Press, 1951), remains deeply insightful. In a similar vein, see the more recent work of Louis Dupré, *The Enlightenment and the Intellectual Foundations of Modern Culture* (New Haven, CT: Yale University Press, 2004), chap. 4 ("Towards a New Conception of Art").

32. The English commentator was Richard Blackmore, *A Treatise of the Spleen and Vapours, or Hypocondriacal and Hysterical Affections* (London: J. Pemberton,

1725), 257. See also Abbé Jean-Baptiste Dubos, *Critical Reflections on Poetry, Painting, and Music*, trans. Thomas Nugent, 3 vols. (London: John Nourse, 1748), 2:10 (Abbé Dubos's popular *Réflexions critiques* were first published in French in 1719); Diderot, "Sur le génie," in *Oeuvres complètes de Diderot: Revues sur les éditions originales*, ed. Jules Assézat, 20 vols. (Paris: Garnier frères, 1875–1877), 4:26–27. On the displacement of humoral theory and the development of vitalism, see Catherine Packham, *Eighteenth-Century Vitalism: Bodies, Culture, Politics* (London: Palgrave, 2012); Michel Delon, *L'idée d'énergie au tournant des lumières (1720–1820)* (Paris: Presses Universitaires de France, 1988), esp. chap. 8 on genius; Peter Hanns Riell, *Vitalizing Nature in the Enlightenment* (Berkeley: University of California Press, 2005).

33. For a recent introduction to the extensive literature on the sublime, see Timothy M. Costelloe, ed., *The Sublime: From Antiquity to the Present* (Cambridge: Cambridge University Press, 2012).

34. My reading of Boileau here draws on the insightful analysis of Larry Norman in his *Shock of the Ancient*, 4–6, 184–204. Joan DeJean makes a somewhat contrary case for the role of the moderns in formulating a modern conception of genius. See her remarks on Charles Perrault's poem "Le génie," in her *Culture Wars and the Making of a Fin de Siècle* (Chicago: University of Chicago Press, 1997), 50–51.

35. [Nicholas Boileau], *Œuvres diverses du Sieur D . . . avec le traité du sublime ou du merveilleux dans le discours, traduit du grec du Longin* (Paris: D. Thierry, 1674), 24, 34, 87. The ancient Greek employed by Longinus is *phua* or *megalophuia*, somewhat equivalent to the Latin *ingenium*, though less common, and translating roughly as "great natured." See also *The Works of Dionysius Longinus, on the Sublime: Or, A Treatise Concerning the Sovereign Perfection of Writing*, trans. Leonard Welsted (London: Sam Briscoe, 1712), 24; *Dionysius Longinus on the Sublime: Translated from the Greek, with Notes and Observations, and Some Account of the Life, Writings and Character of the Author*, trans. William Smith (London: J. Watts, 1739), 37. The key passages from Longinus, *Peri hypsous*, are 1.4 and 13.2.

36. Longinus, *On the Sublime*, ed. and trans. W. Hamilton Frye and revised by Donald Russell, in *Aristotle, Longinus, Demetrius*, Loeb Classical Library (Cambridge, MA: Harvard University Press, 1995), 163, 279 (*Peri hypsous*, 1.4 and 36.1).

37. Gerard, *Essay on Genius*, 66; Pocock, "Enthusiasm"; Carl Friedrich Flögel, "Vom Genie," *Vermischte Beiträge zur Philosophie und den schönen Wissenschaften* (Breslau: Berlag Johann Jacob Korns, 1762), 21; Johann Georg Sulzer, *Allgemeine Theorie der schönen Künste in einzeln: Nach alphabetischer Ordnung der Kunstwörter auf einander folgenden, Artikeln abgehandelt*, 4 vols. (Leipzig: M. G. Weigmann, 1773–1775), 2:610–614; John Gilbert Cooper, *Letters Concerning Taste*, 2nd ed. (London: R. and J. Dodsley, 1755), 101.

38. Diderot, "Éclectisme," in *Oeuvres complètes*, 14:322; Diderot, "Entretiens sur le fils naturel," in *Oeuvres complètes*, 7:103.

39. Milton C. Nahm, *The Artist as Creator: An Essay of Human Freedom* (Baltimore: Johns Hopkins University Press, 1956), esp. Book I ("The Great

Analogy"); Jan Goldstein, *The Post-Revolutionary Self: Politics and Psyche in France, 1750–1850* (Cambridge, MA: Harvard University Press, 2005), chap. 1 ("The Perils of the Imagination at the End of the Old Regime"); Goldstein, "Enthusiasm or Imagination," 30; Samuel Johnson, cited in Dupré, *Enlightenment and Intellectual Foundations*, 87; William Duff, *An Essay on Original Genius and Its Various Modes of Exertion in Philosophy and the Fine Arts, Particularly in Poetry*, ed. John L. Mahoney (Gainesville, FL: Scholars' Facsimiles and Reprints, 1964), 23–24.

40. Diderot is cited in Jaffe, "The Concept of Genius," 594. See also Young, *Conjectures*, 24. Sulzer is cited in Abrams, *Mirror and Lamp*, 203.

41. Duff, *Essay on Original Genius*, 86; Voltaire, "Génie," *Œuvres de Voltaire*, 30:33; Young, *Conjectures*, 16; Immanuel Kant, *Critique of Judgment*, intro. and trans. Werner S. Pluhar (Indianapolis: Hackett, 1987), 175–176. See, more generally, Paul Bruno, *Kant's Conception of Genius: Its Origin and Function in the Third Critique* (New York: Continuum, 2010).

42. William Wordsworth, "Essay Supplementary to the Preface to *Poems*" (1815), in *William Wordsworth: The Major Works*, ed. and intro. Stephen Gill (New York: Oxford University Press, 1984), 659; Georg J. Buelow, "Originality, Genius, Plagiarism in English Criticism of the Eighteenth Century," *International Review of the Aesthetics and Sociology of Music* 21, no. 2 (1990): 117–128.

43. Cooper, "Soliloquy," 1:129.

44. John Wesley's "Thoughts on Genius" (1787) are interesting in the context of the Christian reception of the cult of genius. Prompted by a reading of William Duff's *Essay on Original Genius*, and dated "Lambeth, November 8, 1787," the notes are an informed summary of European reflection on the subject by one of the century's most influential clergymen. They provide no indication that Wesley thought of genius and his Methodist faith as being incompatible. See "Thoughts on Genius," in *The Works of John Wesley* (New York: J. Emory, 1831), 460–461. On the "Jewish Socrates" and the "Vilna Gaon" as two contrasting embodiments of Jewish genius, see Eliyahu Stern, "Genius and Demographics in Modern Jewish History," *Jewish Quarterly Review* 101, no. 3 (2011): 347–382, as well as Stern's fine study *The Genius: Elijah of Vilna and the Making of Modern Judaism* (New Haven, CT: Yale University Press, 2013).

45. Franz Xaver Niemetschek, *Mozart: The First Biography*, intro. Chris Eisen, trans. Helen Mautner (New York: Berghahn Books, 2007), 3 (Niemetschek's *Leben des K. K. Kapellmeisters Wolfgang Gottlieb Mozart* was first published in Prague in 1798); Friedrich Melchior von Grimm, *Correspondance littéraire*, December 1, 1763, in Otto Erich Deutsch, *Mozart: A Documentary Biography*, trans. Eric Blom, Peter Branscombe, and Jeremy Noble (Palo Alto, CA: Stanford University Press, 1965), 26; Claude Adrien Helvétius to Francis, 10th Earl of Huntingdon, London, April 1764, in ibid., 32; *Public Advertiser*, June 26, 1764, cited in ibid., 36.

46. On Mozart as a "symbol of genius," see Paul Henry Lang, "Mozart After 200 Years," *Journal of the American Musicological Society* 13 (1960): 197; Beda Hübner, *Diarium Patris Bedae Hübner*, December 8, 1766, in Deutsch, *Mozart*, 70; *Gazzeta di Motova*, January 12, 1770, in ibid., 105. On the *Miserere*, see Piero

Melograni, *Wolfgang Amadeus Mozart*, trans. Lydia G. Cochrane (Chicago: University of Chicago Press, 2006), 37–38.

47. On this point, see Simon Schaffer, "Natural Philosophy and Public Spectacle in the Eighteenth Century," *History of Science* 21 (1983): 1–43; *Public Advertiser,* July 9, 1765, cited in Deutsch, *Mozart*, 45.

48. Daines Barrington, "An Account of a Very Remarkable Young Musician," a letter from the Honourable Daines Barrington, F.R.S., to Mathew Maty, M.D., Sec. R.S., *The Philosophical Transactions of the Royal Society 1770*, 60:54–64, accessed July 12, 2012, http://rstl.royalsocietypublishing.org/content/60/54.

49. Christian Friedrich Daniel Schubart, "Concerning Musical Genius" (1784), trans. Richard W. Harpster, in *German Essays on Music*, eds. Jost Hermand and Michael Gilbert (New York: Continuum, 1994), 15–16.

50. See Gladwell, *Outliers*, 40–68, as well as the British psychologist Michael Howe, *Genius Explained* (Cambridge: Cambridge University Press, 1999), 2–7.

51. Christoph Wolff, "Defining Genius: Early Reflections of J. S. Bach's Self-Image," *Proceedings of the American Philosophical Society* 145, no. 4 (2001): 474–481; Kivy, *Possessor and the Possessed*, esp. 37–56; Albert Einstein, *Mozart, His Character, His Work*, trans. Arthur Mendel and Nathan Broder (Oxford: Oxford University Press, 1965), 129. Norbert Elias argues, by contrast, that Mozart was "a genius before the age of [Romantic] genius," who suffered in a society that "had no legitimate place for the highly individualized artist" in its midst (Elias, *Mozart*, 19). That was certainly true of his adult career, but as a child prodigy, Mozart benefited from the timing of his prodigious debut.

52. As two of the foremost historians of European science in this period have written, "the vanguard of European intellectuals . . . came to disdain both wonder and wonders in the first half of the eighteenth century," setting the tone of the age. See Lorraine Daston and Katharine Park, *Wonders and the Order of Nature, 1150–1750* (New York: Zone Books, 2001), 329, and, in general, chap. 9 "The Enlightenment and the Anti-Marvelous," 329–363; Leopold Mozart, in a letter of July 30, 1768, cited in Elias, *Mozart*, 72; "Marvelous," *The Encyclopedia of Diderot & d'Alembert: Collaborative Translation Project*, trans. Virginia Swain (Ann Arbor: Scholarly Publishing Office of the University of Michigan Library, 2007), accessed August 31, 2012, http://hdl.handle.net/2027/spo.did2222.0000.598.

53. *Aristide ou le citoyen* (Lausanne), October 11, 1766, cited in Deutsch, *Mozart*, 62; Diderot, "Sur le génie," in *Oeuvres complètes,* 4:26–27.

54. Jean-Jacques Rousseau, *Dictionnaire de la musique* (Paris: Duchesne, 1768), 227; Johann Caspar Lavater, *Physiognomische Fragmente*, 4:80. Lavater's "one in a million" quotation is cited in *Laconics, or the Best Words of the Best Authors*, 3 vols. (Philadelphia: Carey, Lea, and Carey, 1829), 2:33. Lavater's ratio was regularly included in collections of famous quotations in Britain and the United States in the nineteenth century. On Galton, see chap. 5, below.

55. Kant, *Critique of Judgment*, 187, 175–177.

56. Ibid., 176–177.

57. Johann Wolfgang von Goethe, *Poetry and Truth from My Own Life*, intro. Karl Bruel, rev. trans. Minna Steele Smith (London: George Bell and Sons, 1908), 2:285–286; Duff, *Essay on Original Genius*, 91. Duff included the "mechanical arts" as well. See Gerard, *Essay on Genius*, 14; Duff, *Essay on Original Genius*, 140.

58. Edmond Halley, cited in Patricia Fara, *Newton: The Making of a Genius* (New York: Columbia University Press, 2002), 163; David Hume, *The History of England from the Invasion of Julius Caesar to the Revolution of 1688*, foreword William B. Todd, 6 vols. (Indianapolis: Liberty Fund, 1983), 6:542; "Isaac Newton," *Historic Gallery of Portraits and Paintings, or Biographical Review*, 7 vols. (London: Vernor, Hoode, and Sharpe, 1807), 1:20.

59. The ardent admirer, John Conduitt, is cited in Fara, *Newton*, 16. In what follows, I draw heavily on Fara's incomparable study. For other assessments of Newton's reception as a "genius," see Richard Yeo, "Genius, Method, and Morality: Images of Newton in Britain, 1760–1860," *Science in Context* 2 (1988): 257–284.

60. Robert Iliffe, "'Is He Like Other Men?' The Meaning of the *Principia Mathematica*, and the Author as Idol," in Gerald Maclean, ed., *Culture and Society in the Stuart Restoration* (Cambridge: Cambridge University Press, 1995), 159–179. On Newton as a saint, see Fara, *Newton*, chap. 1 ("Sanctity"). "Genius," Fara rightly observes, "resembles sanctity." The line on Newton's Cambridge statue is from Lucretius, who intended it originally to celebrate Epicurus. The statue was sculpted by Louis-François Roubiliac in 1755. It still stands.

61. Fara, *Newton*, 34–49.

62. Colman is cited in Andrew Elfenbein, *Romantic Genius: The Prehistory of a Homosexual Role* (New York: Columbia University Press, 1999), 35. Colman in fact made his declaration in jest, ridiculing the habit in others. Wilde is cited in Richard Ellmann, *Oscar Wilde* (New York: Knopf, 1988), 160. Wilde's line may well be apocryphal: no contemporary account of it exists.

63. See, for example, Koselleck, *Futures Past*; Gauchet, *Disenchantment of the World*, esp. 176–180.

64. The origin of celebrity in the eighteenth century is a topic that is drawing cutting-edge research. See, for example, Antoine Lilti's forthcoming *Figures publiques: Aux origines de la célébrité* (1750–1850) (Paris: Fayard, forthcoming), as well as Fred Inglis, *A Short History of Celebrity* (Princeton, NJ: Princeton University Press, 2010), esp. chaps. 1–3. Chamfort is cited in Antoine Lilti, "The Writing of Paranoia: Jean-Jacques Rousseau and the Paradoxes of Celebrity," *Representations* 103 (2008): 53–83.

65. Sébastien-Roch-Nicolas Chamfort, *Combien le génie des grands écrivains influe sur l'esprit de leur siècle*, in *Oeuvres complètes de Chamfort*, 5 vols. (Paris: Chaumerot Jeune, 1824–1825), 1:203–204; Johann Gottfried Herder, "Vom Erkennen und Erfinden der menschlichen Seele," in *Schriften zu Philosophie, Literatur, Kunst und Altertum [1774–1787]*, vol. 4 of *Werke*, eds. J. Brummack and M. Bollacher, 10 vols. (Frankfurt: Deutscher Klassiker, 1994), 4:381.

66. Diderot, *Le neveu de Rameau*, ed. and intro. Jean-Claude Bonnet (Paris: Flammarion, 1983), 49–50. See also Otis Fellows, "The Theme of Genius in

Diderot's *Neveu de Rameau*," *Diderot Studies*, no. 2 (1952): 168–199; James Mall, "*Le Neveu de Rameau* and the Idea of Genius," *Eighteenth-Century Studies* 11, no. 1 (1977): 26–39. Diderot speaks of geniuses as monsters in his *Elémens de physiologie*, ed. J. Mayer (Paris: M. Didier, 1964), 296. He also refers to "le monstre appelé homme de génie" in his *Réfutation de l'ouvrage de Helvétius intitulé L'Homme* in *Oeuvres complètes*.

67. Diderot, *Le neveu de Rameau*, 101.

THE DAWN OF THE IDOLS

1. Benjamin Franklin to Mrs. Sarah Bache, June 3, 1779, in *The Papers of Benjamin Franklin*, eds. Leonard W. Labaree et al., 40 vols. (New Haven, CT: Yale University Press, 1959–1999), 29:613. On monuments to men of genius, see Judith Colton, *The Parnasse François: Titon du Tillet and the Origins of the Monument to Genius* (New Haven, CT: Yale University Press, 1979); Alfred Neumeyer, "Monuments to 'Genius' in German Classicism," *Journal of the Warburg Institute* 2, no. 2 (1938): 158–163. On images of genius in crockery and other forms, see Samuel Taylor, "Artists and *Philosophes* as mirrored by Sèvres and Wedgwood," in Francis Haskell, Anthony Levi, and Robert Shackleton, eds., *The Artist and the Writer in France: Essays in Honour of Jean Seznec* (Oxford: Clarendon Press, 1974), 21–40, and the many excellent articles in Thomas W. Gaehtgens and Gregor Wedekind, eds., *Le culte des grands hommes, 1750–1850* (Paris: Editions de la Maison des Sciences de l'Homme, 2010). The scriptural reference is to 1 Corinthians 13.8–11 and 1 John 5:21. Franklin's line on idol worship is from his essay "On the Providence of God in the Government of the World" (1732) in the *Papers of Benjamin Franklin*, 1:267.

2. Joyce E. Chaplin, *The First Scientific American: Benjamin Franklin and the Pursuit of Genius* (New York: Basic Books, 2006), 136; Honoré-Gabriel Riquetti, Comte de Mirabeau, "Éloge funèbre de Benjamin Franklin," delivered on June 11, 1790, accessed October 23, 2012, www.assemblee-nationale.fr/histoire/Mirabeau 1790-BFranklin.asp; Joseph Aude, *Le journaliste des ombres, ou Momus aux Champs Elysées* (Paris: Gueffier, 1790), 61. The play was performed at the Theater of the Nation in Paris on July 14, 1790, and featured Franklin, Voltaire, and Rousseau conversing together in the Elysian fields.

3. John Adams, *Diary of John Adams*, vol. 2, entry for June 23, 1779, accessed on November 14, 2012, www.masshist.org/publications/apde/portia. php?id=DJA02d484.

4. On the process of pantheonization, see Jean Claude Bonnet, *Naissance du Panthéon: Essai sur le culte de grands hommes* (Paris: Fayard, 1998); Mona Ozouf, "The Pantheon: The École Normale of the Dead," in *Realms of Memory: Rethinking the French Past*, ed. Pierre Nora, trans. Arthur Goldhammer, intro. Lawrence D. Kritzman, 3 vols. (New York: Columbia University Press, 1998), 3:325–429. Ozouf distinguishes carefully between the eighteenth-century use of "hero" and "*grand homme*," but says nothing about genius. *Mercure de France*, December

4, 1790, cited in James A. Leith, "Les trois apotheoses de Voltaire," *Annales historiques de la Révolution française* 51 (1979): 161–209 (citation on 205).

5. Condorcet is cited in François Azouvi, *Descartes et la France: Histoire d'une passion nationale* (Paris: Fayard, 2002), 130. Condorcet's text was read in the National Assembly by his nephew on April 12, 1791. See Jean Le Rond d'Alembert, *Preliminary Discourse to the Encyclopedia of Diderot*, trans. and intro. Richard N. Schwab (Chicago: University of Chicago Press), 60.

6. Sébastien-Roch-Nicolas Chamfort, *Combien le génie des grands écrivains influe sur l'esprit de leur siècle*, in *Oeuvres completes de Chamfort*, 5 vols. (Paris: Chaumerot Jeune, 1824–1825), 1:203–204. Thomas is cited in Jean-Claude Bonnet, "Les morts illustres: Oraison funèbre, éloge académique, nécrologie," in *Lieux de mémoires*, 2 (Part 3): 217–241.

7. On revolutionary almanacs, see Serge Bianchi, *La révolution culturelle de l'an II: Élites et peuple, 1789–1799* (Paris: Aubier, 1982), 200. Fabre d'Églantine is cited in *Archives parlementaires*, 78:503. The other proposed holidays were consecrated to virtue, work, opinion, and gratitude (*récompense*). Although plans to celebrate the *fête du génie* were entertained, and it is possible that celebrations were actually held locally in the provinces, I have not found any mention of this in the relevant documents held in F/1cI/84–102 at the Archives Nationales in Paris.

8. For a careful analysis of the legislation on intellectual property, see Carla Hesse, *Publishing and Cultural Politics in Revolutionary Paris, 1789–1810* (Berkeley: University of California Press, 1991), chap. 3.

9. *Rapport fait par Marie-Joseph Chénier, sur la translation des cendres de René Descartes au Panthéon*, séance du 18 floréal, l'an 4 (Paris: De l'imprimerie national, Messidor, an 4 [1796]), 2. On the association of liberty and genius in the Revolution, see Paul Bénichou, *Le sacre de l'écrivain, 1750–1830: Essai sur l'avènement d'un pouvoir spiritual laïque dans la France moderne* (Paris: José Corti, 1985), 45. On the use of Longinus in apologies for the Glorius Revolution, see Jonathan Lamb, "The Sublime," in *The Cambridge History of Literary Criticism*, vol. 4, *The Eighteenth Century*, eds. H. B. Nisbet and Claude Rawson (Cambridge: Cambridge University Press, 1989), 396. The line in question is from Longinus, *Peri hypsous*, 44.2. See also "Genius," *The Encyclopedia of Diderot & d'Alembert: Collaborative Translation Project*, trans. John S. D. Glaus (Ann Arbor: Scholarly Publishing Office of the University of Michigan Library, 2007), accessed August 19, 2010, http://hdl.handle.net/2027/spo.did2222.0000.819. On the widespread interpretation of the French Revolution as a sublime event, see Mary Ashburn Miller, *A Natural History of Revolution: Violence and Nature in the French Revolutionary Imagination, 1789–1794* (Ithaca, NY: Cornell University Press, 2011), esp. 39–40, 117–121, 169–170.

10. Immanuel Kant, *Critique of Judgment*, intro. and trans. Werner S. Pluhar (Indianapolis: Hackett, 1987), 174. Reverence, terror, awe, and the fear of death were passions directly associated with the sublime, according to the celebrated analysis (much criticized by Kant) of Edmund Burke in his *A Philosophical*

Enquiry into the Origin of Our Idea of the Sublime and the Beautiful (1757). Robespierre's comments are from the séance of October 24, 1793 in *Archives parlementaires*, 77:508. For good measure, Robespierre made the same point with reference to the classical republican hero Brutus and the author of a celebrated modern play about him, Voltaire. "The author of *Brutus* had genius," Robespierre noted, "but Brutus was worth more than Voltaire" (ibid.).

11. *Archives parlementaires*, 77:508. The speaker was Claude Bazire, who sat with the Mountain. The conviction that "true genius" was of the people was given a pointed articulation in the Jacobin phrase "true genius is almost always *sans culotte*." See the reference in Simon Schaffer, "Genius in Romantic Natural Philosophy," in *Romanticism and the Sciences*, eds. Andrew Cunningham and Nicholas Jardine (Cambridge: Cambridge University Press, 1990), 82–98 (85). For Condorcet's thoughts about genius, merit, and equality, see his *Esquisse d'un tableau historique des progres de l'esprit humain*, ed. Alain Pons (Paris: Flammarion, 1988), 229. See also John Carson, *The Measure of Merit: Talents, Intelligence, and Inequality in the French and American Republics, 1750–1940* (Princeton, NJ: Princeton University Press, 2007), 32–35.

12. Carson, *Measure of Merit*, esp. chaps. 1–2. The citations are from Joseph de Maistre's *Considérations sur la France* (1797), and may be found, along with an analysis of Maistre's thinking about genius and its evils, in my article "The Genius of Maistre," in *Joseph de Maistre and the Legacy of the Enlightenment*, eds. Carolina Armenteros and Richard A. Lebrun (Oxford: Voltaire Foundation, 2011), 19–30.

CHAPTER 4

1. Alexander von Humboldt, "The Vital Force; or, The Rhodian Genius," in *Aspects of Nature, in Different Lands and Different Climates, with Scientific Elucidations*, trans. Mrs. Sabine (Philadelphia: Lea and Blanchard, 1850), 402–410. All subsequent citations from the piece are taken from this translation in consultation with Humboldt's original German, "Die Lebenskraft oder rhodische Genius: Eine Erzählung," in *Ansichten der Natur: Mit wissenschaftlichen Erläuterungen* (Stuttgart: J. G. Cotta, 1874), 317–321.

2. Richard Holmes, *Age of Wonder: How the Romantic Generation Discovered the Beauty and Terror of Science* (New York: Pantheon, 2009). Fisher Ames is cited in Edward Cahill, "Federalist Criticism and the Fate of Genius," *American Literature* 76, no. 4 (2004): 687. See also William Hazlitt, "Lectures in English Philosophy," in *Complete Works of William Hazlitt*, ed. P. P. Howe, 21 vols. (London: Frank Cass, 1967), 2:153; Lucy Delap, "The Superwoman: Theories of Gender and Genius in Edwardian Britain," *Historical Journal* 47, no. 1 (2004): 101–126, esp. 104–105.

3. On the genius as an "archetype" of the "Romantic mind," see Warren Breckman, *European Romanticism: A Brief History with Documents* (Boston: Bedford/St. Martin's, 2008), 12. And on Napoleon as its prime illustration, see Howard Mumford Jones, "The Doctrine of Romantic Genius," in *Revolution and Romanticism* (Cambridge, MA: Harvard University Press, 1974), 294; J. W. Goethe, *Conversations with Eckermann (1823–1832)*, trans. John Oxenford (San Francisco:

North Point Press, 1984), 199 (Conversation of Tuesday, March 11, 1828). The last line of this paragraph is a paraphrase of Natalie Petiteau, *Napoléon, de la mythologie à l'histoire* (Paris: Editions de Seuil, 2004), 75.

4. One of Napoleon's foremost biographers, Steven Englund, observes that, while the French of this period "were not short on smart statesmen and generals," Napoleon "stood out for the impression he made on people for his brains." See Steven Englund, *Napoleon: A Political Life* (Cambridge, MA: Harvard University Press, 2004), 146, and also 104. Rémusat is cited in Englund, *Napoleon*, 319.

5. Kléber is cited in Englund, *Napoleon*, 129.

6. Paul Metzner, *Crescendo of the Virtuoso: Spectacle, Skill, and Self-Promotion in Paris During the Age of Revolution* (Berkeley: University of California Press, 1998); Tia DeNora, *Beethoven and the Construction of Genius: Musical Politics in Vienna, 1792–1803* (Berkeley: University of California Press, 1995). Metzner describes Napoleon as the "archetypal performer-genius of the Age of Revolution," for whom "winning battles became an end in itself" (Metzner, *Crescendo*, 294).

7. Petiteau, *Napoléon*, 25; Jean Tulard, *Le mythe de Napoléon* (Paris: Collin, 1971), 31 (*Courrier de l'armée* quotation); Annie Jourdan, *Napoléon: Héros, imperator, mécène* (Paris: Aubier, 1998), 109–110; [Louis Dubroca], *Histoire de Bonaparte, premier consul, depuis son naissance jusqu'à la paix de Lunéville* . . . , 2 vols. (Paris: Brasseur, 1801), 1: xiv. The mayor of Feurs's remarks may be found in the Archives départementales de la Loire, 1M593, PV du maire de Feurs, le 20 germinal an IX (April 10, 1801). I am extremely grateful to Cyril Triolaire for sharing this reference with me, along with those that follow in this paragraph, which are drawn from his fine dissertation, "Fêtes officielles, théâtres et spectacles de curiosités dans le Massif Central pendant le Consulat et l'Empire-Pouvoir, artistes et mises en scène" (PhD diss., University of Clermont-Ferrand II, 2008). The local priest's comments may be found in the Archives nationales, Series F1CIII Loire 7, Discours du curé d'Yssingeaux, August 15, 1806. On addresses to Napoleon as "the genius," see the close analysis in Triolaire, "Fêtes officielles, théâtres et spectacles de curiosités," Part 2, "Discours à la fête." The "Omniscient, omnipotent," quotation is cited in Jourdan, *Napoléon*, 109–110. On Napoleon's "star," see my article "Die Kometenbahn eines Genies: The Case of Napoleon Bonaparte," forthcoming in *Wahsinn und Methode: Zur Funktion von Geniefiguren in Literatur und Philosophie*, eds. Hans Stauffacher and Marie-Christin Wilm (Bielefeld, Germany: Transcript Verlag, 2014).

8. Jacques-Olivier Boudon, "Grand homme ou demi-dieu? La mise en place d'une religion napoléonienne," *Romantisme: Revue du dix-neuvième siècle*, no. 100, *Le grand homme* (1998): 131.

9. On the "epiphany of the ancients," see Luigi Mascilli Migliorini, *Le mythe du héros: France et Italie après la chute de Napoléon* (Paris: Nouveau Monde, 2002), 10.

10. Max Weber, *Economy and Society: An Outline of Interpretive Sociology*, eds. Guenther Roth and Claus Wittich, 2 vols. (Berkeley: University of California Berkeley Press, 1978), 1:241–246 ("Charismatic Authority").

11. Edward Berenson and Eva Giloi, eds., *Constructing Charisma: Celebrity, Fame, and Power in Nineteenth-Century Europe* (Oxford: Berghahn Books, 2010); Weber, *Economy and Society*, 1:244, 249; Goethe, *Conversations with Eckermann*, 200, 317 (March 11, 1828, and March 2, 1831).

12. Claude-Henri de Saint-Simon, "Introduction aux travaux scientifiques du dix-neuvième siècle," in *Œuvres de Claude-Henri de Saint-Simon*, 6 vols. (Paris: Éditions Anthropos, 1966), 6:201–202.

13. On Napoleon's youthful dream of becoming another Newton, see the account in Michel Foucault, *Discipline and Punish: The Birth of the Prison*, trans. Alan Sheridan (New York: Vintage, 1977), 140–141. Saint-Hilaire's anecdote is recounted in Englund, *Napoleon*, 146. Saint-Hilaire referred to Napoleon as the "four-thought Caesar" in reference to his ability to maintain multiple lines of reflection simultaneously. For Carl von Clausewitz on Napoleon, see his *On War*, trans. and eds. Michael Howard and Peter Paret (Princeton, NJ: Princeton University Press, 1976), 112.

14. Georg Wilhelm Friedrich Hegel, *Lectures on the Philosophy of World History: Introduction*, trans. H. B. Nisbet, intro. Duncan Forbes (Cambridge: Cambridge University Press, 1975), 84–85. I cite from the second draft of Hegel's lectures of 1830, though they were first delivered in 1822.

15. Kim Wheatley, "'Attracted by the Body': Accounts of Shelley's Cremation," *Keats-Shelley Journal* 49 (2000): 162–182; Trelawny gives a detailed, if much stylized, account of the cremation in his *Recollections of the Last Days of Shelley and Byron* (London: Edward Moxon, 1858).

16. Trelawny, *Recollections*, 137; Shelley, *Adonais*, 1.8–9; On the posthumous fate of Shelley's body parts, including his ashes and heart, see Sylva Norman, *The Flight of the Skylark* (London: Max Reinhardt, 1954), esp. 182–183, 262–267.

17. Norman, *Flight of the Skylark*, 264. On the fate of Byron's remains, see Brian Burrell, *Postcards from the Brain Museum: The Improbable Search for Meaning in the Matter of Famous Minds* (New York: Broadway Books, 2004), 59–79.

18. See Russell Shorto's lively *Descartes' Bones: A Skeletal History of the Conflict Between Faith and Reason* (New York: Doubleday, 2008), 107. On the other episodes of reliquary fascination, see chaps. 5 and 6 below, as well as my article "Relikwieen van genieën" [Relics of Genius], trans. Jan Willem Reitsma, *Nexus* 52 (2009): 149–161.

19. Shelley, "A Defence of Poetry," in *Shelley's Poetry and Prose*, eds. Donald H. Reiman and Neil Fraistat (New York: Norton, 2002), 535, 512. On Shelley's use of the term "poet," see Richard Holmes, *Shelley: The Pursuit* (London: Weidenfield and Nicolson, 1975), 642.

20. On prophecy in the Romantic period, see Ian Balfour, *The Rhetoric of Romantic Prophecy* (Palo Alto, CA: Stanford University Press, 2002); Murray Roston, *Prophet and Poet: The Bible and the Growth of Romanticism* (Evanston, IL: Northwestern University Press, 1965). On prophecy and poetry generally, see James L. Kugel, *Poetry and Prophecy: The Beginnings of a Literary Tradition* (Ithaca, NY: Cornell University Press, 1990). On Lowth, see Jonathan Sheehan, *The Enlightenment Bible* (Princeton, NJ: Princeton University Press, 2005), 148–182;

Samuel Taylor Coleridge, *The Table Talk and Omniana of Samuel Taylor Coleridge*, ed. T. Ashe (London: G. Bell and Sons, 1884), 174. Schlegel and Novalis are cited in Balfour, *Rhetoric of Romantic Prophecy*, 40, 43. On "time of the prophets," see Paul Bénichou, *Le temps des prophètes: Doctrines de l'âge romantique* (Paris: Gallimard, 1977). On the "consecration" of the writer more generally in this period and the artistic appropriation of religious functions, see Bénichou's classic *Le sacre de l'écrivain, 1750–1830:Essai sur l'avènement d'un pouvoir spiritual laïque dans la France moderne* (Paris: José Corti, 1985).

21. Shelley, "A Defence of Poetry," 513.

22. Ibid.; James Engell, *The Creative Imagination: Enlightenment to Romanticism* (Cambridge, MA: Harvard University Press, 1981), 256–264.

23. William Hazlitt, "Whether Genius Is Conscious of Its Powers," in *The Plain Speaker: Key Essays*, intro. Tom Paulin, ed. Duncan Wu (Oxford: Blackwell, 1998), 90; F. W. J. Schelling, *System of Transcendental Idealism*, trans. Peter Heath, intro. Michael Vater (Charlottesville: University Press of Virginia, 1978), 222.

24. William Wordsworth, "The Tables Turned," ll. 21–24, in *The Collected Poems of William Wordsworth* (Ware, Hertfordshire: Wordsworth Editions, 1995), 574.

25. On Romantic epistemology and the master metaphor of the lamp, see M. H. Abram's classic analysis in *The Mirror and the Lamp: Romantic Theory and the Critical Tradition* (New York: Oxford University Press, 1974). On Shelley, see Engel, *The Creative Imagination*, 259; August Wilhelm Schlegel, *Lectures on Dramatic Art and Literature*, trans. John Black, 2nd ed. (London: George Bell and Sons, 1904), 359 (Lecture XXIII).

26. William Blake, "All Religions Are One," in *The Complete Poetry and Prose of William Blake*, ed. David V. Eardman, rev. ed. (New York: Anchor Books, 1988), 1.

27. On Blake's idiosyncratic Christianity, see Robert M. Ryan, *The Romantic Reformation: Religious Politics in English Literature, 1789–1824* (Cambridge: Cambridge University Press, 1997), 43–80. F. W. J. Schelling, *Philosophie der Kunst* (Darmstadt, Germany: Wissenschaftliche Buchgesellschaft, 1960), 104 (section 63).

28. Charles-Louis de Secondat, Baron de Montesquieu, "Des Anglais et des Français," in *Oeuvres complètes de Montesquieu* (Paris: Chez Firmin Didot, 1838), 626; William Robertson, *The History of Scotland During the Reigns of Queen Mary and King James VI*, 2 vols. (London: T. Cadell, 1769), 2:301; Marc Fumaroli, "The Genius of the French Language," in *Realms of Memory: Rethinking the French Past*, ed. Pierre Nora, trans. Arthur Goldhammer, intro. Lawrence D. Kritzman, 3 vols. (New York: Columbia University Press, 1998), 3:555–605. On the relation between the universal and the particular in Romantic thought, see Breckman, *European Romanticism*, 31–33.

29. On the "brotherhood of genius," see Edgar Zilsel, *Die Geniereligion: Ein kritischer Versuch über das moderne Persönlichkeitsideal*, intro. Johann Dvorak (Frankfurt: Suhrkamp, 1990), 83ff. Zilsel's work, first published in 1917, drew largely on nineteenth-century examples in establishing this doctrine of the

"Brüderschaft der Genies." See also William Wordsworth, "The Prelude," Book 13, ll. 300–305, in *Collected Poems*, 882; Arthur Schopenhauer, *The World as Will and Representation*, trans. E. F. J. Payne, 2 vols. (New York: Dover Publications, 1969), 2:377; Max Scheler, *Exemplars of Persons and Leaders (Vorbilder und Führer)*, in *Person and Self-Value: Three Essays*, ed. and partially trans. M. S. Frings (Dordrecht, Netherlands: Martinus Nijhoff, 1987), 182–183. Scheler originally began this work, which analyzes the ideal types of the "genius," the "hero," and the "saint," in 1911, and worked on it intermittently until 1921, though it was not published until 1933.

30. Scheler, *Exemplars*, 184–186. Scheler also invokes Kant and Schopenhauer.

31. For a succinct summary of Herder's views, see Elisabeth Décultot, "Le génie et l'art poétique dans les textes du jeune Herder: Examen d'une tension," in *Le culte des grands hommes, 1750–1850*, eds. Thomas W. Gaehtgens and Gregor Wedekind (Paris: Edition de la Maison des Sciences de la Homme, 2009), 103–116.

32. Thomas Carlyle, *On Heroes, Hero-Worship and the Heroic in History*, ed. and intro. Carl Niemeyer (Lincoln: University of Nebraska Press, 1966), 114.

33. Delacroix's letter is cited and translated in Hugh Honour, *Romanticism* (New York: Harper and Row, 1979), 266. Delacroix actually painted two pictures of Tasso. The first was begun in 1823 and displayed in the Salon of 1824. A second, described here, is dated 1839. See Eugène Delacroix, *Journal*, ed. Michèle Hannosh, 2 vols. (Paris: José Corti, 2009), 1:106n39.

34. Gilles Néret, *Eugène Delacroix, 1798–1863: The Prince of Romanticism* (Cologne, Germany: Taschen, 2000). On Tasso's use of *genio*, see Edgar Zilsel, *Die Enstehung des Geniebegriffes: Ein Beitrag zur Ideengeschichte der Antike und des Frühkapitalismus*, intro. Heinz Maus (Hildesheim, Germany: Georg Olms, 1972), 296–297. Hazlitt and Shelley are cited in C. P. Brand, *Italy and the Romantics: The Italianate Fashion in Early Nineteenth-Century England* (Cambridge: Cambridge University Press, 1957), 91–92. For Byron's lament, see George Gordon, Lord Byron, "The Lament of Tasso," 1.3–5; Germaine de Staël, *De l'Allemagne*, cited and translated in Maurice Z. Schroder, *Icarus: The Image of the Artist in French Romanticism* (Cambridge, MA: Harvard University Press, 1961), 32.

35. Frederick Burwick, *Poetic Madness and the Romantic Imagination* (University Park: University of Pennsylvania Press, 1996), 21–42; Dino Franco Felluga, *The Perversity of Poetry: Romantic Ideology and the Popular Male Poet of Genius* (New York: State University of New York Press, 2005), 13–32; Alexander Gerard, *An Essay on Taste* (London: A. Millar, 1759), 176–177.

36. Schlegel is cited in J. Hillis Miller, "Friedrich Schlegel and the Anti-Ekphrastic Tradition," in *Revenge of the Aesthetic: The Place of Theory in Literature Today*, ed. Michael P. Clark (Berkeley: University of California Press, 2000), 58–76 (citation on 71). Miller does not cite the last sentence included here, which I have added back in from the original, Schlegel's "Dialogue on Poetry." For the quotation by Schiller, see his *On the Aesthetic Education of Man*, trans. and intro. Reginald Snell (Mineola, NY: Dover Publications, 2004), 58.

37. Heine is cited in Honour, *Romanticism*, 256–258. Lamartine, from the *Méditations poétiques* (1820), is cited in Pascal Brissette, *La malédiction littéraire: Du poète crotté au génie malheureux* (Montreal: Presses Universitaires de Montréal, 2003), 302.

38. Arthur Schopenhauer, *World as Will*, 1:190–191 and 2:376. The first volume of Schopenhauer's work was published in 1819; the second volume, an elaboration of themes set forth in the first, followed in 1844. Chapter 31 of the second volume is entitled "On Genius."

39. On Staël, see the detailed analysis in Kathleen Kete, *Making Way for Genius: The Aspiring Self in France from the Old Regime to the New* (New Haven, CT: Yale University Press, 2012), chap. 2; Isaac Disraeli, *The Literary Character of Men of Genius Drawn from Their Own Feelings and Confessions*, new ed., ed. Benjamin Disraeli (London: Frederick Warne, 1850 [1818]), 50. For Carlyle quotations, see his *On Heroes, Hero-Worship*, 188–195.

40. Beethoven is cited in Leo Braudy, *The Frenzy of Renown: Fame and Its History* (New York: Oxford University Press, 1986), 426. On genius and the literary press, see David Higgin's careful study, *Romantic Genius and the Literary Magazine: Biography, Celebrity, and Politics* (Milton Park, UK: Routledge, 2005). On Byron and the travails of celebrity, see the lively account in Fred Inglis, *A Short History of Celebrity* (Princeton, NJ: Princeton University Press, 2010), 62–70. See also George Gordon, Lord Byron, "Detached Thoughts," *The Works of Lord Byron, in Verse and Prose*, ed. Fitz Green Halleck (Hartford, CT: Silas Andrus, 1846), 270.

41. The reference to "multitudes" is an allusion to Walt Whitman's celebrated poem "Song of Myself," which contains the line "I am large, I contain multitudes" (section 51); Thomas Carlyle, "Count Cagliostro: In Two Flights," *Historical Essays*, ed. Chris R. Vanden Bossche (Berkeley: University of California Press, 2002), 35; Schopenhauer, *World as Will*, 1:191; Felluga, *Perversity of Poetry*, 13–32; George Becker, *The Mad Genius Controversy: A Study in the Sociology of Deviance* (London: Sage, 1978), 21–75. On the medical and psychological investigation of the alleged links between genius and madness, see chap. 5 below.

42. As George Becker rightly observes, "the semireligious quality surrounding the notion of genius constitutes a cornerstone in the association of genius with madness" (Becker, *Mad Genius*, 21).

43. Charles Baudelaire, "Sur Le Tasse en prison d'Eugène Delacroix," first published in *Les épaves* in 1866 and available on line at http://fleursdumal.org /poem/318. Baudelaire was a great admirer of Delacroix's work, and of this painting in particular. See Rebecca M. Pauly, "Baudelaire and Delacroix on Tasso in Prison: Romantic Reflections on a Renaissance Martyr," *College literature* 30, no. 2 (2003): 120–136; Giacomo Leopardi, "Dialogo di Torquato Tasso e del suo genio familiare," *Operette Morali: Essays and Dialogues*, trans. and intro. Giovanni Cecchetti (Berkeley: University of California Press, 1982), 166–183.

44. Jean Paul actually employed two terms, *Doppeltgänger* and *Doppelgänger*, in his novel *Siebenkäs*, using the first in the sense that we now reserve for the

second, and thus giving the word, as it were, its own double. See Paul Fleming, "Doppelgänger/Doppeltgänger," *Cabinet* 14 (2004); Percy Bysshe Shelley's *Prometheus Unbound*, in *Shelley's Poetry and Prose*, 215. On the Shelleys' collaboration on *Frankenstein* and other texts, see Mary Shelley (with Percy Bysshe Shelley), *The Original Frankenstein*, ed. and intro. Charles E. Robinson (New York: Vintage, 2009).

45. Marie Hélène Huet, *Monstrous Imagination* (Cambridge, MA: Harvard University Press, 1993), esp. 132; John Hope Mason, *The Value of Creativity: The Origins and Emergence of a Modern Belief* (Burlington, VT: Ashgate, 2003), 1–4; Mary Wollstonecraft Shelley, *Frankenstein, or the Modern Prometheus*, ed. Susan J. Wolfson (New York: Longman, 2007), 201–202 (these phrases were added to the revised edition of 1831) and 32.

46. Carl Grosse, *Der Genius*, afterword Günter Dammann (Frankfurt: M. Zweitausendeins, 1982).

47. Samuel Taylor Coleridge, *Biographia Literaria, or Biographical Sketches of My Literary Life and Opinions*, eds. James Engell and W. Jackson Bates (Princeton, NJ: Princeton University Press, 1983), 32–33; Coleridge's *Lay Sermons*, as cited in Simon Bainbridge, *Napoleon and English Romanticism* (Cambridge: Cambridge University Press, 1995), 32. Bainbridge is good on Coleridge's complicated and shifting views of Napoleon. Hugo and Chateaubriand are cited in Jean-Baptiste Decherf's original and insightful "Napoleon and the Poets: The Poetic Origins of the Concept of Charisma," *Studies in Ethnicity and Nationalism* 10, no 3 (2010): 362–376. Coleridge is cited in Bainbridge, *Napoleon and English Romanticism*, 24–26.

48. Christine Battersby, *Gender and Genius: Towards a Feminist Aesthetics* (Bloomington: Indiana University Press, 1989), 6–10, 18, 86–92; Andrew Elfenbein, *Romantic Genius: The Prehistory of a Homosexual Role* (New York: Columbia University Press, 1999), 1–7, 27–35; Lucy Delap, *The Feminist Avant-Garde: Transatlantic Encounters of the Early Twentieth Century* (Cambridge: Cambridge University Press, 2007), 249–292.

49. On the association between genius, originality, and eccentricity, see Miranda Gill, *Eccentricity and the Cultural Imagination in Nineteenth-Century Paris* (Oxford: Oxford University Press, 2009). The theme of genius and obsession is treated nicely in Lennard J. Davis's engaging *Obsession: A History* (Chicago: University of Chicago Press, 2008). On the "aesthetic rewriting of crime" as a privilege of great men, and the birth of a "literature in which crime is glorified, because it is one of the fine arts," see Foucault, *Discipline and Punish*, 68–69. For Sir Arthur Conan Doyle's "The Final Problem" (1893), see *The Complete Sherlock Holmes*, intro. Loren D. Estleman (New York: Bantam Classics, 1986), 471.

50. The citation from Goethe is often attributed to him, both in English and in German, including by reputable sources, but I have been unable to find its origin and suspect that it may be apocryphal. For the Emerson quotation, see Ralph Waldo Emerson, "Experience," in *Essays and Lectures*, ed. Joel Port (New York: Library of America, 2009), 488–489.

51. Hegel, *Lectures on the Philosophy of World History*, 89.

52. Shelley's lyric drama *Prometheus Unbound* was first published in 1820. Shelley is cited from "A Defence of Poetry," 526. Shelley adds, in reference to Milton's refusal "to have alleged no superiority of moral virtue to his God over his Devil," that this "bold neglect of a direct moral purpose is the most decisive proof of the superiority of Milton's genius" (527). For the Byron quotation, see his "Ode to Napoleon Buonaparte," 1.6. On the fallen Napoleon as a figure of pity and fascination even in his nemesis, Britain, see Stuart Semmel, *Napoleon and the British* (New Haven, CT: Yale University Press, 2004), chap. 8 ("Fallen Greatness"). Byron, like Napoleon, was frequently described as a "satanic hero," or, as one of his contemporaries, Sir Samuel Egerton Brydges, noted in 1837, "a great genius . . . [who] had a good deal of the devil in him." See Higgins, *Romantic Genius*, 35; Felluga, *Perversity of Poetry*, 81–87.

53. Johann Wolfgang von Goethe, *The Autobiography of Goethe: Truth and Poetry from My Own Life*, trans. John Oxenford, 2 vols. (London: George Bell and Sons, 1897–1900), 2:157.

54. On Hamann's and Herder's interpretations of Socrates's *daimonion* and their influence on Goethe, see Angus Nicholls, *Goethe's Conception of the Daemonic: After the Ancients* (New York: Boydell and Brewster, 2006), 77–106.

55. Goethe, *Conversations with Eckermann*, 317–318 (March 2, 1831), 319 (March 8, 1831), and 199–205 (March 11, 1828). See also the discussions of December 6, 1829, and March 2, 1831.

56. Ibid., 203 (March 11, 1831). On genius as a key concept of German culture, see the insightful discussion of Hans-Georg Gadamer in *Truth and Method*, rev. ed., trans. Joel Weinsheimer and Donald G. Marshall (London: Continuum, 1989), esp. 52. Strangely, the importance of the idea of genius in German idealist philosophy has been underappreciated. See, however, Hans Stauffacher, "Von 'der seltenen Erscheinung' zum 'ganz allgemeinen Ausdruck': Die Systemstelle des Genies im Deutschen Idealismus," *Philotheos* 10 (2010): 195–204.

57. Thomas Carlyle, *Sartor Resartus*, eds. and intro. Kerry McSweeney and Peter Sabor (Oxford: Oxford University Press, 1991), 135; David Friedrich Strauss, "Über Vergängliches und Bleibendes im Christentum" (1838), in *Zwei friedliche Blätter* (Altona, Germany: J. F. Hammerich, 1839), 101. Elsewhere, Strauss described this phenomenon as a "new paganism" or "new Catholicism" in Protestant Germany, noting that "one incarnation of God is now not sufficient, and there has arisen a desire for a series of ever more complete avatars such are found in Indian religion. . . . This is a mark of the time, to venerate the spirit of God in all the spirits who have affected humanity in a vital and creative way." Cited in Marilyn Chapin Massey, *Christ Unmasked: The Meaning of the Life of Jesus in German Politics* (Chapel Hill: University of North Carolina Press, 1983), 118. On the Schiller statue, see the account in George Williamson's fine *The Longing for Myth in Germany: Religion and Aesthetic Culture from Romanticism to Nietzsche* (Chicago: University Chicago Press, 2004), 175.

58. Goethe, *Conversations with Eckermann*, 200 (March 8, 1831); William Jackson, "The Bard," in *The Four Ages; Together with Essays on Various Subjects* (London: Cadell and Davis, 1798), 216. See, in addition, Jackson's essay "Whether

Genius Be Born or Acquired" (188–202). For William Duff's quotation, see his *An Essay on Original Genius and Its Various Modes of Exertion in Philosophy and the Fine Arts, Particularly in Poetry*, ed. John L. Mahoney (Gainesville, FL: Scholars' Facsimiles and Reprints, 1964), xviii, 186–187.

CHAPTER 5

1. For an astute analysis of the development of the myth of Van Gogh as a neglected and misunderstood genius, see Nathalie Heinich, *The Glory of Van Gogh: An Anthropology of Admiration*, trans. Paul Leduc Browne (Princeton, NJ: Princeton University Press, 1996).

2. See the discussion of the difficulties of establishing Newton's likeness in the eighteenth century in Patricia Fara, *Newton: The Making of Genius* (New York: Columbia University Press, 2004), 30–59. The artistic depiction of the genius figure deserves further treatment. For the eighteenth century, see Desmond Shawe-Taylor, *Genial Company: The Theme of Genius in Eighteenth-Century British Portraiture* (Nottingham, UK: Nottingham University Art Gallery, 1987). For the nineteenth century, see Susan P. Casteras, "Excluding Women: The Cult of the Male Genius in Victorian Painting," in *Rewriting the Victorians: Theory, History, and the Politics of Gender*, ed. Linda M. Shires (New York: Routledge, 1992), 116–146; Brandon Brame Fortune, "Portraits of Virtue and Genius: Pantheons of Worthies and Public Portraiture in the Early American Republic, 1780–1820" (PhD diss., University of North Carolina, Chapel Hill, 1986).

3. Johann Caspar Lavater, *Physiognomische Fragmente, zur Berförderung der Menschenkenntnis und Menschenliebe*, 4 vols. (Leipzig und Winterthur, 1775–1778), 4:81–83.

4. Johann Caspar Lavater, *Essays on Physiognomy, Designed to Promote the Knowledge and the Love of Mankind*, trans. Henry Hunter, 3 vols. (London: John Murray, 1789), 1:14. When the translations are passable, I have made use of contemporary English editions of Lavater's writings, reverting to the original when they are not. See Lavater, *Physiognomische Fragmente*, 4:80, 86–89, 91, 84–85. Lavater first offers his own variation on the theme: "Was ist Genie? Wer's nicht ist, kann nicht; und wer's ist, wird nicht antworten," and then proceeds to cite Rousseau, in French, in a note: "'Ne cherchez point, jeune artiste, ce que c'est le Genie. En as-tu: tu le sens en toi-même. N'en tu pas: tu ne le connoitras jamais' (Rousseau, Dict. de Musique)."

5. Lavater, *Essays on Physiognomy*, 3:249–251, 1:218, 2:390. The lines regarding Rubens may be found in *The Whole Works of Lavater on Physiognomy*, trans. George Grenville, 4 vols. (London: W. Butters, [1800]), 4:199.

6. Lavater, *Essays on Physiognomy*, 2:390. On the similarity of Lavater's methods with that of later scientists, see Michael Hagner, "Skulls, Brains, and Memorial Culture: On Cerebral Biographies of Scientists in the Nineteenth Century," *Science in Context* 16 (2003): 195–218 (esp. 199).

7. On Gall's foundational role, see Michael Hagner, *Geniale Gehirne: Zur Geschichte der Elitegehirnforschung* (Munich: Deutscher Taschenbuch, 2007), esp. 53–80.

8. S. Zola Morgan, "Localization of Brain Function: The Legacy of Franz Joseph Gall (1758–1828)," *Annual Review of Neuroscience* 18 (1995): 359–383; John Carson, *Measures of Merit: Talents, Intelligence, and Inequality in the French and American Republics, 1750–1940* (Princeton, NJ: Princeton University Press, 2007), 85; Stephen Jay Gould, *The Mismeasure of Man*, rev. and expanded ed. (New York: W. W. Norton, 1996), esp. 21–23, 268–269.

9. Franz Joseph Gall, "Des Herrn Dr. F. J. Gall Schreiben über seinen bereits geendigten Prodromus über die Verrichtungen des Gehirns der Menschen und Thiere an Herrn Jos. Fr. von Retzer" (1798), in *Franz Joseph Gall: Naturforscher und Anthropolog*, ed. Erna Lesky (Bern: Huber, 1979), 47–59 (citation on 55).

10. Hagner, *Geniale Gehirne*, 61.

11. Gall and Spurzheim are cited in Hagner, "Skulls, Brains, and Memorial Culture," 199–201.

12. Colin Dickey, *Cranioklepty: Grave Robbing and the Search for Genius* (Cave Creek, AZ: Unbridled Books, 2010); Keith Thompson, "For Sale: Beethoven's Skull," *Huffington Post*, January 18, 2010.

13. The trade in relics was not confined to that of geniuses, but included monarchs, stars, and other celebrities. See Eva Giloi, *Monarchy, Myth, and Material Culture, 1750–1950* (Cambridge: Cambridge University Press, 2010); Stuart Semmel, *Napoleon and the British* (New Haven, CT: Yale University Press, 2004), 226; Stanley M. Bierman, "The Peripatetic Posthumous Peregrination of Napoleon's Penis," *Journal of Sex Research* 29, no. 4 (1992): 579–580. See, as well, the account in Robert B. Asprey, *The Rise and Fall of Napoleon Bonaparte*, 2 vols. (London: Abacus, 2001), 2:440–443. The alleged penis was, until recently, in the collection of the Columbia University urologist John K. Latimer, who died in 2007. On the fascination with the relics of geniuses in the first decades of the twentieth century, see my article "Relikwieen van genieën [Relics of Genius]," trans. Jan Willem Reitsma, *Nexus* 52 (2009): 149–161.

14. On Schiller's skull, see the account in Hagner, *Geniale Gehirne*, 69–75. The skull was reunited with the body after a year, in the Duke of Weimar's family tomb.

15. G. W. F. Hegel, *Phenomenology of Spirit*, trans. A. V. Miller, foreword J. N. Findlay (Oxford: Oxford University Press, 1977), 197. Hegel's lengthy discussion of phrenology and physiognomy is found in section C.V.c, "Observations of self-consciousness in relation to its immediate actuality. Physiognomy and Phrenology."

16. Brain weights are taken from the figures reported, and critically analyzed, in Gould, *Mismeasure of Man*, 120–128. For a recent, critical take on some of Gould's findings, see Jason E. Lewis et al., "The Mismeasure of Science: Stephen Jay Gould Versus Samuel George Morton on Skulls and Bias," *PLoS Biol* 9, no. 6 (2011). On the Society of Mutual Autopsy, see Jennifer Michael Hecht, *The End of the Soul: Scientific Modernity, Atheism, and Anthropology in France* (New York: Columbia University Press, 2005), 6–7, 41. On Spitzka, see Ann Fabian, *The Skull Collectors: Race, Science, and America's Unburied Dead* (Chicago: Chicago University Press, 2010). On brain museums and brain collecting more generally, see

Brian Burrell, *Postcards from the Brain Museum: The Improbable Search for Meaning in the Matter of Famous Minds* (New York: Broadway Books, 2004).

17. Broca is cited in Gould, *Mismeasure of Man*, 115. For E. A. Spitzka, see "A Study of the Brain of the Late Major J. W. Powell," *American Anthropology* 5 (1903): 585–643 (citation on 604).

18. The French scientist is cited in Hecht, *End of the Soul*, 226.

19. Among Lélut's many works attacking phrenology, see his *Qu'est-ce que la phrénologie? ou Essai sur la signification et la valuer des systèmes de la psychologie en général, et celui de Gall en particulier* (Paris: Trinquart, 1836), and *Rejet de l'organologie phrénologique de Gall et de ses successeurs* (Paris: Fortin-Masson, 1843).

20. L. F. Lélut, *Du démon de Socrates, specimin d'une application de la science psychologique à celle de l'histoire* (Paris: Trinquart, 1836).

21. Lélut, *Démon de Socrates*, 17.

22. See Baudelaire's "Assommons les pauvres!" in *Le spleen de Paris*. The poem, written in the mid-1860s, reflects the prominent position that Lélut had by that point acquired. L. F. Lélut, *L'amulette de Pascal pour servir à l'histoire des hallucinations* (Paris: J. B. Baillière, 1846); L. F. Lélut, *Du démon de Socrate, spécimen d'une application de la science psychologique à celle de l'histoire. Nouvelle édition revue, corrigée et augmentée d'une préface* (Paris: Chez J. B. Baillière, 1856); Jacques-Joseph Moreau, *La psychologie morbide dans ses rapports avec la philosophie de l'histoire, ou De l'influence des névropathies sur le dynamisme intellectuel* (Paris: Victor Masson, 1859), xi–xii.

23. Moreau pays homage to Lélut and his work in several places in *Psychologie morbide*, notably on xi–xii, 7, 25–26, and 474; see also 20–24.

24. Moreau, *Du Hachisch et de l'aliénation mentale: Études psychologiques* (Paris: Librairie de Fortin, Masson, 1845).

25. Moreau, *Psychologie morbide*, 18, 463.

26. On Napoleon, see Moreau, *Psychologie morbide*, 559. Moreau relies here on the work of the doctor and psychologist Alexandre Brière de Boismont, whose *Des hallucinations, ou Histoire raisonnée des apparitions, des visions, des songes, de l'extase, du magnétisme et du somnambulisme* (Paris: G. Baillière, 1845) discusses the case of Napoleon's belief in his star. The story was widely repeated by those alleging a close relation between madness and genius. The physiological account of inspiration is provided in *Psychologie morbide*, 494–495. The passage is actually taken from that of the French doctor Joseph-Henri Réveillé-Parise's *Physiologie et hygiène des hommes livrés aux travaux de l'esprit* (Paris, 1834), although that is not immediately clear from the way Moreau cites the work.

27. Moreau provides a long passage from Diderot's article "On Theosophy," from the *Encyclopédie* in *Psychologie morbide*, 567; see also 496–497.

28. On the scientific appropriation of the Romantic construction of mad genius, see George Becker, *The Mad Genius Controversy: A Study in the Sociology of Deviance* (Beverly Hills, CA: Sage, 1978); Ernst Kretschmer, *The Psychology of Men of Genius*, trans. and intro. R. B. Cattell (New York: Harcourt Brace, 1931). The original German *Geniale Menschen* appeared in 1929.

29. Émile Zola, *Dr. Pascal*, trans. Mary J. Serrano (New York: Macmillan, 1898), 121–122. The German psychologist William Hirsch went so far as to call Zola a "Max Nordau in the form of a novelist." See his *Genius and Degeneration, a Psychological Study*, trans. from the 2nd ed. of the German work (London: W. Heinemann, 1897), 322. On the analysis of Zola, see the nice account in Daniel Pick's astute *Faces of Degeneration: A European Disorder, c. 1848–1918* (Cambridge: Cambridge University Press, 1993), 74–97.

30. Cesare Lombroso, *The Man of Genius*, rev. ed. (London: Walter Scott, 1917), 137, 5–9.

31. Ibid., 8, 151, 6–7. The diagram is provided on p. 125.

32. Ibid., 122–130, 112. On Lombroso's high regard for quantification, see David G. Horn, *The Criminal Body: Lombroso and the Anatomy of Deviance* (London: Routledge, 2003), 8.

33. See, for example, William James's unsigned reviews of a German translation of Lombroso's *Genius and Degeneration* and Max Nordau's *Degeneration* in *Psychological Review* 2, no. 3 (1895): 288–290. Caroline J. Essex emphasizes that Great Britain was, on the whole, an exception to the thesis put forth by George Becker in his *Mad Genius Controversy*, which argues for a widespread link between genius and madness in the nineteenth- and early twentieth-century psychological literature. See her "In Pursuit of Genius: Tracing the History of a Concept in English Writing, from the Late Enlightenment to the Dawn of the Twentieth Century" (PhD diss., University College London, 2002), chap. 4.

34. Pick, *Faces of Degeneration*, 2; Irina Sirotkina, *Diagnosing Literary Genius: A Cultural History of Psychiatry in Russia, 1880–1930* (Baltimore: Johns Hopkins University Press, 2002).

35. On the discourse of monstrosity, see Miranda Gill, *Eccentricity and the Cultural Imagination in Nineteenth-Century Paris* (Oxford: Oxford University Press, 2009), 207–239.

36. J. Sully, "Genius and Insanity," *Nineteenth Century* 17 (1885): 948–969 (citation on 952); Lombroso, *Man of Genius*, 145, 334, 361; Henry T. F. Rhodes, *Genius and Criminal: A Study in Rebellion* (London: John Murray, 1932), 59–61. Rhodes was an admirer of Lombroso.

37. Francis Galton, *Memories of My Life* (London: Metheun, 1908), 249–250. Galton initially organized the anthropometric laboratory for the International Exhibition of 1884 and then moved it to a room in the Science Galleries of the South Kensington Museum for six years. On Galton's use of composite portraits in isolating the faces of criminals, see Lorraine Daston and Peter Galison, *Objectivity* (New York: Zone Books, 2007), 168–171; Francis Galton, *Hereditary Genius: An Inquiry into Its Laws and Consequences* (New York: Prometheus Books, 2006).

38. Galton, *Hereditary Genius*, 9, 307, 13.

39. Ibid., 34.

40. Ibid., 28–29, 12. Galton arrived at the ratio of one to a million by comparison with other classes of exceptional human beings. So-called "men of the times" appeared at the rate of roughly 425 to 1 million, while "men of eminence" were

250 to 1 million. But he wasn't always so exact, speaking variously of genius as "one in a million," "one in many millions" or "one in ten millions" (ibid., 18, 41).

41. Galton, *Hereditary Genius*, 11, 39–40.

42. On historimetrics, see Dean Keith Simonton, *Genius, Creativity, and Leadership: Historimetric Inquiries* (Cambridge, MA: Harvard University Press, 1984).

43. Raymond E. Fancher, "Alphonse de Candolle, Francis Galton and the Early History of the Nature-Nurture Debate," *Journal of the History of the Behavioral Sciences* 19, no. 4 (1983): 341–352; Emel Aileen Gökyight, "The Reception of Francis Galton's *Hereditary Genius* in the Victorian Periodical Press," *Journal of the History of Biology* 27, no. 2 (1994): 215–240; Charles Darwin, *The Variation of Animals and Plants Under Domestication*, 2nd ed., 2 vols. (London: John Murray, 1875), 1:451. Darwin expresses similar sentiments in his *Autobiography* and *The Descent of Man*.

44. Samuel Smiles, *Life and Labour or Characteristics of Men of Industry, Culture, and Genius* (London: John Murray, 1907), 75. Smiles's discussion of genius as "intense energy," "inspired instinct," an "inspiration, a gift, an afflatus," which "brings dead things to life" and "begins where rules end" provides a nice summary of reigning assumptions (75–77).

45. Galton, *Hereditary Genius*, 61. See Galton's discussion of the many bizarre tests administered in his anthropometric laboratory in *Memories of My Life*, chap. 17.

46. In addition to the excellent scholarly accounts provided in Gould, *Mismeasure of Man*, and Carson, *Measure of Merit*, see Raymond E. Fancher, *The Intelligence Men: Makers of the IQ Controversy* (New York: W. W. Norton, 1985), and Steven Murdoch, *IQ: A Smart History of a Failed Idea* (Hoboken, NJ: Wiley, 2007).

47. Binet is cited in Carson, *Measure of Merit*, 137. Carson provides a general account of Binet's methods and interest in great calculators like Inaudi (*Measure of Merit*, 131–137).

48. Alfred Binet, "Historique des recherches sur les rapports de l'intelligence avec la grandeur et la forme de la tête," *L'année psychologique* 5 (1895): 245–298. Vaschide is cited in Carson, *Measure of Merit*, 133.

49. Lewis M. Terman, ed., *Genetic Studies of Genius*, 5 vols. (Palo Alto, CA: Stanford University Press, 1925–1959), 1:1–2; Lewis M. Terman, *The Measurement of Intelligence: An Explanation of and a Complete Guide for the Use of the Stanford Revision and Extension of the Binet-Simon Intelligence Scale* (New York: Houghton Mifflin, 1916), 12. The *Measurement of Intelligence* was dedicated to the memory of Binet.

50. Terman, ed., *Genetic Studies of Genius*, 1:vii, 1.

51. Ibid., v.

52. Kurt Danziger, *Naming the Mind: How Psychology Found Its Language* (London: Sage, 1997), 66–83. My account of the changing fortunes of intelligence draws heavily on Carson's excellent discussion in *Measure of Merit*, esp. chap. 3.

53. Gretchen Kreuter, "The Vanishing Genius: Lewis Terman and the Stanford Study," *History of Education Quarterly* 2, no. 1 (1962): 6–18 (citation on 15); Terman, ed., *Genetic Studies of Genius*, 4:352.

54. Fancher, *Intelligence Men*, 95.

55. Terman, ed., *Genetic Studies of Genius*, 1:111, 82, 54.

56. Terman, "The Intelligence Quotient of Francis Galton in Childhood," *American Journal of Psychology* 28 (1917): 209–215.

57. Terman, ed., *Genetic Studies of Genius*, 2:47–87. The IQ estimates of the three hundred geniuses are summarized in Table 12A, "Individual IQ Ratings of Young Geniuses."

58. Hans Eysenck, *Genius: The Natural History of Creativity* (Cambridge: Cambridge University Press, 1995), 53. On the laughable speculations of the Cox study, see the amusing account in Gould, *Mismeasure of Man*, 214–218. For Cox's comments, see Terman, ed., *Genetic Studies of Genius*, 2:3.

59. All citations here and below from Blavatsky are taken from H. P. Blavatsky, "Genius," *Lucifer* 5, no. 28 (1889): 227–233.

60. On the prevalence and centrality of spiritualism to modern culture and the endurance of beliefs in spiritual guardians, see Alex Owen, *British Occultism and the Culture of the Modern* (Chicago: University of Chicago Press, 2004); Corinna Treitel, *A Science for the Soul: Occultism and the Genesis of the German Modern* (Baltimore: Johns Hopkins University Press, 2004); Marco Pasi, "Anges gardiens et esprits familiers dans le spiritisme et dans l'occultisme," in Jean-Patrice Boudet, Philippe Faure, and Christian Renoux, eds., *De Socrate à Tintin: Anges gardiens et démons familiers de l'Antiquité à nos jours* (Rennes: Presses Universitaires de Rennes, 2011), 249–267. On Hugo, see John Warne Monroe, *Laboratories of Faith: Mesmerism, Spiritism, and Occultism in Modern France* (Ithaca, NY: Cornell University Press, 2008), 50–52. I am grateful to Professor Monroe for bringing this episode to my attention.

61. On the question of the modernity of occult practices, see the insightful essay of Thomas Laqueur, "Why the Margins Matter: Occultism and the Making of Modernity," *Modern Intellectual History* 3 (2006): 111–135.

62. Terman, ed., *Genetic Studies of Genius*, 1:v. To point out the similarities between the mystifying effects of nineteenth-century science and those of theosophists and practitioners of the occult is by no means to equate the two, as if the assertions of a Blavatsky were of a kind with those of a Broca. Nor is it to deny that there are essential differences between the fantasies of a Lavater or Lombroso and that of a Terman or Galton. Those who would deny these differences altogether, dismissing the possibility of objective scientific truths, have only themselves to blame when politicians deny the existence of global warming or demand that our schoolchildren be taught that the earth was created in six days and nothing more. And yet it will not do to whitewash the science, as one reputable scientist has done, complaining of the subjectivity of philosophers and historians while writing a "natural history" of genius that leaves out all of the embarrassing bits (see Hans Eysenck, *Genius: The Natural History of Creativity*, 4).

If I have dwelled on those embarrassments here, it is to emphasize how deeply the science of genius was implicated in the "mismeasure of men."

63. Friedrich Nietzsche, *The Twilight of the Idols*, section 44, in *The Portable Nietzsche*, ed. and trans. Walter Kaufmann (New York: Penguin, 1982), 547.

CHAPTER 6

1. Søren Kierkegaard, *The Present Age and Of the Difference Between a Genius and an Apostle*, trans. Alexander Dru, intro. Walter Kaufmann (New York: Harper and Row, 1962), 89–90. "Of the Difference Between a Genius and an Apostle" was written in 1847. It was first published in 1849, along with "The Present Age," in *Two Minor Ethical-Religious Essays*, under the pseudonym "H. H."

2. Bautain is cited in James C. Livingston and Francis Schüssler Fiorenza, eds., *Modern Christian Thought*, vol. 1, *The Enlightenment and the Nineteenth Century*, 2nd ed. (New York: Prentice Hall, 2006), 156. For illustrative examples of the discussion of Jesus as a genius, see Charles Binet-Sanglé, *La folie de Jésus*, 4 vols. (Paris: Maloine, 1908–1915); Constantin Brunner, *Unser Christus: Oder das Wesen des Genies* (Berlin: Oesterheld, 1921); J. Middleton Murry, *Jesus: Man of Genius* (New York: Harper and Brothers, 1926). See also Friedrich Nietzsche, *The Anti-Christ*, section 29, in *The Portable Nietzsche*, ed. and trans. Walter Kaufmann (New York: Penguin, 1982), 600–601. For Renan's account, see *La vie de Jésus* (1863), esp. chap. 28, "Caractère essential de l'oeuvre de Jésus."

3. Kierkegaard, "On the Difference Between a Genius and an Apostle," in Kierkegaard, *The Present Age and Of the Difference Between a Genius and an Apostle*, 96–101.

4. On the Kierkegaard renaissance in the early twentieth century, especially in Weimar Germany, see Dustin Feddon, "Apostles, Prophets, Geniuses: The Tragic Romantic Politics of the Extraordinary Individual in Søren Kierkegaard's Production and Weimar Reception" (PhD diss., Florida State University, 2013). For an introduction to the now substantial literature on "political religions," see Emilio Gentile, *Politics as Religion*, trans. George Staunton (Princeton, NJ: Princeton University Press, 2006). On the related subject of "political theology," see Mark Lilla, *The Stillborn God: Religion, Politics, and the Modern West* (New York: Knopf, 2007).

5. Edgar Zilsel, *Die Geniereligion: Ein kritischer Versuch über das moderne Persönlichkeitsideal*, intro. Johann Dvorak (Frankfurt: Suhrkamp, 1990), 51–53.

6. Edgar Zilsel, *Die Entstehung des Geniebegriffes: Ein Beitrag zur Ideengeschichte der Antike und des Frühkapitalismus,* intro. Heinz Maus (Hildesheim, Germany: Georg Olms, 1972), first published in 1926; Robert Currie, *Genius: An Ideology in Literature* (New York: Schocken Books, 1974). On the theme of *Erlösungskraft*, see the comments of a contemporary critic, the Swiss scholar Jacob Cahan, in his published doctoral dissertation, *Zur Kritik des Genebegriffs* (Bern: Universität Bern, 1911), 32. See also Hermann Türck, *Der geniale Mensch*, 4th ed. (Berlin: Dümmlers Verlagsbuchhandlung, 1896/1899), 271, 275. The material comparing Napoleon and Jesus, in Chapter 9, "Das Weltliche Ubermenschentum

Alexanders, Cäsars, Napoleons," first appeared in the 3rd ed., published in 1898. The work went through at least fourteen German editions by 1931. In his depiction of Napoleon, Türck draws heavily on the influential writings of Karl Bleibtreu, author of numerous hagiographic accounts, including the revealingly entitled *Die Genie-Kaiser und die Welt* (1905).

7. Thomas Carlyle, *On Heroes, Hero-Worship and the Heroic in History*, ed. and intro. Carl Niemeyer (Lincoln: University of Nebraska Press, 1966), 155–157; Ralph Waldo Emerson, "The Over-Soul," in *Essays and Lectures*, ed. Joel Port (New York: Library of America, 2009), 396; see also "The Method of Nature" and "Literary Ethics" in the same volume, esp. 123 and 109, respectively. On Emerson's complicated understanding of genius, see Richard Poirier, "The Question of Genius," *Raritan* 4 (1986): 77–104.

8. Zilsel, *Geniereligion*, 129–130, 214. On the use of the phrase "great geniuses reveal us to ourselves," a truism since Shaftesbury, see Benedetto Croce, "Intuition in Art," in *The Aesthetic as the Science of Expression and of the Linguistic in General*, trans. Colin Lyas (Cambridge: Cambridge University Press, 1992), 15. See also Emerson's reflections on genius in his essays "Self Reliance" and "Literary Ethics." On the theme of the relationship between the genius and the people, see Kerry Charles Larson, "Betrayers and the Betrayed: The Cult of Genius in the Age of Emerson" (Phd diss., Johns Hopkins University, 1983); John Stuart Mill, *On Liberty*, eds. David Bromwich and George Kateb (New Haven, CT: Yale University Press, 2003), 129–130.

9. Bob Perelman, *The Trouble with Genius: Reading Pound, Joyce, Stein, and Zukofsky* (Berkeley: University of California Press, 1994). See also Barbara Will, *Gertrude Stein and the Problem of 'Genius'* (Edinburgh: University of Edinburgh Press, 2000).

10. Zilsel, *Geniereligion*, 59–61, 77–78; Arthur Rimbaud, "Adieu," *Un saison en enfer* (1873); Henry Maudsley, *Heredity, Variation, and Genius, with an Essay on Shakespeare* (London: John Bale, Sons, and Danielson, 1908), 75.

11. Zilsel, *Geniereligion*, 89–99.

12. For Nietzsche on religion, see John Hope Mason, *The Value of Creativity: The Origins and Emergence of a Modern Belief* (Burlington, VT: Ashgate, 2003), 213; Michael Tanner, "Nietzsche on Genius," in Penelope Murray, ed., *Genius: The History of an Idea* (Oxford: Blackwell, 1989), 128–140. For Nietzsche on creativity, see Mason, *Value of Creativity*, 209–227; Nietzsche, "On Old and New Tablets," *Thus Spoke Zarathustra*, trans. and intro. Walter Kauffman (New York: Penguin, 1978), 196.

13. Nietzsche, *Human, All Too Human: A Book for Free Spirits*, trans. R. J. Hollingdale, intro. Richard Schacht (Cambridge: Cambridge University Press, 1996), 115 (section 241), and, more generally, sections 157–165; Nietzsche, "Why I Am a Destiny," *Ecce Homo*, trans. R. J. Hollingdale, intro. Michael Tanner (London: Penguin, 1992), 96. On Nietzsche's reception, see Steven E. Aschheim, *The Nietzsche Legacy in Germany, 1890–1990* (Berkeley: University of California Press, 1992).

14. Robert Schumann, *On Music and Musicians,* trans. Paul Rosenfeld, ed. Konrad Wolff (New York: McGraw-Hill, 1964), 64; Celia Applegate and Pamela Potters, eds., *Music and National Identity* (Chicago: University of Chicago Press, 2002); Max Nordau, "The Richard Wagner Cult," in *Degeneration,* trans. from the 2nd ed. of the German work (New York: D. Appleton, 1895), 171–214; Houston Stewart Chamberlain, *The Foundations of the Nineteenth Century,* trans. John Lees, intro. Lord Redesdale, 2 vols. (New York: John Lane, 1912), 1:167–168, 83, 234, xc. On the *Foundations* and Chamberlain's thought and career more generally, see Geoffrey C. Field, *Evangelist of Race: The Germanic Vision of Houston Stewart Chamberlain* (New York: Columbia University Press, 1981).

15. Otto Weininger, *Geschlecht und Charakter: Eine prinzipielle Untersuchung* (Vienna: Wilhelm Braumüller, 1920), 130.

16. Zilsel, *Geniereligion,* 52; Egon Friedell, *A Cultural History of the Modern Age,* trans. Charles Francis Atkinson, 3 vols. (New York: Knopf, 1931), 1:25–27, 65, 169, 229.

17. Croce, "Intuition and Art," 15–16; José Ortega y Gasset, "Ideas sobre la novela" (1925), in *Obras completas,* 12 vols. (Madrid: Alianza, 1983), 3:388; Wilhelm Lange-Eichbaum, *The Problem of Genius,* trans. Eden and Cedar Paul (New York: Macmillan, 1932), xvii–xviii. The original German edition was published in 1931. See, as well, Albert Solomon, "Zur Soziologie des Geniebegriffs," *Die Gesellschaft: Internationale Revue für Sozialismus und Politik* 3, no. 2 (1926): 504–513.

18. The Soviet commission is cited in Jochen Richter, "Pantheon of Brains: The Moscow Brain Research Institute, 1925–1936," *Journal of the History of Neuroscience* 16 (2007): 138–149 (citation on 140). On the Vogts, see Igor Klatzo and Gabriele Zu Rhein, *Cécile and Oskar Vogt: The Visionaries of Modern Neuroscience* (New York: Springer, 2002).

19. Richter, "Pantheon of Brains," 140. On Vogt's Russian episode and the analysis of Lenin's brain, see the detailed account in Michael Hagner, *Geniale Gehirne: Zur Geschichte der Elitegehirnforschung* (Munich: Deutscher Taschenbuch, 2007), 249–264.

20. Charles Fourier, *The Theory of the Four Movements,* trans. Ian Patterson, eds. Gareth Stedman Jones and Ian Patterson (Cambridge: Cambridge University Press, 1996), 87; Irina Sirotkina, *Diagnosing Literary Genius: A Cultural History of Psychiatry in Russia, 1880–1930* (Baltimore: Johns Hopkins University Press, 2002), 71–73. Already in his 1872 novel *The Possessed,* Fyodor Dostoyevsky saw fit to ridicule the widespread pretension among the leftist intelligentsia that higher men could be bred, placing chilling lines in the mouth of the nihilist Kirilov, who declares that with the coming death of God, "there will be a new life, a new man, everything will be new. Man will be God. He'll be physically transformed." Equally chilling are the lines of the raving Verkhovensky, who observes that in a reign of absolute equality, "men of the highest ability" will have to be "either banished or executed," because they cannot help being despots: "A Cicero will have his tongue cut out, Copernicus will have his eyes gouged out, a Shakespeare will be stoned." Fyodor Dostoevsky, *The Possessed,* trans. David Magarshack (London:

Penguin, 1971), 126, 418. See also Leon Trotsky, *Literature and Revolution*, trans. Rose Strunsky, ed. William Keach (Chicago: Haymarket Books, 2005), 207–208. On Segalin and the project for the Institute of Genius, see Sirotkina, *Diagnosing Literary Genius*, 145–180.

21. Paul Gregory, *Lenin's Brain and Other Tales from the Secret Soviet Archives* (Stanford, CA: Hoover Institution Press, 2008), 27; Michael Hagner, "The Pantheon of Brains," in *Making Things Public: Atmospheres of Democracy*, eds. Bruno Latour and Peter Weibel (Cambridge, MA: MIT Press, 2005), 126–131.

22. Richter, "Pantheon of Brains," 143–144.

23. Evdokimov and Zinoviev are cited in Bernice Glatzer Rosenthal, *New Myth, New World: From Nietzsche to Stalinism* (University Park: Pennsylvania State University Press, 2002), 184. For descriptions of Lenin, see Nina Tumarkin, *Lenin Lives! The Lenin Cult in Soviet Culture* (Cambridge, MA: Harvard University Press, 1997), 89, 218. Mayakovsky is cited in Rosenthal, *New Myth, New World*, 185–186.

24. Nicolas Berdyaev, *The Meaning of the Creative Act*, trans. Donald A. Lowrie (New York: Harper, 1955), 172–174.

25. Comte expounded his entire religious system, including the calendar, in the *Catéchisme positiviste*, first published in 1852, and recently republished in a fine English translation as *The Catechism of Positive Religion*, trans. Richard Congreaves (Cambridge: Cambridge University Press, 2009).

26. Lenin is cited in Tumarkin, *Lenin Lives*, 84, 90. For Marx's comments, see Karl Marx, "Review of *Latter-Day Pamphlets*, ed. Thomas Carlyle, no. 1, *The Present Time*, no. 2, *Model Prisons*," first published in the *Neue Rheinische Zeitung Politisch-ökonomische Revue*, no. 4, April 1850, available at www.marxists.org /archive/marx/works/1850/03/carlyle.htm. See also Jan Plamper, "Modern Personality Cults," in *Personality Cults in Stalinism—Personenkulte im Stalinismus*, eds. Klaus Heller and Jan Plamper (Göttingen, Germany: Vandenhoek and Ruprecht, 2004), 28.

27. Loren R. Graham, "The Eugenics Movement in Germany and Russia in the 1920s," *American Historical Review* 82, no. 5 (1977): 1133–1164 (citation on 1150).

28. H. J. Muller to Comrade Joseph Stalin, May 5, 1936, printed in *The Mankind Quarterly* 34, no. 3 (2003): 305–319. On the life of Muller, see Elof Alex Carlson, *Genes, Radiation, and Society: The Life and Work of H. J. Muller* (Ithaca, NY: Cornell University Press, 1981); Mark B. Adam, "Eugenics in Russia," in *The Wellborn Science: Eugenics in Germany, France, Brazil, and Russia*, ed. Mark B. Adam (New York: Oxford University Press, 1990), 153–216.

29. Gregory, *Lenin's Brain*, 31; Richter, "Pantheon of Brains," 147.

30. Semashko is cited in Hagner, *Geniale Gehirne*, 249. See also Gregory, *Lenin's Brain*, 34. Gregory points out that the Central Committee's secret files pertaining to Lenin's brain were later deposited by Russian archivists working during the Yeltsin years in a collection labeled "The Communist Party on Trial." The "crime" in this case was the "extreme elitism" of the Soviet regime. Trotsky is cited in Gregory, *Lenin's Brain*, 34.

31. Engels's comment on Marx's genius was included as a footnote in the 1888 edition of Engels's *Ludwig Feurbach and the Outcome of German Philosophy* (New York: International Publishers, 2009), 43. See also Engels, "Speech at the Grave of Karl Marx," March 17, 1883, available at www.marxists.org/archive/marx /works/1883/death/burial.htm.

32. J. V. Stalin, "Lenin," speech delivered at a Memorial Meeting of the Kremlin Military School, January 28, 1924, and printed in *Pravda*, no. 34, February 12, 1924, in J. V. Stalin, *Works*, 13 vols. (Moscow: Foreign Language Publishing House, 1954–1955), 6:63. Dzhabaev is cited in Turmarkin, *Lenin Lives*, 253.

33. As Irina Paperno aptly remarks, "Stalin's contemporaries felt that their lives had been crossed by a world-historical genius, akin to Napoleon on horseback." See her "Intimacy with Power: Soviet Memoirists Remembering Stalin," in *Personality Cults in Stalinism*, eds. Heller and Plamper, 360. For the Mikhail Gorbachev quotation, see his *On My Country and the World*, trans. George Shriver (New York: Columbia University Press, 2000), 32.

34. Adolf Hitler, *Mein Kampf*, trans. Alvin Johnson, eds. John Chamberlain et al. (New York: Reynal and Hitchock, 1941), 402–403 (translation altered slightly). Although I have used this version of the text, freely available at www.archive .org, as the basis for my own translations, I have consulted the German original throughout and have frequently made changes. On the complicated publishing history of *Mein Kampf* and its many foreign translations, see Othmar Plöckinger, *Geschichte eines Buches: Adolf Hitlers "Mein Kampf," 1922–1945* (Munich: Oldenbourg Wissenschaftsverlag, 2006).

35. A notable exception to the earlier tendency to discount Hitler's artistic interests was Joachim C. Fest, *Hitler*, trans. Richard Winston and Clara Winston (New York: Harcourt Brace Jovanovich, 1973). The play on Clausewitz's famous observation that politics is "war by other means" is that of Hans Rudolf Vaget, whose article "Wagnerian Self-Fashioning: The Case of Adolf Hitler," *New German Critique 101* 34, no. 2 (2007): 95–114, is itself an important contribution to the new literature recognizing the importance of aesthetic concerns to Hitler and the Nazis. In addition, see Richard A. Etlin, ed., *Art, Culture, and Media Under the Third Reich* (Chicago: University of Chicago Press, 2002); Eric Michaud, *The Cult of Art in Nazi Germany*, trans. Janet Lloyd (Palo Alto, CA: Stanford University Press, 2004); Jonathan Petrapoulos, *Art as Politics in the Third Reich* (Chapel Hill: University of North Carolina Press, 1996); Frederick Spotts, *Hitler and the Power of Aesthetics* (New York: Overlook, 2003); Birgit Schwarz, *Geniewahn: Hitler und die Kunst* (Vienna: Bohlau, 2009); Otto W. Werckmeister, "Hitler the Artist," *Critical Inquiry* 23 (1997): 270–297. For all its richness, this body of work pays surprisingly little attention to the subject of genius.

36. Thomas Mann, *Pro and Contra Wagner*, ed. Allen Blunden (Chicago: University of Chicago Press, 1985), 210. Hitler is cited in Vaget, "Wagnerian Self-Fashioning," 100–101, 103. Hitler repeated the allusion to the Wagnerian sword of Siegfried in *Mein Kampf*.

37. Hitler is cited in Ian Kershaw, *Hitler, 1889–1936: Hubris* (New York: W. W. Norton, 2000), 151. See also Houston Stewart Chamberlain to Adolf

Hitler, October 7, 1923, in Chamberlain, *Briefe 1882–1924 und Briefwechsel mit Kaiser Wilhelm*, 2 vols. (Munich: F. Bruckmann, 1926), 2:124–126. The encounter is described in Vaget, "Wagnerian Self-Fashioning," 105–106. The reference to Goethe is from *Faust* II, 2, *Am untern Peneios*.

38. Georg Schott, *Das Volksbuch vom Hitler* (Munich: Hermann Weichmann, 1924), 48–54. Goebbels is cited in Kershaw, *Hitler, 1889–1936*, 283–284; Robert Gellately, *Lenin, Stalin, and Hitler: The Age of Social Catastrophe* (New York: Knopf, 2007), 127. Hitler is cited in Kershaw, *Hitler, 1889–1936*, 289.

39. Haller and Müller are cited in Klaus Schreiner, "Messianism in the Political Culture of the Weimar Republic," in *Toward the Millennium: Messianic Expectations from the Bible to Waco*, eds. Peter Schäfer and Mark Cohen (Leiden: Brill, 1998), 327. On political messianism more generally in this period, see Lilla, *The Stillborn God*, esp. chap. 6.

40. Hitler, *Mein Kampf*, 479, 403, 396–398. The importance of genius to Hitler's appeal is a point that surprisingly few scholars have emphasized. A notable exception is Jochen Schmidt, *Die Geschichte des Genie-Gedankens in der deutschen Literatur, Philosophie und Politik, 1750–1945*, 2 vols. (Heidelberg: Universitätsverlag, 2004), 2:194–195.

41. John S. White, "Taine on Race and Genius," *Social Research* 10, no. 1 (1943): 76–100; Gustave Le Bon, "Recherches anatomique et mathématique sur les lois des variations du volume du cerveau," *Revue d'anthropologie*, 2nd ser., 2 (1879): 27–104; Gustave Le Bon, *La psychologie des foules* (1895). Though there are numerous more recent works on the question, George L. Mosse's *Toward the Final Solution: A History of European Racism* (Madison: University of Wisconsin Press, 1978), remains a fine introduction. See also Hitler, *Mein Kampf*, 417–418.

42. Hans F. K. Günther, *The Racial Elements of European History*, trans. G. C. Wheeler (New York: E. P. Dutton, 1927), 56. On Hitler's interest in Günther, see Timothy Ryback, *Hitler's Private Library* (New York: Knopf, 2008), 69, 111. See also Hitler, *Mein Kampf*, 489, 412.

43. Sander L. Gilman, *Smart Jews: The Construction of the Image of Superior Jewish Intelligence* (Lincoln: University of Nebraska Press, 1996). On Jewish genius, see, in addition to the works by Eliyahu Stern cited in other chapters, Noah B. Strote, "The Birth of the 'Psychological Jew' in an Age of Ethnic Pride," *New German Critique* 39, no. 1 (2012): 199–224; John Efron, *Defenders of the Race: Jewish Doctors and Race Science in Fin-de-Siècle Europe* (New Haven, CT: Yale University Press, 1994), 47–55, 71–73; Francis Galton, *Hereditary Genius: An Inquiry into its Laws and Consequences* (New York: Prometheus Books, [1869] 2006), 13. And yet, at the same time, Galton could write to Alphonse de Candole, observing, "It strikes me that the Jews are specialized for a parasitical existence upon other nations." Cited in Jennifer Patai and Raphael Patai, *The Myth of the Jewish Race* (Detroit: Wayne State University Press, 1989), 146. See also Cesare Lombroso, *The Man of Genius*, rev. ed. (London: Walter Scott, 1917), 136; Joseph Jacobs, *Studies in Jewish Statistics* (London: D. Nutt, 1891), esp. Appendix B, "The Comparative Distribution of Jewish Ability." On Jewish performance on intelligence tests and percentage of Nobel prizes, see the discussion in Patai and Patai,

Myth of the Jewish Race, 146–149, 158. See also Lewis M. Terman, ed., *Genetic Studies of Genius*, 5 vols. (Palo Alto, CA: Stanford University Press, 1922–1956), 1:56.

44. Hitler, *Mein Kampf*, 489; Chamberlain, *Foundations*, 1:488, 1:269–270.

45. The allusion to the "comet path of genius" is from the title of a work by the high-ranking Nazi official Philipp Bouhler, *Napoleon: Kometenbahn eines Genies* (Munich: Georg D. W. Callwey, 1942), which was one of Hitler's "favorite bedtime reading books," according to Robert S. Wistrich, "Philipp Bouhler," *Who's Who in Nazi Germany* (New York: Routledge, 2011), 11.

46. Adolf Hitler, speech of July 10, 1938, in *Speeches and Proclamations, 1932–1945*, trans. Chris Wilcox and Mary Fran Gilbert, ed. Max Domarus, 4 vols. (Waucanda, IL: Bolchazy-Carducci, 1990–2004), 2:1126. Hitler on genius is cited in Michaud, *Cult of Art*, 37. See also Jon A. Mjöen, "Genius as a Biological Problem," *Eugenics Review* 17, no. 4 (1926): 242–257. The genius's tendency to sterility was a point emphasized particularly (although not exclusively) by degeneration theorists. On Nazi brain research, see Hagner, *Geniale Gehirne*, 276–282; Hans-Walter Schmuhl, "Hirnforschung und Krankenmord: Das Kaiser-Wilhelm-Intitut für Hirnforschung, 1937–1945" (2000), a report of the findings of the Max-Planck Institute Forschungsprogramm, "Geschichte der Kaiser-Wilhelm-Gesellschaft im Nationalsozialismus," available at www.mpiwg berlin.mpg.de/KWG/Ergebnisse/Ergebnisse1.pdf.

47. Hitler on "dictatorship of genius" and Hans Schemm are cited in Michaud, *Cult of Art*, 38, 104. See also Robert Scholz, "Kunst als Grundlage politischer Schöpferkraft: Die Aquarelle des Führers," *Völkischer Beobachter*, April 24, 1936; Joseph Goebbels, "Der Führer als Staatsmann," in *Adolf Hitler, Bilder aus dem Leben des Führers* (Leipzig: Altona/Bahrenfeld, 1936), 44–55.

48. Bonhoeffer is cited in Fritz Stern, *Dreams and Delusions: The Drama of German History* (New Haven, CT: Yale University Press, 1999), 163. On the Nazis' extensive use of Christian symbolism, imagery, and rhetoric, see Michaud, *Cult of Art*, 52–64, 75–84. For Goebbels, see his "Der Führer als Staatsmann," 44. Nietzsche is cited in Mason, *Value of Creativity*, 217. See also Ryback, *Hitler's Private Library*, 126–131; Hitler, *Mein Kampf*, 669. Goebbels is also cited in Schmidt, *Die Geschichte des Genie-Gedankens*, 2:207.

49. Hermann Heller, "Genie und Funktionär in der Politik," *Politische Wissenschaft* (Schriftenreihe der Deutschen Hochschule für Politik in Berlin und des Instituts für Auswärtige Politik in Hamburg), no. 10, *Probleme der Demokratie*, vol. 2 (Berlin: Rothschild, 1931), 57–68 (citations on 62, 65).

50. Thomas Mann, "That Man Is My Brother," *Esquire*, March 1939, 31, 132–133; Thomas Mann, *The Beloved Returns: Lotte in Weimar*, trans. H. T. Lowe-Porter (New York: Alfred A. Knopf, 1940), 82–83.

51. The phrase "organized contempt of the mind" is that of Joachim Fest in his *The Face of the Third Reich*, trans. Michael Bullock (New York: Pantheon, 1970), 250.

52. On the numerous "genius films" produced by the Nazis, see Linda Schulte-Sasse, *Entertaining the Third Reich: Illusions of Wholeness in Nazi Cinema*

(Durham, NC: Duke University Press, 1996), esp. Part II, "Aestheticized Genius"; David Welch, *Propaganda and the German Cinema, 1933–1945* (London: I. B. Taurus, 2001). On representations of the German genius, see Michaud, *Cult of Art*, 74–181. For Hitler's quotations, see *Hitler's Table Talk, 1941–1944*, ed. and intro. Hugh Trevor Roper (New York: Enigma Books, 2002), 250–251 (entry for night of January 25–26, 1942).

53. *Time*, July 1, 1946. On Einstein as Prometheus, see Alan J. Friedman and Carol C. Donley, *Einstein as Myth and Muse* (Cambridge: Cambridge University Press, 1985), 154–156.

54. *New York Times*, November 10, 1919. Thomson, speaking on November 6, 1919, is cited in Walter Isaacson, *Einstein: His Life and Universe* (New York: Simon and Schuster, 2007), 261.

55. Isaacson, *Einstein*, 261–283. English and Palestinian receptions are cited in Jürgen Neffe, *Einstein: A Biography*, trans. Shelley Frisch (New York: Farrar, Straus, and Giroux, 2005), 310. The eyewitness report from Austria is cited in Hans C. Ohanian, *Einstein's Mistakes: The Human Failings of Genius* (New York: W. W. Norton, 2008), 266.

56. Einstein on the public's incomprehension is cited in Ohanian, *Einstein's Mistakes*, 259. See also Einstein, "My First Impression of the U.S.A," *Nieuwe Rotterdamsche Courant*, July 4, 1921, cited in Isaacson, *Einstein*, 273.

57. On the way in which Newton was described in keeping with broader conceptions of genius, see Richard Yeo, "Genius, Method, and Morality: Images of Newton in Britain, 1760–1860," *Science in Context* 2 (1988): 257–284. On Davy, see Jan Golinski, *Science as Public Culture: Chemistry and Enlightenment in Britain, 1760–1820* (Cambridge: Cambridge University Press, 1992), esp. chap. 6; Christopher Lawrence, "Humphry Davy and Romanticism," in *Romanticism and the Sciences*, eds. Andrew Cunningham and Nicholas Jardine (Cambridge: Cambridge University Press, 1990), 213–227. On mathematicians in the nineteenth century, see Amir Alexander, *Duel at Dawn: Heroes, Martyrs, and the Rise of Modern Mathematics* (Cambridge, MA: Harvard University Press, 2010).

58. On both the eighteenth-century "genius of observation" and the nineteenth-century "scientific self," see Lorraine Daston and Peter Galison, *Objectivity* (New York: Zone Books, 2007), esp. 229–233, 238.

59. On Einstein's "mystical, intuitive" approach to problem-solving, see Ohanian, *Einstein's Mistakes*, 215, 332. Planck is cited in Fritz Stern, *Einstein's German World* (Princeton, NJ: Princeton University Press, 1999), 40. On Einstein and the spirit of the age, see David Cassidy, *Einstein and Our World* (Atlantic Highlands, NJ: Humanities Press, 1995). On Einstein's "deep religious vein," see Stern, *Einstein's German World*, 163.

60. Einstein on Hitler is cited in Neffe, *Einstein*, 287. Einstein on faith in authority is cited in Stern, *Einstein's German World*, 91. On relativity as a "Jewish fraud," see Alan D. Beyerchen, *Politics in the Physics Community in the Third Reich* (New Haven, CT: Yale University Press, 1977), 93. The most prestigious leveler of this charge was the Nobel Laureate and "Aryan physicist" Phillip Lenard. Hitler is cited in Beyerchen, *Politics in the Physics Community*, 10.

61. The Nazi condemnation of Einstein appears in Armin Hermann, *Einstein: Der Weltweise und sein Jahrhundert. Eine Biographie* (Munich: Piper, 1994), 395–412. Einstein is cited in Neffe, *Einstein*, 285.

62. Hermann, *Einstein*, 407 ("Einstein war einer der grossen Gegen-spieler Hitlers"). The line about Einstein as a "maker of universes" is George Bernard Shaw's, from a banquet speech in 1930, and is cited in Friedman and Donley, *Einstein as Myth and Muse*, 173. For the Hitler and Einstein poll, see Isaacson, *Einstein*, 445, 624n60. The results of the poll were reported in the *New York Times*, November 28, 1939. The line on heroes is attributed to Einstein in *The Ultimate Quotable Einstein*, ed. Alice Calaprice, foreword Freeman Dyson (Princeton, NJ: Princeton University Press, 2011), 480.

63. Fred Jerome, *The Einstein File: J. Edgar Hoover's Secret War Against the World's Most Famous Scientist* (New York: St. Martin's Press, 2002).

CONCLUSION

1. My account of Thomas Harvey draws heavily on Carolyn Abraham, *Possessing Genius: The True Account of the Bizarre Odyssey of Einstein's Brain* (New York: Saint Martin's Press, 2001).

2. Haymaker's comments to the press are cited in ibid., 88.

3. Michael Paterniti, *Driving Mr. Albert: A Trip Across America with Einstein's Brain* (New York: Random House, 2000); M. Diamond, A. Scheibel, G. Murphy, and T. Harvey, "On the Brain of a Scientist: Albert Einstein," *Experimental Neurology* 88 (1985):198–204; Sandra F. Wittelson, Debra L. Kigar, and Thomas Harvey, "The Exceptional Brain of Albert Einstein," *Lancet* 353 (1999): 2149–2153.

4. Frederic Golden, "Albert Einstein," *Time*, December 31, 1999.

5. Roland Barthes, "Einstein's Brain," in *Mythologies*, selected and trans. Annette Lavers (New York: Hill and Wang, 1972), 68–70.

6. Hannah Arendt, *The Human Condition* (Chicago: University of Chicago Press, 1958), 210–211; Robert Musil, *The Man Without Qualities*, ed. Burton Pike, trans. Sophie Wilkins, 2 vols. (New York: Vintage International, 1995), 1:41. The lines are from the famous chap. 13, "A Racehorse of Genius Crystallizes the Recognition of Being a Man Without Qualities."

7. The description of Ramanujan is that of C. P. Snow in his foreword to G. H. Hardy's *A Mathematician's Apology* (Cambridge: Cambridge University Press, 1967), 12, 33. See also Robert Kanigel, *The Man Who Knew Infinity: A Life of the Genius Ramanujan* (New York: Washington Square Press, 2011); Alfred L. Kroeber, *Configurations of Culture Growth* (Berkeley: University of California Press, 1944); Barbara Will, *Gertrude Stein and the Problem of 'Genius'* (Edinburgh: University of Edinburgh Press, 2000); Lucy Delap, *The Feminist Avant-Garde: Transatlantic Encounters of the Early Twentieth Century* (Cambridge: Cambridge University Press, 2007), esp. 249–292; and Victoria Olwell, *The Genius of Democracy: Fictions of Gender and Citizenship in the United States, 1860–1945* (Philadelphia: University of Pennsylvania Press, 2011).

8. I owe the observation about American uses of genius to John Carson, who developed it in "Equality, Inequality, and Difference: Genius as a Problem and

Possibility in American Political/Scientific Discourse," an unpublished talk delivered at the Huntington Library on May 18, 2012. For an example of the broad use of genius in the United States in the nineteenth century, see Gustavus Sadler, *Troubling Minds: The Cultural Politics of Genius in the United States, 1840–1890* (Minneapolis: University of Minneapolis Press, 2006); Charles Spearman, *The Abilities of Man: Their Nature and Measurement* (New York: Macmillan, 1927), 221.

9. Marjorie Garber, "Our Genius Problem," *The Atlantic*, December 2002; Joshua Cooper Rama and Debra Rosenberg, "The Puzzle of Genius," *Newsweek*, June 28, 1993, 47; *Esquire*, "The Genius Issue," November 1, 1999, 2; Andreas Sentker, "Genies die unser Leben verändert haben," *Die Zeit*, no. 42, October 13, 2011, 37–39. On Jobs, see the cover of *Newsweek*, November 5, 2011, which reads "American Genius Steve Jobs. How He Drove Apple to Victory. How He Changed Our World"; Malcolm Gladwell, "The Tweaker: The Real Genius of Steve Jobs," *New Yorker*, November 14, 2011.

10. Ford is cited in Randall Stross, *The Wizard of Menlo Park: How Thomas Edison Invented the Modern World* (New York: Crown, 2007), 234.

11. All these actual titles were available on Amazon.com at the time of this writing.

12. Einstein's letter is cited in Walter Isaacson, *Einstein: His Life and Universe* (New York: Simon and Schuster, 2007), 522.

13. Kadya Molodovsky, "God of Mercy," 1945. I am grateful to David A. Bell for calling this poem to my attention and for transliterating it from the original Yiddish. See also Mao Tse-Tung, "Talks with Responsible Comrades at Various Places During Provincial Tour, from the Middle of August to 12 September 1971," in *Selected Works of Mao Tse-Tung*, vol. 9 (Secunderabad, India: Kranti Publications, 1990), accessed on October 23, 2012, at www.marxists.org/reference /archive/mao/selected-works/volume-9/mswv9_88.htm.

14. The Arthur D. Little research director is cited in Steven Shapin, *The Scientific Life: A Moral History of a Late Modern Vocation* (Chicago: University of Chicago Press, 2008), 183. On Bell Labs, see Jon Gertner, *The Idea Factory: Bell Labs and the Great Age of American Innovation* (New York: Penguin, 2012).

15. Keynes is cited in Freeman Dyson, *Disturbing the Universe* (New York: Basic Books, 1979), 8. Dyson, who was present at Keynes's lecture, comments himself on the mythology of scientific geniuses as "magi" and "deliverers and destroyers" (9). On the postwar use of the word "genius" among scientists, see the nice account in James Gleick, *Genius: The Life and Science of Richard Feynman* (New York: Vintage, 1992), 311–329 (esp. 322).

16. In addition to the works by Barthes, Foucault, and others cited in my Introduction, see Jacques Derrida's arresting *Geneses, Genealogies, Genres, and Genius: The Secrets of the Archive*, trans. Beverly Bie Brahic (New York: Columbia University Press, 2006), which fittingly complicates the claims made in this paragraph.

17. The current psychological interest in genius is best represented by the work of the highly prolific Dean Keith Simonton. A nice distillation and presentation of the work on collective intelligence is provided in James Surowiecki,

The Wisdom of Crowds: Why the Many Are Smarter Than the Few and How Collective Wisdom Shapes Business, Economies, Societies and Nations (New York: Bantam, 2004), and Steven Johnson, *Where Good Ideas Come From: The Natural History of Innovation* (New York: Riverhead Books, 2010). See also the cover story, "The Genius Problem," in *Time*, August 27, 2007, on the putative failure to properly educate our smartest kids.

18. Garber makes this point nicely in "Our Genius Problem."

19. I am grateful to Anders Ericsson for sharing his thoughts with me on the psychological factors that help preserve a belief in genius.

20. David Plotz, *The Genius Factory: The Curious History of the Nobel Prize Sperm Bank* (New York: Random House, 2005). On Allan Snyder, see Tanya Lewis, "Unlock Your Inner Rain Man by Electrically Zapping Your Brain," *Wired*, July 20, 2012, and Snyder's own website, www.creativitycap.com. David Bates is now engaged in a fascinating project, tentatively entitled *Human Insight from Descartes to Artificial Intelligence*, that traces the rationalist genealogy of the effort to understand human and artificial intelligence. See also R. Keith Sawyer, *Explaining Creativity: The Science of Innovation* (New York: Oxford University Press, 2007), esp. chap. 6, "Computational Approaches," and Nancy C. Andreasen, *The Creating Brain: The Neuroscience of Genius* (New York: Dana Press, 2005). For a particularly upbeat assessment of the future possibilities of artificial and human intelligence, see Ray Kurzwell, *How to Create a Mind* (New York: Viking, 2012).

21. Alexis de Tocqueville, *Democracy in America*, ed. Eduardo Nolla, trans. James T. Schleifer, 2 vols. (Indianapolis: Liberty Fund, 2010), 2:722, 785, 1281, and 1:490.

22. Ralph Waldo Emerson, "Uses of Great Men," in *Essays and Lectures*, ed. Joel Port (New York: Library of America, 2009), 631.

23. Ibid.

INDEX